# Laywomen and the Making of Colonial Catholicism in New Spain, 1630–1790

In the first history of laywomen and the church in colonial Mexico, Jessica L. Delgado shows how laywomen participated in and shaped religious culture in significant ways by engaging creatively with gendered theology about women, sin, and guilt in their interactions with church sacraments, institutions, and authorities. Taking a thematic approach and using stories of individuals, institutions, and ideas, Delgado illuminates the diverse experiences of urban and rural women of Indigenous, Spanish, and African descent. By centering the choices these women made in their devotional lives and in their relationships to the aspects of the church they regularly encountered, this study expands and challenges our understandings of the church's role in colonial society, the role of religion in gendered and racialized power, and the role of ordinary women in the making of colonial religious culture.

Jessica L. Delgado is Assistant Professor in the Department of Religion at Princeton University in New Jersey.

CAMBRIDGE LATIN AMERICAN STUDIES

General Editors
KRIS LANE, Tulane University
MATTHEW RESTALL, Pennsylvania State University

Editor Emeritus
HERBERT S. KLEIN
Gouverneur Morris Emeritus Professor of History, Columbia University
and Hoover Research Fellow, Stanford University

Other Books in the Series

(Continued after the index)

# Laywomen and the Making of Colonial Catholicism in New Spain, 1630–1790

## JESSICA L. DELGADO

*Princeton University*

CAMBRIDGE
UNIVERSITY PRESS

# CAMBRIDGE
## UNIVERSITY PRESS

University Printing House, Cambridge CB2 8BS, United Kingdom

One Liberty Plaza, 20th Floor, New York, NY 10006, USA

477 Williamstown Road, Port Melbourne, VIC 3207, Australia

314–321, 3rd Floor, Plot 3, Splendor Forum, Jasola District Centre,
New Delhi – 110025, India

79 Anson Road, #06–04/06, Singapore 079906

Cambridge University Press is part of the University of Cambridge.

It furthers the University's mission by disseminating knowledge in the pursuit of
education, learning, and research at the highest international levels of excellence.

www.cambridge.org
Information on this title: www.cambridge.org/9781107199408
DOI: 10.1017/9781108185639

First published 2018

Printed and bound in Great Britain by Clays Ltd, Elcograf S.p.A.

*A catalogue record for this publication is available from the British Library.*

*Library of Congress Cataloging-in-Publication Data*
NAMES: Delgado, Jessica L., 1972– author.
TITLE: Laywomen and the making of colonial Catholicism in New Spain, 1630–1790 /
Jessica L. Delgado, Princeton University.
DESCRIPTION: New York : Cambridge University Press, 2018. | Series: Cambridge Latin
American studies
IDENTIFIERS: LCCN 2017052814 | ISBN 9781107199408
SUBJECTS: LCSH: Catholic Church – Mexico – History – Spanish colony, 1540–1810. |
Catholic women – Mexico – History – Spanish colony, 1540–1810.
CLASSIFICATION: LCC BX1428.3 .D45 2018 | DDC 282/.7208209032–dc23
LC record available at https://lccn.loc.gov/2017052814

ISBN 978-1-107-19940-8 Hardback

*For Kaya*

# Contents

# Acknowledgments

It would be impossible to properly thank everyone who deserves my gratitude here. This book was written with the help and support of countless friends and colleagues and is the culmination of a very long journey. What follows is by necessity utterly inadequate.

To my many mentors, there is a part of each of you in this book. Please know that you have taught and given me much more than what I can express here.

I began my graduate studies at the University of California at Santa Cruz and incurred many debts there. Akasha Hull inspired and affirmed my interest in women and spirituality. David Sweet showed me the importance of individual life stories built from fragments and the possibility of good history as a form of justice making. Farnaz Fatemi first taught me to write and then taught me to believe in where my writing could take me. Her friendship then sustained me through the years. Marilyn Westerkamp modeled determined and precise scholarship about religion and early modern women, and she supported my work, even when it led me to leave her program. Lisbeth Haas taught me that research could and should be nourishing; her unfailing support followed me far beyond my days at UCSC. Bettina Aptheker, Emily Honig, Tyler Stovall, Alice Yang-Murray, Edmund Burke, María Elena Díaz, Pedro Castillo, Sonia Alvarez, and Guillermo Delgado each played an important role in my formation as a scholar and in the long path to this book. I am grateful also to the wonderful History Department staff for the years of support. My fellow graduate students, too numerous to mention, also inspired and supported me. Tiffany Wayne, Rebecca Hall, and Rick Warner stand out as exceptional intellectual compañeros and lifelong friends.

I completed my doctorate and the dissertation version of this book at UC Berkeley, where I was blessed with exceptional mentors and colleagues. My advisor, William B. Taylor, deserves more gratitude than anyone else for my ability to be a teacher and scholar. Though I have accepted that I will never achieve the standard of excellence his example reflects, I will continue to strive toward it. This book owes much to his gentle pushing, generous critique, and infinite curiosity. I trust that he knows how grateful I am for his ongoing support, collaboration, and friendship. Margaret Chowning has challenged, inspired, and fortified me in equal parts throughout graduate school and beyond. Her precision, astute guidance, and loyal friendship have been indispensable. I thank Walter Brem for years of archival support and lessons. Working as his curatorial assistant at the Bancroft Library was a great honor and aided my research in countless ways. I am also indebted to David Kessler for his expert assistance, his warmth and humor, and the delicious sandwiches made from his famous homemade bread that got me through long days of work. I am eternally grateful to the wonderful and amazing Mabel Lee and the fantastic Barbara Hayashida for their incredibly generous administrative support and help through numerous logistical problems. Dalia Muller, Camilo Trumper, Celso Castilho, and José Refugio de la Torre will know that this brief expression of thanks for their companionship, intellectual engagement, and unforgettable friendship could never do justice to what we shared and built together in our Berkeley years. I thank them anyway, from the bottom of my heart. I thank Jennifer Hughes, the trickster genius of our field and my partner in mischief and discovery, for sharing resources, research travails, and friendship. I want to thank Sylvia Sellers-Garcia, Brian Madigan, Sean McEnroe, Paul Ramirez, Karen Melvin, Kristin Huffine, and especially Brianna Leavitt-Alcantara for their friendship, support, company, critique, suggestions, and continued collaboration. May it continue for years to come.

I am deeply indebted to many scholars, friends, and archivists in Mexico. Gabriela Cano and Brian Connaughton sponsored me as a Fulbright scholar when I began my research, and their assistance and good advice were indispensable. The Portilla family has provided shelter, wonderful food, important intellectual connections, warmth, and friendship for all of the years of research that went into this book and every year since. To Tina, Santiago, Dulce, and Anita, I truly could not have written this without you. This is also true for Lourdes Juarez Marusich, whose friendship and generous hospitality has supported me for more than a decade. I am grateful to the Colegio de Mexico and UNAM Itztapalapa for institutional sponsorship. I owe an enormous debt to the skilled and generous archivists and staff at the AGN, Condumex, AHAM, and Vizcainas. I cannot possibly name everyone individually who helped me with their expertise, time, and energy, but I am grateful to them all. Berenise Bravo Rubio and Marco Antonio Perez Iturbide of AHAM deserve special mention, however. Large parts of this book would not have been possible without their generosity and the depth of their knowledge. Many historians of Mexico will understand what I mean when I say that it was tempting to spend all of my time working at AHAM under the excellent care of Bere and Marco.

I am grateful to the faculty and staff in the History Department and the Program in Latin American Studies at Smith College and to the Five College Women's Studies Research Center for the two years I spent in the Pioneer Valley writing my dissertation. I want to thank my writing companions and friends there, known among ourselves as the Forbes Library Crew. The company and support of Asha Nadkarni, Nerissa Balce, Dayo Gore, and Richard Chu made a crucial difference in those years and beyond. I am also grateful to Dana Liebsohn, Ann Zulawski, Nina Scott, Laura Lovett, Babette Faehmel, and Nela Trivkofic for their friendship and years of intellectual support.

The colleagues and friends at Princeton University to whom I owe a significant debt of gratitude could fill a chapter of this book. I am very grateful to Jenny Legath, Anita Kline, Robert Wuthnow, and the rest of the faculty and staff of the Center for the Study of Religion for the material and intellectual support during and beyond the three years I spent as a CSR fellow. My work owes so much to the conversations, friendship, and suggestions of the many fellows with whom I collaborated. Amy Kittelstrom's friendship has become a lifeline, and her intellectual acumen, scholarly rigor, and genuine vocation for what we do continue to inspire me. Phil Habberkern's humor and careful reading kept me afloat many a time, and his pointed questions made these chapters better. Manu Radhakrishnan and I shared drinks, ideas, and solidarity, and he offered key insights at crucial moments in my revisions. Annie Blazer, aka "the instigator," always got me to "do stuff" that I was later very glad I did, and she somehow got me to write both faster *and* better. Grace Yukich, Rebecca Sager, Martha Finch, and Hillary Kaell all offered important suggestions, which, along with their warmth and friendship, all improved my work.

I want to thank the entire faculty and staff in the Religion Department for nurturing an exceptionally stimulating and supportive environment in which to work. I will always be grateful to Leigh Schmidt and Marie Griffith for bringing me into this wonderful community and for their early mentorship at the start of my postgraduate career. Judith Weisenfeld, Wallace Best, Kathryn Gin Lum, Seth Perry, and John Gager all read and commented on my work extensively and have accompanied me through all stages of revision and publication with unwavering support and friendship. Eddie Glaude, Jeff Stout, Eric Gregory, Anne Marie Luijendijk, Shaun Marmon, Leora Batnitzky, Stephen (Buzzy) Teiser, Moulie Vidas, Naphtali Meshel, Al Raboteau, and Liane Carlson have all offered support and guidance in numerous ways throughout the process of revising and expanding the manuscript. I am grateful to the participants of the

Religion in the Americas Workshop; the Gender, Sexuality, and Religion Working Group; and the Religion and Culture Workshop for years of critical suggestions and intellectual community. Rachel Lindsey, Rachel Gross, Nicole Kirk, Vaughn Booker, Ryan Harper, Kelsey Moss, Alyssa Maldonado-Estrada, Leslie Ribovich, Beth Stroud, Andrew Walker-Cornetta, Eden Consenstein, Madeline Gambino, Ahmad Green-Hayes, and Ireri Chavez Barcenas deserve particular mention among them. I am grateful as well to my research assistants, Valeria Lopez Fadul and Sophia Nuñez, for their invaluable work that stretched across several years. To BM Pietsch, who made me promise to call him that in these acknowledgments, I owe an immense debt of gratitude, not only for his close reading and excellent suggestions, but also for tirelessly coaching me through the final stretches of revisions when I was greatly in need of some tough love. And to those other steadfast coaches, my fellow "Deadline Oriented Productivity Experiment" members, Annie Blazer, Nicole Kirk, Kathryn Gin Lum, and Judith Weisenfeld, I offer thanks for hilarity and friendship and for keeping me on track over the long haul. They will understand everything encompassed in the now famous phrase: "DOPE, it works!"

I have been blessed with an intellectual home away from home in the History Department of the Ohio State University, and I am grateful to the faculty and staff for all of their help and guidance. I am especially grateful to Birgitte Solange and her daughter, Anna, and to Lucy Murphy and Tom Murphy for friendship and support, as well as intellectual and creative companionship, that have made a critical difference for me and for my family. Birgitte invited me to participate in a conference on the History of Kinship and the Family, and my respondents, Kristina Sessa and Mary Thomson, asked provocative questions that will continue to push me beyond what I have written here. I am also grateful to many other colleagues and friends who have enriched my work and time at OSU in many ways. Among them I especially want to mention Azita Ranjbar, Stephanie Smith, Thomas (Dodi) McDow, Margaret Newell, Randy Roth, Steve Kern, Nate Rossenstein, David Brakke, Jane Hathaway, Kathryn Marino, Robin Judd, Alexander Kaye, and Susan Hartmann. I am grateful for my talented research assistant, Dani Anthony, for the important work she did for me in the sabbatical year I spent at OSU completing this book. And of course, to Shalya Harrison, I could not have finished this book without the love and care you extended to my daughter and to me.

Scholars at other institutions have offered important support as well. I am grateful to a number of scholarly collectives, including La Patrona Collective for the Study of Colonial Latin America, Yale's Material Economies of Religion in the Americas, and the Tepoztlan Institute of Transnational Studies, for inspiration and collaboration that injected new life into my work at key moments. Ken Mills, Matt O'Hara, Donna Guy, Jocelyn Alcott, Pamela Voekel, Jennifer Hughes, Kirstie Dorr, and Sara Clarke Kaplan have all read or heard parts of my manuscript and engaged deeply with my arguments in ways that helped me to sharpen them. I am very grateful to the two anonymous readers for Cambridge University Press who offered extremely helpful suggestions and critique.

At Cambridge University Press's New York office, my editor Debbie Gershenowitz and her assistant Kris Deusch have guided me through the process of publication from start to finish. I am grateful to both of them and to the series editors, Matthew Restall and Kris Lane, for their interest in this project and the work they did to bring it to fruition. I am also grateful to Bronte Rawlings, my content manager at the London office; Indhumathi Kuppusamy and Rogini Rajendiran, the project managers at Integra; and the copyeditor, Karin Kipp, for their time and skill. And for the best indexer I could ask for, Tiffany K. Wayne, I give many thanks and praises.

This project has benefited from the institutional and financial support of a number of programs and organizations. I am grateful for generous fellowships from the Bancroft Library, Fulbright-Hayes, and UC Berkeley's history department, and the Five College Women's Studies Research Center at Mt. Holyoke College for making the research and writing possible during the dissertation stage of this work. I would like to thank Princeton's Center for the Study of Religion, the Department of Religion, the Humanities Council, and the Program in Latin American Studies for research funding and fellowships that supported revision and expansion of the manuscript. I am grateful to the National Endowment for the Humanities for a summer fellowship that supported crucial final revisions.

I also owe a debt of gratitude to programs at a number of universities that invited me to present parts of the book and to the scholars who attended these talks and offered important feedback. At Princeton, these include the American Studies Workshop, the Latin American Studies Works in Progress Lunch Seminar, and the Davis Center for Historical Studies. Elsewhere, they include the Gender and Sexuality History Workshop at the Ohio State University, the Feminist Research Alliance and Early Modern Research Workshops at SUNY at Buffalo, and the Society for the Study of Women and the Renaissance at CUNY Graduate Center.

I am blessed beyond measure by a group of friends and extended family without whom I could not have done any of this. To my CCC sisters, for your unconditional love and support, I can never repay you, and I know that you will never ask me to. Jennifer Hamelburg, Emily Leys, Kirstie Dorr, Vanessa Zelenak, Erica Steiner, Heather Murphy, and Sara Clarke Kaplan, this book belongs to you in so many ways. And to our second generation, Odile, Lily, Ava, Sara, Max, Abby, Miles, and of course, Kaya, you have helped me keep it all in perspective. And there are many more treasured friends who helped: Hilary Bryant, for her endless support and belief in me; Farnaz Fatemi, for inspiration and refreshing my spirit; Marla Hoffberg and Sutton Pierce, for their exceptional loyalty and ever-available cheer; Mary Ader, for her interest in my work and support in innumerable material and emotional ways; Conlaodh Guy, for more than I can find words for; Tanya and Greg Madigow, for taking care of my family and me when we needed it; my cousin Kirsten Delgado, for inspiring conversations, love, and appreciation; my sister-cousin Amanda Ferguson, her wonderful wife (and my dear friend), Jennifer Pariseau, and their two beautiful children, Oliver and Elodie, for years of friendship, food, fun, and shelter in both good and bad times throughout my writing and research. Without each of these people, this book would not exist.

My grandparents, Scott and Kel Ferguson, Rogelio Rodriguez Delgado, and Eva West Delgado, each inspired in me a love of learning and supported me in spiritual and material ways. My "baby" brother, Nathan Roger Delgado, has been my greatest champion through it all. My parents, Linda Ferguson Delgado and Roger Rodriguez Delgado, deserve at least one hundred pages of thanks. Your faith in me; your material, emotional, and intellectual support; your vast patience; and your unconditional love have meant more than any words I could find to describe them, so I will have to make do with saying thank you and that I will strive to make good use of them always. My life partner, Daniel Winunwe Rivers, has accompanied me from start to finish and helped me in more ways than I can enumerate. A brilliant historian and scholar, he blessed me with his insight at every stage of research and writing. As a friend and companion, he lifted my flagging spirits, quelled my doubts, and picked up the slack when the research and writing took me away from our family. For his understanding, love, and loyalty, I will be forever grateful.

But there is one person who has blessed my life more than anyone else, and that is my daughter, Kaya Linda Delgado-Rivers. Her light is brighter than anything I have seen, and her presence infuses everything I do. I dedicate this book to her. May her future benefit in some way from the lives and struggles of the women whose stories fill its pages.

PART I

# Introduction
## Troubling Devotion

The image of the highly pious Mexican woman – devoted to priest, sacraments, and saints; clutching her rosary; and attending daily mass – is a familiar one in film and print and the cultural imaginary of both the United States and Mexico. It has a timeless quality; the women this image conjures appear to be living in a past that, for them, has not changed. Scholars of the national period have historicized the origins of this image, linked to nineteenth- and twentieth-century Mexican nationalism and its discontents more than to the nonspecific colonial past it seems to represent. Rather than an unbroken tradition of female piety from the Spanish conquest to the present, the reality that this stereotype conceals is one of great dynamism and change in women's postcolonial relationship to the church. As we learn more about these changes, it becomes clear that they were a significant part of larger shifts in the church's role in society and its relationship to the rapidly changing Mexican state. Women's participation in these processes has begun to garner some of the attention it deserves, but the colonial precedents of this participation are still largely a mystery.[1]

This gap in our knowledge about women's participation in colonial religious culture has been partially filled by the important scholarship on convents and nuns; literary and historical studies of the past two or three decades have rightfully placed these elite institutions and exceptional women at the center of the Catholic Church's colonial history.[2] However, in doing so, it has also cast a long shadow over our understanding of what it meant to be a woman in colonial Catholic culture. The idea that women in

---

1 Margaret Chowning, "The Catholic Church and the Ladies of the Vela Perpetua: Gender and Devotional Change in Nineteenth-Century Mexico," *Past and Present*, 221 (November 2013); Edward Wright-Rios, *Revolutions in Mexican Catholicism: Reform and Revelation in Oaxaca, 1887–1934* (Durham, NC: Duke University Press, 2009) and *Searching for Madre Matiana: Prophecy and Popular Culture in Modern Mexico* (Albuquerque, NM: University of New Mexico Press, 2014).

2 For an overview of this scholarship, see Margaret Chowning, "Convents and Nuns: New Approaches to the Study of Female Religious Institutions in Colonial Mexico," *History Compass* 6, no. 5 (2008): 1279–1303.

the colonial period had only two viable options – marriage or the convent – remains a fallback assumption in much of our scholarship and teaching, even though scholars have shown that consensual cohabitation, illegitimate children, and economically independent (though perhaps struggling) women were not unusual.[3] This is understandable because, while the notion of women as either wives or nuns may not entirely square with historical realities, it does reflect a powerful colonial ideal that remains salient for historians precisely because of the way it shaped all women's experiences and, in particular, their relationship to the religious culture that permeated colonial society. In other words, while it may have been unattainable, the proscription that a good woman should be either a cloistered nun or a secluded, pious, and obedient wife was familiar to everyone in New Spain. And women of all walks of life knew that they were being measured against this ideal in some context of their lives.

The day-to-day particulars of women's complex negotiations with this largely unattainable social and spiritual mandate, along with many other aspects of the church's ubiquitous role in colonial life, have remained relatively unknown. Only when the church was threatened – its traditional roles and privileges challenged after Mexico ceased to be a Spanish colony – did laywomen's intense attachments to the church become more visible to historians; and yet this happened in an era in which they were also changing tremendously. What appear to be the historical actions of women defending the church in the context of liberal opposition may be more accurately described as both women and the church seeing new opportunities, in each other, for increased civic engagement in a period of crisis, rupture, and redefinition. The affiliations, public activities, and passionate engagement that lay behind the anticlerical image of a conservative woman wedded to an antiquated, backward institution actually represented new dynamics in women's relationship to the church.[4]

3   On the distance between sexual and marital behavior and church proscriptions, see Asunción Lavrin, "Sexuality in Colonial Mexico: A Church Dilemma," in *Sexuality and Marriage in Colonial Latin America*, ed. Asunción Lavrin (Lincoln, NE: University of Nebraska, 1989). On the realities of women's lives and choices, see Pilar Gonzalbo Aizpuru, "Las mujeres novohispanos y las contradicciónes de una sociedad patriarcal," in *Las mujeres en la construcción de las sociedades Iberoamericanas*, eds. Pilar Gonzalbo Aizpuru and Berta Aires Queija (Mexico City: El Colegio de México, Centro de Estudios Históricos, 2004).

4   Margaret Chowning, "The Catholic Church and the Ladies of the Vela Perpetua"; "La femenización de la piedad en México: Género y piedad en las cofradías de españoles: Tendencias coloniales y pos-coloniales en los arzobispados de Michoacán y Guadalajara," in *Religión, política e identidad en la época de la independencia de México*, ed. Brian Connaughton (Mexico City: UAM, 2010); and "Liberals, Women, and the Church in Mexico: Politics and the Feminization of Piety, 1700–1930." Paper presented at the Harvard Latin American Studies seminar, Cambridge, MA, 2002; Silvia Marina Arrom, "Las Señoras de la Caridad: pioneras olvidadas de la asistencia social en México, 1863–1910." *Historia Mexicana* 57, no. 2 (Oct.–Dec. 2007): 445–90; and "Mexican Laywomen

But how do we explain the willingness of women to seize upon these new opportunities? What was it that made women inclined to seek them out and to lend their support to the church in the first place? Nineteenth-century changes alone do not suffice as an explanation, nor does the exclusion of women from the masculinist state and its nation-building projects. Historians need to also reckon with the long history of women seeking and finding a significant portion of the scarce emotional and material resources available to them in their relationship to the church and their participation in religious culture. If we accept the story of colonial Catholicism as uniformly oppressive to all but the most elite women and, even then, offering only very limited avenues of participation, we cannot fully understand the phenomenon of so many ordinary women publicly defending the church in the early national period.

The fuller explanation is not a simple one, however. Neither is it found clearly in stories of resistance or accommodation. Rather, to understand the colonial history of the possibilities women sought, found, and created in the national period, we have to examine the gradually forged relationships, day-to-day interactions and practices, and cumulative knowledge that constituted women's participation in colonial religious culture. This history is one of troubling devotion in two senses of the words: troubling, as an adjective, because women's devotion was significant even when it seems to have reinforced the very ideas and power dynamics that caused them harm; and troubling, as a verb, because the history that results from examining laywomen's role in shaping religious culture challenges the usual understanding of what counts as religious devotion. Women of all geographies, racial categories, and social positions participated in a spiritual economy that was both transcendent and material and that involved institutions and social networks as much as it did intimate and emotionally charged relationships. "Devotion" gets at some of the affective potency of women's connections to religious ideas, authorities, images, and sacraments and other embodied practices. But it falls short of explaining the depth to which these things shaped the whole of women's lives and possibilities, the urgency of women's negotiations and interpretations of them, and thus the impact women had on them.

Understanding women's participation in colonial religious culture has the power to change the way we think about the church's role in colonial society in general. Throughout the course of my research, I encountered a number of things that challenged what I had previously thought about colonial dynamics and processes more generally. Taking women's

Spearhead a Catholic Revival: The Ladies of Charity, 1863–1910," in *Religious Culture in Modern Mexico*, ed. Martin Austin Nesvig (Lanham, MD: Rowman and Littlefield Publishers Inc., 2007), 50–77.

interactions with the church as the point of departure can nuance and sometimes transform time-honored interpretations of religious practices and cultural change. Most of these shifts are subtle, and yet they engage with important debates in the historiography. Things as varied as the development of the individual in early modern history, the relative strength and effectiveness of the Inquisition in New Spain, jurisdictional divisions in ecclesiastical justice, the shape of convent reforms, and the development of prisons and other disciplinary institutions all look somewhat different when seen through the lens of women's engagement with the church.[5]

This book explores women's participation in religious culture through their engagements with rituals, authorities, institutions, and ideas. Throughout, it pays attention to how colonial understandings of sexuality, gender, race, and social status shaped those interactions. It makes four general arguments: the first is that, over time, the church developed a distinct body of ideas and practices related to laywomen; the second is that laywomen absorbed, sometimes embraced, and always strategically engaged with these practices, even as they were deeply meaningful; the third is that women's understanding of and responses to these ideas and practices constituted an additional recognizable, though informal, body of knowledge; and the fourth is that this body of knowledge was something that church authorities and institutions engaged with in ways that in turn subtly altered institutional and sacramental practice. It is through this back-and-forth exchange that laywomen became essential players – in partnership and tension with many aspects of the church – in creating and shaping colonial religious culture. The details of this process, its varying contexts, and the specific content it produced fill the rest of these pages.

Documenting this dialogic relationship between laywomen and church authorities, infrastructure, and ritual reveals important aspects of the daily elaboration of cultures of religiosity and the social contracts that supported, challenged, and shaped the Catholic Church's role in colonial society. By the mid-seventeenth century, church courts' broad jurisdiction over marriage and sexuality, together with a long discursive tradition of theological and social concern over women's spiritual, physical, mental, and emotional capacities, led to an expansive body of pastoral, institutional, and juridical ideas and practices aimed specifically at laywomen. Ecclesiastical authorities were especially concerned with the perceived contagion of sin and scandal and with women's roles either as dangerous vectors of such contagion or as protective bulwarks against it. Images, ecclesiastical

---

5   Each of these subjects warrants focused research that centers women's experiences and religiosity, which may very well lead to important interpretive shifts.

communication, and official religious discourse depicted women as existing on a continuum in relation to this question – from those who posed the greatest threat to society (the defiantly corrupt woman, the fallen but redeemable woman, and the vulnerable but protectable woman) to those whose sanctioned position and model behavior actually strengthened society (the securely protected woman and the exceptionally virtuous woman capable of sanctifying others). Women of diverse social locations engaged with these concepts in their devotional lives and interactions with church authorities and institutions; they embraced, challenged, and interpreted these ideas in ways that helped them create meaning, solve problems, and navigate disciplinary forces. These efforts constituted a layer of lay religious culture that clergymen and institutional authorities then had to contend with to do their jobs effectively.

Seeing laywomen's experiences and choices in New Spain requires paying attention to both formal and informal interactions, mining fragmentary evidence, and incorporating both marginal and mundane contexts and events. It is helpful in this process to think of the colonial church as a web of social relationships, practices, ideas, moral obligations, and beliefs rather than as a discrete institutional entity or even a collection of interlocking institutions. "The church" in New Spain (and other early modern places) was at once an institutional network, a community, and a culture. Seen this way, the boundaries of what was "church" and what was not become porous, which is precisely how people living in colonial Mexico most likely experienced them.

Historians over the past two decades have increasingly challenged the separation of "popular" and "elite" religiosity and troubled the demarcation of clear boundaries between an official, orthodox, institutional church and an informal realm of practice.[6] In spite of this important shift, it remains methodologically challenging to focus on the role of devotional practice in people's daily lives while also attending sufficiently to the workings of church institutions within colonial society. However, this is the very challenge we must continue to meet if we are to accurately reflect the history of "religion" and "church" in the early modern era. In colonial Mexico, this means attending to the human exchanges that forged the social contract between the church and society, which simultaneously limited and validated ecclesiastical power. It means keeping in mind the

---

6　The analytical lens of "local religion" has been particularly helpful in moving beyond these binaries. See, for example, William Christian, *Local Religion in Sixteenth-Century Spain* (Princeton, NJ: Princeton University Press, 1981); Martin Austin Nesvig, ed., *Local Religion in Colonial Mexico* (Albuquerque, NM: University of New Mexico Press, 2006; Amos Megged, *Exporting the Reformation: Local Religion in Early Colonial Mexico* (New York: Brill Press, 1996); and Jennifer Scheper Hughes, *Biography of a Mexican Crucifix: Lived Religion and Local Faith from the Conquest to the Present* (Oxford: Oxford University Press, 2010).

material and economic aspects of religious culture. And it means remaining alert to the ways that emotions and affective states like fear, respect, reverence, desire, guilt, relief, and joy brought meaning to and motivated people's decisions.[7]

Imagining an interlocking history of institutions, ideas, practices, and embodied, emotional experience and holding in productive tension concepts like devotion and coercion, belief and negotiation, and power and intimacy are essential in this history. While many laywomen identified profoundly with church teachings and practices, these same women also learned to interpret and navigate them strategically in order to find protection, assistance, and comfort. A key way that they did so was by expressing their needs and desires as consistent with the purposes of the church – particularly as manifested in attitudes toward sin and guilt, practices related to sacraments and the seclusion of women, and the proper role of priests in communities.

This expression both challenged and strengthened the constrictive force of Catholicism on women's lives. Confessors, ecclesiastical judges, and administrators of church-supported cloisters and shelters for laywomen found themselves having to accommodate women's interpretations in the day-to-day execution of their jobs. In this dynamic and ongoing exchange, women learned to see themselves as female parishioners with gender-specific obligations owed to them, and religious authorities learned to see their vocations as including specific responsibilities to laywomen. Through this mutually constitutive learning process, laywomen contributed to, elaborated upon, and helped shape the devotional landscape and religious culture of colonial Mexico.

### Laywomen: Clarification of Terms

"Laywomen" is an inherently problematic term for this time period. Though some scholars of modern Catholicism consider all women part of the laity because they are excluded from the clergy, this is not the way the term was used in colonial Mexico. *Laicas,* or laywomen, referred to women who had not taken binding religious vows to live as black-habited nuns, living in a convent, after completing a novitiate period and professing to a particular religious order. There was nonetheless some slippage in this term. Laicas included a whole range of women, some of whose lives looked very much like nuns – namely, novitiates, white-habited nuns, and *beatas*

---

7  Javier Villa-Flores and Sonya Lipsett-Rivera, eds., *Emotions and Daily Life in Colonial Mexico* (Albuquerque, NM: University of New Mexico Press, 2004); Pilar Gonzalbo Aizpuru, ed., *Historia de la vida cotidiana en México*, Vols. I–III (Mexico City: El Colegio de México, Fondo de Cultura Económica, 2004).

living in convent-like institutions called *beaterios*.[8] In some instances, the language used to describe these women combined the language of the laity with that used for professed nuns. The terms "lay sisters" and even "nuns of the white habit" show up in convent records and other documents, and scholars of nuns and convents do not always agree about their meaning. *Donadas*, for instance – women who were "donated" or who "donated" their own bodies and labor to convents but who wore habits and participated in the devotional life of the convent to a greater degree than other servants – sometimes appear in both primary and secondary sources as nuns who could not afford a dowry and found another path to a permanent, second-tier, cloistered religious life, while at other times they appear more like ordinary servants or even slaves.[9] Contemporary observers and scholars alike reflect a certain fluidity between the terms "lay sisters," "beatas," "donadas," and "nuns of the white habit." In addition, laywomen living in convents – including servants, slaves, and *niñas* (girls and women who lived as dependents of individual nuns) – often shared space and daily routines with professed nuns. All of this renders the distinction between these groups of women more or less relevant, depending on the question at hand.

With all of this ambiguity and blurriness around the category of "laywomen," my use of the term requires some justification. First, the term "laywomen" is simply a more elegant way of saying "non-nuns." Nuns appear in this study, but they are not the focus. Nuns were an important but unusual group of women in colonial Mexico, and their prestige and education resulted in a rich body of sources that has led to a layered historiography. This study seeks to place the "other" women at the center – the majority of women who did not take binding religious vows and live as a class of cloistered religious elites. My second reason for using the term "laywomen" is its capaciousness. Using laywomen as my broadest organizing category allows me to see the variety of factors that shaped women's lives within and aside from their lay status. In other words, rather than making a claim that laywomen's lives were more like one another's lives than that of nuns, my hope is that by excluding nuns from my main focus but including everyone else, I can highlight the diversity of experiences and practices that existed among laywomen. Race/*casta*, class/social status, geography, and spiritual status are the primary categories of analysis through which I understand the choices available to different laywomen

---

8 Beatas were laywomen who took nonbinding vows of celibacy and devotion. Some lived independently, some took additional vows of poverty and obedience to a particular religious order and lived adjacent to them, and some lived in cloisters exclusively for beatas called beaterios.

9 Kathryn Burns, *Colonial Habits: Convents and the Spiritual Economy of Cuzco, Peru* (Durham, NC: Duke University Press, 1999); Asunción Lavrin, *Brides of Christ: Conventual Life in Colonial Mexico* (Stanford, CA: Stanford University Press, 2008); and J. Holler, *"Escogidas Plantas": Nuns and Beatas in Mexico City, 1531–1601* (New York, NY: Columbia University, 2005).

and the varying ways they participated in the making of colonial Catholicism.[10]

The very imprecision of the term "laywomen" is also useful; like the boundaries of church and not-church, complete clarity is not possible, nor should it be. Some laywomen's lives and associations placed them squarely within the world of nuns and clergy, while others had very little contact with these manifestations of church authority. These differences, and the fact that some women are more accurately thought of as inhabiting a liminal space between professed nun and laica, make "laywomen" a productive category for highlighting the way that gendered understandings of piety and reputation shaped women's social status, alongside and entangled with racialized, economic, and geographic differences.

## Spiritual Status

A theoretical proposition that underlies many of the arguments in this book is that there existed a historically specific category of social power that was related to one's reputation for piety and virtue, together with one's concrete connections to the church. Elsewhere I have proposed using the term "spiritual status" to describe this nexus of social difference and argued that doing so helps us better understand the co-constitutive nature of racialized, gendered, and economically shaped colonial hierarchies.[11] When historians approach "religion" as a category of analysis rather than simply an object of study or a description, it becomes clear that what I am calling spiritual status was something that accrued and could be lost through relational interactions. It was both entangled with and distinct from other forms of

---

10   I use the word "casta" throughout the book in three ways: (1) together with race, to indicate the workings and hierarchies of power mapped onto the differences between colonial categories such as: *Españoles, Indios, Negros, Mulatos, Mestizos, Castizos, Moriscos,* and *Lobos*; (2) in the plural, "castas," to refer collectively to people of "mixed" descent; and (3) with the phrase "casta category" to refer collectively to the recognized colonial racial/ethnic categories that people used and assigned to one another. For various approaches to the workings of casta in colonial Latin America, see Ilona Katzew, *Casta Painting: Images of Race in Eighteenth-Century Mexico* (New Haven, CT: Yale University Press, 2004); María Elena Martinez, *Genealogical Fictions: Limpieza de Sangre, Religion, and Gender in Colonial Mexico* (Stanford, CA: Stanford University Press, 2008); and Rachel Sarah O'Toole, *Bound Lives: Africans, Indians, and the Making of Race in Colonial Peru* (Pittsburgh, PA: University of Pittsburgh Press, 2012).

11   Jessica Delgado, "Virtuous Women and the Contagion of Sin: Race, Poverty, and Women's Spiritual Status in Colonial Mexico," unpublished essay; "Public Piety and *Honestidad*: Women's Spiritual Status in Colonial Mexico," Annual Meeting of the American Academy of Religion, Chicago, IL, November 2012; and "Contagious Sin and Virtue: Race, Poverty, and Women's Spiritual Status in Colonial Mexico," Annual Meeting of the American Academy of Religion, Chicago, IL, November 2012.

social power and difference and thus worthy of analysis in and of itself. When we look carefully at the practices, modes of expression, qualities, ideas, relationships, and structures that modern people tend to associate with religion – which in colonial Mexico were intrinsically bound with politics, culture, law, economics, and social structures – it becomes clear that "religion" in colonial Mexico was not merely something people believed in or practiced but was also a field of relations that produced and was productive of social hierarchy.

Like race, class, and gender, "spiritual status" is not a phrase that colonial Latin Americans would have recognized or used in the way modern scholars may understand it. Recent scholarship seeking to better integrate the specificities of colonial Latin America and the Iberian early modern world in general into our understanding of modern concepts of race and racism has yielded productive and provocative arguments about the utility of the various categories and languages of difference that circulated in the colonial period as well as those historians of Latin America have used. These include *raza*, casta, *vecindad, razon, educación, limpieza de sangre*, old and new Christian, *miserable*, and *natural*, as well as the modern English language terms "race," "class," and "social status."[12]

I am particularly compelled by the usefulness of imagining all of these historical terms and the hierarchies they implied as being a part of the ubiquitous colonial category of *calidad*, or, literally, quality, which was used in a holistic way to refer to someone's social position as well as their personal characteristics. My contribution to this understanding of calidad is to encourage us to be attentive to the unnamed yet materially and socially significant category of social power and difference based on one's reputation for piety and virtue, which may have been particularly significant for women.[13] Spiritual status was fundamentally gendered. For women, it was essentially a combination of one's public reputation for piety and

---

12   For a definition and discussion of these and other terms, an overview of recent scholarship related to them, and a critical analysis of the role of religion in colonial racial formation, see Jessica Delgado and Kelsey Moss, "Race and Religion in the Early Modern Iberian Atlantic," in *The Oxford Handbook of Religion and Race in American History*, eds. Kathryn Gin Lum and Paul Harvey (Oxford: Oxford University Press, 2018). For examples of recent debates about race, class, and the colonial languages and hierarchies related to these modern terms, see the essays in María Elena Martínez, Max-Sebastián Hering Torres, and David Nirenberg, eds., *Race and Blood in the Iberian World* (Zurich: Lit Verlag, 2012).

13   There is a strong argument for thinking of calidad as a broad field of power and difference for colonial Latin America and spending our analytical time and energy trying to understand how people's individual qualities and group identities – understood as social, biological, or behavioral life circumstances, choices, and locations – operated together to produce people's perceived and experienced calidad. It may be that once such a framework is broadly utilized, we will no longer need to use modern terms except in the service of comparative and cross-regional histories of the terms and concepts themselves.

one's public reputation for sexual virtue or honor.[14] The most historically appropriate word to describe the latter part of this equation would be *recogimiento* – a complex word that, among other things, described the qualities of modesty, obedience, sexual continence, and withdrawal from public view.[15] However, women whose economic circumstances made withdrawal and seclusion impossible, nonetheless claimed the term, calling themselves *muy recogida* and asserting that they lived lives of *mucho recogimiento*. By this they meant that they avoided scandal, behaved in ways appropriate to their gender, and were sexually virtuous as fitting their role as either married or single.[16]

Historians have previously spoken about the "honor/shame" complex in ways that relate to spiritual status.[17] The benefit of using the honor/shame complex as an analytical tool is that it highlights the way *vergüenza* (shame) worked as both a positive and negative quality for women and that it reveals the social mandate for men to control women's behavior and reputation. A key part of men's honor, according to this scholarship, was their ability to ensure that the women in their families exhibited vergüenza. The limits of the honor/shame complex as a lens, however, is that it does not allow us to talk about the productive elements of social status for women as it related to sexual reputation nor about the way this status could accrue in relation to both sexual and gendered virtue and a reputation for piety. Seen through the honor/shame complex, only men were truly able to lay claim to honor; vergüenza was a female quality upon which men's honor depended but it did not accrue independently for women. Men's honor certainly affected the women in their families, but this formulation of gendered power does not take into account anything other than referential status for women. In other words, the shame/honor complex reveals something important about patriarchal relations, but it does not reveal the connection between women's own social status and gendered behaviors of modesty, "honesty," obedience, and reserve. These characteristics are connected to vergüenza, but they are not exactly the same thing.

The term "recogimiento," on the other hand, does much of this work for us. Women laid claim to recogimiento as something they had and

---

14   I have yet to work out the usefulness and limits of the term for men, and I invite others to join me in this task.

15   For an excellent history of the concept and practice of recogimiento in colonial Peru, see van Deusen, *Between the Sacred and the Worldly: The Institutional and Cultural Practice of Recogimiento in Colonial Lima* (Stanford, CA: Stanford University Press, 2002).

16   In New Spain, this is particularly visible in women's testimonies before diocesan courts.

17   Ramón Gutiérrez, *When Jesus Came, the Corn Mothers Went Away: Marriage, Sexuality, and Power in New Mexico, 1500–1846* (Stanford, CA: Stanford University Press, 1991); Verena Martinez-Alier, *Marriage, Class, and Colour in Nineteenth-Century Cuba: A Study of Racial Attitudes and Sexual Values in a Slave Society* (Ann Arbor, MI: University of Michigan Press, 1989).

something they expressed, and men and women both used it to describe women. Recogimiento, by some evaluations, might require possessing the proper amount of "shame" (scrupulousness, modesty, caution, even squeamishness), but overall, it operated much like the English word "virtue" does now. In other words, a woman described as "muy recogida" or "de mucho recogimiento" was not merely a woman who had shame but was a virtuous woman – a woman of honor. Her honor may have been determined in large part by her degree of modesty, seclusion, and self-containment, but the word nonetheless also implied a level of moral righteousness that vergüenza does not quite convey.[18]

One's public reputation for recogimiento was part of what defined women's spiritual status, but another was women's public reputation for piety. These two things were interrelated; if a woman was known to frequent the sacraments, have close but appropriate relationships with priests, and otherwise exhibit signs of devotional piety, the reigning presumption was that she was also chaste, modest, reserved, and obedient. And if she was known as a woman of great recogimiento, observers would likely assume that she was also pious and that her piety was orthodox. Conversely, if it was known that a woman had been sexually active outside marriage – especially in a public or scandalous way – her piety would also be suspect, even if she was openly devoted to the sacraments. And if a woman's piety was in doubt – if she had been accused of religious error, was suspected of unorthodox religious practices, or was simply openly lax about fulfilling religious requirements – the assumption that she was also sexually incontinent tended to follow.

Spiritual status was a ubiquitous category that marked a woman's degree of privilege and prestige in colonial Mexico, but it operated in interlocking ways with other social status indicators. Race/caste, class/social status, gender, and spiritual status were co-constitutive and reinforcing. Concretely, this means that while in theory, the spiritual status of a woman of African descent with a reputation for great piety and recogimiento could partially mitigate her subordinate position within the

---

18  Peter Bakewell and Jaqueline Holler define the relationship between honor, vergüenza, and recogimiento in the following way: "Both men and women inherited honor from their families, yet the nature of the virtue demanded of the sexes was quite distinct. Men's honor resided in manliness, loyalty, honesty, and zealous concern for the reputation of their families ... Women's honor, by contrast, was primarily conceived of as *vergüenza*, or shame, a quality that manifested itself in modesty, sexual propriety, and, among the higher classes, *recogimiento*." Peter Bakewell and Jaqueline Holler, *A History of Latin America to 1825*, third edn. (Malden, MA: John Wiley & Sons, 2010), 333. This use of "recogimiento" takes at face value the elite definition, which includes literal seclusion, however, as van Deusen found for Peru and I have found for Mexico, women in the lower social classes also claimed this term for themselves as exactly those qualities attributed in the above quote to vergüenza – that of modesty and sexual propriety. However, they did so in a way that implied the possibility of owning, accruing, and recovering recogimiento as a positive quality.

colonial racial hierarchy, in practice it was very difficult for a woman of African descent to arrive at such a reputation. The presumption that black women were promiscuous and prone to religious error was widespread and difficult to surmount.

Nonetheless spiritual status was a factor in determining one's life circumstances and position in the colonial society, and it had the potential to both reinforce and undercut other categories of difference and power. Just as some people of African, Indigenous, and mixed descent did achieve unusual levels of wealth and social power, so did some poor and nonwhite people come to be admired for their piety or some wealthy people lose their social status when sexual or spiritual scandal destroyed their reputations. Spiritual status could sometimes alter the social perception of a woman's race or caste. However, the most important insight that comes of employing "spiritual status" as an analytical category is not the revelation that there was sometimes some wiggle room in colonial social hierarchies but rather that "religion" in this time and place – alongside race/caste, gender, class/social status, and other factors – shaped people's social and material possibilities and was implicated in relations of power. Spiritual status had material ramifications that varied in relation to other aspects of a woman's social position and circumstances; one's reputation for piety and sexual and gendered propriety mattered for laywomen and all the more so if they lacked the shield that whiteness, wealth, and effective male protection could provide.

This is not to reduce religion to class, however; there was certainly more to piety and virtue than reputation and more to reputation than its material implications. The point of naming spiritual status as such, rather, is to highlight the way in which concerns we might think of as spiritual were intricately intertwined with concerns we might think of as social and material. For instance, greater spiritual status provided increased access to spaces and practices that had salvific and transcendent value. And public reputation for virtue and piety protected laywomen's ability to enjoy a vibrant and fulfilling devotional life, which in turn deepened their relationships to God and the saints and assured them safety in the afterlife.

This study does not focus primarily on women's accrual and loss of spiritual status, but both were important factors in the constraints and opportunities through which laywomen engaged with the church and shaped colonial Catholicism. Furthermore, laywomen's efforts to protect, gain, or regain spiritual status were in and of themselves an important way they participated in and shaped religious culture. In order to understand what spiritual status meant to women, it is crucial to understand colonial ideas about the contagiousness of sin, scandal, and virtue and the gendered nature of this contagion.

## Contagion of Sin; Contagion of Virtue

Another set of assertions that are folded into the main arguments of this study include the following: (1) women occupied a particular place in colonial notions of the self in relation to the community, (2) sin and scandal were experienced as contagious, (3) women were understood as particularly dangerous vectors of this contagion, and (4) under certain circumstances, women's virtue could also be contagious. Religious authorities and laypeople alike discussed and related to sin, scandal, and spiritual health as if they spread from person to person and from individuals to the collective. Furthermore, institutional practice and cultural discourse alike placed all women on a spiritual continuum that spanned from especially dangerous contaminants to powerful forces for sanctification, and these seemingly dichotomous positions were in fact intimately linked.

Seen as particularly susceptible to corruption and temptation, women represented a weak link in the community's defenses against the forces of Satan, a notion visible in trials against women for witchcraft, false visions, and other religious crimes.[19] Furthermore, clergymen, religious institutions, and pious society operated out of an awareness of the spiritual liability that women's subordinate social position represented for the collective. In a sexual economy that prized the appearance of virginity for marital prospects and a social context that included limited economic possibilities for women outside marriage, the belief that women were physically, emotionally, and spiritually weaker than men meant the ever-present danger of "fallen" women who had been forced to turn to a life of sin in order to survive. Even when a woman was virtuous, social weakness, especially when compounded by poverty, could lead her to ruin, and this ruin threatened the spiritual well-being of society as a whole. Concern about this vulnerability gave rise to a variety of "solutions" to the social problem of unprotected women, including institutional cloisters, funds to provide dowries for marriage or entry into a convent, and the practice of *depósito* – an official transfer of legal guardianship of a woman, either temporary or indefinite, to an institution or private residence.

19 Solange Alberro, "Herejes, brujas, y beatas: mujeres ante el tribunal del Santo Oficio de la Inquisición en la Nueva España," in *Presencia y transparencia: la mujer en la historia de México*, ed. Carmon Ramos Escandón (Mexico City: El Colegio de México, 1987), 79–94; Mary Giles, *Women in the Inquisition: Spain and the New World* (Baltimore, MD: Johns Hopkins University Press, 1998); Stacey Schlau, *Gendered Crime and Punishment: Women and/in the Hispanic Inquisitions* (Boston, MA: Brill, 2013); Nora Jaffary, *False Mystics: Deviant Orthodoxy in Colonial Mexico* (Lincoln, NE: University of Nebraska Press, 2004); Martha Few, *Women Who Live Evil Lives: Gender, Religion, and the Politics of Power in Colonial Guatemala* (Austin, TX: University of Texas Press, 2002); and Laura Lewis, *Hall of Mirrors: Power, Witchcraft, and Caste in Colonial Mexico* (Durham, NC: Duke University Press, 2003).

Laywomen were constantly interacting with these ideas and the practices and institutions to which they gave rise. They encountered them in their relationships with priests and their experiences of confession. They both suffered and benefited from them in the context of ecclesiastical courts. And they utilized and contested the possibilities and constraints they found in systems and institutions designed for the seclusion of women. These choices and the dialogues of which they were a part affected and helped construct colonial Catholic religious culture in an ongoing way.

## Place, Periodization, and Change over Time

The approach of this study is more thematic than chronological. While I maintain a historian's interest in change over time and try to note it when it is most visible, diachronic analysis is not the primary mode of story-telling here. This was not my original intent, but as I deepened my research, the narrative became more and more synchronic. Rather than changes, I focused on the relational dynamics I saw played out for a more than a century, and I sought to understand how laywomen shaped and participated in religious culture in New Spain in the mid-colonial period.

Nonetheless, the periodization of the study is an interpretive choice. The bulk of my material is from the early to mid-seventeenth century to the mid- to late eighteenth century. Most of it falls between 1640 and 1770, though the more expansive dates of 1630 to 1790 reflect the smaller number of sources and examples that stretch beyond this core time period. My rationale for choosing these dates was twofold. One was my interest in what scholars have deemed the long seventeenth century as a useful time to study societal dynamics and social relations. In between the tumultuous-ness of the formative period following conquest and establishing colonial society throughout the sixteenth century and the dramatic changes brought by the most aggressive Bourbon reforms in the last two or three decades of the colonial period, the mid-seventeenth to the mid-eighteenth centuries provide an opportunity for historians to study the workings of a colonial Catholic society that was fairly well established. Because I wanted to be able to highlight the mechanisms through which laywomen shaped, enforced, challenged, and negotiated religious culture in an ongoing way, this time period provided a fruitful though challenging opportunity. Nonetheless, some sources, particularly those coming from the Inquisition and petitions related to cloisters, do not demonstrate significant changes in kind or quantity around 1770. This is in contrast with local diocesan ecclesiastical courts, the sources from which reveal a dramatic decline in women's engagement after 1775.

In the future, in addition to taking a closer look at change over time, I hope that scholars will pick up the various themes, subjects, and sites of interaction represented by each of these chapters and look more closely at how they mapped on to particular places. The bulk of the sources for this book come from central Mexico, but I did not exclude material from any part of New Spain. For the same reason that change over time became less important than taking the whole of what I could see into account, so did a commitment to local context give way to a broad lens that attends more to generalizable differences in place – such as differences between urban and rural locations, small and large cities, indigenous towns and Spanish or mixed-race communities – than to a deep grounding in particular local histories. The next step for further research would be to look for variations in the context of focused local and comparative histories.

The difficulty in finding material that elucidates the lives and choices of laywomen and the fragmented and often decontextualized nature of what sources do exist led me to cast a wide net in terms of both time and place, to allow my arguments to be more synchronic than diachronic, and – with the notable exception of one chapter that is set in the town of Toluca – to focus on general categories of space rather than the contours of particular places. These choices also responded to the scope of the study and the questions I am asking. There has been no book-length study of laywomen and the church, and I wanted to understand this relationship broadly by engaging with various sites of interaction.[20] I wanted to look at married and single women together, in both urban and rural spaces, and to include laywomen of the fullest range of status and life experience. However, I hope this attempt to address the gap in our knowledge of ordinary women's lives and contributions to religious culture will open the way for future scholars to look more closely at the many individual subjects and themes this book takes up, with heightened attention to particularity of location and change over time.

## Organization and Logic

The book is divided into two sections: Part I consists of three chapters that examine laywomen's experiences and interactions with sacraments, clergy, and courts; and Part II is made up of three chapters about laywomen's engagements with places, practices, and ideologies of cloister and containment. Both sections are tied together by three things: the importance of colonial notions of sin, scandal, piety, and virtue as contagious and of women as particularly significant agents of these spiritual and diabolical

---

20  Brianna Leavitt-Alcantara's important new book will also significantly remedy this gap by improving our understanding of unmarried laywomen's devotional practice in the late colonial and early independence era Guatemala. Brianna Leavitt-Alcantara, *Alone at the Altar: Single Women and Devotion in Guatemala, 1670–1870* (Stanford, CA: Stanford University Press, 2018).

contagions; the way in which women's navigation of these ideas shaped their spiritual status; and the ways laywomen's choices, responses, and interpretations of the world around them shaped the religious culture of colonial Mexico.

The logic of a tryptic consisting of sacraments, clergy, and courts might not seem evident at first glance, but in the lives and experiences of laywomen, these three elements of the church and colonial Catholicism were intertwined in revealing ways. The sacraments of confession and communion constituted a fundamental learning ground for the ideas that shaped women's religiosity as well as the primary site for their engagement with clergymen. Priests understood their sacramental roles as including those of teachers, fathers, and healers first but secondarily that of judges. Local diocesan courts, on the other hand, were explicit manifestations of clergymen's judicial powers. Though women's interactions with these courts were less frequent and regular than was their exposure to confession and communion, they took ideas and sensibilities worked out in the confessional and expressed them in these courts in ways that were sometimes to their benefit. As confessors, clergymen were charged with didactic, regulatory, and restorative duties at the level of individual penitents, and they enacted these in particular ways with women. As ecclesiastical judges in local diocesan courts, clergymen were charged with the protection of the local community from public sin, which allowed women opportunities to seek their help in their conflicts with men. The first two chapters look at these two aspects of women's relationships with priests as well as their engagement with the ideas that threaded their way through these sacramental and judicial contexts.

Local investigatory mechanisms of the Inquisition are the focus of the third chapter. These practices relied heavily on the contexts of confession and diocesan courts and, specifically, on the relationships that women and priests forged within them. The Inquisition imposed itself onto women's sacramental experiences and relationships in order to gather information, and it sometimes co-opted ecclesiastical judges for this purpose as well. But most importantly, the Inquisition utilized women's emotional, spiritual, and social experiences related to sin and scandal in ways that turned women into agents of an Inquisitorial culture.

Part II picks up the thread of ideas related to female contagion and looks at practices of containment and women's engagement with them. The subjects of Chapters 4, 5, and 6 are the practices, ideologies, and actual places involved in the cloister, control, containment, and protection of laywomen. All of the places and practices studied in Part II developed out of the belief that it was necessary both to protect society from the coercive impact of some women and to benefit society by protecting others and concentrating their sanctifying power. I argue in this section that religious authorities and pious society envisioned these cloistering and containment practices as connected and existing on a continuum, whether they dealt with highly pious or highly suspect women.

## Part I: Chapters and Sources

Chapter 1 explores women's diverse experiences of the twin sacraments of penance and Eucharist with a particular focus on women's relationships with the priests who acted as sacramental facilitators and gatekeepers. It approaches these sacraments as learning contexts for both laywomen and priests through which both parties communicated and expressed expectations, gathered knowledge, and developed repertoires of behavior and practice. The didactic function of confession and the repetitive, physical, and somatic nature of these ritual interactions forged and deepened women's understandings of church teachings and how to interact with church authorities. In turn, these same interactions forged and deepened clergymen's understanding of women and how to relate to them in these contexts.

While some scholars have explored the oft-contested significance of these sacraments in Indigenous communities and in the complicated relationships between uniquely visionary nuns and their confessors, there has been little written about the role of confession and communion in laywomen's lives, particularly nonelite laywomen.[21] Patriarchal social relations, gendered ideas about sin, and beliefs about women's particular vulnerabilities and weaknesses distinguished women's sacramental experiences from those of men. At the same time, great diversity in life circumstances and status among laywomen meant that their engagement with confession and communion was far more varied than that of cloistered religious women. Differences in geography, wealth, social and spiritual status, and caste and race shaped laywomen's experiences with these sacraments as well as the ways priests related to their female penitents. For some women, these rituals represented nearly the only contact they had with priests, and this contact may have been limited to the annual Lenten requirement to complete a single confession followed by communion. For other women, frequent confession and communion were significant aspects

21 For confession in Indigenous communities, see Nicholas Griffiths and Fernando Cervantes, eds., *Spiritual Encounters: Interactions Between Christianity and Native Religions in Colonial America* (Birmingham, AL: University of Birmingham Press, 1999). For nuns and beatas and their confessors, see Jodi Bilinkoff, *Related Lives: Confessors and Their Female Penitents, 1450–1750* (Ithaca, NY: Cornell University Press, 2005); Elsa Sampson Vela Tudela, *Colonial Angels: Narratives of Spirituality and Gender, 1580–1750* (Austin, TX: University of Texas Press, 2000); and Kristine Ibsen, *Women's Spiritual Autobiography in Colonial Spanish America* (Gainesville, FL: University Press of Florida, 1999).

of their regular interactions with priests – interactions that may have included social visits, family connections, and female networks of piety grounded in relationships to particular clergymen.

These sacraments pose challenges to social historians. While ideals about confession and communion can be found in didactic literature, what actually transpired was documented only in the breach. Historians' ability to see what took place within the actual events of confession and communion is limited by the private nature of confession and the lack of description of ordinary examples of communion in the historical record. If sacramental relations and procedures were unproblematic and uncontested, they rarely left written traces. Documentation of them generally happened only when something went wrong enough to warrant court testimonies, official complaints, and clerical investigations. The resulting judicial and institutional sources reflect the importance of these sacraments as places of learning, but they do so in a refracted manner.

Nonetheless Inquisition records produced in response to unsanctioned sacramental behavior offer the most detailed window into what happened during confession and communion. In spite of the distortions inherent in these kinds of cases, the testimonies they contain allow us to see patterns in women's experiences and the meanings they ascribed to them. Inquisitors asked open-ended questions about their histories with clergymen and sacraments, and in response, laywomen spoke broadly about their experiences, referencing practices, emotions, and learned strategies that often went beyond what the Inquisitors were looking for. In particular, the richest body of sources for learning about women's experiences and expectations of confession and communion come from testimonies the Inquisition gathered in relation to the crime of *solicitación*. Solicitación was a minor heretical offense in which a confessor used the sacrament to engage in sexual acts or express sexual desires. While these sources clearly contain distortions in terms of their depiction of "normal" confessional practices, the structure of these testimonies still conveys aspects of the significance and meaning of both sacraments in women's lives as well as revealing important aspects of their relationships with priests.

The experience and threat of sexual violence and violation were a part of women's experiences of confession, but the sources that provide a window into these sacraments unavoidably over-represent this aspect of sacramental relationships. There is no way to avoid this, and readers will inevitably be powerfully affected, as I have been in doing this research, by the painful histories of trauma that cases of solicitación captured. It is a difficult task to glean information about ordinary interactions from evidence produced by largely disturbing and often violent ones and then to write about both in a way that neither overemphasizes nor minimizes the abusive possibilities of these sacraments. Imagining how to do this is a part of my ongoing work as a scholar of women's lives.[22] I have not yet found a satisfactory balance, and I look forward to the questions and critiques this chapter in particular will undoubtedly provoke.

It is important to understand how women came to testify in solicitación cases in order to read them with the necessary caution and to recognize what makes them valuable sources of information. Most laywomen came to testify against their confessors either because the Inquisition specifically called them to do so or because a priest – usually another confessor – told them they were obligated to present a denunciation. In fact, the majority of women who appeared "voluntarily," meaning without having been called by the Inquisition, had actually been compelled to do so in the course of an actual confession. The Inquisition asked confessors to help regulate religious error by looking for evidence of particular sins or crimes, including solicitación. If a penitent mentioned something that fell into the category of religious errors under the Inquisition's jurisdiction, confessors were not allowed to absolve the penitent until she or he had informed the Inquisition. This was true whether the penitent had committed the sin themselves or merely suffered from a troubled conscience as a result of knowing about someone else's crime. In the sacramental theology of colonial Catholicism in New Spain, both of these states required confession and absolution. This meant that the penitent would remain in the spiritually perilous state known as *enhoramala* until they presented a formal denunciation before a local *comisario*, or Inquisition representative.[23] Sometimes this was done in person, but other times, confessors would take a penitent's dictated denunciation and then deliver it to the comisario.

Chapter 2 examines another aspect of laywomen's relationships with clergymen, namely their interactions with priests as judges. To get at these interactions, this chapter looks at women's initiation of court cases related to sexuality, marriage, and gendered violence in the *Juzgado Eclesiástico de Toluca* – a regional ecclesiastical court under the authority of the archbishop of Mexico. Through this local case study, I explore women's interpretations of the court's stated purposes, their engagement with ideas about sin and scandal, and their expectations of and communications with priests as judges. In these court cases, women engaged with the notions of spiritual

22  Jessica Delgado, "Foregrounding Marginal Voices: Writing Women's Stories Using Solicitation Trials," in Sylvia Sellers-Garcia and Karen Melvin, eds., *Imagining Histories of Colonial Latin America: Synoptic Methods and Practices* (Albuquerque, NM: University of New Mexico Press, 2017).

23  The literal translation of "enhoramala" is "unfortunate, in a bad hour," or sometimes as an exclamation, "damn the hour." But in the sacramental context it referred to a dangerous state of the soul in which a person had sin on their conscience and had not completed confession. In this state, taking communion was forbidden, and if the individual died, she or he would have to pay for this unconfessed sin in purgatory. Its opposite, *enhorabuena*, connotes being in a fortunate state and is also used as a statement of congratulations or blessing.

health as collective and communal, of sin and scandal as contagious, and of women as particularly dangerous vectors in this equation. In their efforts to appeal to ecclesiastical judges for help and support, they invoked rather than contested these ideas but did so in a way that spurred judges to act on their behalf. Rather than simply presenting themselves as weak and in need of protection, these women reminded ecclesiastical judges of their obligations to protect the community from damage caused by unchecked sin and scandal, and they did so by positioning *themselves* as the unwitting sources of this scandal. Forced into a position in which their very circumstances threatened the health of the community, these women sought restitution for the crimes committed against them by the men ultimately responsible for the damage inflicted by women's compromised bodies and souls.

The archive of the Toluca court is unique among repositories of diocesan court records; whereas the records of most regional and local branches of the bishops' *Audiencia* have been either lost or scattered, the records of the Toluca court have remained largely intact. While women's use of this court to navigate their sexual and domestic relationships with men is striking, it is important to keep in mind that it was also still probably a last resort. Women in the region brought perhaps only two such cases a year. Nonetheless, women utilized the court in particular ways and significantly more than men did. In addition, testimonies from cases related to sexuality and marital conflict reflect that knowledge about these types of cases was more extensive than was the practice of bringing them, suggesting that women in the community knew it was a possible resource for them. In other words, the relatively few cases brought to court had a wider impact than the numbers might suggest. Whatever the case, these court documents themselves provide uncommonly clear examples of women articulating their own interpretations of church teachings about themselves.

The third chapter explores the ways that laywomen became entangled in the Inquisition's investigatory mechanisms and how this entanglement interrupted and affected their devotional lives and relationships with clergymen. This interruption reflects an important dynamic in women's experiences of "church" – namely, the distinctions, overlapping boundaries, and sometimes contradictory purposes and styles of different church institutions and authorities. Whereas women were able to engage with the purposes and priorities of diocesan courts with relative success, those of the Inquisition were rarely conducive to women's needs. Rather, the Inquisition's investigatory activities and methods utilized women's sacramental, judicial, and social relationships with priests – as well as women's informal homosocial communication networks – in ways that compromised laywomen's sacramental experiences and access, damaged their relationships with priests, and threatened their reputations and standing in their communities.

What made it possible for the Inquisition to tap into women's sacramental and social relationships was women's own engagement with church rituals and practices. Women's belief that sin and scandal were indeed contagious and that confession was necessary to restore one's spiritual health after being exposed to the sins of another led them to spread information – turning for comfort to each other as well as priests – in ways that the Inquisition could then utilize. And the importance of confession and communion in women's lives allowed the Inquisition to coerce them into testifying by threatening to interrupt their access to these sacraments. Thus, in addition to reflecting some of the complications of women's interactions with a multifaceted church, a focus on the Inquisition reveals elements of women's piety and the intersections of their devotional and social lives.

This chapter also complicates the view of women's participation in colonial religious culture presented in previous chapters. In Chapter 3, women themselves become agents of local Inquisitorial cultures of guilt, catharsis, and rumor. These cultures were bounded by time and place, and women's participation in them was largely the result of coercion, fear, and anxiety; nonetheless, the mechanisms and results were widespread enough to make up a significant aspect of women's contribution to colonial religiosity. Though women often unwittingly contributed to the Inquisition's methods of gathering information, and in spite of the fact that they were frequently harmed by the process and the resulting spread of suspicion and scrutiny, these dynamics remain a part of laywomen's role in the making of colonial Catholicism.

However, in order to see this, it is necessary to look beyond the usual scholarly emphasis on women as defendants in Inquisition trials and instead examine their roles as witnesses. It is also important to take into account the enormous amount of fragmentary evidence and testimony produced by dead-end local investigations rather than focusing on the relatively rare instances of full trials that arrived to the main tribunal of the Holy Office in Mexico City. Though scholars of the Inquisition in New Spain have correctly argued that the number of actual trials and convictions was in fact very small, the gathering of local denunciations and follow-up testimonies was far more widespread. When inspired by a particularly vigilant clergyman, the periodic publication of edicts, or even the fluctuations of informal communication practices and networks themselves, the processes examined in Chapter 3 could lead to a flurry of activity that could affect a community for years. Seen through the resulting fragmentary and incomplete records, women's engagement with the Inquisition appears far less rarefied and spectacular than a focus on trials would make it appear. Instead, it emerges as one factor among many that shaped women's devotional lives and relationship to the church.

## A Note on Ecclesiastical Justice

The Inquisition serves as a major source of documentation for all of the chapters in Part I, and the role of ecclesiastical justice in general looms large throughout the entire book. While it is not my primary purpose to enter into the historiographic debates related to the Inquisition and other ecclesiastical courts in New Spain, it is unavoidable that some of my arguments both build on and have implications for this scholarship. For this reason, it may be helpful to address some of these questions up front and to clarify the relationship between the two main branches of ecclesiastical justice represented in Part I.

Starting in the 1960s and increasing after the 1980s, scholarship about the Mexican Inquisition began to move against the legacy of the "black legend" that had previously shaped so much of the historical memory of the Spanish Inquisition as a whole. Scholars reassessed the significance of the Inquisition in colonial Mexican society, arguing that it was not the all-powerful institution of successful repression that this legend implied and increasingly turning to Inquisition trial records primarily as sources of social history.[24] While these have been important correctives and research directions, they have not fully addressed the local and informal impact of the Inquisition within Mexican communities. It is true that very few people found themselves the focus of an Inquisition trial; Richard Greenleaf found that only 5 percent of the population was subject to an Inquisition accusation; that of this 5 percent, only one-sixth of these cases ever came to trial; and that of these few trials, only about 2 percent of defendants were convicted.[25] However, these numbers do not reflect the much greater numbers of people who testified before a comisario as witnesses or accusers, nor can they measure the more widespread and indirect impact of the Inquisition's methods of gathering information. These mechanisms mobilized both clergy and laypeople in ways that encouraged the spread of information, along with guilt and surveillance, and had the potential to damage reputations, families, and communities.

A focus on trials rather than local investigations also gives the impression that Indigenous women and men rarely interacted with the Inquisition by the seventeenth century. However, this is not the case because Indigenous people frequently testified as witnesses. Royal and religious authorities

---

24   See, for example, Richard Boyer, *Lives of the Bigamists: Marriage, Family, and Community in Colonial Mexico* (Albuquerque, NM: University of New Mexico Press, 1995); Few, *Women Who Live Evil Lives;* Jaffary, *False Mystics;* Villa-Flores, *Dangerous Speech: A Social History of Blasphemy in Colonial Mexico* (Tucson, AZ: University of Arizona Press, 2006); and, for the Iberian world, Stuart Schwartz, *All Can Be Saved: Religious Tolerance and Salvation in the Iberian Atlantic World* (New Haven, CT: Yale University Press, 2008).

25   Richard Greenleaf, "Historiography of the Mexican Inquisition: Evolution of Interpretations and Methodologies," in *Cultural Encounters: The Impact of the Inquisition in Spain and the New World,* ed. Mary Elizabeth Perry and Anne J. Cruz (Berkeley, CA: University of California Press, 1991), 249–73.

debated the correctness of Native Americans being subjected to the harsh scrutiny of the Inquisition throughout the monastic and Episcopal Inquisition periods but finally decided against it in 1571, when the independent tribunals of the Holy Office of the Spanish Inquisition opened their doors in Mexico and Peru. At this time, King Philip decided that Native Americans, as a class of childlike subjects and neophytes in the faith, should be formally excluded from the Inquisition's jurisdiction for the time being, perhaps indefinitely. This meant that bishops and archbishops – and in practice, local clergymen as well – retained the primary authority to police the boundaries of orthodoxy in Indigenous communities. Formally, these duties belonged to the bishops' audiencias, known collectively as the *Provisorato de Indios y Chinos*.[26] However, in practice, heresy, idolatry, and other religious errors that the Inquisition regulated constituted only a small part of the work local ecclesiastical courts undertook in these communities. Rather, parish priests and regular clergy tended to take most of the responsibility for disciplining and educating the Indigenous population through confession, public penance, and didactic sermons.[27]

This being said, there remained a fair amount of fluidity and even confusion in how Inquisitorial authority was supposed to function for the Indigenous population.[28] The Provisorato de Indios y Chinos was one-third of a larger judicial apparatus under the bishop, shared by the *Provisorato de Españoles* and the *Juzgado de Testamentos, Capellanías, y Obras Pías*. Local tribunals of this apparatus, like the Juzgado Eclesiástico de Toluca and smaller parish courts, heard cases brought by and against members of both the Indigenous and non-Indigenous population within their jurisdiction and tended to have their hands full with matters other than religious heterodoxy. Only when a case was too serious or when the court wanted the advice of a superior did the local judge have to decide which central court had jurisdiction. On the other hand, in its formal inquisitorial function, the Provisorato de Indios continued to operate as an *Inquisición Ordinaria* and its *provisores* as *Inquisitores de Indios*, terms to which the Inquisition strongly objected but that the diocesan tribunals continued to claim throughout the colonial period.[29]

26  This was the umbrella court that supervised the Juzgado Eclesiástico de Toluca, the local tribunal that is the subject of Chapter 2.

27  Jorge Klor de Alva, "Colonizing Souls: The Failure of the Indian Inquisition and the Rise of Penitential Discipline," in *Cultural Encounters: The Impact of the Inquisition in Spain and the New World*, ed. Mary Elizabeth Perry and Anne J. Cruz (Berkeley, CA: University of California Press, 1991), 3–21; Greenleaf, "The Inquisition and the Indians of New Spain"; and Richard Greenleaf, "The Mexican Inquisition and the Indians: Sources for the Ethnohistorian," *The Americas* 34, no. 3 (Jan. 1978): 315–44.

28  Greenleaf, "The Inquisition and the Indians."

29  Greenleaf, "The Inquisition and the Indians" and "The Mexican Inquisition."

It is also the case that such trial records are scarce, due perhaps to some combination of poor bookkeeping, a tendency to leave all but the most serious cases of Indigenous heterodoxy in the hands of confessors and parish priests, and the loss of documentation in the nineteenth century when the state appropriated the bulk of church property and records. All of these factors have most likely contributed to the paucity of evidence of the Provisorato de Indio's Inquisitorial activity in all but the most notorious extirpation of idolatry campaigns. During the life of the Juzgado Eclesiástico de Toluca from 1680 to 1825, there were a total of three cases of idolatry, eighteen of witchcraft, one of superstition, two of blasphemy, and six of bigamy. All of these proceedings were very short, as they were primarily concerned with gathering testimony to be forwarded on to the Provisorato de Indios. The relatively few cases of religious crimes heard in this tribunal, which had jurisdiction over the largely Indigenous Valley of Toluca, suggest that it was parish priests who most often dealt with these issues through penitential discipline.

J. Jorge Klor de Alva has argued that penitential discipline was ultimately more important than the Inquisition or the inquisitorial activities of the diocesan tribunals in dealing with heterodoxy in Indigenous population.[30] This argument is borne out by Klor de Alva's evidence, but in the case of Indigenous people called to testify as witnesses before the Inquisition and for the non-Indigenous population in general, the division it makes may be too clear-cut. The impact of the Inquisition was in fact intimately linked to penitential discipline through the practice of confession and the activities of local clergy. The Spanish Inquisition in Mexico depended on the work of confessors and parish priests and would not have had the impact it did without incorporating both into its mechanisms of local investigation. It may be, therefore, that some of the patterns of laywomen's interactions with the Inquisition as witnesses might be relevant in complex ways for Indigenous people who lived among Spaniards and castas. It will take the research of many more scholars focusing on witnesses, rather than defendants, to understand this and other aspects of the Inquisition's impact on local communities – a task I suspect would be well worth the effort.

## Part II: Chapters and Sources

Part II of the book examines places and practices designed explicitly for the control, protection, and seclusion of laywomen, namely, those encompassed in the terms depósito and recogimiento. "Depósito" was a general term describing the legal transfer of guardianship of a dependent, usually

30    Klor de Alva, "Colonizing Souls."

a woman, from father or husband to either an institution or another private household. It was mediated and mandated by a range of judicial forces, sometimes at women's own request, sometimes at the behest of husbands, and sometimes at the discretion of ecclesiastical or civil authorities themselves. "Recogimiento" was a related and expansive term that referred to a broad range of institutional cloisters, the practice of gathering and secluding women in a range of locations, and the illusive ideology and set of characteristics that both described and proscribed the qualities of modesty, seclusion, and obedience in women. Protecting virtuous and vulnerable women, reforming those who were lost but still redeemable, punishing and quarantining those who needed to be controlled, and gathering together unusually virtuous women in order to concentrate and spread their sanctifying power were all connected and interrelated projects central to religious authorities' and other elite men's treatment and imagination of women.

However, laywomen themselves interpreted and attempted to shape depósito and recogimiento in a variety of ways – sometimes in contradiction to the intentions of founders and regulators. Though women's engagement with depósito and recogimiento was mediated by ecclesiastical and civil authorities, women attempted to use them to their benefit and define them in their own ways as much as possible. In some instances, women themselves sought out depósito in private homes and institutions and chose to celebrate and claim aspects of the ideology of recogimiento. In other situations, judicial authorities imposed the constraints of depósito and recogimiento on them, often at the behest of husbands. The reasons and circumstances involved in all of these situations were diverse, but the practices, ideas, and places of depósito and recogimiento were always connected to a nexus of issues related to sexuality, marriage, theologies of contagion, and women's spiritual status. As the chapters in Part II illustrate, this nexus represented a contested field of ideas and relations.

Together, Chapters 4, 5, and 6 include a wide range of experiences: relatively elite laywomen living in convent-like lay cloisters; women voluntarily and involuntarily placed in depósito within private homes or a range of protective, disciplinary, or rehabilitating institutions; and laywomen living and working in convents for nuns all appear in these three chapters. When referring to institutions, the word "recogimiento" could be either a general term for any kind of cloister or a specific term for places meant only for laywomen. The latter included *colegios*, or schools for girls; prestigious and exclusive lay cloisters; shelters for "poor but virtuous" women and girls; rehabilitative and disciplinary institutions; and asylums for women labeled as deranged or insane. A combination of religious and civil authorities authorized and administered these places, while religious brotherhoods, bishops, and pious individuals contributed financially to their support. Finally, judicial authorities of every kind received and decided on requests and petitions related to women's entrances and exits.

Chapter 4 looks at laywomen and girls living voluntarily in *colegios* and prestigious recogimientos. Though these were meant to house laywomen temporarily in preparation for marriage or profession as nuns, they also housed a significant minority population of permanent residents. Another portion of the residents moved between these places for years, occasionally spending time in convents as well. For these women, such institutions represented a kind of third option – a way to survive outside marriage or the convent while still maintaining or enhancing their spiritual status.

This chapter contains case studies of three of the most prestigious lay cloisters for women in colonial Mexico: *the Colegio de las Niñas de Nuestra Señora de la Caridad*, run by one of the largest *cofradías*, or confraternities, in New Spain; the *Recogimiento y Colegio de San Miguel de Belem*, which was under the authority of the archbishop of Mexico; and the *Colegio de San Ignacio de Loyola*, founded and administered by the Basque *Cofradía de Nuestra Señora de Aránzazu* exclusively for daughters and widows of Basque men and their descendants, all in Mexico City. Founders and supporters of all three of these places imagined their target residents as virtuous girls and women whose ability to protect their spiritual statuses had been compromised by poverty or the death of fathers or husbands. The histories of all three institutions also reflect changes over time in both the ideal and reality of whom these places served and how they did so.

The stated goal of all of these institutions was to educate, protect, and socially and spiritually elevate worthy but vulnerable women in preparation for marriage or the convent or, in the case of virtuous widows, to maintain their family's reputation. However, a close look at the alternate forms of community, family, and female authority forged within these cloisters reveals a more diverse range of possibilities and a greater diversity of residents than founders and regulators imagined. Additionally, the ways these institutions fit within the institutional landscape of female cloister suggest that like professed nuns, these virtuous laywomen could, when properly secluded and gathered together, become a sanctifying force for surrounding communities and the colonies in general.

Chapter 5 looks at cloistering practices aimed at a very different population of women – those thought to require containment, correction, and repentance, either in private homes or in less prestigious recogimientos. Some of the institutions included in this category were originally founded for repentant prostitutes or other women who had voluntarily turned away from sexually "disordered" lives. However, in reality many of the women living in these places were seeking divorce or escaping marital conflict, had been sent by their husbands as punishment for disobedient behavior, or were seeking temporary shelter because of their husbands' absence.

In addition, and increasingly in the eighteenth century, these types of recogimientos also served as places of punishment for women accused of nonsexual crimes like theft, selling prohibited liquors, drunkenness, or violence. The ideal of voluntary repentance as the purpose of these institutions was intertwined from the start with the goals of upholding patriarchal authority and offering practical solutions to marital problems, and increasingly over time, with indefinite punishment and correction as well.

The residents of these less prestigious cloisters were generally not as successful in engaging with them on their own terms, but this was not for lack of trying. Petitions and complaints presented to a wide range of judicial authorities illustrate the often-intense negotiations with husbands, other family members, religious and civil authority figures, and the *rectoras* – the female residential supervisors of the institutions themselves. Ideas about contagion and containment are prominent in founding documents but less visible in the record of women's actual experiences of and negotiations with them. The function these cloisters served within colonial society was contested from both within and without and was linked to the role of convents and prestigious lay cloisters on one hand as well as with the gradual development of prisons, asylums, and poorhouses on the other.

Chapter 6 focuses on the large population of laywomen who lived and worked as servants, slaves, dependents, and temporary residents in convents of nuns. This population overlapped with those in Chapters 4 and 5, sometimes moved between convents and recogimientos, and engaged in similar ways with the ideals of female cloister as did many residents of lay cloisters. However, the emphasis in this chapter is on laywomen's relationship with the nuns themselves. The ideology of recogimiento that nuns represented, and the crucial work of sanctification that nuns and convents provided, was in fact dependent on the labor, company, and mobility of the laywomen who lived and worked in these prestigious cloisters. Because of this, these laywomen's personal spiritual status, in some ways, lay outside the logic of recogimiento; their own exposure facilitated and bolstered elite women's claims to exceptional spiritual status. In practice, however, many of them were there exactly because of that logic in their own lives, and the line between servant, dependent, and nun was never as clear as bishops and other religious authorities would have liked.

As religious authorities' and pious society's priorities shifted in relation to how best to respond to the problem of women's special relationship to the contagion of sin and scandal, opportunities for voluntary cloister for laywomen narrowed. Ironically, protecting the pure seclusion of elite religious women in convents facilitated some kinds of voluntary cloister for a wider range of laywomen than did lay cloisters; the complete seclusion and heightened piety of nuns depended on the presence of women of lesser spiritual status who could perform labor while nuns prayed and who could facilitate necessary communication with the outside world. The intense struggle that resulted when reformers tried to limit the number of lay-women living in convents reflected nuns' own sense of this dependence.[31] What is less clear is what these reforms meant for the laywomen themselves who had previously experienced the convents as places of work and residence.

Though it is difficult to learn about convent laywomen before, during, and after the eras of reforms – they were anonymous in most convent records – it is clear that they played a crucial role in cloistered female piety and thus in religious culture in general. This chapter builds on the work of other historians who have successfully illuminated the conventual context in which these laywomen lived. Its new contributions are found largely outside convent records. Nuns' petitions about servants and slaves, testimony of convent laywomen themselves, and testimony and communication by priests about convent laywomen are scattered throughout various kinds of ecclesiastical court records, both inquisitorial and diocesan. This chapter works with this fragmented record to explore the way these women helped make colonial Catholicism.

The sources for the chapters in Part I differ in some significant ways from those in Part II. For both parts, many of the sources are judicial in nature, which reflects both the nature of colonial authority and the practical realities of doing women's history for the early modern world. But the differences in the forms of justice, kinds of testimonies, and ways the sources have been preserved present distinct opportunities and challenges. The sources for Part I consist primarily of either Inquisition documents, in which women appear as witnesses, or diocesan court cases, in which women are primarily the ones presenting complaints and seeking justice. In contrast, the judicial sources for Part II are as often petitions and complaints initiated against women as by them.

The sources for Chapter 4 are not judicial records in the same sense as the rest of the chapters. Rather they are *visita* records and other institutional documentation internal to the three recogimientos studied. Archbishop visita records come the closest to judicial records in their style and content, but in general, the records of "visits" to cloisters, be they of archbishops or men of the founding cofradías assigned to supervise and regulate the cloisters, are quite different than documents produced by an interaction between a petitioner, judge, notary, and witnesses. There is more narrative about the institution, record of authorities' choices, and information about

---

31  For the history of this conflict, see Margaret Chowning, "Convent Reform, Catholic Reform, and Bourbon Reform in Eighteenth-Century New Spain: The View from the Nunnery," *Hispanic American Historical Review*, 85 (2005); and *Rebellious Nuns: The Troubled History of a Mexican Convent, 1751–1863* (New York, NY: Oxford University Press, 2006).

the daily lives of the female residents. And yet women's actual words play a smaller role than they do in documents in which they testified.

The sources for Chapter 5, on the other hand, are judicial. But they are far more miscellaneous and fragmented than those of Chapters 1, 2, and 3. They do not represent consistent institutions or judicial traditions, and there is very little continuity between the various sources of the paper trails. This is part of the shape and context of women's engagement with recogimientos; any authority figure could act as a judge, which led husbands, wives, sisters, mothers, brothers, and fathers to utilize a range of judicial powers, pitting judges against each other when necessary or simply seeking out other options when initial efforts failed.

The miscellaneous, decontextualized quality of these sources also has to do with the way colonial archives were translated by nineteenth-century bureaucrats. The petitions that make up the source base for this chapter are not organized by the judicial entities receiving them, in relation to particular cloisters, nor even by type of petition. They are scattered throughout a wide number of collections organized through other logics. Most of the individual documents name the title of the authority to whom the petition is presented, but in contrast to the archives of the ecclesiastical court of Toluca or the Inquisition, these petitions are not surrounded by other cases heard by the same judge nor even in the same court. For this reason, it is very difficult to find patterns in judges' responses and even to learn about the particular procedures involved. Thus, these sources do not lend themselves to a study of how women engaged these particular courts or judges. Rather, what is most visible are the actions and arguments of the men and women pitted against each other and the ways each of them was relating to the practices and places of recogimiento.

Chapter 6 draws primarily on a range of judicial records to expand what we know about convent laywomen. Convent sources themselves are generally less helpful for this task, and the surprising nuggets revealed elsewhere help bring the anonymous laywomen to the foreground. What is lost through this approach, however, is a vision of the particular convents themselves. A general picture of daily rhythms and possible relationships emerge, but not a close look at any one specific place or specific relationships within that space.

The differences in these kinds of sources result in a different style of narrative in the two parts of this book. In Part I, there is more possibility for constructing stories that takes into account the experiences and representations of emotion and affect, and particular choices, rationales, and relationships are also more visible in the first half of the book. All of these things are harder to see in the sources for Part II. Particular material environments and institutional goals are visible in Chapter 4. Patterns emerge from the petitions used for Chapter 5. Chapter 6 illustrates possibilities through varied examples that were nonetheless sparsely recorded. In all three chapters of Part II, generalizations about laywomen's relationships with female family members, nuns, and other female authority figures also emerge as central.

## Troubling Devotion

This is, in the end, a story of devotion as much as a story of negotiation and dialogue. The communication and interactions I examine all took place in a devotional context; some of this devotional communication is troubling. It is troubling to see women risk sexual assault in order to receive confession and communion. It is troubling to see the naked power that husbands could exercise with the support of ecclesiastical judges when they sent their wives to less than desirable recogimientos. And it is troubling to see the Inquisition require confessors to betray the trust of their penitents, compelling them to become witnesses when they were only seeking to privately unburden their consciences before God and a trusted clergyman. But the stories and arguments set forth here also trouble the notion of devotion itself. Devotion still calls to mind a force that is nonrational and separate from material and social concerns. But this is not how laywomen's relationship with the church and religious culture in general worked in the colonial era; devotion motivated their choices but did so within a social context that was shaped by forms of power that modern readers might not recognize as religious.

Colonial laywomen's devotion may be troubling to us sometimes, but by troubling our very notion of devotion, it is also possible to see the ways it could also be life affirming, strategically beneficial, and materially necessary. To understand how so many Mexican women in the postcolonial period came to imagine themselves as defending something crucial that had been lost, it is necessary to explore the possibilities of what women in the colonial era felt they had prior to this moment. Rather than evaluating whether the colonial church was good or bad for women, the most fruitful way of understanding their choices is to examine the ways they participated in the making of colonial Catholicism. Colonial laywomen were both savvy and sincere; they were involved in a complex, paradoxical relationship with the Catholic faith and culture that enlivened their lives and to the ecclesiastical institutions, symbols, authorities, and practices that supported and gave structure to that faith and culture. Perhaps the answer to why so many laywomen felt so strongly about protecting and defending the church in the face of a hostile state was less about the church itself and more about the time and energy they had invested. In the following chapters, I hope to bring to life some of what they built – both for good and for ill – over time, with their bodies, hearts, and minds, through their practices, emotions, and interpretations.

# I

# Sacramental Learning

María Antonia Samariego, a thirty-year-old, married Indigenous servant woman from the village of San Ignacio de Tamazula in Durango, testified in 1774 that Padre Fray Domingo Mauriño was guilty of *solicitación*. Samariego appeared before the *comisario* – a local Inquisition representative – in the Villa de Culiacan. She told him that some years prior, she had gone to the nearby mission to confess with Mauriño; Samariego told the comisario that during this confession, she had mentioned a rumor she had heard that a local *curandera* – a female healer – was practicing witchcraft. In response, Mauriño told her that he would give her something to protect her from this woman's diabolical magic. After finishing the confession, Mauriño and Samariego agreed on a time for her to come to get the promised talisman.

When Samariego arrived, she found Mauriño outside smoking, drinking, and chatting with a local man. He told her to wait for him inside his room, but she did not want to do so and sat down outside the door instead. When Mauriño finished his conversation, he beckoned her inside and directed her to sit next to him on his bed. Samariego testified that she remained standing, "out of shame," protesting that she did not want to sit on his bed.[1] When he continued to insist, she finally sat next to him. He took out two cigarettes and offered one to her. Again, she protested this gesture of familiarity, but after he repeatedly urged her to smoke with him, she finally accepted the cigarette, "with shame," she told the comisario.[2]

At this point, smoking their cigarettes and seated on his bed, Mauriño asked her how Saramiego knew about the woman who practiced witchcraft. Samariego told Mauriño that a man from out of town had come to this woman, seeking a cure for his illness; he had heard rumors that the curandera used spells and incantations to heal illnesses. The outsider had relayed his conversation with the curadera to Samariego, telling her that when he assured the curandera that he would protect her secrets if she would help him, the healer had replied that she had nothing to hide. She insisted that she cured with herbs alone.

1  "Por vergüenza."  2  "Con vergüenza."

Noting that this man had revealed a private, sensitive conversation to her in some detail, Mauriño asked if Samariego had been sexually involved with the man from out of town. When she admitted that she had, Mauriño asked her: "Well, couldn't you want me in the same way you wanted this man?" Saramiego testified that she leapt up, frightened, and said to Mauriño, "No, Father, never would I do such a thing with you, because you are Christ on earth." Mauriño responded that for his part, he would have sex with her if he had the chance. At that, Samariego left, saying that her husband would be wondering where she was. She told the comisario that, from then on, she avoided Mauriño, making sure she was never alone with him again.[3]

There is a fundamentally dialogic learning process visible in this fraught exchange between Samariego as penitent and Mauriño as clergyman in which preexisting expectations were asserted, challenged, and negotiated. This kind of process is visible in laywomen's testimonies across geographical and social differences in New Spain. Confession and communion were foundational moments in which clergymen and women forged relationships and understandings that both shaped and transcended the sacramental contexts in which they developed.

Women learned how to confess properly, how to behave correctly in the presence of priests, and about doctrine and theological ideas more generally. They also developed a repertoire of sacramental practices, patterns of responses to the variety of possible experiences, and strategies for getting what they needed and avoiding potential dangers. Priests taught women normatively correct extra-sacramental feminine behavior in ways that conformed to these elite men's notions of the proper colonial hierarchies of race and class, and they expected women to conform to the sacramental version of orthodox femininity in response to their own rights and obligations as confessors and priests.

Priests also learned in the contexts of these sacraments. They gathered experience and knowledge about women in different life circumstances that sometimes challenged their previous expectations. Some priests learned how to be effective confessors for women and how to respond to their particular needs. Others learned strategies for taking advantage of the power they had in these women's lives. Female penitents pushed confessors to be what they needed them to be as best they could. Within the constraints of the sacramental power relationship, laywomen asked for certain kinds of help and guidance. They complained when confession

---

3   "y tu tubiste alguna cosa con ese hombre que curo la muger? Y respondiéndolo que haber tenido que ver con el referido hombre, le dijo el padre, 'pues como quisiste a ese hombre, no me quisieras así tambien?' a lo que asustada le respondió, 'no padre nunca hiziera yo con Vuestra merced eso porque es Cristo de la Tierra.'" Banc. mss 96/95m 1774, Padre Fray Domingo Mauriño.

did not go as they hoped it would. And they pressured and pleaded with confessors to hear their confessions, or reconfess them, when they felt it was necessary. In varying ways, laywomen and priests taught each other about their roles and how to relate to each other through these sacramental contexts.

María Antonia Samariego's testimony was one of many against Father Mauriño, who had solicited and harassed many women in the towns and villages he had served as a confessor. Though cases like these present a skewed picture of priestly interactions with penitents, they also gathered hundreds of women's voices together and reveal much about the meaning of confession and communion in women's lives. Samariego's testimony contains a striking but not uncommon example of a rural Indigenous woman giving a theology refresher to a priest who was failing to live up to his sacramental role. The shock and assertiveness Samariego expressed may have challenged commonly held assumptions about the docility and passiveness of Indigenous women, yet they appeared in the testimonies of many Native women from places similar to Samariego's village.

This is less surprising in light of these women's sacramental realities. María Antonia Samariego, like most people she lived near, probably encountered relatively few priests over the course of her life. She was the servant of a local priest she referred to only as the *cura*, don Miguel. She may have normally confessed with him, which would mean she had more regular access to the sacraments than many rural women. In her testimony, Samariego said she did not remember what year the events with Mauriño had taken place "because she did not know how to count," but she did know it was the year that her employer, don Miguel, had fallen ill and gone to the nearby Villa de Culiacan to seek medical treatment. It is possible that this is why Samariego had gone the mission to find a priest with whom to confess. The way she recalled the timing suggests that both she and the comisario understood that the story was about the annual Lenten requirement: The comisario only asked her what year it was and if she remembered the day of the week but did not ask what month or date it was; Samariego was unaware of the year by number but was clear that it was when her employer was out of town; and she did not remember what day of the week it was, suggesting that it was not a Sunday. Most likely, given these questions and answers, Samariego was referring to the week of Lent and the yearly obligation to confess at this time rather than to an instance of traveling to confess something that was particularly troubling her or to confess in anticipation of attending weekly mass and taking communion.

Many women living in places like San Ignacio de Tamazula pertained to parishes that were without priests for much of the year and therefore only confessed at Lent, either when a traveling priest came to town to serve these needs or when they themselves traveled to find a confessor. In other words,

María Antonia Samariego and other women like her might have only experienced a small number of priests in this sacramental context. And if these sparse experiences had not challenged the idealized notions of clergymen that they had absorbed from sermons, catechism, and religious images, it follows that they would be shocked when faced with something like a drinking, smoking, lascivious priest. And even if Samariego had already been familiar with some less than righteous priests, she still apparently expected that her confessor would at least uphold certain boundaries. And when Mauriño did not conform to these expectations, according to her testimony, she was frightened but forceful. She reminded the sacrilegious priest that he was God's proxy, and she asserted that she would never cross the line he was suggesting because she understood that he was *Cristo de la Tierra*.

The urban women who testified against Father Mauriño told different kinds of stories. Rather than recalling indignant, shocked, or frightened responses, they described strategies that were passive but savvy. Nonconfrontational in their avoidance techniques, most urban women demurred and quietly resisted whenever possible, and in their testimonies, they did not report surprise at what had transpired. This does not mean that Mauriño's behavior was the norm nor that these particular women had necessarily experienced it before. But it does suggest that they knew it was a possible risk.

Samariego and Mauriño's story also reveals the significance of the physical space of the confessional and those where extra-sacramental exchanges took place. Confession happened in various locations: hidden corners; right next to the altar; in a confessional that partially hid the priest; or utilizing only a chair, with the priest seated and the penitent kneeling. These differences made a difference for the women confessing, not only in the case of abusive priests like Mauriño, but in orthodox confessions, as well, in relation to privacy and the proximity of observing, listening parish and community members. But in all cases, the space of the confessional might only be the first place female penitents interacted with priests. Like María Antonia Samariego, many women had further communication with their confessors outside confession. Women sought extra-sacramental advice and help from clergymen, and it was common for priests to make social calls and to allow local families to honor them with humble meals or a drink of chocolate.

And finally, Saramiego's testimony offers evidence of a poor, rural, Indigenous woman devoted to the sacraments – at least to the point of fulfilling the yearly requirement and understanding sacramental theology in relation to the role of the priest – but who nonetheless interpreted her own obligations in a slightly unorthodox way. It is notable that she did not mention her sexual relationship with the man from out of town in the course of confession. This might reveal a lack of trust in this confessor or the confidentiality of the confession, an unorthodox understanding of sexual morality, an unorthodox understanding of the requirements for confession, or simply fear and shame too great to overcome, even in this sacramental context. In spite of this omission, which went directly against the expectation that she must confess every sin, the rest of her behavior and recalled statements suggest a relatively solid understanding of sacramental theology and practice.

The sorts of expectations, fears, joys, and responses represented in the many women's testimonies in the long case against Mauriño had been learned through the embodied experiences of confession and communion. In these ritualized but intensely personal exchanges, laywomen enacted a central aspect of Catholic theology in a highly scrutinized way. For some of these women, these were nearly their only interactions with a priest. For others, like the urban women who testified against him, confession was only a part of their multilayered relationships with the many clergymen they interacted with socially and spiritually. But for all of them, these sacraments had both transcendent and pedagogical elements.

While Inquisition investigations and trials for solicitación make up the primary source base for this chapter, my focus is not primarily the abuse these cases so often represented. It is difficult to peel back the layers of the painful stories embedded in these cases to learn about the breadth of laywomen's sacramental experiences, but it is necessary in order to understand women's participation in the culture of religiosity of New Spain. The power imbalances, threat of danger, and emotionally charged dynamics revealed in cases of solicitación were central to women's "normal" experiences of clergymen and sacraments as well, even if they never experienced an abusive priest. In addition, part of the tragedy of these sources is the fact that women's intense devotion to these sacraments – whether they experienced them once a year or more often – is still very visible in spite of the usually painful situation that brought it to light. Documentation for cases of solicitación captures the words of women of all economic levels, geographical locations, and racial, social, and spiritual status. And these women spoke, sometimes extensively, about their relationships with priests, their sacramental experiences, and the spiritual and gendered ideologies that shaped so much of their lives.

It would be overstating the case to say that the twin sacraments of confession and communion were the origin point of all lessons that women and priests learned about each other, but they were a very important site of such learning. Within a decentralized, didactic colonial context, confession and communion were among the very few consistently shared church rituals, and because of their particular social and spiritual significance for women, they are important entry points into understanding laywomen's roles in the making of religious culture.

## The Sacraments in New Spain

Religious authorities in Europe and the New World understood sacramental rituals as centerpieces of the Counter-Reformation. In the Spanish colonies, confession arguably rivaled baptism as the most important tool at the local clergy's disposal for the Christianization and correction of Indigenous communities and was essential for the ongoing supervision of *castas* and colonial Spaniards, both Iberian Peninsula and American born. Ideally, it was a direct way for priests to convey doctrinal and moral lessons to individual parishioners and to monitor whether these lessons had been understood and how well they were being followed. Communion, while less emphasized in the explicitly didactic literature, was considered the final step in the reconciliation that lay at the heart of confession. It was an embodied lesson in two central mysteries of the Catholic faith: the incarnation of Jesus as fully human and fully divine and the transubstantiation of Christ's body and blood into the host and wine. It was also an essential moment of reintegration of the sinner into the church. And finally, it served as a visual representation of religious authority and the importance of clergymen in the absolving of sins and realignment of souls with God.

For this historical period, confession and communion are best understood as two rituals that belonged to a single sacramental complex. Officially, of course, each was considered its own sacrament, but this separation was only theoretical. They were intrinsically connected; to partake in either one without the other – unless explicitly following clerical instructions – was a doctrinal error. Communion without confession was a serious sacrilege and was never sanctioned. Confession without communion might be temporarily called for but nonetheless implied an incomplete sacrament. For instance, religious authorities might require a penitent to complete a certain number of confessions while abstaining from communion as a part of their penance or to correct a spiritual imbalance. Inquisitors prescribed this kind of path for a woman named Ysabel de Salazar when they determined that her unorthodox behavior was the result of prolonged spiritual melancholy, for instance.[4] Or a spiritual mentor might suggest a period of daily or otherwise frequent confessions for the purposes of spiritual instruction but not think it was appropriate for his penitent to take communion that often. This is what the confessors of both María Anastasia González and Marta de la Encarnación did when faced with these women's potentially unorthodox spiritual longings and experiences.[5]

---

4   This case will be discussed in greater detail later in this chapter. AGN Inq. V. 498, exp. 21.
5   The case of María Anastasia González will be discussed later in this chapter as well as in Chapter 3. AGN Inq. V. 1, 312 exp. 2 and Banc. mss 72/57m 1790, María Anastasia González. María de la Encarnación's story will be discussed at greater length later in this chapter. AGN Inq. V. 788, exp. 24, María de la Encarnacíon.

And in the case of newly converted peoples, evangelizers might consider confession an essential part of the learning process but not believe that these neophytes in the faith were ready for the privilege and divine intimacy of communion.[6] These exceptions, however, highlight the fact that communion was imagined as a reward for and completion of the spiritual process begun in confessional.

The confession-communion sacramental complex was also unique as the only sacramental experience meant to be repeatedly enacted. All other sacraments were supposed to happen only once and marked a particular spiritual milestone. Confession and communion, on the other hand, constituted a spiritual discipline through which human beings regularly renewed and maintained their relationship with God, the church, and the parish community, whether it was annually, monthly, weekly, or daily. Theologically and pedagogically, the repetitive nature of confession and communion was meant to anchor people both individually and communally to God and the church. This anchoring was accomplished socially, somatically, and emotionally through the embodied learning of ritualized repetition and shared physical experiences among parishioners.

Doctrinally, it was important that this process required the mediation of properly licensed clergy. Parishioners learned, through sermons, ubiquitous religious images, and the practice of the sacraments themselves, that confession and communion were the required and exclusive mechanisms for atonement, redemption, and the restoration of God's grace in the context of the ever-present reality of human sinfulness. And they further learned that this only worked with the participation of a priest licensed to perform these rituals. Even when this priest was of dubious character or mediocre quality, participants in these sacraments seemed to feel that his position itself held a sacred potency and that as long as he said the right words and performed the right gestures, divine power would infuse the sacrament, making it efficacious. Clergymen were trained to think of these sacraments as the primary site of their ordained right to teach, judge, guide, and heal. Not every priest had this privilege and right, and it formed an important part of the hierarchy among ordained men.[7]

---

6  In the early colonial period, some theologians and clergyman called for denying communion to Africans and Native Americans on the grounds that they either inherently lacked or had not yet developed the spiritual, mental, or emotional capacity to correctly comprehend and engage in such a complex mystery of faith. For an innovative discussion of the implications of these debates and policies for the deep historical imbrication of race and religion, see Kelsey Moss, "Instructions in Faith: Constructing Religious and Racial Difference through Evangelizing Discourse in the Early Americas," presented at the AAR annual meeting, Atlanta, November 2015, and "On Earth As It Is in Heaven: Spiritual Racialization and the Atlantic World Economy of Salvation in the Colonial Americas," dissertation, Princeton University, 2018.

7  Taylor, *Magistrates*.

For many people in colonial Latin America, confession and communion were also the most intimate experiences they ever had with priests, and in some settings, they were the *only* personal experiences they had with them. New Spain, like other parts of colonial Latin America, was plagued by a chronic imbalance between properly educated and licensed clergymen and the sprawling territory and the majority Indigenous and casta populations they served. The scarcity of priests in rural areas throughout the colonial era was notorious and presented challenges for evangelization and conveying the doctrinal orthodoxy of the sacraments. This was partially remedied by traveling and temporarily stationed confessors, but there remained parishes and small towns that had to get by without clergy for much of the time.

In spite of the significance of the priest in these sacraments, the character of confession and communion made people's experiences and interpretations of them somewhat difficult to control. By their nature, the twin sacraments were profoundly experiential; instructions for proper confession and communion included heightened attention to thoughts and feelings as well as gestures. They were performative embodiments of expression. While the goal of this instruction was maintaining orthodoxy of belief and practice, the importance placed on the mental, emotional, and sensual experience of these sacraments also made them vulnerable to personal interpretation and introduced an internal arena of practice that was hard to regulate. And finally, the social significance of the sacraments – their effect on public reputation for piety – added another element of meaning to them. While church authorities tried to teach people the "right" way to confess and receive communion, parishioners' own needs, desires, and social contexts also shaped both their practice and understanding of them.

Marked as they were by tensions and fraught power dynamics, the sacraments of confession and communion in colonial New Spain were nonetheless sites of dialectical learning. The relationships laypeople and clergymen forged and the lessons they learned about and from each other over the course of these rituals reflected and shaped the broader culture of religiosity. These sacraments made up a particularly didactic sacramental exchange: Clergy dispensed knowledge through words and actions in the confessional and through the Eucharist, and parishioners learned by listening and through repetitive, embodied practice. However, priests also learned in these interactions. Through intimate but unequal interactions, clergymen learned what they could expect from parishioners of various social positions, how best to respond to them, and how to understand themselves as ministers and supervisors of the faith.

## Laywomen and Sacramental Subjectivity

Studies of the history of Catholic confession in early modern Europe and colonial Latin America have emphasized the importance of the sacrament in an early modern shift in subjectivity away from a collective orientation and toward an enlightenment focus on the individual.[8] However, a focus on laywomen's contributions to religious culture in colonial Mexico reveals that a heightened focus on the interior (thoughts, emotions, and privately experienced bodily sensations) as an important realm of sin and repentance was very much still embedded within widespread concerns about collective spiritual health and a porous understanding of self and community. Sin and atonement in colonial Mexico remained deeply social; what was felt in the body and thought in the mind had an impact far beyond the boundaries of the individual "self," spreading into the surrounding society in spiritual and material ways.

Ideas of contagion and disease communicability had been circulating since at least the early sixteenth century, and metaphors of health and illness were widespread in confessional discourse in New Spain. [9] Priests spoke about confession as medicine and confessors as doctors attending to the spiritually ill. Theologians and religious authorities talked about and understood the spread of heresy, the communicability of religious error through the blood, and the idea of women as transmitters of impurity both metaphorically and literally.[10] These concepts, along with the added worry that the physical and moral environment of the New World was

8 Michel Foucault, *History of Sexuality, V. I;* Abigail Firey, ed., *A New History of Penance* (Boston, MA: Brill Press, 2008). See also Jean Delumeau, *Catholicism Between Luther and Voltaire: A New View of the Counter-Reformation* (London: Burns and Oates, 1987); Virginia Krause, *Witchcraft, Demonology, and Confession in Early Modern France* (New York, NY: Cambridge University Press, 2015); Thomas Tentler, *Sin and Confession on the Eve of the Reformation* (Princeton, NJ: Princeton University, 1977); Patrick J. O'Banion, *The Sacrament of Penance and Religious Life in Golden Age Spain* (University Park, PA: Pennsylvania State University Press, 2012); Jodi Bilinkoff, *Related Lives,* and "Confessors, Penitents, and the Construction of Identities in Early Modern Avila," in *Culture and Identity in Early Modern Europe: Essays in Honor of Natalie Zemon Davis,* ed. Barbara B. Diefendorf and Carla Hesse (Ann Arbor, MI: University of Michigan Press, 1993); Stephen Haliczer, *Sexuality in the Confessional: A Sacrament Profaned* (New York, NY: Oxford University Press, 1996); Serge Gruzinski, "Individualization and Acculturation: Confession among the Nahuas of Mexico from the Sixteenth to the Eighteenth Centuries," in Asunción Lavrin, ed., *Sexuality and Marriage in Colonial Latin America* (Lincoln, NE: University of Nebraska Press, 1989); J. Jorge Klor de Alva, "'Telling Lives': Confessional Autobiography and the Reconstruction of the Nahua Self," in *Spiritual Encounters: Interactions Between Christianity and Native Religions in Colonial America,* ed. Nicholas Griffiths and Fernando Cervantes (Lincoln, NE: University of Nebraska Press, 1999).

9 Hieronymi Fracastorii, *De Contagione Et Contagiosis Morbis Et Eorum Curatione, Libri III,* translation and notes by Wilmer Cave Wright (New York, NY: The Knickerbocker Press, 1930); and Vivian Nutton, "Seeds of Disease: An Explanation of Contagion and Infection from the Greeks to the Renaissance," in *Medical History* 1983, 27:1–34.

10 Martinez, *Genealogical Fictions.*

a corrupting influence to American-born Spaniards, produced an intellectual atmosphere in which women's spiritual and social vulnerabilities became a heightened focus of anxiety. In the colonial context, if women's weaknesses and the dangers they posed to society were not properly rectified and their contagion contained, they could threaten collective spiritual health and, ultimately, the strength and success of Spain's Christian empire.[11]

All of humanity shared the experience of being divided into two warring parts – a spirit that longed for intimacy with God and a body whose urges and desires created an insurmountable distance from God and threatened the soul's salvation.[12] Women were thought to be ill-suited to maintain spiritual health within the context of this battle, however. The body was the primary site of temptation; the devil had the greatest success when preying upon people's physical natures, and the spirit was vulnerable precisely because of its proximity and dependency on the body for its earthly life. Women were widely imagined as more physical than men and less able to rise above or resist their bodies' demands.[13] An individual whose spirit was corrupted by the body's weakness (a fate that women were supposedly especially prone to experience without sufficient male protection and control) threatened the spiritual health of others in turn. Like a rotten apple spreading its decay through an entire barrel, a "fallen" individual could infect the community, thus weakening its defenses against the devil. And women, this logic went, fell more often than men.

Concretely, this collective process happened through the individual but fundamentally social and contagious experiences of *escándalo* and *escrúpulo*. These words translate to "scandal" and "scruples," respectively, but their usage in this historical and religious context implies more than is contained by these English words. People spoke of being *escandalizado*, or

---

11   I am grateful to Kristy Wilson Bowers for directing me to ideas of contagion in sixteenth-century medical discourse. For an excellent study of health and disease in early modern Spain, see her book, Kristy Wilson Bowers, *Plague and Public Health in Early Modern Seville* (Rochester, NY: University of Rochester Press, 2013).

12   For helpful discussions of the relationship of body to soul, see Rosalie Osmond, *Mutual Accusation: Seventeenth-Century Body and Soul Dialogues in their Literary and Theological Content* (Toronto: University of Toronto Press, 1990).

13   For a succinct discussion of ideas about women in the early modern West, see Merry E. Wiesner-Hanks, "Ideas and Laws Regarding Women," chapter one of *Women and Gender in Early Modern Europe* (Cambridge: Cambridge University Press, 2008). On concepts of women in early modern Spain, see Georgina Dopica Black, *Perfect Wives, Other Women: Adultery and Inquisition in Early Modern Spain* (Durham, NC: Duke University Press, 2001); and Margaret Boyle, *Unruly Women: Performance, Penitence, and Punishment in Early Modern Spain* (Toronto: University of Toronto Press, 2014). For ideas about women and gender difference in early modern Catholicism, see Kathleen Comerford and Hilmar Pabel, eds., *Early Modern Catholicism: Essays in Honor of John W. O'Malley* (Toronto: University of Toronto Press, 2001).

scandalized, by something they witnessed or heard about, and they described this experience as one that caused internal harm. From that experience, or sometimes without it, but simply following an awareness that something they witnessed was sinful, the experience of escrúpulo could follow. Escrúpulo named a state that today we might think of as having a troubled conscience, but with a deeper and longer-lasting spiritual impact.

Confessors and penitents alike talked about coming into contact with the sinful behavior of another as something that caused strong feelings of guilt and pain; those who witnessed or learned about someone else's misdeeds were not innocent but rather implicated in and tainted by what she or he had observed. This impact brought concrete spiritual danger; God could not be in the presence of sin, whether that sin lay in one's conscience as a result of one's own mistake or of that of another. Spoken of as having "formed" or "entered into" escrúpulo, this state of mind resulted in the absence of God's grace.

Among theologians, this idea was a bit more complex; biblically speaking, Jesus was often in the presence of sinners, and there are early modern examples in which religious authorities recognized God as illustrating his presence to people who had sinned and not yet been absolved. And yet practical confessional theology did convey the notion that being *enhoramala* meant being without God's protective grace in some measurable form. This distance led to further moral weakness if not rectified, and this weakness could then influence others in turn. A soul thus estranged could not partake of the sacrament of communion and risked damnation or added time in purgatory in the case of untimely death. A community full of individuals embroiled in the experience of escrúpulo was a community whose defenses against the disorderly forces of sin and excess were weakened.

In other words, while early modern penitential practices did create an increasingly internal sphere of scrutiny and regulation, far from turning parishioners into atomized individual "selves," this dynamic only *reinforced* collective and communal responsibility for sin and redemption in colonial Mexico. The way sin was experienced as contagious meant that the increasingly dangerous internal world that existed within highly porous "selves" became a constant threat to a fragile and vulnerable collective. And within this fraught relationship between "private" sin and "public" spiritual health, priests stood as powerful mediators.

As judges, priests tried to protect the collective from public scandal by halting its spread – something that Chapter 2 will explore in depth. But as confessors, priests also had the more intimate task of healing the spiritual damage that members sustained through their exposure to sin, not only in order to rectify individual relationships with God but also to protect the broader community from the corroding influence of escrúpulo. In testimonies, confessors talked about their penitents as having formed escrúpulo and then suffering and, as a result, being weakened in the face of further temptation and sin. Yet they did not generally speak of themselves in this way, even though they were "witness" to more sins than anyone. Presumably this was part of the near-magic quality of their position from the perspective of penitents – that they managed to remain unscathed by all they heard.

Laywomen encountered and engaged with these ideas regularly in sacramental contexts, together with the notion of themselves as spiritually, physically, and socially weaker than men and thus more vulnerable to sin. This understanding of women shaped expectations for both confessor and penitent. It colored women's internal experiences as well as their interactions with priests, each other, their families, and their communities. The Inquisition exploited these dynamics for the purpose of gathering information – turning women into affective agents of local inquisitorial cultures, damaging their sacramental experiences and relationships, and in the process, producing documentation that inadvertently reveals much about confession and communion. Women's guilt, anxiety, and fear are visible through the refracted lenses these sources offer, but so are experiences of cathartic release and relief provided by these sacraments.

## Gendered Sacraments

Among the things priests had to confront as confessors was the diversity of laywomen's specific needs. Shaped by their own elite and racialized worldview, clergyman came to this interaction with assumptions and beliefs about the relative moral strength, trustworthiness, and spiritual capacity of urban and rural women, wealthy and poor women, unmarried and married women, and *españolas, mestizas, mulatas, indias*, and other castas. But those who took this part of their job seriously also learned and were sometimes surprised by what they saw in their female penitents. Some might even find themselves acting outside their strictly sacramental duties to forge friendships or act as counselors and defenders of women in extra-sacramental capacities.

For their part, laywomen learned important aspects of what it meant to be female parishioners according to their racial, social, and geographical circumstances from the intimate sacramental exchanges that took place in confession and communion. They learned how they were expected to enact and experience the sacraments and how they ought to relate to priests in this and other contexts. Humility before the confessor and obedience to his commands, along with an experience of *dolor verdadero*, or the true pain of remorse, was a requirement for all penitents. But for women in a sex-segregated and deeply patriarchal society, the gendered tensions and power dynamics of confession, along with the notion that women were more emotional than intellectual, underlined these particular requirements for them. Confession was also the most direct way the church extended its reach into laywomen's daily lives. Sermons conveyed ideals of feminine piety and fears about feminine weakness, but confessors elaborated on these ideas through practical instruction aimed at particular situations.[14]

Confessors counseled women on marital relations, their obligations to husbands and fathers, and properly gendered behavior in ordinary social interactions and life circumstances. In one such example, a confessor working in the late eighteenth century became involved in the marital conflict of his penitent, María Anastasia González, who wanted to pursue a spiritual path at the expense of her marriage. González was a woman of Spanish descent and modest means living in the medium-sized town of Sayula, near Guadalajara, in the late eighteenth century. She had married very young and given birth to ten children, yet she had experienced a powerful call to dedicate herself to God ever since she was a child. Once her children reached a certain age, she wanted to take a vow of celibacy and dedicate herself to prayer. Her husband strongly objected, and conflict ensued between the couple. Father Zendejas, the confessor who had agreed to serve as spiritual guide for González and lead her through an intense regimen of prayer, nonetheless took the husband's side on this question. He told her that she was obligated to obey her husband over and above her spiritual longings. Even when González reported that she was physically unable to take communion when she had been sexual with her husband and that she felt that God was angry with her for not following the call he had placed in her heart, Zendejas insisted to the contrary that God's will was always for wives to be subservient to their husband's authority.[15]

Confession entailed unequal power relations for both men and women, but for laywomen, these were compounded in a number of ways. The gendered social distance between educated clergyman and most laywomen was dramatic. The specific kind of feminine shame and fear women were expected to feel when discussing intimate thoughts and feelings in confession must have often created a painful tension. And the required stance of submission before all men only intensified the priests' recognized authority as spiritual fathers and judges.

In spite of these fraught power dynamics, anecdotal evidence suggests that in the mid-colonial period, women in urban areas of New Spain sought

---

14  For gendered discourse in sermons, see Charles Witschorik, *Preaching Power: Gender, Politics, and Official Catholic Church Discourses in Mexico City, 1720–1875* (Eugene, OR: Pickwick Publications, 2013).

15  AGN Inq. V. 1312, exp. 2 and Banc. mss 72/57m.

out confession more than men did.[16] They did so in response to gendered social and spiritual pressures like their own internalized notions of women's spiritual frailty and the social rewards or punishments women experienced in relation to their sacramental habits. They also sought confession because of the unique opportunities it provided them for emotional release, spiritual guidance, and close relationships with learned and powerful clergymen. Confessors made casual references in their testimonies to women making up the preponderance of penitents on any given day, and women's testimonies offhandedly mention that they had been waiting in groups of women to confess.[17] Confession and confessors emerge as a common topic of women's conversations, and when it was available, going to confession was something women seem to have frequently done together, in pairs or groups.[18] To the extent that it is possible to see glimpses of women's confessional dialogues in court testimonies, spiritual and emotional suffering is visible alongside cathartic redemption, communication, and guidance.

What happened during communion was in many ways an extension of the learning processes that took place in the confessional. The Eucharist was a completion of the work of confession. It was also a consummation of the relationship the priest facilitated between God and parishioner. Together, confession and communion consolidated the authority of the priest, who in both instances acted as Christ's proxy.

As performed in the early modern era, communion does not look very dialogic. Priests were at the center of the ritual with exclusive power to handle the sanctified host. Taking on Christ's role in the last super, the priest became an essential part of the transubstantiation miracle itself. Many parishioners were left only gazing at the host and the holy hands that held it high while the owner of those hands kept his back turned to them.[19] And those parishioners who had completed confession recently enough to partake did so supposedly as grateful and passive recipients – vessels, cleansed by the priest acting as Christ's proxy, receiving Christ's body often from the hands of the same priest, acting again as Christ's proxy.

There was limited room for negotiation and interpretation in the Eucharist ritual, but they did exist. Those who had options could refuse

---

16  Scholars of early modern Spain have concluded that the same was true in Spain for this period. Haliczer, *Sexuality in the Confessional*; Bilinkoff, *Related Lives*.

17  Banc. mss 96/95m. AGN Inq. V. 295, exp. 1.

18  AGN Inq. V. 373, exp. 2; AGN Inq. V. 482, f. 154–170.

19  For a discussion of the significance of beholding the host, see Miri Rubin, *Corpus Christi: The Eucharist in Late Medieval Culture* (Cambridge: Cambridge University Press, 1991); and Andrew Castor, "Display and Devotion: Exhibiting Icons and their Copies in Counter Reformation Italy," in *Religion and the Senses in Early Modern Europe*, ed. Wietse de Boer and Christine Götler (Boston, MA: Brill Press, 2013), pp. 51–55.

to take communion at some clerical hands and could choose to receive it from others, challenging the idea that the sacrament was equally valid regardless of a priest's personal characteristics. Such ordinary choices either undermined or legitimized particular priests' authority within communities and became part of the body of information shared about them. González Calderón, the resident parish priest of San Andres Mixquic, a village outside Mexico City, was an example of such a priest. He was known locally as corrupt, crass, and abusive, largely because of the information that women in the town had spread about him. When he came under investigation for solicitación in 1613, it came out that a large number of women had been refusing to take communion from him for some time because they disapproved of his behavior.[20] Because San Andres was not a large town, in practical terms, this choice may have meant that these women either went without communion or had to travel to another town to receive it. Their actions implicitly resisted the notion that they were bound to accept the sacrament by whatever hand offered it and directly went against the church's requirement that parishioners take Easter communion in their own parish. These women's refusal to relate to a misbehaving priest illustrates the tensions present between clerical control of the sacrament of communion and the ability of women to negotiate that control.

Women's own understandings of the Eucharist may have opened a bit of space for negotiation as well. The theology of transubstantiation offered a counter discourse to the idea of women as fundamentally and especially flawed, tainted, and weak. Deeply felt religious and cultural conceptions of women as closer to body and emotions than men led some women to identify with the embodied theology and wordless devotion of the Eucharist. Studies of nuns, female mystics, and holy women in New Spain, as in other early modern Catholic places, illustrate this possibility.[21] Women's supposedly more embodied nature justified their exclusion from many aspects of religious life, but it also meant they might be particularly well suited for some other, less intellectual forms of piety. While acknowledging that men could also participate in emotional, mystical, and physical piety, studies of female spirituality have shown that some women took special advantage of the openings created by otherwise misogynist and constrictive religious and cultural ideas about womanhood in order to rise to great spiritual heights, particularly in the seventeenth and early eighteenth centuries.

---

20  AGN Inq. V. 295, exp. 23.
21  Moshe Sluhovsky, *Believe Not Every Spirit: Possession, Mysticism, and Dicerment in Early Modern Catholicism* (Chicago, IL: University of Chicago Press, 2007); Richard Kagan, *Lucrecia's Dreams: Politics and Prophecy in Sixteenth-Century Spain* (Berkeley, CA: University of California Press, 1990); Bilinkoff, *Related Lives*; Jaffary, *False Mystics*.

This elevated spiritual path often included a passionate, even frenzied and otherworldly, devotion to the Eucharist. Central to Marta de la Encarnación's mystical piety that led to the 1725 Inquisition trial against her as a false mystic was a passionate devotion to the Eucharist. An española of humble economic origins, Marta was living as a cloistered laywoman at Nuestra Señora de la Merced, where she took informal vows but also performed menial labor for room and board. Marta took daily communion after praying the rosary and meditating on the stations of the cross, weeping for an hour at each station. She said she felt the suffering of Jesus so deeply that she was constantly battling illness. She experienced communion as medicinal for her struggling body as well as for her spirit. When she began having visions, her confessor sternly ordered her to stop taking daily communion but did not intervene in any of her other practices.[22] The Eucharist was also a central problem in the trial against Gertrudis Rosa Ortís, a widowed mestiza accused and found guilty of false visions in 1723. Most worrisome to her confessor and Inquisitors was the fact that Gertrudis frequently saw Christ's passion followed by his transubstantiation in the Eucharist. The Inquisitors ultimately decided that these particular visions were the result of Satan taking advantage of her weak mind.[23] By the late 1770s, María Anastasia González, the woman from Sayula discussed earlier, had become a widow and was finally free to pursue her religious pretensions. She fell prey to the Inquisition's suspicions in part because of her passionate yearning for daily communion. She sometimes sought it twice in one day, and when her confessor denied her, she fell into uncontrollable shaking, sighing, and moaning. When this happened, her confessor punished these "excesses" with whippings that he himself administered. Eventually, González began to receive communion at the hands of the saints and Jesus himself in her embodied mystical experiences.[24]

Though we know more about these kinds of dramatic cases because they came to be documented by the Inquisition, we can imagine that there were other women who also felt a powerful devotion to the Eucharist but whose lives and practices did not cause the same kind of concern. The discursive and metaphorical connections made in sermons and religious images between the Eucharist and food, the Eucharist and nursing, and the figuring of the Eucharist as making one "pregnant with God," must have had a particular kind of significance for women as food-makers and child bearers. While it is easier to see this in the lives of unusually pious women and mystics, some ordinary laywomen were also particularly drawn to the

---

22   AGN Inq. V. 788, exp. 24.     23   AGN Inq. V. 805, exp. 1.
24   AGN Inq. V. 1, 312 exp. 2; Banc. mss 72/57m 1790, María Anastasia González.

experience of physical and spiritual nourishment and to the notion that literal communion with Christ was possible by taking his body into their normally denigrated female ones.

Colonial laywomen's relationships to the Eucharist are more difficult to trace than their relationships to confession because there was not the same kind of sustained attention to regulating its abuse. Nonetheless, clues about the intensity of some laywomen's devotion to the sacrament lie in the documented stories of interrupted confession. In their testimonies, women appear willing to risk a number of personal dangers in order to take communion, and they speak about finding ways to compel reluctant confessors to provide it. And when all else fails, some of them described experiencing the Eucharist in supernatural ways that the clergy could not control. While there was not much space for parishioner's open and varied expression within the ritual of communion itself, women nonetheless sometimes interpreted the meaning of communion, or their own readiness for it, in ways that were at odds with church teachings or the instructions of their own confessors.

The clearest evidence of a widespread desire for communion on the part of laywomen from all places and circumstances is the concern and anxiety they expressed when they could not receive it. Women across racial, socio-economic, and geographical differences testified about these fears. They worried about the spiritual impact of taking communion when they felt their confessions had been inadequate but also about other people noticing that they did not take communion when they were supposed to. Some women admitted to having taken communion without a proper confession in order to avoid community suspicion, while others struggled to be *bien confesada* before taking communion, sometimes at great risk or difficulty.[25] Women's material, spiritual, and social concerns intermingled in their testimonies.

When María Josefa Fernández testified before the Inquisition in 1793 in the course of a trial against a priest named Joaquin García, she wove together all of these concerns. A twenty-four-year-old servant in the convent of Santa Isabel, Fernández had gone to confess with García, the convent's chaplain, because her regular confessor did not arrive on the day she normally confessed and took communion. Before hearing her confession, García had reportedly asked whether he could come visit her at her family's home sometime. She replied affirmatively, offering to serve him chocolate when he came to call. He rebuffed this offer, saying he was certain that her family did not have any good-quality chocolate, but went on to say that he would come anyway because what he wanted was to be alone with her. He also offered to

---

25  Well or properly confessed.

continue confessing her instead of her regular confessor. She declined his offer and completed her confession.[26]

Fernández told Inquisitors that after leaving García, she worried that the confession had been "bad" because she had been too distracted by the uncomfortable conversation that had preceded it. She worried in particular that she had not been able to feel the required "dolor verdadero."[27] She returned to García and asked him to confess her again in order that she be ready to take communion the next day. He refused, and she pleaded with him, saying she needed to be "bien confesada" in preparation for the Eucharist. He told her that he no longer wanted to hear her confession but just wanted to "continue communicating with" her. Eventually she agreed to do so if he would just confess her this one time.[28]

Clearly, Fernández was not only concerned about the social impact of not taking communion, or she would have – as some women did – gone ahead and taken communion in spite of her belief that her confession had been incomplete. She seems to have been genuinely afraid of the spiritual consequences of partaking without being truly readied for the sacrament. But neither was she solely concerned about the spiritual impact, nor she could have simply skipped that week and waited until her confessor returned the following week. This would have put her soul in danger in the case of her sudden death, but she did not express concern about that, and given that she was not ill, that was probably not her biggest concern. Rather, Fernández was very anxious to ready her soul to take communion the following day as scheduled because, as she explicitly told García, she was afraid that her mistress would notice that she had not taken communion after making her confession and would assume that the priest

26  " ... la preguntó si tenía gentes, o era sola: y respondiéndole que tenía Padre y hermanos, la dixo; podré venir a verte y hablarte? Contestándole qye sí, que lo que era bueno podía lucir Delante de Dios, y de todo el Mundo. Pues ahí vendré, la repusó, a decía una misa: Venga Vm. Quando quisiera, le dixo, y con satisfacción pidame chocolate que se lo daré. Me darás chocolate de oreja, porque bueno no lo tendrás dixo el Padre: no obstante yo vendré, porque mi fin es comunicarte, pero a solas, y así quando quisieres te seguiré confesando: a que le dixo ella que no, porque tenía confesor que venía cada ocho dias: y con esto la confesó, y se fue."

27  "Que en la segunda occasión, rezelosa de que la primera confesión havía sido mala, le dixo a dicho Padre García, quería volverse a confesar de nuevo, por no haver quedado contenta la primera vez, porque creió no havía llevado dolor verdadero."

28  " á que la contestó el Padre: pues yo no quiero confesarte, lo que quiero es comunicarte: a que ella le dixo: confiéseme Vm. Que yo quiero quedar bienconfesada, porque me precisa comulgar mañana: á que el Padre la repitío, no quiero confesarte, anda á un Cuerno: y ella viendo esta resistencia, quiso convencerlo con ruegos, y no consiguiéndolo, le dixo: confiéseme Vm. Ahora no mas: que yo le prometo sequir comunicandolo: para asi precisarlo a que la confesara: a lo que contestó el Padre: pues de no seguir confesandote conmigo te irás mucho de enoramala: porque yo no quiero confesarte: a que ella le dixo que no mas esta vez, y ya no volvía á confesarse con el."

had determined her sins to be too grave to absolve without further penance.[29]

Confession and communion were both public sacraments and for women they were intricately tied to reputation and honor. For Fernández, who lived in the closely supervised environment of a convent, being improperly confessed entailed either the spiritual risk of taking communion incorrectly or the social and material risk of her employers and community members wondering why she had not partaken of the Eucharist after having confessed. But even in less scrutinized places, women's reputations could be affected by their relationships to the sacraments, and reputation could have significant material consequences for women in New Spain.

When religious authorities measured women's honor and virtue, they used women's sacramental habits as key indicators. Inquisitors and other ecclesiastical judges determined women's credibility as witnesses by initiating investigations into their reputations and sacramental practices. Judges and confessors alike presumed that women who skipped the sacraments or completed them in unorthodox or lackluster ways were also morally suspect and probably sexually unchaste. For the authorities evaluating the characters of these women, this made them untrustworthy as witnesses, more likely to commit sexual and religious crimes themselves, and potential dangers to their communities.

At a local level, confession and communion also had an impact on women's status, even if church authorities never formally evaluated their spiritual qualities. Failure to confess and take communion once a year in the post-Tridentine era was a serious religious error and evidence of poor education, dubious morality, or both. But where it was possible, communities expected their virtuous members to partake even more regularly. Ideally, the Eucharist lay at the heart of the celebration of every mass. Wherever there was a priest licensed to consecrate and administer the Eucharist, those parishioners attending had the opportunity to take it. Theoretically this meant that it would be available not only on weekly Sunday celebrations but also during the large numbers of festivals and religious feast days. In urban settings or in rural towns that enjoyed a resident priest licensed to enact the sacraments, each of these events offered the opportunity for everyone to gaze upon the consecrated Eucharist as the priest held it over his head during the sacred ritual that only he could enact. To actually receive the host, parishioners had to

29 "porque el la dixo: que de no darle gusto no volvía mas, y que se fuera en horamala: y en vista de esto, ella prometió darselo, pero que por la presente no podía ser, y así que la confesara, porque su Ama, quando venía el confesor, si no comulgaba, la reconvenía, y a estas instancias la confesó . . . " Banc. mss 96/95m 1973, Fray Joaquin García. For a longer discussion of this case and of the process of reading the documents related to it, see Delgado, "Foregrounding Marginalized Voices."

complete a proper confession in the days immediately prior to the mass and not commit any sin after that. In places where communion was regularly available, therefore, community awareness of who received it would have particular significance. Refraining from doing so, particularly on important feast days, could start rumors and speculations about one's actions and character.[30]

Devotion to the sacraments did not always protect women from suspicion, however. In spite of the growing popularity and acceptance of frequent communion, as well as its accepted utility in assessing moral characteristics, church authorities also remained suspicious of women they saw as overly enthusiastic in their Eucharistic piety.[31] Becoming known for one's devotion to communion could make women vulnerable to accusations of pride, hypocrisy, and even heterodoxy. For women of Spanish descent, this was particularly true if they were poor or if they were not publicly understood to be virgins. Women of African descent and Native women along with mestizas and other castas who could not claim purity of blood were especially suspect in these ways. Church authorities were quick to presume religious error on the part of non-Spanish descended women.[32] Women's spiritual devotion to confession and communion was intertwined and inseparable from this racialized and uneven experience of community and ecclesiastical scrutiny and of the material consequences of reputation.

These gender-specific pressures caused great anxiety, as documented frequently in cases where women's access to the sacraments was interrupted. But women also suffered from the opposing pressures both to frequently and publicly participate in the sacraments and to experience them with great depth and intensity of feeling each and every time. The widespread belief in women's inherent weaknesses exacerbated this pressure and could lead to fear and self-doubt. The case of Ysabel de Salazar, a woman of Spanish descent and modest means living in Valladolid in 1691, provides a vivid, if perhaps extreme, example of these tensions. Salazar was troubled by her lack of feeling in the sacraments. In her own self-evaluation, she did not ever experience the "dolor verdadero" she thought she should, nor did she feel the love and gratitude upon taking communion she believed she should. Her muted emotions led her to doubt that she had ever been baptized, and she began pleading with her confessor to baptize her. Though her confessor obtained her baptism records, Salazar

---

30    Stephen Haliczer has found for seventeenth-century Spain that taking communion was particularly popular among women on feast days. Haliczer, *Sexuality in the Confessional*, 30–33.

31    On women, indigeneity, and debates about frequent communion in colonial Mexico, see Sampson Vera Tudela, *Colonial Angels*, 85–87.

32    The story of the mulata Juana Navarro, discussed in Chapter 3, is a good example of these tendencies. Banc. Inq. Mss. 96/95, 1750 Fray Tomás de Sandoval.

was not convinced and continued to ask for this first sacrament that was meant to bring Christians into the church and enable salvation. Her confessor told investigating Inquisitors that Salazar had always been *mui escrupulosa* but also that she had very little religious understanding. Complicating all of this was the fact that her husband, a man the confessor described as "imprudent," "beyond stubborn," and "very ignorant," had forced her some twenty times to take communion without having confessed. Perhaps he was motivated by social anxieties that his own honor would be stained if his wife's reputation was marred by her failure to take communion. In some of these instances, Ysabel found herself choking on the host, and she spat it out. In others, she simply suffered debilitating guilt for her own lack of pious feeling. In one instance, after she failed to take communion on the festival of the Virgin of Carmen, she tried to take her own life by throwing herself into a river.

Her spiritual anxiety eventually led to several other attempts at suicide, and ultimately the Inquisition determined that Ysabel had suffered so much escrúpulo that it had sickened her. They determined that she was afflicted by *melancolía* – a religious and mental ailment that could afflict both men and women but that was gendered in its manifestations and claimed more women than men in New Spain.[33] The cure Inquisitors proscribed was frequent confession but without communion until her confessor felt she was ready.[34] This abstinence, though it may have brought spiritual relief, must have had negative social consequences for Ysabel. It would have made her struggle even more public than it had been, as people would inevitably notice that she was completing multiple confessions and never taking communion.

Though Ysabel's de Salazar's experience was extreme, many women questioned their experiences of remorse in confession and feared they might have received communion without the proper contrition and purification of the spirit. The emotional experience of Ysabel de Salazar would most likely have gone undocumented if it had not resulted in her visibly spitting out the Eucharist and her suicide attempts. But women's testimonies as witnesses in cases of interrupted sacraments reflect that some degree of these painful anxieties and sacramental doubts was widespread.

## Sacramental Geographies

The differences between urban and rural geographies of devotional practice shaped laywomen's experiences of confession and communion. Urban

33  Roger Bartra, *Transgresión y melancolía en el México colonial* (México, D.F.: UNAM-Centro de Investigaciones Interdisciplinarias en Ciencias y Humanidades, 2004).
34  AGN Inq. V. 498, exp. 21.

environments, with their parishes, convents, monasteries, hospitals, and other religious institutions, provided women far greater sacramental access and options. Theoretically, this meant having the ability to confess regularly, to "shop around" for a willing and skilled confessor, and to avoid returning to a confessor who had behaved or performed badly. Testimonies of urban women reflect this reality, painting a picture of a landscape of chapels and confessionals housing a diversity of clergymen. Women describe seeking out confessors at convents, colegios, monasteries, and other institutions. They admit to avoiding communion at the hands of priests they thought unworthy of the sacrament. They report trading information with each other about good and bad confessors. And they mention receiving domestic visits – both sacramental and social – from priests who were clearly a part of these women's social networks and communities.

For laywomen with especially pious inclinations, urban environments could also provide the opportunity to establish a special relationship with a confessor who might serve as a spiritual director.[35] María Anastasia González was one such woman. Her hometown, Sayula, boasted many clergymen, both regular and secular. When her husband was still alive and she knelt before the statue of the Virgin of Guadalupe in the chapel of Sayula's Franciscan Colegio in 1779 to ask for guidance in her search for the right confessor and spiritual director, she had quite a few options to choose from. During her tumultuous relationship with Father Zendejas, the priest God guided her toward that day, she also confessed with at least three other clergymen in town.[36] Marta de la Encarnación of Mexico City, the cloistered laywomen living in the convent of Nuestra Señora de la Merced, was known for her piety even before she moved into the convent. This reputation and the urban environment in which she lived allowed her to find a father confessor, Juan Manuel de Vega, who could be her spiritual director. She confessed weekly with him for many years, sometimes even daily, until her visions caused concern among her acquaintances, and her beloved confessor was called to testify against her in 1725.[37]

Laywomen's access to and experiences of confession and communion were not equal, even in these settings where priests were plentiful; differences in social, economic, racial, and spiritual status shaped sacramental choices and possibilities. In Querétaro in 1658, two domestic servant women, one a mulata slave named Margarita and the other a *morisca*[38]

---

35    On spiritual directors, see Bilinkoff, *Related Lives;* and Sluhovsky, "General Confession."

36    AGN Inq. V. 1, 312 exp. 2; Banc. mss 72/57m 1790, María Anastasia González.

37    AGN Inq. V. 788, exp. 24.

38    Morisca here most likely refers to the colonial casta category, meaning the offspring of a mulata and española, or to the color of the servant's skin rather than to the original Spanish meaning of the word, which was a Christian convert from Islam.

servant named María, asked Alonso Pérez, an *indio ladino*,[39] to accompany them at midnight to the Franciscan monastery of San Juan to find a priest to hear the confession of a fellow servant woman who was gravely ill and to administer communion to her. This journey, though not so far in distance, implied danger and vulnerability for these women. While there was certainly no shortage of priests licensed to confess in their urban environment, neither the woman sick in her bed nor Margarita or María seem to have enjoyed an ongoing relationship with a confessor upon whom they could call in an emergency. In fact, when they arrived at the monastery, Alonso Pérez had to talk to a few different priests in order to find someone willing to travel to the woman's house in the middle of the night, in spite of the seriousness of her illness and the possibility that she could die without confessing.

In spite of the fact that many nonwhite urban women were devoted to the sacraments, urban priests' testimonies nonetheless reflected the widespread idea that Spanish women were more spiritually capable, trustworthy, and morally sound than other women.[40] These biases made finding a regular father confessor or even confessing frequently a different prospect for Indigenous and casta women living in urban areas than their white counterparts. However, even among españolas there were differences; poor women, unwed mothers, or women known for scandalous behavior – even when they could claim *limpieza de sangre* and "old Christian" status – faced more limited options than those who were recognized for their piety or whose wealth and social status had protected their reputation.[41]

Rural women had very different sacramental circumstances than those who lived in cities. The scarcity of priests in many rural parts of New Spain meant that many rural women had little choice of confessor and limited access to the Eucharist. A trusted local confessor who took his position seriously could garner great influence in a small town or village – earning the devotion and loyalty of poor and wealthy women alike.[42] But when the one priest available for miles was neglectful or abusive, pious rural women might find themselves at his mercy. María Antonia de la Luz, a nineteen-year-old Indigenous woman of humble means, had to travel a half-day's

39   Hispanicized Native American, usually referring to dress, language, and place of residence.
40   On the intersection of racial and gendered biases about spiritual capacity, see Sampson Vera Tudela, *Colonial Angels.*
41   *Limpieza de sangre* meant purity of blood and referred to someone whose genealogy did not contain any "stains" of non-Christian peoples, heretics, or tainted "races." *Old Christian* was a term that referred to people who were not descended from converts from either Judaism or Islam. For examples of the range of opinions confessors held of their white and nonwhite female penitents, see Few, *Women Who Live Evil Lives*; Jaffary, *False Mystics;* and Sampson Vera Tudela, *Colonial Angels.*
42   For examples of confessors becoming trusted mentors, see Taylor, *Magistrates*, 191–96.

journey to the villa of Sacramento del Ojo Caliente in order to confess during Lent. The man she sought out to hear her confession was a visiting Franciscan missionary named Pedro Rebuelta. On her first visit, Fr. Rebuelta assaulted her, and she narrowly escaped being raped. Nonetheless, she returned again the next day, because she had fled without receiving communion. She confessed with Rebuelta again and received absolution and communion, this time without incident. Later, in 1775, when she testified about this terrible event in the context of a solicitación investigation, she said that though she was devoted to the sacraments and had continued to confess and take communion as often as she could, she did not tell another priest for years about what had transpired with Rebuelta "because of the enormous fear and sense of shame she felt towards confessors."[43] Women like María Antonia de la Luz might distrust confessors but remain committed to the sacraments themselves. This created great sacramental vulnerability for these rural women who had to depend on whatever clergyman was available.

## Physical Space and Public Penitence

In both rural and urban areas, variations in the physical space in which confession took place was also an important factor in laywomen's experience of this sacrament. In some instances, confession took place in a public and visible location, while in others, the venue was dark and secluded or included relatively private confessionals. The closed confessional, in which the penitent was hidden not only from the view of the listening priest but from the eyes and ears of nearby observers, was rare in the seventeenth century and by no means universal in the eighteenth.[44] In fact, concerns about clerical abuses of the sacrament encouraged a move toward more open arrangements. Depending on the architectural sophistication of the church or chapel where the confession took place, the "confessional" could range from a simple chair upon which the priest sat while the penitent knelt before him to some form of an actual structure, perhaps with a curtain partially hiding the priest with the penitent kneeling outside. The locations of these arrangements varied: Some were in quiet, darkened rooms of chapels – out of the way of the main traffic – while others were front and center – just off of the main altar and in no way hidden.

The space in the chapel where the aforementioned priest, Pedro Rebuelta, was hearing confessions was one of the latter arrangements –

43    "Por el sumo temor y vergüenza que tenia a los confesores." Banc. mss 96/95m 1775, Fray Rebuelta.

44    For a useful discussion of the physicality of the confessional and its implications on the sacrament, see de Boer, *The Conquests of the Soul*, 84–125.

visible to everyone in the small chapel. Thus María Antonia de la Luz was relatively protected from her abusive confessor during confession itself. The problem arose after confession because Rebuelta had convinced her to come to his room for a spiritual "remedy" that he said she needed to resist some particular temptations that were troubling her. It was in the privacy of his room that Rebuelta sexually assaulted her. The cynicism or purposeful innuendo of priests claiming that sexual acts with them would serve as spiritual remedies for women who had confessed to sexual sins is a reoccurring theme in solicitación cases. However, it is not clear that María Antonia de la Luz had confessed about a sexual sin, and would-be solicitors used similar strategies in other situations as well. These predatory tactics depended on the availability of private space. When women spoke about fearing the effects of witchcraft, soliciting confessors sometimes used the promise of magical protection to lure women to more private quarters, as took place with María Antonia Samariego, whose story opened this chapter. In other cases, a pious woman simply seeking extra spiritual guidance might be vulnerable to a priest's suggestion that he teach her spiritual exercises outside confession or tutor her in a private place.

These informal locations and extra-sacramental interactions were potentially dangerous for female penitents but less so for the confessors; if sexual behavior took place outside confession and the confessional, the crime of solicitación had not officially taken place. This was part of the learning that happened in the context of confession and confessional relationships, as sordid and transgressive as it was. Those clergymen inclined to take advantage of their power learned strategies for doing so while trying to avoid punishment. In turn, women learned strategies for responding to such an unholy repertoire and trying to protect themselves.

While it must have been emotionally traumatic for María Antonia de la Luz to return to receive the sacraments again from her assailant, she also probably knew that as long as she remained in the chapel this time, where Rebuelta was hearing confessions and other penitents were waiting, she would most likely be physically safe. What is more, because the confessions were out in the open and there would almost certainly be witnesses present, by returning, María Antonia de la Luz was publicly communicating to Rebuelta that he had not fulfilled his obligations to her and was demanding that he complete the sacraments. Perhaps in a way she was also letting him know that he should not presume that he could get away with his sacramental abuse. Whatever she did or did not intend to communicate by her actions, María Antonia de la Luz did manage to get Rebuelta to complete the sacramental work she needed, and she did so with witnesses nearby and in a relatively visible space. During this second visit, Luz testified that Rebuelta confessed her and gave her communion without any problematic behavior.

Though public locations could serve as a protection against would-be abusive confessors, in general, many women probably preferred the privacy of a less public confessional space. Though the content of confession was always meant to be secret, the physical space in which it took place could make this a practical impossibility, and this, too, could have consequences for penitents' reputation and safety. The sorrow and remorse required of a proper confession were measured by audible and visible bodily expression. When confession was in a public setting, people standing or waiting nearby could hear sighing and crying – or could note the absence of it. If the priest was visible, the physical gestures of absolution were also recognizable to all, and even if these actions were hidden, the words of absolution were sometimes audible. When this part of the ritual did not happen, it was clear to witnesses that something was amiss. Priests and women both testified about female penitents' fears and anxieties about being observed by people nearby when confessors denied them absolution.

In addition to the semipublic nature of confession itself, confessors sometimes assigned penitential exercises that entailed noticeable changes in public devotional practices. These could be as dramatic as ordering a penitent to approach the altar on their knees while offering particular prayers aloud but could also include subtler changes, like attending mass more frequently than usual or saying the rosary every day in the chapel for a month.[45] All of these changes and additions would be visible to one's community, and the interpretation could be either that the person in question had become extremely pious or that she or he had something serious to atone for.[46] The confessional, therefore, in addition to being a place of potential release and spiritual comfort, was also a place of social risk. Its public and performative nature could damage even a very pious woman's reputation, but it also reinforced a culture of religiosity that imbued daily practices and social interactions with opportunities for demonstrating that piety.

## Sexual Violence and Sacramental Abuse

As the stories in this chapter have already illustrated, confession implied the risk of sexual exploitation or physical violence, as it brought women

45    For a useful, though modern, discussion of Catholic penitential practices, see David Mellot, *I Was and I Am Dust: Penitente Practices as a Way of Knowing* (Collegeville, MN: Liturgical Press, 2009). For a discussion of penitential practices in the context of evangelization in the colonial Americas and early modern Europe, see Gretchen Starr-Lebeau, "Lay Piety and Community Identity in the Early Modern World," in Firey, *A New History of Penance*, 395–419.

46    When María Anastasia González was ordered to perform public acts of penance consisting of prayers and other devotional acts in church, her female friends and acquaintances noticed and testified to this fact. AGN Inq. V. 1, 312 exp. 2 and Banc. mss 72/57m 1790, María Anastasia González.

into close contact with men who could abuse their position in this way if they were so inclined.[47] The Inquisition cases that offer a rare window into women's experiences of the sacraments most likely overrepresent the extent to which this kind of abuse happened and cast a long shadow over any discussion of women's sacramental lives, as they inevitably have also here in this chapter. But they also reveal that awareness of this possibility was a part of many laywomen's sacramental experience, even if they themselves had never encountered a soliciting priest. Rumors of sexual advances made in the confessional, awareness of ongoing illicit relationships between priests and laywomen, and even the publication and reading of Inquisition edicts about the obligation to report instances of solicitación introduced the specter of sacramental abuse into at least urban women's ordinary frame of reference.

Though no class of women was invulnerable to sexual advances in the confessional, poorer women, particularly servants, seem to have been at greater risk, and women of African or Indigenous descent were more vulnerable than Spanish women. Priests' probably engaged in this racialized, class-stratified pattern in part because of their own perceptions of the risks involved in soliciting some penitents versus others. Creole and peninsular priests had reason to presume that elite women had greater familial and social protection, and religious authorities commonly expressed the presumption that racially pure women from reputable families had a more well-developed sense of piety and escrúpulo, leading them to be more likely denouncers of wrongdoing. Perhaps priests would also presume that elite women had access to more concrete information about the proper channels through which to denounce an errant priest. All of these assumptions would have made wealthy españolas appear more threatening to would-be solicitors than their less privileged counterparts. This did not completely dissuade sexual advances with elite women, by any means, but it probably did cause some soliciting priests to act with more caution with them than with others.

However, this sense of having greater immunity with poor, nonwhite women did not accurately reflect the reality of sacramental dynamics in New Spain. Though it was the case that wealthy, white women enjoyed

---

47 Priests could certainly solicit men during confession as well, although the reported cases are relatively few. Haliczer argues that this is the case in Spain because whereas women's limited mobility made confession one of the few opportunities for priests to have unfettered access to women, priests wanting to sexually engage men had plenty of other less professionally and spiritually risky opportunities to do so. Haliczer, *Sexuality in the Confessional*, 107–9. For an earlier history of solicitación in Spain, see Adelina Sarrión Mora, *Sexualidad y confesión: Solicitación ante el Tribunal del Santo Oficio (siglos XVI–XIX)* (Madrid: Alianza Universidad, 1994). For more recent studies of cases of solicitación involving male penitents, see Zeb Tortorici, "Contra Natura: Sin, Crime, and 'Unnatural' Sexuality in Colonial Mexico, 1530–1821," doctoral dissertation, 2010.

greater social protection, poor, nonwhite women were not necessarily any less likely to end up testifying against their confessors. In part, this was because the mechanisms through which the Inquisition gathered testimony did not rely on women's own initiative and therefore did not require the sense of status or entitlement that soliciting priests feared in elite women. Most laywomen did not voluntarily initiate solicitación cases on their own, whatever their class or racial background; in general, laywomen testified only after a clergyman informed them that it was their obligation to do so – usually by denying them absolution in their role as their current confessor – or when the Inquisition directly called them to testify in a trial already under way. These investigatory processes ensnared women of all social classes and positions – even those who did not confess frequently.

In the case of rural, Indigenous women, the relationship between urbanity and spiritual status, combined with racist attitudes, created the potential for a particularly pronounced imbalance of power in the sacramental context. A pattern emerges from solicitación accusations and trials of blatant sexual violation of rural *indias* at the hands of some traveling confessors administering sacraments in missions, haciendas, ranchos, rural villas, or pueblos, as well as vicars stationed in remote parishes for a year or two. This is not to say that most such priests were soliciting ones, only that those who were inclined to treat their penitents this way seem to have been particularly aggressive when they were farther away from supervision and interacting with rural Indigenous women.

In these soliciting confessors' testimonies, there is a palpable sense of resentment toward their assignments in the hinterlands and of disdain and dismissal of their penitents. Sometimes they could not even remember the names of the women they admitted to having sexually assaulted. Carelessness and a sense of immunity come through in these testimonies; by their own admission, these accused confessors were more reckless, used cruder language, and handled these women more roughly than they reported doing with the urban women they had also solicited.[48] The women's presumed lack of recourse, the exclusive sacramental power a visiting priest enjoyed, and the relative lack of supervision in these remote areas, together with the racial and cultural attitudes of these urban, Creole priests toward rural Indigenous women, facilitated a pattern of more overt sacramental abuse. In the records of trials and investigations for solicitación, rural, anonymous women outnumber urban women as victims, even when the accused priests worked for greater lengths of time in cities.

48   For particularly clear examples, see Banc. Mss 96/95m, 1792, Fray Juan de Ortega and Banc. Mss 96/95m, 1774, Fray Pedro Rebuelta.

## Sacramental Expectations

The historical record does not capture the work of individual good pastors as often as the deeds of those who abused their positions. Nonetheless, reading between the lines, it is possible to see that many women expected and had experienced comfort and respectful treatment from other confessors and priests in general. Soliciting confessors often spoke about their rural, indigenous penitents in ways that conveyed their negative attitudes toward the populations they were forced to serve, but we know from other kinds of sources that not all priests felt this way. In fact, many considered their roles in these communities to be their primary vocation. A similar paradox is visible in solicitación testimonies from urban women; they had more experience and exposure to priests and confessors in general, which led to a greater awareness of the possibility of sacramental abuse but also to more positive experiences.

Information about who was a good and bad confessor circulated among networks of women, in both domestic and public settings. In 1631, four women of Mexico City testified against Diego de Cuéllar for improper sacramental behavior. In the course of their testimonies, they mentioned several occasions in which three or more women had gone together to confess with the accused priest as well as conversations with other women during which they shared their concerns and suspicions about this priest. One of the women who testified had noticed her niece acting strangely after confession, while another had been concerned when her daughter refused at the last moment to enter the confessional. As a result of hushed speculations, private conversations, and rumors, it eventually came to light that de Cuéllar had solicited the first young woman who had then confided in her cousin, causing the latter's reticence to enter the confessional.[49]

In places where women had the option to choose confessors, these channels of communication could work against the uneven power dynamics of the confessional, protecting women to some extent from the possibility of abuse and encouraging decent confessors to become especially talented ones. The authority of the church was both supported and limited by its parishioners in everyday ways when people chose whether to attend mass, affirmed the skill of one particular confessor over another, or quietly criticized a priest who abused his power. Laywomen played an important role within communities in sustaining this social contract and holding clergymen accountable. In a case against the confessor Diego González Calderón, many women in the town of San Andres refused to confess with him, thereby expressing their fear and condemnation and communicating

49  AGN Inq. V. 373, exp. 2.

to him that his sacramental authority in their community was predicated on his staying within the boundaries of acceptable sacramental behavior.[50]

For Indigenous women living in rural areas, community criticism of priestly behavior was sometimes a part of collective resistance to colonial interference and imposition. John Chuchiak has written about accusations against priests in Mayan towns in the colonial diocese of Yucatan, finding examples of entire communities coming forward to complain about a particular priest.[51] In these cases, the discussion among the priests and Inquisitors reveals that this was a fairly common scenario. The authorities' interpretation was that Mayans were using accusations of clerical misbehavior to get the priests out of their communities, but Chuchiak cautions us to keep in mind that the frequent accusations could also represent a pattern of abuse by priests stationed in Native communities, not unlike the pattern my own research has suggested. Whatever the case may have been in each individual setting, the accusations illustrate the sexual and religious tensions that existed between church authorities and Native people throughout the colonial period and the ways that expectations of religious behavior were a part of individual and communal negotiations of ecclesiastical power.

Inquisition cases from central Mexico support Chuchiak's findings in the Yucatan and suggest that women's experiences in the confessional could become rallying points for Indigenous communities to protest priests whose presence had become offensive. In 1613, a Native woman from the town of Reymango appeared voluntarily before the nearest comisario of the Inquisition. She reported that the local priest, Pedro de Ayllón had solicited her along with many other women. This comisario wrote to Inquisitors in Mexico City that though this particular witness appeared to be an honest woman, the residents of Reymango had a reputation of being "bad, perverse" people who practiced witchcraft and brought false charges of solicitación against priests who try to correct them. Whether Pedro de Ayllón had been soliciting women or merely meddling in the spiritual and healing practices of the people of Reymango, this lone Native woman was speaking not only for herself but also for her community when she testified before the comisario that this priest had become a problem.[52]

---

50   AGN Inq. V. 295, exp. 23.

51   John Chuchiak, "Secrets behind the Screen: Solicitantes in the Colonial Diocese of Yucatan and the Yucatec Maya, 1570–1785," in *Religion in New Spain*, ed. Susan Shroeder and Stafford Poole (Albuquerque, NM: University of New Mexico Press, 2007), 83–110.

52   AGN Inq. 295, f. 62. This kind of testimony was highly unusual among non-Indigenous women or urban Indigenous women, as it went against the usual pattern of laywomen only testifying when directed to do so by another confessor or when called forward after an investigation had revealed their names. This kind of proactive coming forward on the part of some Indigenous women who then become involved in campaigns to oust a priest from their towns was probably linked to community decisions and community support.

However, not all of rural, Indigenous women's resistance to sacramental abuse was communal. Like women of other racial categories, many Native women objected to bad priestly behavior within the semiprivacy of the confessional, and their responses only became visible outside it through the mechanisms of an Inquisition case. On the one hand, the stories contained within these testimonies are tied to the pattern of racist rural abuse by recently arrived or traveling confessors and reflect rural Indigenous women's sacramental vulnerability. On the other hand, they also contain examples of shock and outrage, suggesting that these particular women expected something different from their confessors. These responses contrasts with the patterns of urban women's responses to soliciting priests, which tended to reflect a greater awareness of the dangers the sacraments could pose.

Rural Indigenous women's testimonies also sometimes speak to how they felt about the sanctity of the confessional or the sacrament itself. Cases against traveling confessors often include testimonies of Native women expressing surprise, shock, and fear when describing a misbehaving priest. These same narratives also include penitents' overt rebukes and condemnations. The offending confessors, in response, often tried to reassert their power within the sacramental space, presuming religious ignorance on the part of their rural, Indigenous female penitents.

In 1612, María, a Native woman from Huatulco, Oaxaca, relayed to the comisario her memory of expressing shock and clear objections when Diego de Paz Monterey abruptly began groping her breasts during confession and said that he wanted to have sex with her. She told the comisario that she gestured to the religious images in the confessional, exclaimed that God was watching, and asked how the priest could do such a thing in God's presence. Diego de Paz Monterey responded by saying that these things were only images of God but that he himself was, in fact, God on earth – referring to the doctrine that in a sacramental context, priests stood in for Christ.[53] This kind of exchange was not uncommon in these testimonies; for some of these penitents, God was physically present in the images of Christ and the saints that watched over their interactions with confessors. The transgressing confessors, on the other hand, responded to this assertion by correcting what they saw as an idolatrous notion of religious images among Indigenous parishioners and contrasting the representation of God in these images with their own power as the human representation of God.[54] Though this assertion was technically correct in

---

53  AGN Inq. V. 295, f. 6.
54  For a discussion of the role of immanence in objects and images in Indigenous Christianity, see William Taylor, *Shrines and Miraculous Images: Religious Life in Mexico Before the Reforma* (Albuquerque, NM: University of New Mexico Press, 2010).

the context of the sacrament they were performing, the implication in these cases was that as God's representative, they had the power to do as they would, even if it contradicted church teaching. In spite of the fact that this put them at even greater risk of punishment by the Inquisition, these priests may have calculated that by invoking this doctrine, they would placate or intimidate these penitents enough that they would not speak of what had transpired to anyone else.

However, some rural Indigenous women seem to have absorbed the doctrine that priests were standing in for Christ when acting as confessors or presiding over the transubstantiation miracle of the Eucharist. The story of María Antonia Samariego suggests that she was aware of this theological concept, though she may have understood it to mean that priests always occupied this semidivine status. When she said that she would never engage in a sexual act with father Mauriño, she gave as her reason that "he was Christ on earth" – not that in the moment of performing confession, he was Christ on earth, but that in his position as a priest, he always was. [55]

Even if they did not explicitly mention this theological point, some rural indigenous women responded to soliciting priests with a similar level of shock to learn that someone inhabiting this sanctified position could behave in this manner. In 1775, a year after Saramiego testified to the comisario of the Villa de Culiacán, another woman, described only as an *india viuda*, relayed a similar response in her testimony before the comisario of Zacatecas. This unnamed widow had gone to confess with Pedro Rebuelta – the same priest who had solicited María Antonia de la Luz. Like Mauriño, Rebuelta had told this anonymous penitent to come to his room the next day because he had something important to tell her. Thinking it was some kind of spiritual advice, she went and then was startled and frightened when he pulled her into a dark corner of his room and attempted to rape her. The widow told the comisario that she struggled free and ran for the door but that she stopped as she reached it in order to turn and ask her confessor, "How could you commit such a terrible sin?" Rebuelta replied that "everything would be made all right through confession," at which the widow fled and never returned to confess with him again. [56]

Though not all rural Native women responded in this way, the surprise these testimonies express is notable. There is a paradox in the contrast between the sense of shattered expectations that their individual

---

55  Banc. mss 96/95m 1774, Padre Fray Domingo Mauriño.
56  "De el se fue para la puerta, desde donde le dixo que como havía de cometer un pecado tan grande, y la respondió, que estará todo compuesto con confesando." Banc. mss 96/95m 1775, Fray Rebuelta.

testimonies present and the evidence of a widespread pattern of clerical abuse in the countryside overall. At least as they represented themselves to their examiners, these women had expected transcendent priestly behavior and moved rapidly from respect and deference to frightened but indignant shock when the priests behaved so differently. These women reported that after these events they felt wary of confessors, suggesting that their expectations had changed and that this event was probably the first time they had encountered the possibility of sacramental abuse.

Clearly, these testimonies must be read with care and skepticism; these penitents could very well have been performing the kind of innocence and naivety prevalent in some strains of colonial discourse about Native neophytes as childlike and in need of protection. But even if they do represent sincere reactions of surprise, they should not be taken to mean that it was rare for rural Indigenous women to have heard of the possibility of sacramental abuse. Reports of priests sexually abusing Indigenous women in rural areas are too frequent to believe that rumors and carefully shared information about the need to be careful in the presence of temporarily stationed or traveling priests did not spread in many Indigenous communities. Nonetheless, because the scarcity of priests was so widespread, it is feasible that these particular women in these particular communities had not ever experienced or heard of behavior like this. Perhaps there had been a beloved confessor serving their communities, and he had only recently left. Or perhaps these women had simply not encountered many priests, and ones they had encountered had all been trustworthy and competent. Time and location are also significant factors here. While this pattern emerges from cases that span the seventeenth and eighteenth centuries, each geographical location has its own history of engagement with missionaries and priests – both those of religious orders and diocesan priests. A closer look at local circumstances and contexts would undoubtedly reveal a greater or lesser exposure to a variety of clergymen in each of these communities, which might shed light on women's responses to soliciting confessors.

In the absence of this more finely grained discussion, what remains most striking is the fact that this kind of surprise is largely absent from urban women's testimonies across time and place. This suggests that there may have been a significant difference between rural Indigenous women's expectations of priestly behavior in general and those of the women who had consistently been exposed to a greater diversity of sacramental possibilities in urban areas. Urban women's testimonies rarely reflect surprise about sacramental abuse, even when the incident reported appeared to have been the first such experience for the woman testifying. When confessors pressured their urban female penitents to meet with them outside the confessional, these women often suggested places and times they knew would be crowded with people, or they simply did not show up.[57] Sometimes they told confessors that they would be alone in their homes when in fact they knew that a parent or other relatives would be present.[58] Such women seemed prepared for and aware of some of the common methods used by soliciting priests.[59] This kind of passive resistance seems especially common among women solicited by a confessor who was well known to them, particularly when they were members of his parish or lived in a cloister in which he worked.

These same testimonies also provide ample evidence of beneficial relationships with confessors, however. In fact, urban women's testimonies suggest that the majority of priests these women had encountered did their jobs well. It was often to another priest that an injured woman would turn when she felt victimized by a confessor, for instance, and brief mentions of "good" confessors pepper the pages of the cases that are focused on the bad ones.[60] These sources rarely give us the stories or even names of these good pastors, but taken together, a picture emerges of an urban landscape full of trustworthy priests that also included a significant minority of abusive ones. Urban women learned from each other that sacramental dangers existed alongside the possibility of fulfilling spiritual experiences and competent spiritual guides.

In addition to reflecting rural and urban women's varying expectations and experiences of priestly behavior, solicitación testimonies also reveal that many laywomen had internalized the church's expectations of them. Women's words suggest they knew how much they needed a full and proper confession but that they were also aware of the frailty and moral weakness that supposedly made this difficult for them. But confession – and women's communication about confession – was one of the primary places where women learned such expectations in the first place. Women learned that confession could alleviate the experience of escrúpulo and was required to remedy its negative spiritual consequences. Eventually a feedback loop between emotional experiences within and outside confession became part of women's devotional practices, and communion became the culmination and fulfilment of this spiritual journey. In this context, women's dependence on confessors could lead to intense relationships of both vulnerability and support.

---

57  Banc. Mss 96/95m, 1771, Padre Fray Domingo Mauriño.
58  Banc. mss 96/95m 1775, Fray Rebuelta.
59  For other examples of these kinds of avoidance techniques, see Banc. Mss 96/95m 1793 Fray Joaquin García and AGN Inq. V. 295, exp. 1.
60  A particularly rich example of women sharing information about confessors is found in AGN Inq. V. 482, f. 154–70.

## Sacramental Power, Guidance, and Intimacy

The relationship between father and daughter of confession was potentially one of genuine spiritual guidance that provided much-needed emotional relief. We know about such relationships through literate nuns' spiritual autobiographies, whereas much of what we know about laywomen's enduring relationships with spiritual directors comes from Inquisition cases – either against the confessor or against the penitent. These cases imply a rupture of that relationship, making it more difficult to see positive experiences. Nonetheless, they do emerge. One woman gushed about a confessor who caused her to feel the depth of her sins and how skilled he was at providing her spiritual solace.[61] Another woman mentioned how long the wait was to confess with a particular confessor because he was known by the women in her community as being particular comforting to them and wise in relation to their particular concerns.[62] This sense also comes indirectly from evidence of women's friendships with their confessors. Many priests paid visits to their penitents' houses, where family members served them chocolate and they spent long afternoons catching up on the latest gossip and family events.[63] Some expected hospitality as they passed through a familiar town in their travels, and the women who hosted them talked about these clergymen in ways that conveyed trust and intimacy.[64] These glimmers of admiration and devotion or of uneventful, easy relationships between laywomen and priests do not capture our attention in their brevity as much as the detailed descriptions of abuse. But the number of priests accused of sacramental abuse is vastly smaller than the number of priests who toiled away in colonial Mexico and never made their way into the historical record. Without denying the risks and realities of gendered, racialized power dynamics and violence, these little glimpses of successful, ordinary sacramental relationships remind us that many – perhaps most – of laywomen's ordinary interactions with confessors were relatively positive within the cultural expectations of the sacraments.

However, the deeply intimate exclusive relationship between an *hija de confesión* and her father confessor and spiritual director was complex. Though we do not know how common such a profound connection was for laywomen, narratives of these spiritual friendships and special mentorship relationships do surface in court cases of various kinds and suggest a range of possibilities. The stories of Marta de la Encarnación and Gertrudis Rosa Ortís, both discussed earlier, demonstrate some of the kinds of relationships that could develop – from trust to suspicion,

---

61  Banc. Mss 96/95m, 1792, Fray Juan de Ortega.  62  AGN, V. 295, exp. 1.
63  Banc. Mss 96/95m, 1793, Fray Joaquin García.  64  AGN Inq. V. 380, f. 2–230.

encouragement to harsh punishment – and the meaningfully fraught nature of spiritual and emotional intimacy.

Though he eventually testified against her, turning over all of his notebooks in which he had written about her over the years, Juan Manuel de la Vega had heard the confessions of Marta de la Encarnación since her childhood. An española from a humble economic background, Marta had always been exceptionally pious, though she also sickened easily and was therefore unable to complete all of the strenuous spiritual practices she longed to undertake. Her confessor had mostly been a stabilizing and encouraging influence on her. When she was young, he encouraged her to read the lives of saints and to eventually take up the habit of a beata and live in the convent in which he worked as a confessor. Even when her Eucharistic piety seemed excessive to him, he still encouraged her to continue her disciplined prayers and meditations.

When Marta began to report seeing visions, Juan Manuel did not doubt her, but he ordered her not to speak to the visions until he was sure whether they were of heavenly or diabolical origin. The visions kept coming, and for the span of a year, between 1718 and 1719, Marta's confessions about them became increasingly urgent. Every night during this period, Mary and St. Peter would come to her, sometimes teaching her various prayers even though she told Mary that her confessor had forbidden her to speak to them, defying this order in the process of this communication. More disturbing to her were the visions of people in flames, crying to be released from purgatory. In an effort to quell them, her confessor told her to take communion less frequently and to make sure that any physical mortifications she practiced were sufficiently mild. He kept careful track of her spiritual activities and experiences in his notebook and seemed unsure whether she was suffering from the torments of the devil or the blessings of God. However, when he testified against her years later, he did not describe her as possessed, ignorant, or even tricked. He cooperated with the Inquisitors but remained as noncommittal as he could about her guilt, suggesting that he felt a loyalty to her in spite of his need to protect himself.[65]

This was not the case with Gertrudis Rosa Ortís's confessor, however. Ortís was a deeply pious widowed mestiza, and she had a relationship with her spiritual director, a man she referred to only as *el Señor Deán*. Ortís came to hear mass every day at the convent of Nuestra Señora de la Encarnación in Mexico City and cultivated a mentorship relationship with her confessor that eventually led to him accusing her of false visions. Upon her confessor's orders, Ortís denounced herself to the Inquisition in 1723, initiating a trial that ended in her death in the tribunal's secret prisons.

65    AGN Inq. V. 788, exp. 24.

The pair had contentious relationship throughout, and yet Ortís did not venture to confess with anyone else. She, like Marta de la Encarnación, was troubled by often-disturbing visions, and she went to her spiritual director for counsel. In addition to regularly seeing the baby Jesus, Christ's passion and visions of transubstantiation, Gertrudis began to have visions of a more macabre nature. Churches burning, people drowning, and premonitions of the deaths of specific, powerful individuals were among the things she anxiously brought to her father confessor.

His responses varied greatly over time. She first told him that during her nightly prayers she had seen all of the churches in Mexico in flames and that she had asked God what the visions meant. Rather than advise her, her spiritual director angrily told her that he did not believe her and that she was a diabolical spirit trying to fool him. He told her to ask God to forgive her lies, and then he absolved her. But when the vision returned, her director changed his tune, telling her that he now believed her and thought that God was trying to tell her that he wanted to punish Mexico for its sins and that he would start with the churches. His faith in her visions did not continue when they began to include blood flowing in the streets. Again, he accused her of being diabolical, telling her that she "was not a woman, but rather a woman of all of the demons" and that he did not want to hear her confession anymore. For four months, she went without confessing to him or anyone else. During this period, her visions continued, and she took communion elsewhere without license to do so. Eventually she returned to her spiritual director, who heard her confession but then sent her to the Inquisition and to certain condemnation.[66]

These two cases, though anecdotal and both featuring highly pious women, suggest the ways in which spiritual status interacted with racial and casta differences, along with other measures of social power. Marta de la Encarnación was described as white, but she was not an elite woman and did not have the means to pay the dowry needed to profess as a nun. A beata and never-married doncella, she had a great deal of spiritual status, but she also ran the risk of appearing arrogant to religious authorities, as her piety was not supervised by a religious order or bishop. Gertrudis Rosa Ortís was also deeply pious, and her piety was publicly acknowledged as well. However, as a mestiza and a previously married woman, she was vulnerable to the judgments that came from racialized notions of spiritual capacity as well as the suspicions that sexually active women no longer under the control of a husband were dangerous and potentially contagious vectors. Both women were ultimately tried for their unorthodox piety, but Ortís's confessor was much more erratic in his support of his penitent than was de

66   AGN Inq. V. 805, exp. 1.

la Encarnación's and seemed more predisposed to suspect her of heresy from the beginning.

Though they both ended in prosecution by the Inquisition, these stories nonetheless capture the possibilities that the penitent-confessor relationship could offer for emotional and spiritual guidance, long-term intellectual and religious companionship, and cathartic release from existential and burdensome internal experiences. We generally only learn about the sacramental bonds that go awry and lead to court cases or become semifamous because of the literary and spiritual ambitions of the confessors of exceptionally pious women. But these unusual stories suggest that such close relationships were possible, and it is only logical to imagine that many such intimacies existed without ever leaving the kind of mark that would become part of the historical record.

## Conclusions: Sacramental Learning

María Guadalupe Ortiz, with permission from her husband and accompanied by her three brothers, traveled overnight to a rural mission outside Queretaro in order to find a priest to hear her confession. She stayed in the mission for a full day and an additional night, unburdening herself to Fray Juan de Ortega multiple times, with tears and sighs and expressions of great spiritual suffering. When her conscience was finally cleared, she received communion and made the long journey back to her hometown, where presumably there was either not currently a priest licensed to hear her confession or else not one to whom she was willing to go.

Ortiz was a married, Spanish-descent woman with three brothers available to travel with her. Though little is directly revealed about her life, her story suggests that she probably enjoyed a relatively comfortable economic status and a reputation for piety and modesty. And yet she had to go to great lengths to obtain the sacramental access she longed for. Though Fray Juan de Ortega was later tried by the Inquisition for abusing his sacramental power, in her testimony, Ortiz raved about his skills as a confessor. She claimed that he had provided much needed spiritual comfort that she could not receive anywhere else.[67]

Though Ortiz and Ortega may never have crossed path's again, this priest fulfilled Ortiz's particular expectations of spiritual healing and added to her understanding of what such an experience could and should be like. Ortiz, for her part, illustrated the ideal emotional and spiritual pain necessary to assure the confessor that her remorse and repentance were sincere. That Ortiz was comforted by her confessor's touch when he made the sign of the cross over her heart and that she only felt ready to take

---

67   Banc, Mss.96/95 1792 Juan de Ortega.

communion after multiple confessions also speak to her expectation that these sacraments be experienced as intimate, highly emotive exchanges.

Ortiz claimed that her experience of Ortega was transformative, and it seems to have relieved her of the suffering she had been experiencing before she met him, but other women had very different kinds of encounters with this particular confessor. In fact, Ortiz is one of only two women among the many who eventually testified against him who described his capabilities as a confessor in positive terms. It turns out that this itinerate friar had made a career of sexually assaulting and molesting women of all castas and economic backgrounds in both rural and urban areas. The testimonies that eventually came forward as a result of Ortega's abuse, in spite of being painful to read, are rich in their representation of both the diversity of sacramental expectations and experiences and the visible patterns within that diversity.

One particularly striking element of these testimonies is that it was not always or only Ortega's behavior that determined these women's experiences. In the case of Ortiz, for instance, Ortega himself, in his own testimony, describes his treatment of her as vulgar and violent. He says he fondled her breasts; she says he made the sign of the cross over her heart. He says he threatened her with a knife; she mentions that he pointed a knife at her in the kitchen but she said she thought he was joking. Another woman of Spanish descent had a similarly benign interpretation of Ortega's admittedly lecherous and exploitative behavior, albeit one that seemed to rely on years of memory to soften. In these two situations in which women remembered Ortega's behavior as innocent, the most powerful element of their experience seems to have been the cathartic sacramental relief they both felt, which they sorely needed and had been difficult to find.

Of course, some of Ortega's behavior was unmistakably abusive, most notably the kind he exhibited toward the often unnamed *indias* in rural areas whose confessions he sometimes heard and sometimes neglected as he frankly took advantage of their vulnerability. But even in these situations, his degree of subterfuge or coarseness varied along with the women's responses. Some of these women, when they could be found and called to testify, described being utterly shocked that a priest would behave this way and verbally condemning him for it. This differed from the responses of most of the urban women who testified against Ortega. These women seemed more familiar with the possibility of this kind of danger and had at the ready a number of passive but ingenious strategies to avoid or resist his salacious aims.[68]

Ortiz's experience of Ortega and the gap between her descriptions of their encounters and his, together with the patterns of surprise on the part

---

68  Banc, Mss.96/95 1792 Juan de Ortega.

of rural Indigenous women and the quiet but savvy subterfuge on the part of urban women, suggest how complex the twin sacraments were for lay-women in seventeenth- and eighteenth-century Mexico. Confession and communion implied particular emotional, spiritual, social, and physical risks for laywomen, but were also crucial events – doctrinally and emotion-ally necessary and at least sometimes deeply affirming, healing, and trans-cendent. These experiences were shaped by differences in geography and status, along with the characteristics of available priests, but they also differed with women's own interpretations and needs.

In the lives of women who had learned to see themselves as particularly sinful, shameful, or weak in the face of temptation because of their sex, confession and communion were profoundly multilayered experiences. Confession required these women to scour their consciences and be scru-pulously honest in evaluating the depth of their own emotions to determine whether they could legitimately take communion. Communion was then a unique moment in which their normally denigrated bodies could be sanctified by the literal physical presence of God. These sacraments also implied an intense and complex relationship with the clergyman who administered them. Some women saw in this relationship the opportunity to seek the counsel of a learned or compassionate man whose job it was to listen carefully to their feelings and experiences. Others suffered an inten-sification of shame in the presence of Christ's proxy in the form of an elite man whose social status greatly outweighed theirs.

Both dangerous and deeply meaningful, then, confession and commu-nion were charged points of learning between priests and laywomen. Highly intimate, unequal, and gendered, they affirmed such seemingly disparate things as the church's authority and the power of elite men in women's spiritual lives, women's own understandings of the sacraments and their place in the devotional culture of their communities, and the possibility of intense relationships with men of God – be they positive or negative. But laywomen's interpretations of sacramental theology – their particular choices, strategies, and responses – also shaped the experiences and sacramental repertoires of confessors. Like all other interactions between laywomen and the church, women's sacramental practices occurred in a context of both conflict and collaboration with church authorities. It was not an equal communication, but through their actions and interpretive choices, laywomen did participate in the sacramental dialogue and learning that lay at the nexus of devotional life, colonial pedagogy, and church authority in New Spain.

## 2

# Public and Scandalous Sin

In 1737, in the Central Mexican city of Toluca, María Guadalupe Quiñones presented a complaint to ecclesiastical judge Br. Nicolás de Villegas charging Andrés Salguero of three crimes.[1] The court called María Quiñones an *española*, and though no racial category was mentioned for Andrés Salguero, they were both most likely part of the class of humble people of Spanish descent, or passing as such, that formed the majority of townspeople in the City of Toluca.[2] The couple had a young child and had been living with Salguero's parents for two years when Quiñones presented her charges. She accused Salguero of "violating" her virginity, reneging on his promise to marry her, and sexual involvement with a married woman. For these crimes, Quiñones asked Villegas to detain Salguero in the local jail until he agreed to marry her or provide a dowry that would help her overcome the stigma of unwed motherhood and allow her to marry in the future.[3]

María Guadalupe's hearing was one of many such cases women presented to the *Juzgado Eclesiástico de Toluca*, a regional branch of the court of the archbishop's *Provisorato Eclesiástico* that was established in the late seventeenth century and functioned until Mexican independence. This chapter looks at women's interactions with the Toluca court and argues that in cases involving marriage and sexuality, women were able to appeal to the Provisorato's stated purpose to oppose "public and scandalous sin" to demand and receive a measure of support and protection.[4] In their petitions, women appealed to ecclesiastical judges' duty to preserve social and sexual order. They drew on the connection the church made between proper

---

1 The archive of this tribunal is located in the *Archivo Histórico del Arzobispado de México* (AHAM) in Mexico City. For this chapter, I consulted 290 cases from this archive.

2 I will include ethnic/racial/casta classification whenever noted, but as with Andrés, this and other courts did not always record them.

3 AHAM, caja 52, exp. 28.

4 Archbishop Juan Zumárraga, the architect of the Provisorato Eclesiástico, described this court's purpose as "la lucha en contra del pecado público y escandaloso." Jorge E. Traslosheros, *Iglesia, justicia y sociedad en la Nueva España: La audiencia del Arzobispado de México, 1528–1668* (Mexico: Editorial Porrúa, 2004), xiii, xi–61.

marital relations and the salvation of souls, invoked the notions that women were vulnerable and in need of ecclesiastical protection and that this vulnerability posed a threat to the spiritual health of their community, and claimed access to what they felt was owed them in the context of marriage, courtship, and sexual behavior.

Cases of sexual and marital conflict show local diocesan courts to be potentially important resources for women; they also offer evidence of a mutual learning process that included both female petitioners and ecclesiastical judges, which was in some ways an extension of and in other ways a variation from the dynamics of the confessional. Familiar with basic church teachings on sexual behavior and marriage – and experientially with how confessors, preachers, and teachers dealt with public sin and scandal – the women approaching this court learned how to express their needs as consistent with the court's purposes. In doing so, they explicitly justified the demands they made on the clergyman serving as ecclesiastical judges. In turn, these judges developed specialized knowledge and a repertoire of strategies for responding to these demands. In the process, women learned to see themselves as parishioners to whom particular debts and obligations were owed, not only from the men with whom they had domestic and sexual relations but also from priests and ecclesiastical institutions. Priests serving as ecclesiastical judges learned to see themselves as protectors and mediators in women's sexual and domestic relationships with men as a part of their role as guardians of public morality.

Asunción Lavrin and others have shown that while the colonial state and church had "overlapping interests" in sexuality, marriage, and the family, "ecclesiastical scrutiny . . . was more comprehensive than that of the state and more intrusive of individual privacy, as it defined the proper engagement rituals and religious taboos of affinity and kinship." Lavrin argues that the church "established a sacramental bonding connecting the material with the spiritual," in which its goal was "to place all actions expressing sexuality within a teleological objective: the salvation of the soul."[5] Clergymen articulated this connection in sermons and confession, while religious art and proscriptive literature supported it. These didactic efforts of the church made up the dominant discourse about sexual norms and ideals in colonial society – a discourse with which women of Spanish, Indigenous, African, and mixed descent were all familiar in seventeenth- and eighteenth-century New Spain.

One of the other ways the church established the link between eternal salvation and proper sexual behavior was through the daily workings of its

5   Asunción Lavrin, "Introduction: The Scenario, the Actors, and the Issues," in *Sexuality and Marriage in Colonial Latin America*, ed. Asunción Lavrin (Lincoln, NE: University of Nebraska Press, 1989), 1–46, 3.

diocesan tribunals. Though people may have accepted church teachings about sexuality as valid, few actually lived up to their stringencies.[6] In addition to problems of conscience, the tension between these realities created social conflicts that could not be resolved through confession and absolution. As a result, ecclesiastical judges found themselves responding to accusations of scandal and the communal problems that arose from illicit sexual behavior.

## The Archbishop's Court in Toluca: Place and Context

Local tribunals of the diocesan court system, to the extent that their records have been preserved, offer a particularly good view of women's interactions with priests in their roles as judges.[7] Women were most active in these

6 Patricia Seed, *To Love, Honor, and Obey in Colonial Mexico: Conflicts over Marriage Choice, 1574–1821* (Stanford, CA: Stanford University Press, 1988); Asunción Lavrin, "Sexuality in Colonial Mexico"; Gutiérrez, *When Jesus Came.*

7 Little has been written about the role of the diocesan court system in the regulation of community or domestic life, and there has been even less attention paid to women's active use of these courts. Juan Javier Pescador's essay about judges' treatment of women in the Provisorato Eclesiástico of Mexico City is the only systematic study of women's interactions with a diocesan court that I am aware of. Juan Javier Pescador, "Entre la espada y el olvido: pleitos matrimoniales en el Provisorato Eclesiástico de México, siglo XVIII," in *La familia en el mundo iberoamericano*, ed. Pilar Gonzalbo Aizpuru (Mexico City: Instituto de Investigaciones Sociales, Universidad Nacional Autónoma de México, 1994), 193–225. Scholars have used evidence from diocesan courts in the service of broader arguments, however. For instance, Asunción Lavrin uses cases heard by the Provisorato to explore church ideology about sexuality and people's actual lived sexual behavior. Lavrin, "Sexuality in Colonial Mexico." Pilar Gonzalbo Aizpuru looks at sexual violence cases in both ecclesiastical and civil courts in her study of violence in society. Pilar Gonzalbo Aizpuru, "Violencia y discordia en las relaciones personales en la Ciudad de México a fines del Siglo XVIII," *Historia Mexicana* 51, no. 2 (2001): 233–59. Women appear before ecclesiastical judges along with their betrothed to obtain licenses to marry or defend themselves against disapproving parents in Patricia Seed's study of marriage choice. Seed, *To Love, Honor, and Obey.* And there is discussion of women requesting dispensation from ecclesiastical judges for religious impediments to their marriages in the work of Ramón Gutiérrez. Gutiérrez, *When Jesus Came.* Caterina Pizzigoni worked extensively with Nahua language testimonies in the Ecclesiastical Court of Toluca. Caterina Pizzigoni, ed., *Testaments of Toluca* (Stanford, CA: Stanford University Press, 2007); Pizzigoni, *The Life Within: Local Indigenous Society in Mexico's Toluca Valley, 1650–1800* (Stanford, CA: Stanford University Press, 2012). Pizzigoni's earlier work also included two essays that looked at individual cases of Indigenous women accused of crimes in these courts. The first looked at the church's treatment of Indigenous women through four bigamy cases, and the second challenged contemporary notions of passivity in Indigenous women through twelve cases of mala vida (seven of which were brought by women) and thirteen cases of broken marriage promises along with evidence of women's involvement in the production of alcoholic beverages. Caterina Pizzigoni, "'Para que le sirva de castigo y al pueblo de exemplo'. El pecado de poligamia y la mujer indígena en el valle de Toluca (siglo XVIII)," in *Las mujeres en la construcción de las sociedades iberoamericanas*, ed. Pilar Gonzalbo Aizpuru and Berta Ares Queija (Mexico City: Colegio de México, Centro de Estudios Históricos, 2004), 193–218; Caterina Pizzigoni, "'Como frágil y miserable': Las mujeres Nahuas en

smaller courts, bringing suits on their own behalf more frequently than they did in civil courts and with a broader range of requests than they did in the *audiencia*, or high court, of the Provisorato Eclesiástico in Mexico City. Their efforts, successes, and failures were shaped in part by local circumstances, the tendencies of particular ecclesiastical judges, and the changing level of autonomy with which the court operated vis-à-vis the central court and the archbishop. But evaluating these dynamics – both in Toluca and in general – requires an understanding of the structure of the diocesan audiencia and its spiritual and legal aims.

Juan Zumárraga, the first archbishop of New Spain and the architect of the audiencia of the archbishopric of Mexico, charged this court with "defending the faith," "reforming customs," and guarding against "public and scandalous sin."[8] The Inquisition shared the first of these goals but in specific ways and for certain crimes.[9] "Reforming customs" and responding to "public and scandalous sin" were really the tasks of the diocesan courts. In practice, this meant mediating conflict between community members and responding to individual petitions and complaints. Receiving such requests and testimonies was in many ways the primary function of diocesan courts and judges, and a great deal of the cases they attended to were related to sexual behavior, conflict, and violence.

Each diocese, or bishopric, had its own audiencia headed by the bishop or archbishop as superior ecclesiastical judge. In function, this high court was divided up into two or three central courts, each with an appointed judge, or *provisor*, acting as the bishop's proxy, and many smaller local and regional courts. In the archbishopric of Mexico City, the central courts were the *Provisorato de Españoles*, *Provisorato de Indios y Chinos*, and the *Juzgado de Testamentos, Capellanías, y Obras Pías*. The Provisorato de Españoles had jurisdiction over españoles and castas for crimes not tried by the Inquisition. The Provisorato de Indios regulated the population classified as indios for all types of crimes. The Juzgado de Testamentos dealt with issues of money and property. Collectively these courts were known as the Provisorato Eclesiástico. The archbishop could turn any parish in the diocese into a court by giving a clergyman, who may or may not have been the beneficed parish priest, the title of *juez eclesiástico*, or ecclesiastical judge. In addition to these parish level courts, the archbishop also set up

el Valle de Toluca," in *Historia de la vida cotidiana en México III: El siglo XVIII: Entre tradición y cambio*, ed. Pilar Gonzalbo Aizpuru (Mexico City: El Colegio de México, 2005), 501–30.

8    Traslosheros, *Iglesia, justicia, y sociedad*, xi–xvi, 43–48.

9    However, it is also important not to overemphasize the distinction between these branches of ecclesiastical justice. Officially, diocesan courts were completely separate from the Inquisition and, in the case of the non-Indigenous population, dealt with different kinds of offenses. However, individual ecclesiastical judges could also be local representatives of the Inquisition, which could muddy the intended separation between the two types of ecclesiastical judicial power.

three separate regional ones in Querétaro, Acapulco, and Toluca with jurisdiction over all the parishes in the areas surrounding these towns. Though the archbishop and provisores were the official supervisors of these parish and regional diocesan courts, distance and circumstance demanded that ecclesiastical judges be fairly self-sufficient. The role of ecclesiastical judge meant the power to police and discipline, to be sure, but it also positioned these clergymen as authorities from whom people expected to receive justice and moral healing in the form of protection, restitution, retribution, and absolution. For much of the colonial period, clergymen enjoyed a great deal of judicial authority as a part of their regular pastoral responsibilities, and the formal title of "juez eclesiástico" was merely an extension of these duties.[10]

The Juzgado Eclesiástico de Toluca had its headquarters in the city of Toluca, a modest city just thirty miles west of Mexico City that lay at the heart of a largely Indigenous grain-producing region.[11] Nahua-, Otomí-, and Mazahua-speaking people made up the majority of the valley's population, and most of them lived in villages designated as Indian pueblos. Native people also lived and worked on the haciendas owned by wealthy Mexico City residents, on smaller ranchos owned by españoles or *mestizos*, and in the commercial and administrative head-towns, or *cabeceras*, of the valley. Most españoles, mestizos, and other castas were townspeople living in the cabeceras, but non-Indigenous people remained the minority, even in these urban areas, with the exception of the city of Toluca itself. Others were small-scale farmers known as *labradores* and lived either in small communities scattered throughout the countryside, on land connected to the large haciendas or owned by Indian pueblos, or as nonnative individuals within Indian pueblos living among the Indigenous population. Some Spaniards and castas also worked as employees on the large haciendas that Mexico City residents owned.[12]

---

10   The gradual erosion of the judicial authority of priests in the late eighteenth-century was one of the significant impacts of the Bourbon era reforms. Taylor, *Magistrates*.

11   The Valley of Toluca had supplied the Mexico City-Tenochtitlan region with maize long before the Spanish conquest. By the eighteenth century, wheat and other grains had been incorporated into the area's agricultural production, as had some livestock. The area's primary market was still the capital, though it also provided for the mining towns to the south.

12   On Toluca, see Peter Gerhard, *A Guide to the Historical Geography of New Spain* (Norman, OK: University of Oklahoma Press, 1993); James Lockhart, "Capital and Province, Spaniard and Indian: The Example of Late Sixteenth-Century Toluca," in *Provinces of Early Mexico: Variants of Spanish American Regional Evolution*, ed. Ida Altman and James Lockhart (Los Angeles, CA: UCLA Latin American Center Publications, 1976), 99–123; Lockhart, *Nahuas and Spaniards: Postconquest Central Mexican History and Philology* (Stanford, CA: Stanford University Press, 1991); Stephanie Wood, "Corporate Adjustments in Colonial Mexican Indian Towns: Toluca Region, 1550–1810" (Ph. D. dissertation, University of California, Los Angeles, CA, 1984); Wood, "Matters of Life at Death: Nahuatl Testaments of Rural Women (Central Mexico), 1589–1801," in *Indian Women of Early*

Though a clear administrative distinction existed between Spanish-style towns and Indian pueblos, there was also a great deal of contact between these groups in both town and countryside. By the eighteenth century, most Indigenous people were versed in Spanish, though women living in pueblos tended to be disproportionately monolingual.[13] Bilingualism and regular interaction facilitated a degree of cultural exchange that connected Indigenous and non-Indigenous communities and individuals. Employment relations, business and social alliances, friendships, and even some marital ties bound the "two republics" together in ways that complicated the designation of the Valley of Toluca as an Indian region.

Parish life in the Valley of Toluca was primarily under the care of the Franciscan order, though Carmelite friars had an important presence there as well, and the region was not secularized until 1859.[14] Nonetheless, by the early eighteenth century, a small but growing number of resident secular priests formed something of a social elite in terms of education, social connections, and orientation toward Mexico City.[15] The appointed ecclesiastic judges for the Juzgado Eclesiástico de Toluca usually came either from outside the valley or from among the ranks of these few diocesan clerics rather than from the Franciscan or Carmelite parish priests, though exceptions would be made if necessary. This undoubtedly led to moments of friction between secular and religious clergy since the latter had presumably acted as judges in their own right before the establishment of the archbishop's tribunal and probably still attempted to do so when not thwarted by diocesan authorities.

Neither Juzgado records nor those of visiting archbishops reveal the exact location of the tribunal in the city of Toluca. Aside from the Franciscan convent and Carmelite church, the colonial town center was located on the sloping hillside above where the modern city lies today. Since most of the valley's parishes belonged to the religious orders, court business was probably not held in a church. Most likely it was situated in a central location and very well could have occupied the same house reserved for visiting archbishops and their staff. During these visits, parishioners from the city and surrounding pueblos, ranchos, and haciendas lined up outside this house to personally present their petitions and complaints to the archbishop, establishing the physical space as a place to

*Mexico*, ed. Susan Schroeder, Stephanie Wood, and Robert Haskett (Norman, OK: University of Oklahoma Press, 1997), 165–84; Wood, *Transcending Conquest: Nahua Views of Spanish Colonial Mexico* (Norman, OK: University of Oklahoma Press, 2003); Pizzigoni, *The Life Within; Testaments of Toluca.* See also Deborah Kanter, *Hijos del Pueblo: Gender, Family, and Community in Rural Mexico, 1730–1850* (Austin, TX: University of Texas Press, 2009).

13    Kanter, *Hijos del Pueblo.*     14    Gerhard, *A Guide to the Historical Geography of New Spain.*
15    James Lockhart, "Capital and Province."

be heard.[16] The archbishop's responses usually included instructions for the ecclesiastical judge to carry out, facilitating ongoing interaction between parishioners and the Juzgado Eclesiástico after the archbishop left town. The autonomy of the Juzgado Eclesiástico de Toluca varied over time, but judges generally claimed the authority to hear petitions and complaints, temporarily jail or detain the accused, gather and send testimony to the Provisorato Eclesiástico, and carry out superior court sentences. Officially, all decisions related to marriage were to be remitted to the Provisorato for disposition, but in practice local ecclesiastical judges frequently made decisions and administered justice in cases related to sexuality and marriage without seeking the permission of their superiors.[17] Even when judges did turn everything over to the Provisorato and await word, the immediate actions they took while doing so often had significant consequences for women presenting complaints. In fact, many women's requests did not go beyond the power these local judges regularly exercised in jailing the accused and admonishing him to change his behavior.

## Women in the Court

For women with relatively few channels for protection in the context of unequal social and sexual relations with men, the church's concern with sexuality and marriage in combination with the local workings of ecclesiastical justice could become an important resource if navigated correctly. Juan Javier Pescador has argued that the Provisorato Eclesiástico in Mexico City operated as a protective institution for women.[18] He suggested that provisores recognized women's sexual, social, and corresponding spiritual vulnerability in the church-supported patriarchy of colonial society and felt it was their responsibility to protect and defend them within that framework. This differs from women's experiences accusing men of physical or sexual violence in colonial civil courts.[19] Though, in theory, rape and

16  See especially AHAM caja 27, exp. 4; AHAM caja 20CL, exp. 1; AHAM caja 20CL, exp. 2; AHAM caja 2CL, exp. 3; and AHAM caja 21CL, exp. 2.

17  Archbishop Don Francisco Antonio de Lorenzana's official appointment of Juez Eclesiástico don Matías José Eguilas Benavidas in 1767 gave Eguilas the power to sentence in cases "que sean de moderada sumo," including criminal cases between "indios," but not in marriage cases, which were to be remitted to the Provisorato for disposition. AHAM caja 97, exp. 2.

18  Pescador, "Entre la espada."

19  Gonzalbo Aizpuru, "Violencia y discordia"; Marcela Suárez Escobar, *Sexualidad y norma sobre lo prohibido: la Ciudad de México y las postrimerías del virreinato* (Mexico City: Universidad Autonoma Metropolitano, 1994); François Giraud, "La reacción social ante la violación: del discurso a la práctica. (Nueva España, Siglo XVIII)," in *El placer de pecar y el afán de normar*, ed. Seminario de Historia de las Mentalidades (Mexico City: Joaquin Mortiz/Instituto Nacional de Antropología e Historia, 1988), 295–352; and William B. Taylor, *Drinking, Homicide, and Rebellion in Colonial Mexican Villages* (Stanford, CA: Stanford University Press, 1979). Deborah Kanter also looks at

virginity theft were serious crimes, civil law made them difficult to prove, and judges tended to assume that women's accounts of sexual violence were false.[20] Probably for this reason, women did not usually pursue these types of cases on their own behalf in civil courts but were rather represented by male relatives and, to a lesser degree, older female ones.[21]

The patterns I have found for women's interactions with the Juzgado Eclesiástico de Toluca more closely resemble those Pescador found in the Provisorato Eclesiástico than those of civil courts, but there are differences as well that suggest particular characteristics of local ecclesiastical justice. Women frequently turned to both central and local ecclesiastical courts with complaints of sexual violence, broken marriage promises, and marital discord and could generally expect judges to support them. However, comparing the evidence from Toluca to that of the Provisorato Eclesiástico suggests that local ecclesiastical courts were more accessible to poor women, more flexible and personal in their responses to women's requests, and, in some instances, more effective in dealing with women's immediate concerns.[22]

Though Pescador and I both found that women brought the majority of these cases on their own behalf, the ratio is somewhat greater in Toluca, with even very young women presenting their own petitions. Women presenting these kinds of cases in Toluca made use of lawyers far less than women did in the centrally located Provisorato. Judges in Toluca responded more swiftly and decisively to jail men in response to women's complaints but were somewhat more reluctant to grant requests of marital separation than provisores in Mexico City. On the other hand, whereas married women facing conflict or abuse in their marriages primarily turned to the central court to request a separation or divorce, wives in Toluca more often sought more intimate and immediate mediation from local courts. Local judges punished and scolded misbehaving husbands, counseled

local civil courts in the Toluca Valley and finds a generally protective attitude toward the Indigenous population and, in some cases, particularly women, but not in cases of sexual or marital conflicts with men. Kanter, *Hijos del Pueblo*. For comparison in another colonial Latin American context, see Kimberly Gauderman, *Women's Lives in Colonial Quito: Gender, Law, and Economy in Spanish America* (Austin: University of Texas Press, 2003). And for an important and provocative discussion of the broader historical implications of nonelites' use of courts in general in colonial Latin America, see Bianca Premo, *Enlightenment on Trial: Ordinary Litigants and Colonialism in the Spanish Empire* (New York, NY: Oxford University Press, 2017).

20   Giraud, "La reacción social."

21   François Giraud found that half of the sexual violence cases in the *Real Sala de Crimen* in Mexico between the years of 1720 and 1820 were brought by men on behalf of a female relative and that mothers brought most of the other half, while victims themselves brought only 17 percent. Giraud, "La reacción social," 318.

22   The majority of relevant Provisorato cases are in the *Ramo Matrimoniales* of the *Archivo General de la Nación* (AGN) in Mexico City.

women to let their spouses cool off in jail, and appointed neighbors to watch over reunited couples as a means of safeguarding domestic and community peace.

Women of diverse social, economic, and racial status made use of the ecclesiastical tribunal in Toluca, ranging from poor women to the local social elite.[23] It is notable, however, that in the cases brought by women against men, the petitioner was rarely identified as being of African descent. The population of African-descent people was relatively low in this largely Indigenous area, but they were not absent. They did appear in other types of cases in this same court, suggesting that women of African descent may not have found this court as helpful in marriage and sexuality cases as did other women. Given the way colonial authorities imagined African and African descent women's spiritual and moral capacities, it is very possible that judges would not have afforded them the credibility and base level of spiritual status needed to find these courts useful.

In her study of violence and social conflicts in colonial Mexico City, Pilar Gonzalbo Aizpuru suggests that in order for women to effectively engage with civil courts, they had to play to judges' expectations of femininity by presenting themselves as innocent, fragile, and in need of protection.[24] This observation applies to the diocesan courts as well, but women were also successful because they appealed to religious teachings about sexuality and marriage along with fears of contagious sin and scandal. In so doing, they moved from a stance of weakness to an assertion of entitlement and even moral defender of their communities.

Though women did describe themselves as victims in need of defense, they simultaneously presented themselves as parishioners who knew and demanded the particular protections, obligations, and debts owed to them. They also spoke as community members offended by the transgressions of the accused and, ironically, as unwitting sources of scandal themselves who were concerned for the well-being of those around them. They suggested that the disgrace these men had brought upon them would harm the community and that the only way to stop its spread was to compel those responsible to rectify the situation and, failing that, to publicly punish them. With this kind of rhetoric, women whose initial testimonies were crafted within a framework of fragility and destitution presented subsequent testimonies with a tone of increasingly righteous indignation to reject the claims of the accused and to remind judges of their spiritual

---

23 The highest levels of New Spanish society are not represented in these cases because members of the large landowner class of the Valley of Toluca had their primary residences in Mexico City and generally turned to the courts in the capital.

24 Gonzalbo Aizpuru, "Violencia y discordia." Kanter also finds this dynamic at work in the civil judicial record of Toluca Valley. Kanter, *Hijos del Pueblo*.

and legal obligations to protect their community from the negative effects of scandal.

However, these women had to walk a fine line to appropriate or employ church goals and teachings in this way without appearing to challenge them.[25] Common sexual practice fell short of the church's ideals, particularly in terms of the prohibition of premarital sex; nonetheless, women seeking judges' help could not appear too far from the mark. By virtue of the conflicts they were involved in, most had broken some of the church's rules, but their success depended on characterizing these mistakes as falling within a socially acceptable margin of error. Those who visibly deviated too much from this standard were likely to find themselves on the wrong side of the justice they sought.

In spite of this ever-present risk, many women were able to use ecclesiastical justice in Toluca as a resource. As is visible in the historical record related to confession and communion, both men and women, clergy and laypeople alike imagined sin, scandal, and shame as contagious and communal forces, and in the context of the ecclesiastical court of Toluca, women found ways of utilizing this notion and the connection between "private" and public sin in a more direct way than can be seen through their engagement with the sacraments. While confessors and penitents may have focused on healing the painful, interior experience of *escrúpulo* (always with the knowledge that this experience had a tendency to spread out beyond the boundaries of the affected individual), for ecclesiastical judges, this "private" experience was not the primary concern. Addressing the sin itself, or even resolving the interior suffering it caused the sinner and those who had come to learn of the sin, was ultimately less of a priority in this judicial context than simply reducing its public visibility. This was the greatest concern for the priests-as-judges charged with "reforming customs" and "guarding against public and scandalous sin." Theoretically, if kept private, sin only endangered the soul of the sinner, whereas publicly visible sin affected and infected everyone who witnessed it. While confessors attended to each person spiritually touched by sin, scandal, and escrúpulo, ecclesiastical judges acted out of a pragmatic effort to contain the contagion in a larger context – working from a belief that the greater the sin's visibility, the greater the damage.

In their testimonies, Tolucan women engaged these concerns and told judges that the men they accused had sinned against God and his church, undermined the sacrament of marriage, and caused public scandal. They charged these men of shirking church-defined obligations to them, which

---

25   In a similar dynamic, Deborah Kanter finds men and women using the language of patriarchy and paternalism to remind civil authorities of their obligations while avoiding any challenge to their authority or the hierarchies it was based on. Kanter, *Hijos del Pueblo*.

they claimed endangered not only their physical and social well-being as women but their immortal souls as well. In addition, these women argued that by forcing them into a visibly immoral and disorderly lifestyle, the offending men were scandalizing the community and thus threatening its overall spiritual health.

The clergymen listening to these women responded to this logic. They operated within a cosmology that saw human beings as essentially weak and fragile and the self as intimately connected to community and corporate identity. As did confessors, ecclesiastical judges understood the spirit as corruptible through its proximity to the body, and they believed that the spiritual integrity of the community as a whole could be damaged by the presence of corrupted souls. Therefore, when a woman claimed that a man was forcing her to lead a life of sin and disorder in full view of the community, she was tapping into genuine fears about the danger of scandal, the social vulnerability of women, and the connection between the two.

Elite families went to great lengths to protect the reputations of female relatives, and ecclesiastical judges and notaries sometimes supported these efforts by not revealing women's names if their situations were not already publicly known; but most women did not have the resources required for this kind of anonymity.[26] Lacking the privacy that large houses and powerful male relatives afforded, nonelite women could rarely hide a premarital pregnancy or avoid market or neighborhood gossip about a sexual affair or broken engagement. A woman with a damaged reputation was a woman with fewer marriage options and therefore less protection, financial support, and supervision. The concern from the perspective of ecclesiastical judges was to prevent a vicious cycle in which such women fell into a state of even greater degradation and "disorder," subjecting the community to more scandal through the visible presence of *mujeres vergonzozas*, or shameful women.

In the Valley of Toluca, women raised the specter of these dangers in their petitions against men with whom that they had sexual and domestic conflicts. It is difficult to know how much these women had internalized these ideas, but by the mid-seventeenth century, women and men of all racial categories and social positions in Mexico were at least aware of them. Since these cases frequently became public knowledge, it is likely that women learned from one another how best to articulate these ideas in their testimonies in a way that would help gain the court's support. In addition, when women were successful, others could use the threat of following in their footsteps as leverage in their informal negotiations with wayward or

26 See Ann Twinam, *Public Lives, Private Secrets: Gender, Honor, Sexuality, and Illegitimacy in Colonial Latin America* (Stanford, CA: Stanford University Press, 1999).

violent lovers, reluctant fiancés or partners, and abusive, unfaithful, or negligent spouses.

The archives of Toluca's ecclesiastical court show local judges spending a significant amount of time receiving petitions related to sexual and marital conflicts, of which women initiated more than twice as many as men did. Roughly two-thirds of all petitions related to sexuality or marriage conflicts or crimes accused men of sexual violence, virginity debt or theft, broken marriage promises, or marital abuse. Of these, unmarried women presented 55 percent and married women presented 20 percent, while men presented less then 10 percent of these cases on women's behalf, and the remainder are cases for which the original petition was anonymous. Men's petitions made up less than a third of all cases related to sexual or marital crimes or conflicts. Of these, 40 percent were cases in which a man accused a woman other than his wife of sexual impropriety; roughly 30 percent were authored by husbands against their spouses, usually for abandonment; 20 percent were cases against other men for sexual violence, virginity theft, or broken marriage promises on behalf of women; and 10 percent accused other men of sexual impropriety not related to the defense of women. Taken together, these ratios suggest that women had a special relationship with this court in the area of sexuality and marriage, in which they used the court more than men did and were complainants more often than they were defendants.

This relationship changed over time, however. In the 1750s and 1760s, Bourbon reforms began to limit the church's judicial powers to regulate marriage.[27] Two new policies, the *Pragmática Real de Matrimonios* of 1778 and a *real cédula* concerning separation and divorce that circulated in 1787, further strengthened this trend.[28] The church itself underwent an internal reorganization in the second half of the eighteenth century in order to "guard its spaces of action that slowly began to be replaced by the power of civil authorities."[29] These larger trends were reflected in Toluca; though the local ecclesiastical court remained active until 1821, its sexuality and marriage conflict cases ended in 1785.

27   Taylor, *Magistrates*; Chowning, "Convent Reform"; D. A. Brading, *Church and State in Bourbon Mexico: The Diocese of Michoacán, 1749–1810* (Cambridge: Cambridge University Press, 1994); and Dora Dávila Mendoza, "Vida matrimonial y orden burocrático. Una visión a través de el quaderno de los divorcios, 1754 a 1820, en el arzobispado de la ciudad de México," in *Historia, género y familia en iberoamérica (siglos XVI a XX)*, ed. Dora Davila Mendoza (Caracas: Konrad Adenauer, 2004).

28   Angela Carballeda, "Género y matrimonio en Nueva España: Las mujeres de la élite ante la aplicación de la Pragmática de 1776," in *Las mujeres en la construcción de las sociedades iberoamericanas*, ed. Pilar Gonzalbo Aizpuru and Berta Ares Queija (Mexico City: El Colegio de México, Centro de Estudios Históricos, 2004), 219–50; Chowning, "Convent Reform."

29   "Cuidar sus espacios de acción que paulatinamente comenzaban a ser sustituidos por el poder de las autoridades civiles." Dávila Mendoza, "Vida matrimonial," 162–63.

The court heard the first of these cases in 1705, but it was most busy with these matters from 1750 to 1759, which were also the years in which women used the court most actively. From 1705 to 1731, women brought six of the ten cases related to marriage or sexual conflicts or crimes. From 1731 to 1749, there were between one and four such cases annually; women brought twenty-one of them, and men brought ten of them on women's behalf. Then from 1750 to 1759, the court heard eight to twenty cases annually; women presented fifty-five, and men presented seventeen on women's behalf.

Between 1760 and 1773, these numbers dropped significantly: there were zero to nine cases annually, with an average of three per year, fourteen of which women brought and eleven of which men brought on women's behalf. From 1774 to 1782, things picked up slightly with five to eleven of these types of cases a year, thirty-five of which women brought and eight of which men brought on women's behalf. Then they dropped again in 1783, when for two years there was only one case per year, both brought by women. With the exception of one divorce case in 1808, these cases finally disappeared in 1785.

The fluctuations in these numbers suggest that local forces were at play in addition to central reforms. Nonetheless, the overall number of petitions for sexual and marital conflict dropped by more than half in the early 1760s, corresponding with a dramatic increase in divorce and separation cases in the civil courts of Mexico City and, ironically, in the Provisorato Eclesiástico as well.[30] The latter probably reflects both better record-keeping, as the church attempted to retain control of what seemed to be slipping from its grasp, and a growing centralization of ecclesiastical authority for the same reason.[31]

The change in women's engagement with the ecclesiastical court of Toluca points to a change in the nature of women's relationship to the church in the late colonial period. If Bourbon reforms supported by crown-appointed bishops "redefine[d] the clergy as a professional class of spiritual specialists with fewer judicial and administrative responsibilities and less independence than in Hapsburg times," this move away from the priest-as-judge also worked to limit the power and autonomy of regional ecclesiastical courts.[32] In the Valley of Toluca and wherever late eighteenth-century reforms began to close down local channels of ecclesiastical justice, particularly around issues of marriage and sexuality, these changes would have had an impact on

---

30  Dora Dávila Mendoza, *Hasta que la muerte nos separe: El divorcio eclesiástico en el arzobispado de México, 1702–1800* (Mexico City: El Colegio de México, 2005); Dávila Mendoza, "Vida matrimonial"; Gonzalbo Aizpuru, "Violencia y discordia"; and Pescador, "Entre la espada."
31  Dávila Mendoza, "Vida matrimonial."   32  Taylor, *Magistrates*, 14.

women's lives, relationships, and ability to access help from colonial authorities.[33]

## Rape, Virginity Debt, and Broken Marriage Promises

In Toluca, the majority of unmarried women's complaints accused men of rape or sexual violence, virginity theft or debt, and broken marriage promises. For the complainant, these accusations usually implied admitting to loss of virginity. In addition to reduced marriage possibilities, a reputation damaged by such an admission could also imply a greater vulnerability to other kinds of accusations, being less able to defend oneself against future coercive relationships with men, and bringing dishonor to their male relatives.[34] Ann Twinam has explored elite women's attempts to protect their honor and that of their families, but she notes that when these efforts failed, sometimes the only recourse for a public loss of reputation was to try to regain it in a fairly public forum, usually a court.[35] Though the majority of women presenting these cases in Toluca did not have the resources elite women enjoyed, they shared the concern about reputation. Lacking the options of their elite counterparts, turning to the ecclesiastical court may have sometimes been the most sensible way for less privileged women to deal with public disgrace.

Nonetheless, testifying to a loss of virginity was a risk, as it made compromising circumstances even more visible than they already were, invited counteraccusations, and risked damning testimony from defendants. For Indigenous women, presenting a complaint to the diocesan court could also increase the danger of being accused of religious misdeeds. Though the Inquisition was in charge of trying non-Indigenous people for heresy, the diocesan judges and courts, along with religious orders, were in charge of regulating Indigenous people's religious practices and punishing unorthodoxy. Indigenous women particularly vulnerable to accusations of witchcraft – like female healers (*curanderas*) or soothsayers, for instance – might be less likely to present a petition to the ecclesiastical judge. Wary of these risks, many women who eventually testified said that they had waited years before doing so, only approaching the judge after other informal efforts had failed to resolve their problem.

---

33  For a different and broader view of Bourbon era changes as seen through subaltern use of colonial courts in Latin America, see Premo, *Enlightenment on Trial*.

34  On the relative importance of virginity, see Lavrin, "Sexuality in Colonial Mexico"; Ann Twinam, "Honor, Sexuality, and Illegitimacy in Colonial Spanish America," in *Sexuality & Marriage in Colonial Latin America*, ed. Asunción Lavrin (Lincoln, NE: University of Nebraska Press, 1989), 118–55; Gonzalbo Aizpuru, "Las mujeres novohispanas"; Gonzalbo Aizpuru, "Violencia y discordia"; Pescador, "Entre la espada"; and Giraud, "La reacción social."

35  Twinam, "Honor, Sexuality"; and Twinam, *Public Lives*.

While the tone and content of unmarried women's petitions indicate that the loss of virginity held real social and economic danger, they also reflect the prevalence of premarital sex and consensual unions. This is one of the ironies of colonial Mexican society and a particularly treacherous one for women. What was actually common practice in most communities could still result in damaged reputations, financial ruin, accusations of sexual misconduct, and punishment under certain circumstances.[36] Women's testimonies in these cases certainly reflect this difficult reality; all of them express clear distress at the prospect of being "lost" and "without remedy," which meant a loss not only of honor but of the hope of marrying anyone other than the man with whom they had lost their virginity.

In cases where premarital sex was part of a long-term consensual union, women primarily expressed this distress only when they faced the possibility of abandonment. Many of these women had lived for years in marriage-like arrangements and filed a complaint only because they thought the relationship might be coming to an end. As long as a stable domestic situation existed, these women did not demand that their partners fulfill their promises of marriage. However, prolonged absences or the presence of another woman sometimes changed that, pushing women to try to force marriage or demand a dowry to aid them in future marriage prospects.[37]

In sexual violence cases, women in Toluca sought various solutions. Some sought marriage with the man they accused of rape rather than face the prospect of dishonorable spinsterhood, particularly when they were in their mid-twenties or older or had become pregnant. Others asked ecclesiastical judges to simply punish their rapist, even when this meant making the crime – and thus their loss of virginity – more public through an extended trial and the calling of witnesses to testify.

Though church teachings officially defined rape, virginity debt or theft, and broken marriage promises as separate violations, women's petitions and ecclesiastical judges' responses to them blurred these categories. In theory, rape was a crime of violence subject to punishment by civil and ecclesiastical authorities, virginity debt or theft obligated the guilty party to repay his debt through marriage or a dowry, and a broken marriage promise constituted a breach of contract that could result in the indefinite

---

36 Lavrin, "Sexuality in Colonial Mexico"; Suárez Escobar, Sexualidad y norma; *Pilar Gonzalbo Aizpuru,* Familia y orden colonial (Mexico City: El Colegio de México, 1998); Gonzalbo Aizpuru, "Violencia y discordia"; Gonzalbo Aizpuru, "Las mujeres"; Lavrin, "La sexualidad y las normas de la moral sexual," in *Historia de la vida cotidiana en México II: La ciudad barroca*, ed. Antonio Rubial García and Pilar Gonzalbo Aizpuru (Mexico City: El Colegio de México, 2005), 489–517.

37 This compensation is always referred to in the historical record as a *dote*, or dowry, but Giraud argues that this is somewhat misleading because unlike other dowries, the giver could not reclaim it if the recipient did not marry. Giraud, "La reacción social," 334–35.

suspension of the right of the accused to contract marriage with someone else.[38] In practice, however, women often interwove the three wrongdoings in their petitions, and the general goals of diocesan courts were not always best served by rigid interpretations of these crimes. When faced with individual women's circumstances and needs, ecclesiastical judges in Toluca often demonstrated a flexibility that allowed women to pursue various resolutions to their predicaments.[39]

Officially, *violación* was defined as nonconsensual sex achieved through physical force, against which a woman struggled consistently to the end; *estupro*, on the other hand, was ambiguously and variously defined as sex with a virgin achieved through some means of coercion but not necessarily physical force, the rape of a virgin, or even taking a woman's virginity in consensual sex.[40] In practice, however, very few of the Toluca cases used the word "estupro," and "violación" tended to describe everything from violent rape to coercive pressure or seduction by trickery. Legally, the question of virginity was irrelevant in a true violación case; if sex was forced, the offender was supposedly subject to punishment.[41] Taking a woman's virginity, on the other hand, carried primarily financial consequences. Even if sex was consensual, if a woman was a virgin, the man owed her compensation in the form of marriage or dowry. The concept was that a woman's virginity was her most valuable possession and could be taken, given, or lost, like property. The man who took it was obliged to pay for it, in effect making up for its loss by giving her a dowry to help secure marriage in the future.[42] Finally, a broken promise of marriage was treated as a failure to fulfill a contract. Ecclesiastical judges could not violate the voluntary nature of the sacrament of marriage by forcing a couple to get married, but they could apply pressure. At this time, a verbal marriage agreement was binding in the eyes of the church and constituted an impediment to contracting marriage with anyone else.[43] When a dispute existed over an alleged betrothal, the judge detained men in jail, placed women in *depósito*,

---

38   These teachings are most readily visible in contemporary confessionals and published tracts on moral theology. See especially Gabino Carta, *Práctica de confesores* (Mexico City: Viuda de Bernardo Calderon, 1653), 62v, 80. For an excellent list of such texts, see Lavrin, "Sexuality in Colonial Mexico," 82, n. 7.

39   Women testifying before the Provisorato Eclesiástico in Mexico City pursued a somewhat more limited range of solutions pointing to a lesser degree of flexibility in the central court. Pescador, "Entre la espada."

40   Giraud, "La reacción social," 304–16.

41   don Joachin Escriche, *Diccionario razonado de legislación y jurisprudencia* (Madrid: Viuda e hijos de D. Antonio Callejo, 1847) and Giraud, "La reacción social," 304–16 and 333–38.

42   Lavrin, "Introduction"; Lavrin, "Sexuality in Colonial Mexico"; Giraud, "La reacción social."

43   Lavrin, "Sexuality in Colonial Mexico"; Seed, *To Love, Honor, and Obey*; Gonzalbo Aizpuru, *Familia y orden*; Pescador, "Entre la espada."

and halted all competing marriage proceedings until the matter was resolved.

Ecclesiastical judges in Toluca varied their responses to these crimes based on how women presented their cases and what resolutions they sought. Women frequently charged that a man had "violated her virginity"[44] sometimes with force, sometimes without, but often "without her complete consent"[45] and "under contract (word or promise) of marriage."[46] In other words, women often accused men of rape, virginity theft, and breaking a marriage promise all at once. From there, the focus of the case depended largely on her needs. If a woman brought all three charges but emphasized violence and demanded punishment, judges tended to treat her complaint as part of a *violación* case. If, on the other hand, she framed her lack of consent primarily as evidence of her virginity and asked only for compensation, the court treated her case as a situation of virginity debt. And even when witnesses confirmed that a violent rape had occurred, if a woman thought her best "remedy" was marrying her rapist, the judge would generally shape his efforts toward that end. The fact that women presented the vast majority of these cases in their own name and without the aid of a lawyer may have contributed to the range of solutions women sought and their tendency to change strategies when the first one was not working.

The following six cases demonstrate the court's flexibility when dealing with unmarried women's petitions. In all of them, women accused men of *violación*, virginity theft or debt, and breaking a promise of marriage.[47] In the first two, the very young complainants sought punishment and financial compensation rather than marriage, and the judges responded supportively. In the four that follow, women emphasized each of the three crimes to varying degrees, but all sought marriage as their preferred solution, and the judges took appropriate action toward this end. Taken together, these cases illustrate the range of strategies unmarried women employed, men's defensive tactics, and the willingness of judges to respond positively to female complainant's specific demands, even if their efforts did not always produce the results women hoped for.

In November 1750, at age thirteen, Rita Marzela Gómez, identified as an española from Toluca, presented a complaint before *Licenciado* Juan de Villar. She accused Joseph Antonio Reboyo, identified as an español, also from Toluca, of *violación*, demanding punishment and compensation for her virginity. Joseph Antonio Reboyo was a stranger Rita Marzela Gómez encountered while fleeing a violent dispute with her mother. Seeing her on

---

44  "Violado su virginidad."   45  "Sin consentimiento totál."

46  "Bajo de la palabra de casamiento."

47  In all of the cases examined, women presented their petitions on their own behalf.

the road, barefoot and sparsely clothed, Reboyo lifted her onto the horse he was riding. Though Gómez begged him to drop her off with relatives in Metepec, her abductor took her on to where he was staying in San Antonio de la Isla, dragged her into the house, and raped her. Struggling against him, Gómez protested that she was a virgin, but Joseph merely replied that he would marry her in that case. In her testimony, Gómez described this event as a violent assault in which she was deeply afraid, and she ended her petition with indignation, saying that Reboyo had made a mockery of God and the church and that she had no desire to marry him. She demanded punishment and a dowry in return for her stolen virginity.

Gómez's father had previously appeared to Villar when his daughter was still missing, having heard from a relative that Reboyo was holding her against her will in his house.[48] However, after she returned home, Gómez came forward on her own, without being called by the judge, to present a new complaint in her own name. It was at this point that the judge jailed the accused. In his declaration, Reboyo claimed Gómez had consented to sex. He told Villar that seeing her *semi-desnuda* caused him to react as "any man would" and that he had taken her virginity *por frágil y por hombre* but with her complete consent.[49] He was willing to pay his debt through marriage, saying this was the "only thing anyone could obligate [him] to do."[50] Villar placed Reboyo in depósito at the house of her relatives in Metepec to ensure that her parents were not influencing her testimony, probably in part because her father had appeared prior to her own complaint.[51] After some time had passed, Villar took Gómez's declaration again, asking what she desired and whether anyone had pressured her to accuse Joseph. Gómez said she spoke of her own volition and that she did not want to marry Reboyo because he was "nothing but a criminal who had stolen her virginity."[52] She told the judge she wanted to go home and reminded him of his duty to punish men who inflicted damage on innocent women *sin temor de Dios*, or "without fear of God."

Though the record of this case is extensive, it does not include a final resolution. Over the months that Reboyo was imprisoned, his defense became increasingly hostile, and his mother appeared to testify on his behalf. Eventually he claimed that Gómez had not seemed to feel very much pain during sex and concluded she had therefore not been a virgin after all. Joseph also told Villar that he was not obligated to marry her because he had not promised to do so. In effect, he owed her nothing, not

---

48  I have not found this original testimony, but it is referred to in the case brought by Rita.

49  "Because he was weak and a man."    50   "Es lo único a q. me pueden obligar."

51  This was a common practice in situations of kidnapping, some of which were in fact staged by the couple in order to circumvent parental disapproval for matrimony.

52  "Nada mas q. un reo q. me ha robado mi virginidad."

even a dowry. He complained bitterly that his detention had cost his job and left his ailing mother without care. Nonetheless, Villar continued to hold him in jail for at least nine months, during which Gómez presented further petitions and more witnesses in her favor.[53]

Another thirteen-year-old girl identified as an española, Luisa María, from the pueblo of Metepec, presented a similar complaint in July 1750 before Br. Joaquín José Aragón de Chacón, who also pursued the legal avenue the young complainant sought.[54] Luisa María claimed she had been *violado con palabra de matrimonio* by Doroteo Antonio, labeled as a mestizo from Metepec.[55] Like Rita Marzela Gómez, Luisa María had no interest in marrying her assailant and demanded punishment and payment "for the damage he had done." Also like Gómez, Luisa María presented her complaint in her own name, but Luisa María's parents did not offer supporting testimony.

In this case, the accused and accuser were not strangers; Luisa María knew Doroteo Antonio through relatives. She told Aragón that before dawn one morning when her parents were asleep, she stepped outside to urinate and found Doroteo Antonio lurking in the shadows. He tried to convince her to have sex with him by promising marriage. When she refused, he raped her with a violence that caused bruising and bleeding, confirmed by witnesses.

Aragón imprisoned Doroteo Antonio and took his declaration. The accused admitted to taking Luisa María's virginity but claimed she had consented to sex and had agreed to marry him. After a few months of Luisa María's petitions, witness testimony, and her steadfast refusals to marry him, Doroteo Antonio grew tired of languishing indefinitely in the local jailhouse and agreed to pay her a dowry. Before judge and notary, Doroteo Antonio promised to pay Luisa María twenty-five pesos. Luisa María promised to drop her complaints. And they both agreed not to pursue any further marriage claims with one another. Aragón admonished them to forgive each other, as God had forgiven them, and sentenced Doroteo Antonio to a period of imprisonment for rape, to be determined in consultation with civic authorities.[56]

Some women did not press for punishment but sought instead to marry the men they accused of rape, and judges tended to follow their lead in these cases as well. In 1748, Teodora Martina from Toluca, whose racial category was not given, accused José Elías, identified as an español and *vecino* from Toluca, of violación, taking her virginity, and defaulting on a marriage promise. Teodora Martina sought the solution of marriage in spite of the

---

53  AHAM caja 68, exp. 40.
54  Many of these cases do not include the surnames of defendants or accusers.
55  "Violated" or "raped" along "with a marriage promise."    56  AHAM caja 68, exp. 17.

violence that began their relationship. She told Villar that her initial sexual encounter with José Elías was not consensual; though she struggled, José Elías overcame and injured her, but in the process, he also promised to marry her. Afterward, she agreed to continue their sexual relationship in order to secure the "remedy" of marriage he had offered. They continued their "illicit friendship" for more than a year, during which time she bore a child. Soon thereafter, Teodora Martina realized that José Elías did not truly intend to marry her. Fearing she would be "lost" and "without remedy," Teodora Martina turned to the ecclesiastical judge for help. The added burden and visibility of a child may have contributed to her decision to seek marriage as her preferred solution.

Villar imprisoned José Elías, not for rape but to detain him until the couple resolved the disputed marriage claim. In his testimony, José Elías admitted to taking Teodora Martina's virginity but denied raping her or promising marriage. He claimed her child was not his because Teodora Martina had been with other men since the start of their relationship. He acknowledged owing her a dowry but said he was too poor to pay. Teodora Martina's response was indignant. She shifted her emphasis from her own helplessness to the seriousness of José Elías's crimes. After several petitions, Teodora Martina stopped asking for marriage and demanded a dowry instead. She told Villar that José Elías's excuse of poverty was not valid and reminded him that as a priest he was "obligated to punish men" like José Elías, who "caused public scandal" and "put women's souls at risk," expertly echoing church teachings linking chastity and matrimony to spiritual salvation. The record of this case ends with the accused still in jail and the complainant still pressing for her demands.[57]

Like Teodora Martina, Juana Josepha Fonseca from Toluca, whose racial identity was not identified, also sought to marry the man she accused of rape. In her 1731 petition, Fonseca told Br. Juan Varón de Lara that Felipe Vargas, identified as a mestizo from Toluca, had been harassing her for weeks, proposing marriage, even after her parents chased him away. Then one day when she was hanging out laundry, Vargas snuck up behind her and demanded that she marry him. When she refused, he grabbed her and violently raped her, "sin temor de Dios" and without respect for her parents. Afterward, Vargas promised to make up for his crime by marrying her. When Fonseca learned that Vargas planned to marry someone else, she made a formal complaint, telling Varón de Lara she feared being left "without remedy." In spite of the rape and her parent's opposition, Fonseca sought "the only option she had left," to demand that Felipe Vargas make good on his marriage promise.

57    AHAM caja 66, exp. 38, f. 5–6.

Varón de Lara imprisoned Felipe Vargas and suspended his current marriage proceedings, treating the case as a marriage dispute rather than a criminal case. Vargas denied all of Juana Josepha Fonseca's charges, claiming he had never promised marriage, she had not been a virgin, and the sex had been consensual. He claimed Fonseca was "a woman of the world" and offered to present witnesses confirming this bad reputation. Fonseca refuted Vargas's claims and demanded the judge pressure him to marry her. However, Fonseca may have then dropped the case for fear that Vargas's witnesses could inflict further damage because the record ends after her assertive response.[58]

Unlike Rita Gómez, Luisa María, Teodora Martina, and Juana Josepha Fonseca, some women accusing men of "violación" were vague about the question of consent in their petitions. In Luisa de Córdoba's 1731 petition against Félix Padilla, both identified as españoles from Toluca, the defendant told Br. Juan Varón de Lara that Padilla tricked her into traveling with him by pretending that her sister was sick. Once they were alone, Padilla told de Córdoba her sister was actually fine and that he had only wanted to have sex with her but promised marriage if she conceded to his desires. Luisa de Córdoba's petition is very unclear about the line between consent and coercion; she said Padilla begged and insisted and that she gave in reluctantly but then summarized by saying that Padilla had *violado su virginidad bajo de palabra de casamiento*.[59] After the incident, Padilla allegedly told de Córdoba he did not plan to marry her but wanted to continue their *torpe amistad*. She told Varón de Lara that "sin temor de Dios" and with great disrespect for the church, the community, and her person, Padilla had continued to solicit sex from her for the past year.

To avoid being "lost," Luisa de Córdoba asked the judge to detain Félix Padilla until he agreed to marry her. Varón de Lara did so, but the accused claimed he owed the defendant nothing. Padilla contended they had an "illicit friendship" for more than a year with no promise of marriage, that de Córdoba had not been a virgin at its start, and that he had not raped her. In fact, he claimed, she voluntarily had sex with him for fifteen days, after which he saw fit to take her to her sister's house "to stop her from offending God." Neither Luisa de Córdoba nor Félix Padilla presented any witnesses, but they argued back and forth for a few months until Padilla was able to pay his bail.

The record ends with a note saying that soon after Félix Padilla was released, the couple got married. In this case, church justice may have played a role within a larger system of community and family negotiations. We have no way of knowing what kinds of pressures Félix Padilla faced upon his release from jail, but Luisa de Córdoba's willingness to turn to

---

58   AHAM caja 44, exp. 59.   59   "Violated her virginity under the promise of marriage."

ecclesiastical authorities may have had a hand in pressuring a reluctant lover into a stable union.[60]

A woman's reputation could be greatly damaged if the man she accused resisted marriage for an extended period of time after she filed her complaint. In such cases, the complainant needed the support of respected community members to vouch for her character and chastity. María Guadalupe Quiñones, whose case opens this chapter, chose to emphasize the public nature of her relationship with Andrés Salguero and downplay the issue of consent and coercion, even though she did claim that their first sexual encounter was "violación." Her words were *como frágil y llevada de sus ynstansias y ruegos, me violó mi virginidad, aunque sin total consentimiento mío.*[61] Quiñones told Br. Nicolás de Villegas that she then agreed to live with Salguero at his parents' house "in the hopes that [she] could find a remedy." Once living together, they did enter into a marriage agreement, which several witnesses said was public knowledge in their community. But Salguero told a different story. He said Quiñones was a corrupt woman who grew up "on the streets" without parental supervision and had been with many men before him. He claimed he had only agreed to marry her in order to "help her lead a better life and stop offending God." However, he had recently heard that a local priest had taken María Guadalupe Quiñones's virginity years before. This changed his mind about wanting to marry her, even though she had borne him a child. He never mentioned the married woman who Quiñones had alleged was his lover.

Quiñones fought this damning testimony. She presented five witnesses, including the father of the priest Salguero said had taken her virginity. Each of the witnesses had known both defendant and complainant since they were children. They all testified to Quiñones's known virginity before her relationship with Salguero and said the couple had lived publicly "as man and wife" for more than two years. Many of them also confirmed Salguero's affair with a married woman. Salguero presented two witnesses who attempted to discredit Quiñones, but in the end their testimonies were far less concrete than those of Quiñones's witnesses.

María Guadalupe Quiñones continued presenting petitions, and Andrés Salguero countered each of them with increasingly outlandish accusations. He said she was a prostitute and was "with two different men every day and night." In response, Quiñones eventually changed her tactic and said she no longer wanted to marry Salguero. She demanded instead that he remain in jail for "violación, stealing her virginity, breaking a marriage promise, committing adultery, and bearing false witness." She told Villegas that

60  AHAM caja 44, exp. 58.
61  "Myself being weak and taken by his insistence and begging, he violated my virginity, although without my complete consent."

Salguero's behavior and disrespect for the sacrament of marriage had scandalized the community. By the end of the record, María Guadalupe Quiñones had not received a dowry, and Andrés Salguero was still languishing in prison.

## Cases of Spousal Mistreatment

Married women in Toluca turned to judges for help, protection, and mediation in their intimate relationships with men less frequently than their unmarried counterparts. The fact that they did engage the ecclesiastical court in Toluca for other matters – such as presenting petitions on behalf of their daughters or in defense of their sons or to impede marriages they felt were inappropriate for their children – demonstrates that married women did think of this court as an effective resource to resolve some problems. Married women could and did seek the Toluca court's help in situations of marital abuse, infidelity, neglect, or abandonment, but their comparatively small number suggests that wives found this a less appealing or less effective option than did unmarried women presenting claims against lovers, fiancés, or assailants. Social and religious understandings of marital relations gave women the right to challenge abusive or negligent husbands, but the legal protections through which they could do so were most accessible in extreme situations.[62] Indeed, married women's petitions in both Toluca and the central Mexico City court usually described either abandonment or brutal, even life-threatening abuse. The gravity and scarcity of these cases together suggest that the ecclesiastical court of Toluca afforded less protection for married women than for their unmarried counterparts. This was probably in part due to the fact that, officially, the local court had less jurisdiction over marital disputes and was supposed to turn them over more quickly to the Provisorato in Mexico City.

Supporting this assumption is the fact that Pescador found married women to be somewhat *more* successful than unmarried women in the high court of the Provisorato Eclesiástico in Mexico City. However, he also noted that these women were usually requesting a separation. In this central court, after separations were granted, women frequently reappeared with a new petition saying they had forgiven their husbands and wished to reunite with them. This kind of strategy, probably aimed at affecting

---

62  See Lavrin, "Introduction"; Richard Boyer, "Women, 'La Mala Vida,' and the Politics of Marriage," in *Sexuality and Marriage in Colonial Latin America*, ed. Asunción Lavrin (Lincoln, NE: University of Nebraska Press, 1989), 252–86; Steve Stern, *The Secret History of Gender: Women, Men, and Power in Late Colonial Mexico* (Chapel Hill, NC: University of North Carolina Press, 1995); Gonzalbo Aizpuru, "Violencia y discordia"; and Pescador, "Entre la espada."

a change in their husbands' behavior rather than seeking permanent separation, was not common in the Toluca court. Rather, most married women directly asked the judge to intervene in the conflict by punishing or pressuring their husbands to change their behavior. This suggests a difference in women's expectations of ecclesiastical judges and the role they ought to play in their marriages. In the larger, central courts, women may have seen these judges as distant authorities from whom they could expect protection primarily in the form of a sanctioned separation, while in Toluca, judges were also seen as mediators who could scold, supervise, and advise.[63]

Married women in Toluca accused their husbands of verbal and physical violence, financial neglect, drinking and gambling, infidelity, and absence. They summed up these charges as *sevicia* (extreme cruelty), *malos tratos* or *tratamientos* (abuse or mistreatment), or giving them *mala vida* (bad life). Some filed criminal charges, asking judges to punish or imprison their husbands until they agreed to change their ways, while others saw no viable solution and sought a permanent separation. Though judges were generally supportive, there were limits to what married women could expect to receive. Only severe abuse or, in some cases, infidelity justified a request for permanent separation, and options were limited for wives living apart from their husbands. Archbishops attempted to regulate ecclesiastical judges' responses through instruction and oversight of individual cases.[64]

If a judge granted a separation, he usually placed the woman in *depósito* in an institution or private home. Sometimes women had a specific home or institution in mind, but this was subject to approval by the judge and, in some cases, the husband as well. Depósito could mean a move into relative freedom for a woman who went to the home of a trusted relative or to a respected institution, but it could be very different if a judge sent her to a stranger's house who treated her as a domestic servant or to an institution that more closely resembled a correctional facility than a shelter for women who sought to protect their reputations.[65] Occasionally ecclesiastical judges in Toluca even placed women in their own homes – themselves taking responsibility for their protection and control and perhaps benefiting from their domestic labor.[66]

In Toluca, when a woman criminally accused her husband, the ecclesiastical judge usually imprisoned him before or soon after taking his testimony. If the wife was willing to reunite with her spouse, the judge

63  Pescador, "Entre la espada."    64   BN Fondo Reservado, 1000 LAF.

65  For an excellent discussion of private households that served as "casas de depósito," see Lee M. Penyak, "Safe Harbors and Compulsory Custody: Casas de Depósito in Mexico, 1750–1865," in *The Hispanic American Historical Review* 79, no. 1 (Feb. 1999): 83–99.

66  This was a practice that eventually came under criticism by Provisoratos and Archbishops. See BN Fondo Reservado, 1000 LAF.

brought the couple to appear jointly. If both parties agreed to reconcile, the court would often appoint a neighbor or acquaintance to serve as a *fiador* (or a guarantor) to watch them and report any backsliding. With this arrangement in place, the judge would release the husband and order the couple to live in peace and stop offending God. Judges also approved some women's petitions to live apart from their spouses, but a husband could make this more difficult by preemptively accusing his wife of abandonment. Some judges hesitated to jail husbands or act decisively without orders from their superiors. Hesitant judges might agree to place a woman in temporary depósito while waiting, but this still left her more vulnerable to reprisal than if her husband was imprisoned while the proceedings took place. Variations in the level of autonomy with which local ecclesiastical judges acted could have a significant impact on women's lives and the balance of power in their marriages.

Though married women's cases were less frequent, I examine more of them in this chapter because the women's strategies and judge's responses varied more than those of unmarried women. The following nine cases illustrate the most common patterns with some interesting variations. In the first five cases, women sought the court's help with the ultimate goal of reuniting with their husbands, while in the last four, women sought to live apart from them. In the cases where women wanted a peaceful reunion, some openly pressed criminal charges and allowed their husbands to remain in jail for some length of time. Others merely asked the judge to admonish husbands to change their behavior, one even requesting that her identity as the complainant be kept a secret during this process. Among the women seeking separation, some sought the protection and material support of depósito, either before or after they had physically left their husbands, while others asked that their husbands be punished as well. Judges' responses ranged from supportive to suspicious, and when they did take action on women's behalf, they varied in their alacrity, their willingness to act without seeking the approval of their superiors, and their apparent concern for the defendants' safety.

Like unmarried women, wives often waited years before turning to the ecclesiastical court and sometimes only did so when husbands abandoned them. This was the case with Úrsula Cayetano de los Reyes, identified as a mestiza from the Indian pueblo of San Andrés Quescoltitlan. In 1758, by the time she presented her complaint to Judge Jorge Martínez, along with the testimony of three witnesses, de los Reyes had survived eleven years of violent marital abuse resulting in multiple injuries and at least one miscarriage. She also accused her husband, an "indio" named Luis Antonio Domingo, of drinking heavily and abandoning her for long periods with their two small children. De los Reyes asked Martínez to jail her husband. She did not initially mention the possibility of a reunion but made it clear that her motive for detaining Domingo was to put a stop to the absences that kept her children hungry. Her witnesses, three "indios" who knew the couple by first name only, confirmed Domingo's violence and frequent absences and mentioned that the community was aware of their problems and of the fact that de los Reyes had brought formal criminal charges against her husband.

Called before the judge, Luis Antonio Domingo countered that it was his wife, along with her mother and sister, who instigated the violence in their household; he claimed that he merely defended himself against their abuse. He also told the judge that his absences were work related and that he only drank occasionally. Nonetheless, Martínez responded by immediately imprisoning Domingo and then sending de los Reyes's petition to the *Provisor de Indios y Chinos* for advice. The provisor sent word to try to reunite the couple, but only if Domingo agreed to cease all verbal and physical abuse, quit drinking, stay at home, and give de los Reyes at least one *real* a day. Domingo promised to comply, and de los Reyes agreed to the reunion. Judge Martínez approved Juan Mateo as a fiador, another "indio" from San Andrés, who promised to report any future problems to the ecclesiastical judge. Martínez then released Domingo from custody. Úrsula de los Reyes' choice to present witnesses may have helped convince the judge to jail her husband, and it certainly let Luis Antonio Domingo know that his community was aware of his behavior, perhaps encouraging him to agree to the court's demands and submit to the supervision of a fiador.[67]

In 1774, Juana María, described as an *india tributaria* from the barrio of San Miguel in the jurisdiction of Toluca, took a similar path but was less successful in negotiating a guarantee of changed behavior. Juana María presented her petition to Dr. Alejo Antonio de Betancourt, criminally accusing her husband, Francisco Nicolás, of abuse, drinking, and gambling. She said the first ten of their twelve years of marriage were happy but that in the last two years, Francisco Nicolás's increased drinking had brought about daily explosions of violence. She said they lived in terrible poverty as a result of his gambling and that Francisco Nicolás had scandalized the community by publicly threatening her life. Nonetheless, Juana María hoped for a reunion with her husband. To this end, she asked the judge to jail Francisco Nicolás until he promised to change but stipulated that she would not live with him again without the guarantee of a fiador.

Betancourt did not involve his superiors in Mexico City but simply imprisoned Francisco Nicolás without taking his declaration. Juana María brought no witnesses; she simply waited a month and then told the judge she had forgiven her husband and wanted to reunite with him. The judge

67   AHAM caja 80, exp. 53.

brought the couple face-to-face but extracted no promises from them. Furthermore, he did not require a fiador, nor did the couple present one. The notary only recorded a "mutual pardon" followed by Francisco Nicolás's release to return home with his wife. Perhaps Juana María decided that life alone was worse than her previous predicament, or maybe she hoped that a month in jail was enough to convince her husband to change his ways. Betancourt's apparent lack of concern for Juana María's future is striking, given both the level of abuse reported and his initial willingness to imprison the offending husband. It would seem that as long as Juana María was willing to rescind her original demand for a fiador, Betancourt was more inclined to settle the case quickly than insist on this protective mechanism.[68]

Sometimes married women accused their in-laws of violence and could be successful in removing them from their households. In 1774, Rosalía Gertrudis from Toluca, whose racial category was not given, accused her husband, Pedro Leonardo Estrada, also of unnamed racial identity, along with his mother and sister, of physical abuse and cruelty. She told Dr. Alejo Antonio Betancourt that not only did her in-laws encourage her husband's anger and violence toward her, but that they themselves physically and verbally assaulted both her and her mother. She asked Betancourt to punish all of them and said she would only reunite with her husband if he agreed to live separately from his family. In the meantime, she was willing to accept whatever depósito Betancourt saw fit for as long as necessary, insisting that there was no possibility for peace in her marriage without a "complete separation" from his family.

Betancourt placed Rosalía Gertrudis in depósito in the house of a reputable family and presented her demands to her husband, Pedro Leonardo Estrada, and his mother and sister. He must have done so forcefully because they immediately agreed, thus avoiding prison. Estrada presented a fiador, and his family rushed to arrange the separate living arrangements. Four days later, Rosalía Gertrudis's own mother appeared to say that Estrada had complied with all that was requested of him. Betancourt released Rosalía Gertrudis from depósito and approved the couple's reunion. Rosalía Gertrudis's tactics were assertive but also astute. Her willingness to place herself under Betancourt's full authority rather than leaving home on her own initiative or insisting on her own choice of depósito, as did some other women, probably served her well in gaining Betancourt's trust and protection.[69]

If in-laws ranked high on the list of accused in marital abuse cases, so did alleged mistresses. In 1750, Manuela de la Asunción, from the Barrio of San Miguel in Toluca, accused her husband, Juan Gonzales, of abuse and infidelity, but she also accused Gonzales's alleged mistress of adultery. She told Lic. Juan de Villar that Gonzales's "injurious, denigrating words" and violence only began when he initiated a sexual relationship with Bárbara María, also from San Miguel. Though no racial identification was given for anyone involved in this case, San Miguel was a largely indigenous neighborhood. Manuela de la Asunción blamed Bárbara María for the continuing conflict with her husband and asked the judge to secretly summon both of them for questioning. De la Asunción described brutal beatings in which Gonzales kicked her until she lost consciousness, threatened her with a knife, and locked her out of the house, all in response to her questions about his mistress. De la Asunción pleaded with Villar to keep her petition confidential; she wanted the judge to stop her husband's affair but feared for her life if he learned that she was the one who had brought his adultery to the judge's attention. She did not ask to be put in depósito in spite of the safety that might have offered because it would have meant notifying her husband.

Though she hoped for secrecy, word nonetheless got out that Manuela de la Asunción had approached the judge because later that same day, Bárbara María appeared before the judge of her own volition to present her side of the story. Bárbara María told Villar she had come to defend her honor because she knew of de la Asunción's accusations. She said she had lived a chaste and honest life, in spite of her own husband's absence, and charged de la Asunción with presenting "false and sinister" testimony. Villar did not call Juan Gonzales for questioning.[70]

Though there is no record of a resolution, the two petitions themselves demonstrate the vulnerability of both women in the close-knit Indigenous community of San Miguel. As a woman living apart from her husband, Bárbara María could easily fall under suspicion of adultery, the punishment for which could include whipping, jail time, labor in a hospital, or cloister in a *recogimiento*. Manuela risked her husband's violent retaliation by turning to the ecclesiastical court, and Villar's failure to detain Juan Gonzales increased this risk. The judge could have held Gonzales in the name of the court while still maintaining Manuela de la Asunción's anonymity. Perhaps de la Asunción's unwillingness to go public caused him to doubt her testimony, which might explain why he was slow to summon her husband.

Villar demonstrated a very different attitude three years later with María Gertrudis, named as an "india" from the neighborhood of San Miguel in Toluca. María Gertrudis accused her husband, Marco Tadeo, whose racial category was not mentioned, of cruelty and physical abuse. María Gertrudis described six separate incidents of brutal whippings and beatings. Nonetheless, even though she said her husband treated her "as if she was his slave," she said she wanted to "enjoy peace and tranquility with her husband" and sought the judge's help. That very day Villar summoned Marco Tadeo, who flatly admitted to the six beatings without excuses or apologies. Villar jailed him immediately.

Three days later, María Gertrudis returned to court to tell Villar she had forgiven her husband and wanted to reunite with him. Villar told her to give it more time and to come back in a few days. This may have emboldened her, or perhaps other matters simply intervened, because she missed several court dates after that, leaving Marco Tadeo in jail for more than a month before finally presenting her petition for his release. Even then, the judge waited, only approving the reunion after María Gertrudis could find and present another member of their community, Domingo Antonio de los Reyes, to serve as a fiador.[71]

Villar's behavior in this case contrasts not only with his own treatment of Manuela de la Asunción but also with Betancourt's handling of Juana María's very similar case two decades later. Whereas Betancourt was willing to follow Juana María's lead even if it was dangerous for her, Villar appears to have offered even more protection than María Gertrudis had initially sought for herself, encouraging her to leave her husband in jail a few more days and insisting on a fiador before reuniting the couple. Though the record does not reflect any greater repentance from Marco Tadeo than from Francisco Nicolás when he was released, both María Gertrudis and the judge probably hoped that a month in jail and the presence of a fiador would deter him from repeating his violence.

Many women who presented these kinds of complaints of abuse and neglect seemed to feel that living alone was more difficult than their previous marital situations. For these women, criminally charging their husbands and leaving them in jail were strategies aimed at eventual reconciliation. By demonstrating their willingness to involve local church authorities, they challenged their husbands' authority and showed them that marriage was more than a private, domestic matter. These women activated the protective mechanisms of local ecclesiastical justice, and in turn, judges relied on community involvement through the appointment of a fiador to ensure that the offending husband knew he was being policed.

However, not all women were interested in reunion, and Toluca judges tended to be more reticent to approve indefinite separations than they were to jail, punish, and scold offending husbands. Andrea Salvador de Albarrán, whose racial identity was not given, approached ecclesiastical judges seeking safety for herself and her children and freedom from a marriage that had become a nightmare. Though the notary labeled Salvador de Albarrán's 1758 petition as a criminal accusation of abuse, it reads more like

71  AHAM caja 72, exp. 40.

a desperate appeal for shelter and protection. She told ecclesiastical judge Lic. Jorge Martínez that she and her daughter had left their home on the *Hacienda de las Malades* some time ago because her husband, Osorio Martín García, whose racial category was also not given, would not cease his "cruel and violent treatment." Since then, they had wandered from "door to door and house to house" supported only by Salvador de Albarrán's own "sweat and work." She told Martínez she was *totalmente desamparada* and pleaded with him to place her in depósito and provide her child with food and clothing. Martínez agreed temporarily but made a note that appropriate efforts ought to be made to reunite Salvador de Albarrán with her husband.[72]

Sometimes women sought permission to live apart from their husbands because their honor was threatened more than their immediate survival. This worked for Petra Rodríguez, of unknown racial identity, probably only because her husband was so clearly an undesirable character. In 1755, Rodríguez asked Lic. Juan de Villar to return her husband to jail to prevent him from wreaking more havoc on her public image and turning her into a source of public scandal. Petra Rodríguez's husband, Antonio José Bernal, whose racial status was unnamed, had served four years in a presidio and soon after returning home found himself in the local jail for new misdeeds. He had recently escaped and taken refuge in the nearby church. When Rodríguez found him there, ensconced with his current lover in the church cemetery, the two of them abused her "in word and deed." She told Villar she feared her husband would commit more crimes, insult her further, and cause more damage to her honor and that of her children. She asked the judge to extradite Bernal from the church property, where he had taken asylum, and send him back to jail but with increased surveillance to prevent another escape. Rodríguez said she had lost all hope of reconciliation. Villar placed the order for Antonio José Bernal to be removed from the cemetery and returned to jail under heavier guard. Surprisingly, the judge did not place Rodríguez in depósito, in spite of her husband's now indefinite imprisonment. Perhaps she was already living with male relatives or perhaps Villar was simply not concerned about her living situation given the seriousness of her husband's crimes. Antonio José Bernal had certainly forfeited his right to control his wife's movements through his flagrantly public adultery and other crimes.[73]

When women sought an officially sanctioned separation, their chances were far better if they sought the court's help early before they had taken

---

72   AHAM caja 80, exp. 70.
73   AHAM caja 74, exp. 47. Often it was to protect the honor of the estranged husband that judges insisted on depósito for wives, though women themselves sought out depósito for other reasons as well.

matters into their own hands. Two women whom judges refer to with the honorific title "doña" but whose racial category is not named both said they had no hope, desire, or willingness to reunite with their husbands, and both sought depósito with their brothers.[74] However, doña Juana Antonia turned to the court while still living at home, while doña María Luisa fled her husband's abuse long before presenting her petition. This difference made doña María Luisa vulnerable to her husband's accusations of abandonment, causing the court to receive her petition with suspicion, whereas it supported doña Juana Antonia's claims and honored her request for separation.

In 1782 doña Juana Antonia asked Judge Alejo Antonio de Betancourt to place her in depósito at her brother's house and to approve a permanent separation, telling Betancourt she had suffered two years of financial neglect, abuse at the hands of her in-laws, and the humiliation of her husband's infidelity. Rather than elaborating on her husband's crimes, however, she focused on her own misery, saying she had no desire to reunite with her husband or to punish him but only wanted to be placed in depósito with her brother, where she could live the rest of her life in peace. Dr. Betancourt agreed to sanction this move.[75]

The same judge had responded very differently to doña María Luisa a year earlier, however, in spite of the fact that she had accused José Murguía of nearly a decade of brutal abuse, molesting her daughter from another marriage, and keeping her from confession and communion. Doña María Luisa was a widow and mother when she married Murguía, and she told Betancourt she had hoped her second husband's "age and experience" would have meant "a corresponding maturity, Christianity, and prudence." However, after six months of marriage, she realized that she was mistaken. Murguía began to exhibit violent fits of rage, during which he beat doña María Luisa senseless, hit her on the head with a water jug, and threatened her daughter with a machete.

The problem was that on various occasions, doña María Luisa had fled to live with a relative or friend, and during these separations, Murguía had charged his wife with filial abandonment. In spite of the fact that her husband had also spied on her, attacked household visitors out of jealousy, and accosted her when she left the houses she was staying in, effectively keeping her from fulfilling her sacramental duties of confession and

74 In spite of the honorific title, neither woman is described as an Española. The court does not mention their racial categories, but it was not uncommon in certain circumstances for those categorized as indias or indios who held positions of prestige within their communities to be referred to as "don" or "doña." Someone of means who was of mixed parentage might also be referred to in this way sometimes, and when this was the case, it would be unusual for them to be openly called a *mestiza* or other mixed casta category.

75 AHAM caja 120, exp. 29.

communion, the judge previous to Betancourt had responded to her husband's abandonment charge by placing doña María Luisa in a disreputable recogimiento for insubordinate women. This history caused Betancourt to hear doña María Luisa's own petition with suspicion. Betancourt did not jail Murguía, nor did he approve the depósito doña María Luisa had requested. Rather, he gathered up all of the material this couple's conflict had generated and sent it off to Mexico City with the recommendation that doña María Luisa be placed in "an honest house" rather than with any of her family members. By waiting to seek the church's help, doña María Luisa may have missed her chance to gain the court's support. The delay gave doña María Luisa's husband time to activate the ecclesiastical court's mechanisms of control in his favor before she could activate its mechanisms of protection in hers.

### The Role of the Judge

Six judges appear in the fifteen cases discussed here: Juan de Villar, Alejo Antonio de Betancourt, Jorge Martínez, Juan Varón de Lara, Nicolás de Villegas, and Joaquín José Aragón de Chacón. Out of all the cases related to sexuality and marriage in the Juzgado Eclesiástico de Toluca, Betancourt heard forty-five cases by or on behalf of women and twelve cases against them. Martínez heard forty-four cases by or on behalf of women and ten cases against them. Villar heard forty cases brought by or on behalf of women and nineteen cases against women. Villegas heard seventeen cases by or on behalf of women and one case against a woman. Varón de Lara heard seven cases by or on behalf of women and one case against a woman. And Aragón de Chacón heard five cases by or on behalf of women and three cases against them.

Though analysis of these numbers requires caution, they do suggest the possibility that women chose to approach some judges more than others and that some judges were more receptive to cases against women than were other judges. These numbers reflect several things: community dynamics; the interplay between regional judges, local clergy, provisores, and archbishops; and change over time in the level of autonomy Toluca judges enjoyed. However, an individual judge's reputation for being responsive to women's needs or, to the contrary, harsh and suspicious would have also influenced the kinds and numbers of cases women presented to them. Perhaps Betancourt, Martínez, and Villar came to be more trusted by women, or at least rumored to be more sympathetic in certain situations, than did other judges. It is particularly interesting that Betancourt's tenure corresponds exactly with a noticeable upsurge in cases between 1774 and 1782 – after 1760, when these types of cases were generally on the decline as a result of internal ecclesiastical reforms.

As clergymen involved in local affairs but also with powerful ties to Mexico City, these judges were probably well-known and influential figures in the city and valley of Toluca. In other words, there could have been other reasons beyond their performance in court that women and men had learned to trust or distrust them. In a 1756 pastoral letter directed to ecclesiastical judges and other priests in the archbishopric of Mexico, Archbishop Manuel Joseph Rubio y Salinas condemned the practice of ecclesiastical judges taking women into depósito in their own homes.[76] This practice was not uncommon when women had nowhere to turn for support. The archbishop found this practice greatly problematic, and it is easy to see how some judges could have taken advantage of such depositadas either sexually or as domestic laborers. But some judges and priests were most likely acting out of their sense of obligation to protect these women, having witnessed their untenable circumstances and being unable to find a suitable alternative for them. Such behavior may be the kind of out-of-court reasons that judges gained reputations for trustworthiness or untrustworthiness among women.

## Other Days in Court

Though sexual violence, virginity debt, and marital abuse cases form the largest areas of women's involvement with the Juzgado Eclesiástico de Toluca, they were not its totality; women testified before ecclesiastical judges as petitioners, defendants, and witnesses in a variety of other situations. Though married women's complaints against husbands were less frequent and somewhat less successful than unmarried women's complaints against fiancés, lovers, and men who assaulted them, married women still turned to the court to present petitions on behalf of their unmarried daughters, in defense of their accused sons, to impede marriages they felt were inappropriate for their children, or to do battle with other women. Married women might also request depósito if their husbands were absent for an extended period of time, and unmarried women sometimes requested depósito in the process of trying to contract marriage, especially if their families disapproved. Finally, unmarried women frequently appeared alongside their betrothed for the regular, uncontested business of contracting marriage.

The surviving archive of Toluca's ecclesiastical tribunal shows in vivid and varied detail that women sought resolutions to their domestic and sexual conflicts by engaging directly with the aims of the court and the church as a whole, but this engagement does not mean they never found

76  BN Fondo Reservado, 1000 LAF.

themselves on the wrong side of ecclesiastical justice. Women dragged their female rivals before judges, husbands accused their wives of abandonment and adultery, parents protested their daughters' marriage choices and tried to control their movements, and community and ecclesiastical authorities accused both women and men of straying outside sexual or gender norms. Indigenous women also occasionally found themselves accused of witchcraft, superstition, blasphemy, and other religious crimes that the Inquisition handled for the non-Indigenous population.

Judges who found women guilty had a number of disciplinary measures at their disposal. Though women were rarely jailed, judges often placed them in an undesirable depósito in an institution known for housing women of questionable character or in a home in which they would be treated as a domestic servant rather than family member. For serious crimes like bigamy, witchcraft, or even adultery in some cases, judges might punish women by means of public whippings, humiliations intended as penance, or even forced labor. For lesser crimes like simple premarital sex, priest-judges might require less dramatic or public forms of penance. However, even in the less serious cases, women were often required to pay for the cost of their trials, which could lead to debt or servitude to work off their court fees. Whatever the ultimate resolution of their cases, formal accusations had the power to seriously affect women's reputations, marriage prospects, livelihood, and ability to turn to religious authorities for help in the future.

To truly understand the role these courts played in women's lives and what it meant for women to turn to them for help, the real and present danger of falling prey to these courts' disciplinary forces must be kept in mind. Though cases against women were not extremely common, they must have made an impact on the community when they did happen. It was a reasonable fear that bringing forward a complaint could make a woman vulnerable herself to accusations, not only those a defendant might bring in retaliation but also others that might result, even tangentially, from the testimony of witnesses. Women who did not enjoy a favorable reputation in their communities, whose lifestyles or living situation made them particularly vulnerable, or who had volatile secrets in their lives and families may have thought twice before turning to the local church court for help. This would include not only women like María Celestina, a mulata living in Toluca accused of prostitution and causing "scandal to the entire community," but also women who simply did not live with a father or husband or those who may have at one time lived with a male lover and then separated from him.[77]

---

77   AHAM caja 70, exp. 24.

## Conclusions: Laywomen and Local Ecclesiastical Justice

In spite of the dangers, women did use the ecclesiastical court in Toluca to navigate precarious personal circumstances. To do so effectively, they had to deploy gendered religious concepts and teachings to their advantage and be prepared to defend themselves against public defamation. They had to weigh their options carefully. Married women turned to the court strategically to show their husbands they were not without support and would not tolerate extreme mistreatment, gambling that this move would not worsen their situations and leave them with fewer options than before. And unmarried women had to decide whether their reputations would be harmed or helped by making their situation more public than it was before. In their petitions, women called ecclesiastical judges to task, reminding them of their obligation to preserve order, protect the sacraments, and guard the spiritual health of the community. In doing so they demanded, often forcefully, the protections and obligations they felt were owed to them as women, based on their understanding of accepted religious and social codes.

Unmarried women accused men of offending God, causing public scandal, and threatening women's already vulnerable social well-being along with their immortal souls. In extended cases, unmarried women who may have presented themselves as vulnerable victims in the beginning spoke as offended parishioners and members of the community by the end. Married women usually claimed that their husbands' actions had brought dishonor to their families and scandalized the community, sometimes adding that the accused had kept them from participating in communion and confession.[78] They described themselves as good wives, and their petitions reflect an awareness that married couples had an obligation to God and his church to live in peace with one another. Both married and unmarried women emphasized their own sexual and economic vulnerability and the dangers it posed to the collective. They also insisted that their demands were legitimate and righteous, although the latter tone tended to be more prominent in unmarried women's petitions.

Men's defensive strategies affected women's experiences in these cases as well, and they too drew on a gendered understanding of the church's goals and fears. A common strategy men employed in virginity debt, rape, or broken marriage promise cases was to claim that the petitioner was "corrupt" or a "woman of the world" and, if possible, to produce witnesses confirming this characterization. Sometimes men aimed to strengthen their own moral standing by claiming they had tried to "stop her from offending

---

78 See, for example, AHAM caja 113, exp. 2; AHAM caja 114, exp. 72; AHAM caja 80, exp. 70; AHAM caja 74, exp. 47; and AHAM caja 67, exp. 16.

God." In cases presented by very young women – thirteen or younger – accused men usually admitted to virginity debt but claimed that the sex had been consensual.[79] In these cases, men often offered marriage but resisted paying a dowry, at least initially.

When wives accused their husbands of mistreatment, the accused usually denied these claims or made accusations of their own, saying that their wives and in-laws had initiated the conflict. However, the most effective strategy for husbands was to preemptively go on the offense. As in the case of José Murgía and María Luisa, husbands could undermine their wives' petitions by presenting their own first. Abusive husbands whose wives had left home to escape violence frequently accused these women of abandonment before women had presented complaints of their own.[80] Once husbands' complaints were on file, an ecclesiastical judge might look skeptically at women's cases if they later decided to seek help from the court. And in the meantime, husbands could ask the judge to compel his absent wife to either return home or be placed in a depósito against her will.

Many cases do not have final resolutions, and yet some patterns of limited success are still visible. Cases that ended in unmarried women's favor, or at least those prolonged indefinitely by their efforts, were usually ones in which complainants invoked the church's obligations and altered their demands in response to men's testimonies – accepting a dowry instead of marriage or deciding to seek punishment instead. In these extended cases, the tone of unmarried women's testimonies gradually changed from vulnerable victim to offended parishioner and community member. Married women's cases do not tend to be as long, and their success was probably affected by factors not always visible within a given case, like varying degrees of judicial autonomy and the relative social power of the accused and complainant. But generally speaking, married women who filed complaints before leaving home, asked for the

---

79 One man made this claim about an eleven-year-old girl, even though several neighbors said they saw her crying and bleeding. AHAM caja 47, exp. 18. I have not found a consistent age for a transition from "niña" to "mujer" in these or other sources. Canon law at this time permitted marriage starting at twelve for women, and in practice, the years between twelve and fourteen seem to be meaningful ones for how women's virtue was evaluated. However, the most relevant distinction for women seems to have been from *doncella* to a married woman or from doncella to *soltera*; the first implies a change of legal and sexual status, whereas the second implies a (negative) change in sexual and spiritual status. For a very useful reflection on the history of childhood in colonial Latin America, see Bianca Premo, "'The Little Hiders' and Other Reflections on the History of Childhood in Imperial Iberoamerica," in *Raising an Empire: Children in Early Modern Iberia and Colonial Latin America*, ed. Bianca Premo and Ondina González (Albuquerque, NM: University of New Mexico Press, 2007), 238–48.

80 This kind of case is very common in the petitions that led women to be placed in disciplinary recogimientos, like those discussed in detail in Chapter 5.

immediate imprisonment of their husbands, and sought placement in a court-approved depósito were generally more successful than those using other strategies.

Racial and social status is less visible as a factor in women's successes and failures than it is in many other judicial, sacramental, and institutional contexts, including those explored in other chapters of this book. However, the absence of women of African descent presenting these kinds of cases is telling in this regard, and colonial hierarchies of race must have been in operation beyond this absence as well, even if they happened outside the range of the recorded testimonies. Within the institutional context of the Provisorato's local tribunals, and perhaps in the particular context of the Toluca Valley where Spaniards were in the minority, perhaps judges were more inclined to focus on differences of spiritual status and honor than perceived casta and racial categories. The lack of social distance between petitioner and defendant in most of these cases would also have been a factor here. Unlike cases in which women of lower racial and social status testified against priests or other social superiors, most of the women using the Juzgado Eclesiástico de Toluca accused men who were their social equals.

Visible in these court transcripts is a tension-filled interaction between women's needs on the one hand and the purposes of the court and judges on the other; women learned to express their needs as consonant with those purposes, and ecclesiastical judges found ways of responding to women's interpretations of the courts goals. This process shaped women's under-standings of themselves as parishioners with certain protections owed to them in connection to those of the community at large. It also expanded ecclesiastical judges' sense of duty to include specific obligations to women, namely, to protect both them and the community from the men who endangered them all.

This chapter and the previous one focused on laywomen's experiences and interactions with priests, first in their sacramental duties and then in their judicial capacities. These two aspects of women's relationships with clergymen are interconnected: Both were sites of learning, both were contexts in which women were trying to get urgent material and spiritual needs met, and both presented possibilities for assistance and support alongside great risk. The following chapter looks at moments in which a different aspect of church authority and regulation – namely, Inquisition investigations – utilized laywomen's sacramental and judicial relationships with priests as a mechanism of surveillance and control and in the process distorted both.

# 3

## Ambivalent Witnesses

Sometime in the 1630s, when María de Nava y Aguirre was about eleven or twelve years old, she and her mother stayed for several months with her aunt in the mining city of Pachuca, located in the modern state of Hidalgo. While they were there, Nava y Aguirre worked in various households – among them, the home of Isabel Cartado. In the Cartado household, Nava y Aguirre observed some unusual domestic practices. Her employers handled certain foods in ways that she had never seen before, and they washed and replaced all the household linen every Friday evening. María Nava y Aguirre commented on these habits to other domestic servants and slave women with whom she worked in the market and other households – not, she later claimed, because she suspected that there was anything wrong with them but simply because she found them curious. She also mentioned them to her mother, who later said that at the time she had not seen any reason for concern.

These communications took on new meaning two years later when a Franciscan friar the women had known in Pachuca visited them in his travels through their home city, Tulancingo, about thirty miles away from Pachuca. As they shared some humble refreshments and caught up on old acquaintances, the visiting friar mentioned that had heard the Inquisition was investigating Isabel Cartado's brother. Hearing this, María's de Nava y Aguirre's mother called her daughter into the room and asked her to describe the peculiar domestic practices she had observed in the Cartado home. After listening to the girl's stories, Fray Domingo informed her and her mother that they were all now obligated to testify before their town's *comisario* because the practices María had observed were evidence of hidden Judaism.

Both María Nava y Aguirre and her mother did as the friar directed. The comisario pressed the young woman to remember the names of everyone to whom she had mentioned what she had seen. She named six other domestic servants and slaves, all of them women. The comisario then called each of these women forward. In their testimonies, they revealed that they had passed on what Nava y Aguirre had told them to other women they encountered while running errands, delivering things to homes, or buying and selling things in the market. The comisario then called forward this tertiary group of women, asking them to testify and to divulge the names of anyone they might have spoken to as well. This process continued until the circle of witnesses grew beyond domestic servants to include employers and neighbors who had also heard of the Cartados' practices. When all was said and done, the witnesses included twenty-three women and ten men.

The chain of witnesses finally ended with doña María de Pérez, who did not know the Cartados personally but had heard cryptic rumors that something sinister and maybe heretical was happening in Pachuca when she came to visit relatives. She testified that the rumors made her anxious and disturbed her conscience, so she took her concerns to confession. Like the friar who had visited Nava y Aguirre and her mother, Pérez's confessor sent this scrupulous woman to testify. Inquisitors reviewing her testimony decided that what she had heard was merely "hearsay of hearsay," did not bear a direct relation to Cartado's crimes, and therefore did not require further investigation.[1]

It is quite possible that the discomfiting hearsay Perez had encountered had originated from rumors fueled by the Inquisition's investigation itself rather than from María de Nava y Aguirre's discussion of what she saw in the Cartado household. In addition to the fact that witnesses clearly did not always maintain the secrecy Inquisitors commanded of them, rumors were also instigated as a result of the supposedly "secret investigations" the Inquisition undertook to determine witness credibility. To carry out these investigations, comisarios asked local clergymen, Inquisition familiars, and other reputable folks in the community to gather information about the sexual behavior, domestic relations, and sacramental habits of witnesses in an effort to determine their public reputation for virtue or vice and thus their believability. It is easy to imagine how such questioning could stir up suspicion and rumors of the kind that led Perez to her confessor – perhaps wildly different in content from real events but with equal capacity to spread anxiety and to damage the reputations of those who had testified. The testimony of a slave woman from the Cartado household alluded to the not-so-secret character of all of these proceedings when she begged the comisario not to return her to her employers because she feared they would punish her for having testified against them.[2]

Like the previous chapter, this one is concerned with laywomen's encounters with local manifestations of ecclesiastical justice, but rather than diocesan tribunals, the focus here is on the mechanisms of Inquisitorial investigations. The discussion works from a sample of 222 Inquisition *procesos* – documents produced in a given investigation or court proceeding –

---

1 "Oydas de oydas."   2   AGN Inq. V. 380, f. 2–230.

that took place throughout the seventeenth and eighteenth centuries. These include trial records, collections of testimonies, records of partial investigations, and dead-end denunciations.[3] Though very few people experienced a formal Inquisition trial, many more were touched by preliminary investigations, most often as witnesses, and still more were affected by the awareness and fear that such investigations engendered in people who heard about them. The story of the long trail of witnesses testifying against the Cartado family reveals some of the ways that the Inquisition incorporated much larger numbers of people into its information gathering. Though the Cartado case did eventually make it to trial, much of the activity of Inquisitorial justice never went beyond the local level in which it was initiated. But these local mechanisms could still have a profound impact. Through its explicit involvement of local priests and the sacrament of confession and because of the ways that these things intersected with women's communication networks and informal, extra-sacramental practices of spiritual and emotional unburdening, the Inquisition's reach into local communities had a significant impact on women's lives and devotional practices.

The aims of the Inquisition, unlike those of the diocesan court, were very difficult for most laywomen to engage in ways that benefited them, but their participation in Inquisitorial investigatory mechanisms nonetheless had an impact on colonial religious culture. Women who were pulled into these channels became agents of the culture and practices of suspicion, scrutiny, and guilt that the Inquisition tended to foster as it sought to gather information. The opening story illustrates some of the ways laywomen could become entangled in these processes; laywomen became participants through confession, formal and informal interactions with priests, and the ways their personal, homosocial communication practices – both spiritual and social – intersected with their interactions with clergymen. When the Inquisition interrupted these relationships and rituals, women found themselves engaging in practices that helped produce a culture of guilt and suspicion that disproportionately affected them.

In the previous two chapters, I explored laywomen's sacramental and judicial relationships with priests and argued that, in both contexts, women engaged directly with a conceptualization of sin, shame, and scandal as contagious and with the idea that women's spiritual and social vulnerability made them particularly dangerous vectors and thus threatening to collective spiritual health. In their sacramental experiences, women clearly suffered from the guilt and pain these ideas caused. However, they also employed these same concepts to protect their access to confession and

---

3   In most cases, the procesos were selected because they contain testimonies of women speaking as witnesses. They are evenly spread out over the years of 1600–1790.

communion, which, among other things, provided some measure of relief from this very suffering. In a similar way, laywomen utilized these ideas within the structure of diocesan courts by appealing to clergymen's roles as judges to make direct claims for protection and restitution. In both of these sacramental and judicial contexts, laywomen sought and found resources for comfort, protection, or restitution by engaging directly with church teachings and attitudes about women. In this way, laywomen could sometimes find relief and garner support, even as their efforts legitimized the underlying tenants of the religious misogyny that harmed them and constrained their lives.

These negotiations look very different in the context of Inquisitorial processes. In spite of some superficial similarities in the structure of diocesan courts and local manifestations of the Inquisition, there are very few examples of women successfully utilizing the Inquisition to their benefit in the ways possible with the diocesan courts. The underlying purpose of the Inquisition – "defending the faith and Church" against heresy – led to very different priorities and practices than that of diocesan courts, the latter being "guarding against public sin and scandal."[4] These differences meant that the Inquisition was generally not a viable resource for women. In fact, women's direct interactions with the Inquisition were rarely voluntary. Furthermore, the Inquisition's utilization of confession and laywomen's communication networks created a particular kind of sacramental vulnerability, disrupted their piety, and co-opted their communication practices.

Scholars of women's lives, myself included, have sometimes obscured elements of communication practices by subsuming them under the large umbrella of gossip. But when approached with an awareness of the social and spiritual dynamics of *escrúpulo*, other dimensions of the ways and reasons women told each other stories and shared information emerge. Escrúpulo created a demand for confessors and confession, but it also led to informal practices of emotional and spiritual unburdening that official church teaching did not recognize as sacramentally valid. For some women, this meant intimate and informal communication with priests, like that which took place over coffee in the home of María de Nava y Aguirre and her mother in Tulancingo. But for many women, this unburdening happened within the circles of female family, friends, and acquaintances.

At a certain point in my research, I shifted from thinking of these practices as female "gossip," or even less pejoratively as "women's informal communication networks," and began to see some of them as women's efforts to deal with escrúpulo – to ease their troubled hearts and to sort out among themselves what really needed to be taken to confession – not to mention

---

4 Traslosheros, *Iglesia, Justicia y Sociedad.*

which confessors were trustworthy and capable. This is not to say that the titillating spread of rumors we tend to call gossip did not also happen nor even that women did not have a particular relationship to it. But in this particular context, I do want to emphasize the importance of women's extra-sacramental communication that functioned as a kind of informal confessional practice. Within the particular demands of the gendered colonial religious culture in New Spain, female-to-female informal "confession" may have served as an important release valve.

This may have been particularly true in places where confessors were scarce. Though the Inquisition archives are full of cases in which the involvement of one or two confessors exposed a network of women, this does not mean that these confessors were necessarily a regular presence in these communities. Testimonies were often gathered within a relatively short time, but in those testimonies, women often mentioned communications that had gone on for months or years before being overheard by a visiting priest or being intercepted during a Lenten confession.

However, even among laywomen who regularly confessed, many women turned first to their female family members or friends to try to make sense of the meaning and process the emotional impact of things they had seen or heard. This allowed women to sort out their own experiences with people they considered their equals first before taking them to a potentially fraught sacramental context. Some women clearly trusted their confessors and turned to them first, according to the chronologies they laid out in their testimonies. But others doubted the confidentiality of the sacrament or the goodwill of the confessor. They had good reason to be wary; whether or not they knew that the Inquisition asked confessors to compel penitents to testify when they mentioned certain sins, most had heard circulated stories about confessors breaching the secrecy of the confessional.

## Women as Witnesses

Though dramatic trials, including those accusing women of false visions and witchcraft, have captured the greatest amount of scholarly attention, the far more mundane recording and filing of denunciations, gathering of initial testimony, and undertaking of informal preliminary investigations were in fact what constituted the bulk of the Inquisition's work. Both men and women testified before local representatives of the Inquisition. However, doing so implied greater risks to women's reputations, relationships, and devotional practices than that of men.

Though women testified in Inquisition trials of all sorts, some crimes tended to elicit laywomen's testimonies more than others, namely those of *solicitación*, Jewish practices, male bigamy, and cases against women in general. Solicitación and the practice of Judaism almost always resulted in large numbers of female witnesses, most of whom would be laywomen. The number of women who testified in a given bigamy case against a man was rarely numerous, and in fact most of the witnesses tended to be men. However, cases against male bigamists almost always, by necessity, required the testimony of the two or more women married to the accused. Finally, most cases in which women were accused of a crime, whatever that crime was, tended to produce multiple testimonies by other women.

The crime for which the Inquisition gathered the largest number of women's testimonies was that of solicitación. From the perspective of the Inquisition, the victim of this crime was the sacrament itself rather than the penitent, even when the case involved sexual coercion and physical violence.[5] Inquisitors treated priests acting in this way as having violated not the persons and bodies of female penitents, but the sacrament itself. This perspective by no means defined the testifying women's experience of what had transpired, but it did shape their experience of testifying and the impact the Inquisition's investigation had on their lives. Because the Inquisition was concerned about the damage soliciting priests might have on the legitimacy of the sacraments, Inquisitors instructed confessors to ask their penitents whether previous confessors had ever said or done anything sexual in the context of confession. This, along with a tendency for women to share information about confessors and confession, led to large numbers of female testimonies related to solicitación.

As the story of Isabel Cartado's trial exemplifies, another type of case that frequently included an abundance of female witnesses was related to the crime known as *judaizante* – literally, "judaizing" – the secret practice of or belief in elements of the Jewish faith. Such cases were less numerous in colonial Mexico but could be devastating for accused families and deeply disruptive for whole communities when they occurred. In its episodic efforts to find the descendants of converted Jews who secretly maintained Jewish traditions and beliefs, the Inquisition looked for evidence in domestic practices.[6] Many of these practices had to do with food preparation, ways of handling clothing and other linen, and other household rituals that were generally women's responsibilities. Thus, the Inquisition's focus on domestic practices meant that women were particularly vulnerable to initial

---

5  Diocesan courts did consider rape a serious and punishable crime, but it was not under the jurisdiction of the Inquisition. For the relative leniency with which ecclesiastical courts and authorities treated breaches of celibacy versus solicitación, see Taylor, *Magistrates*, 182–91.

6  See Solange Alberro, "El matrimonio, la sexualidad y la unidad doméstica entre los cripto Judíos de la Nueva España, 1640–1650," in *El placer de pecar y el afán de normar*, ed. Sergio Ortega Noriega and the Seminario de Historia de las Mentalidades (Mexico City: Instituto Nacional de Antropolgía e Historia, 1987), 103–66; and Stanley Hordes, "The Inquisition as Economic and Political Agent: The Campaign of the Mexican Holy Office against the Crypto-Jews in the Mid-Seventeenth Century," *The Americas* 39, no. 1 (July 1982): 23–38.

denunciations for "judaizante," though their male relatives would inevitably be accused as well. It also meant, as was the case in the opening story, that female domestic servants were often early witnesses to the behaviors in question. Once an investigation was far enough under way, the Inquisition tended to call female relatives of the accused to testify before male ones, presumably because Inquisitors thought they were privy to the domestic details indicating guilt.

Cases of male bigamy normally required the testimony of at least two women: the wives of the accused. Given women's behavior in diocesan courts like the Juzgado Eclesiástico de Toluca, one might expect jilted or deceived wives to be among the first to denounce their bigamous spouses, but this generally was not the case. It was far more common for wives to appear only after the Inquisition called them to testify. However, some of these women had previously testified in diocesan courts, accusing their husbands of abandonment and hoping to secure judges' help in convincing them to return. In attempting to do so, diocesan judges sometimes discovered that the wandering husband had in fact married again in another location. At this point, if the accused was not classified as an *indio*, the judges were required to turn the case over to the local comisario because bigamy was considered a heretical offense. This transfer effectively turned the petitioner into a passive witness.[7] In areas where clergy was scarce, the diocesan judge may have actually been the same priest who served as the comisario. In these situations, the judge would directly report to Inquisitors in Mexico City and then, wearing a different hat and taking a very different stance with different purposes, would call the petitioning woman to testify again in the context of beginning an Inquisition investigation. This time she would appear as a witness rather than an aggrieved spouse, a position from which she would not have the ability to make demands and would be compelled to answer a systematic, formal set of questions designed with the Inquisition's needs in mind rather than hers.

Finally, any case accusing a woman was likely to result in multiple testimonies by laywomen. This is true whether the accused herself was a laywoman or a professed nun.[8] In a catalog of procesos started against women in the Inquisition collections of the *Archivo General de la Nación* in Mexico City, Adrian Rodríguez Delgado has listed 2,660 entries between the years of 1571 and 1820. These do not represent all the trials heard, of course, since Inquisition records also exist in Spain and are scattered throughout other archives in the Americas and Europe. Nor can we assume

---

7   If the accused was classified as an indio, the case would be sent to the judges' own superiors within the diocesan court structure.

8   Though cases against nuns were predictably full of the testimony of other nuns, they also tended to involve female servants and other laywomen who resided in convents.

that all trial and denunciation records survived to be archived. It also does not seem that Rodríguez Delgado's catalogue includes entries for the collections of individual testimonies filed by particular years, regions, or crimes.[9] Nonetheless, this number still gives us a sense of how relatively rare it was for women to be formally tried by the Inquisition: according to this list, an average of between ten and eleven times a year for all of New Spain. At the same time, these trials represent a much larger number of women who testified as witnesses as a part of the local procedures leading up to these proceedings. For instance, the case against María Anastasia González for false visions contains the witnesses of six other women.[10] This is a relatively small number because the accused was a *beata* (a laywoman who had taken informal vows to live a life of spiritual devotion) and had a small social circle consisting primarily of these six other women – also beatas – and several priests. However, in the case against Isabel Cartado that opened this chapter, twenty-three women testified alongside only ten men.[11] Even the case against the beata Marta de la Encarnación, which was full of testimony by clergymen called in as experts, also contains the testimonies of eleven women.[12] These cases are typical, demonstrating a range in terms of ratios of women to men but illustrating that whenever a woman was accused, there would almost always be several or more laywomen called to testify against her.

The central court of the Inquisition was located in Mexico City, and the Holy Office appointed its comisarios from among the ranks of both regular and secular clergy. In places where clergy was sparse, a comisario often doubled as the bishop's appointed *juez eclesiástico*, therefore serving as representatives of both kinds of ecclesiastical justice. This alone might bring women into greater contact with the Inquisition in these regions. The Inquisition encouraged people to bring denunciations directly to these comisarios by publishing "edicts of faith" and requiring parish priests to read them aloud and to be alert to the crimes they mentioned. The content of these edicts reflected periodic or cyclical shifts in the Inquisition's priorities, but they always contained a strong mandate to report any instances of words, actions, or beliefs subject to correction by the Inquisition along with the reminder that failure to do so was itself a sin that only the Inquisition could absolve.

In practice, local parish priests played a key role in this process of gathering testimony, particularly from laywomen. Whether out of ignorance or fear, many witnesses only reported to the comisario after having

---

9 These collections are particularly useful for studying women as witnesses, as they gather together testimony for particular crimes, between certain years, in a given region.

10 AGN Inq. V. 1312, exp. 2 and Banc. mss 72/57m.

11 AGN Inq. V. 375, exp. 1 and AGN Inq. V. 380, exp. 5.    12 AGN Inq. V. 788, exp. 24.

been directed to do so by their confessor. This was especially true for laywomen. This pattern is easy to miss in the documents because notaries prominently categorized witnesses as either those whom the Inquisition called to testify or those who appeared *sin ser llamada*, (without being called), even sometimes adding the phrase *de su voluntad* (of her or his own will or volition). However, in contrast to men and nuns, the majority of laywomen who appeared "sin ser llamada" explained early on in their testimonies that they were there because their confessor or another priest had sent them.

In theory, Inquisitors wanted everyone to come directly to the Inquisition as soon as they heard about or witnessed something that required testimony, but this stood in tension with Inquisitors' concerns about false testimony and untrustworthy witnesses. Court communication between comisarios and Inquisitors and marginal notes about witness credibility reflect more trust and better treatment afforded laywomen whose confessors sent them than the few that came on their own. This was a double-edged sword, however; since edicts mandated immediately notifying the Inquisition, a delay in doing so required justification. Confessors testifying on behalf of their female penitents often framed these women's initial reticence as proof that they were *muy recogida* – that they possessed the shame and modesty befitting a woman of virtue and were therefore reluctant to travel, appear in public, speak to a man unaccompanied, or perhaps even trust their own intelligence and knowledge to be certain about what required a denunciation. By taking their doubts and concerns to a confessor first, they demonstrated that they were not arrogant and had sufficient recogimiento to be credible, even if they had technically erred in waiting.

It is possible that some women who wanted to make a denunciation intentionally sought out the direction of a confessor in order to cultivate this appearance and avoid being seen as having testified *por malicia*, or out of malice.[13] Theoretically, witnesses could also pretend that a priest had mandated their denunciation, but this would be a risky strategy, since the Inquisition could easily question the clergymen said to have given this order. If a woman purposely sought out the legitimization of a confessor or other priest before testifying, it probably behooved them to allow their confessor to believe it was his suggestion so that he could testify that she was modest and obedient. There may have also been situations in which a woman and confessor decided on this strategy together. Whatever the

---

13   This was a phrase that appeared at the end of almost all testimonies. Comisarios and Inquisitors asked witnesses to swear that everything they had said was true and none of it was said "por malicia." Nonetheless, through witness investigations and reviewing the testimonies themselves, Inquisitors sometimes concluded that "malicia" was in fact the motive.

case, a laywoman who Inquisitors perceived as too ready to denounce someone, particularly someone who was her social superior, was often suspect.[14]

If priests lent credibility when laywomen testified, it was confessors, in particular, who had the most power to compel them to testify. The Inquisition directed confessors to withhold absolution to penitents who mentioned something under the Inquisition's jurisdiction, but this was not merely a request; priests who absolved penitents in these situations before they had made a denunciation were themselves guilty of a heretical error punishable by the Inquisition. However, there was an expedient way to deliver absolution without requiring the penitent to make a physical trip to the comisario: Frequently, confessors would allow their female penitents to dictate a denunciation before they left the confessional, which the confessor would transcribe and submit as written testimony to the Inquisition in the penitents' names.[15] As relieved as a woman in this situation might be, this was not necessarily the end of her engagement with the Inquisition. Not only did it still put her at some risk of a secret investigation into her reputation, she could also still be called to testify in person if the Inquisition took her denunciation seriously.

If she was called forward, she would be asked to reveal the names of anyone else who might have information related to the matter of which she spoke. Women's testimonies usually resulted in more women's testimonies, and the women called forward as a result would generally mention even more women. It was the generative quality of local investigations themselves, whether or not they ever blossomed into full trials, that led many laywomen to participate in the Inquisition's information gathering mechanisms, exposing them all to the risks and dangers these mechanisms implied.

## Communication and Guilt

Women's communication with each other was a key way that they became entangled in these processes. Women experiencing escrúpulo and choosing to unburden their consciences with female relatives, friends, or acquaintances or, like María de Nava y Aguirre, simply sharing what they thought were innocent observations with other women were engaging in common communication practices that were nonetheless vulnerable to the Inquisition's

---

14  For an example of this, see the testimony of Juana Navarro in Banc. mss 96/95m 1750, Fray Tomás de Sandoval. See also the testimony of Mónica Zupaqua in AGN Inq. V. 295, exp. 1. Nuns were not perceived this way as often, and indeed, nuns did more frequently make denunciations before being directed to do so.

15  For examples of this practice, see AGN Inq. V. 295; AGN Inq. V. 334; and AGN Inq. V. 740.

methods of gathering information at a local level. Each time a woman spoke of something illicit, she potentially caused an experience of escrúpulo in the listener, increasing the chances that eventually someone in the chain of communication would feel the need turn to a confessor for relief or might even go directly to the Inquisition.

This was the case in a 1631 investigation against the Jesuit priest Padre Diego de Cuéllar in Mexico City. Padre de Cuéllar had apparently committed solicitación with two sisters, Ysabel and Thomasina, on several occasions. Through a convoluted path of both secrecy and sharing, two cousins, two aunts, and the mother of the solicited sisters came to learn about these events. None of them moved to denounce de Cuéllar, though they did stop confessing with him. They later testified that they did not want to cause him harm even though they no longer trusted him as a confessor. Eventually, one of the cousins, in consultation with one of the aunts, sought out the informal council of another priest, who then sent them to formally confess with another priest. When the cousin did so, this new confessor told her she must denounce de Cuéllar immediately and that everyone else who knew about it must also do so, and none of them could be absolved until they complied. Though the Inquisitors scolded each of the women for having waited so long after the actual events had transpired, they all came forward within days of the cousin receiving this directive in confession.[16]

Women's social and domestic networks were such that they tended to turn first to other women when events like these occurred, but men could also become involved and might be the first ones to bring the information to a priest or comisario. This happened in the 1674 case against Father Domingo de Treto in Sinaloa. A female domestic servant, María de Ariola, had been present when her employer, Pedro Barcelona, told a male visitor what his female relative, Leonor Coronado, had confided in him about a local priest. Leonor Coronado's conscience had been bothering her because her friend, María Fachula, had mentioned that she had heard other female acquaintances saying that a local priest, Domingo de Treto, "was up to his old business again." María Fachula had assumed this meant he was propositioning his female penitents, and she had communicated this suspicion to Leonor Coronado, who eventually told Pedro Barcelona. When Barcelona's servant, María de Ariola overheard him relaying this complicated story to his guest, she then passed it on to several other servants, including her sister. Don Gabriel de Espinosa, yet another male visitor in Pedro Barcelona's house, then overheard a conversation between María de Ariola's sister and another female servant, and he decided to take the whole story to the local comisario. This move on the part of don Gabriel

16   AGN Inq. V. 373, exp. 2.

de Espinosa resulted in the forced testimonies of everyone mentioned previously.[17]

Part of the Inquisition's purpose in pursuing these rumors all the way to their sources was the notion that they had infected all who had heard them. It was therefore necessary to convey to everyone that what they had seen or heard of was in fact a serious crime that the Inquisition must handle and also that they could not be legitimately absolved until they brought what they knew to the Inquisition. In addition, Inquisitors wanted to convey to these witnesses that, if they ever experienced anything similar, they must go straight to a comisario before discussing it with anyone else and that in relation to the current matter, they should immediately stop spreading *escándalo* by talking to other people about it. The irony of all of this instruction to guard secrecy and speak only to the proper authorities is that however damaging Inquisitors thought this kind of rumor spreading could be, they also relied on it to gather as much information as possible. Indeed, the Inquisition's own investigative practices tended to increase rumors and scandal rather than quell them.

Women's testimonies reveal that they did not experience the spread of escándalo as a trivial affair, nor was it necessarily the result of malice on their part. The experience of being *escandalizado*, or scandalized, was described as emotionally painful, and it resulted in the spiritually danger-ous experience of escrúpulo. This was true for any sin, whether the Inquisition considered it a heresy or not, but if the affected person came to learn that the matter troubling them was serious enough to be of concern to the Inquisition, this must have heightened the fear and anxiety.

Whether or not someone had prior first-hand experience with the Inquisition, the Holy Office was a well-known symbol of religious authority and hierarchy. The Inquisitors presiding over the tribunal in Mexico City were among the most educated churchmen in colonial Mexico. They had advanced degrees in theology and law and had sometimes served as bishops and other high church officials. They were all Peninsular Spaniards. This was not the case with the local comisarios they employed, but nonetheless hearing that something "was a matter for the Inquisition" brought to mind the image of the *Santo Officio* and all it stood for.[18] Fear of punishment was certainly part of that, but so also was a genuine sense of religious angst and respect for the learned, powerful men who served the Holy Office. If local priests could be seen as authorities on God's laws and those of the church, Inquisitors were the true experts.

17   AGN Inq. V. 482, f. 154–70.
18   "Es asunto del Santo Oficio" (it is a matter for the Inquisition) is the reoccurring phrase witnesses reported hearing from clergymen who sent them to make denunciations.

Thus, even when comisarios did not call everyone forward, once someone learned that she or he had an obligation to report to the Inquisition, direct or indirect pressure to make a denunciation often moved backward through the chain of communication until it had reached the original source. In the case against Father Domingo de Treto, the comisario summoned all of the people who witnesses mentioned, but the testifying did not stop there. As a result of the "secret" witness investigations under way and the spread of escándalo/escrúpulo that accompanied them, several other women came forward who had not been mentioned.

Female domestic and working spaces fostered both sharing and guarding of information among women. And the experience of guilt and religious responsibility could lead at least one of them – or perhaps one of the men with whom they brushed shoulders – to break this secrecy with a confessor or even directly with a comisario. When this happened, an entire network of women, spanning households and families, might be compelled to testify before the Inquisition.[19]

As these stories show, networks of female domestic workers played a particularly important role in this process. They were privy to families' domestic and religious practices, their private conversations, and their private problems.[20] They also traveled frequently between households and to marketplaces, working temporarily for families other than their main employers, making deliveries, running errands, and selling food or other goods. During these travels, information about what was happening in one home could be easily passed on to another. This did not mean it was these same domestic workers who necessarily exposed the misdeeds being talked about, however. In fact, it was often a *dueña* or *dueño* or a household guest who overheard whispers of suspicious activity and reported it. Other times this kind of information was spread from person to person and household to household for months or even years before someone finally mentioned it in confession and heard the instruction to go to the comisario.

Though women's own guilt and communication compelled many of them to testify, in solicitación cases in particular, the guilt and fear of the accused could also lead to large numbers of female witnesses who might never have chosen to speak of their experiences. Because women shared information about their confessors, female witnesses often mentioned to comisarios the names of other women they knew had also confessed with the accused priests, and these women would then be called forward. Given

---

19  See also AGN Inq. V. 380, exp. 5. In this case, secondhand reports among domestic servants discussing the behavior of one woman's employers eventually led to the questioning of a whole network of female slaves and servants in the neighborhood.

20  For other examples of female domestic workers playing a role in cases of supposed Jewish practices, see AGN Inq. V. 379, exp. 1, and AGN Inq. V. 380, f. 2–230.

the not-so-secret nature of the "secret" investigations that followed, it was only a matter of time until most accused priests learned that their penitents were appearing before the Inquisition. Many priests in this position came forward with an *espontanea*, or a supposedly "spontaneous" confession. Espontaneas could garner mercy from the court, but only if they included everything the court had already heard of and everything that might be revealed by further witnesses; if the accused seemed to be holding anything back, the strategy could backfire. For this reason, accused priests regularly confessed to soliciting more women than had already testified, and the court would then call all of these women forward as well.

## Experience and Consequence

The Inquisition's purposeful employment of priests in its mechanisms of gathering information and investigating witnesses created a potential contradiction in women's relationship to local clergy. María de Nava y Aguirre's description of her mother's conversation with Fray Domingo de Santiago suggests that he was a regular visitor to their home or at least that the women were comfortable with him in an informal domestic setting. Whatever other roles they played, priests were also community members, and many laywomen enjoyed extra-sacramental relationships with priests who behaved like mentors, confidants, and even trusted friends.[21] For a laywoman in such a relationship, it may have felt a bit like entrapment for a priest to respond to something said in casual conversation or a moment of confiding by ordering her to report to a higher authority, even if the clergyman was sincerely trying to save the woman's immortal soul by informing her of her obligations. One can easily imagine that María de Nava y Aguirre and all the women called forward to testify, after witnessing the rumors and disruption caused by this one moment, may have been more careful from then on about what they shared with priests or with people they knew to be close with priests.

The explicit role of confession in Inquisition investigations had an even greater impact on laywomen's relationships to local clergy as it interrupted their sacramental access and success. Whether they enjoyed positive, regular communication with priests or not, laywomen understood that confession and communion were important religious obligations to be undertaken at least once a year. In spite of an awareness that some confessors were not trustworthy, most women probably still expected to find some measure of spiritual relief and comfort through their annual confession and,

---

21   While the purpose of solicitación cases was to punish inappropriate sacramental behavior, the documents they produce also include much evidence of this kind of ordinary, intimate communication between laywomen and priests.

at the very least, recognized that it was necessary in order to receive communion. Some particularly pious, scrupulous, or anxious women may have depended on more frequent confession to alleviate their bouts of escrúpulo and may have been deeply devoted to the Eucharist that followed. All of these varied kinds of expectations were betrayed when a confessor interrupted the normal sacramental process to say to his penitent that he could not absolve her or continue hearing her confession unless she reported what she had just told him – in a supposedly confidential sacramental context – to the powerful Inquisition.

This moment was all the more difficult when the issue at hand was solicitación because of the vulnerability, betrayal, and violence that were so often a part of the original experience. Whether out of shame or fear or because they had not realized they ought to, women often waited for years to confess to a solicitación event. It reportedly took the convent servant María Josepha two years of weekly confession until she trusted her new confessor enough to do so. One can only imagine how she must have felt when he returned that trust by refusing to absolve her and sending her instead to the Inquisition.[22] Monica Zupaqua, a young *india* from a small village near Michoacán, reportedly waited three years to confess about having been raped by a visiting confessor because she had not thought she was at fault and so did not understand the urgency to do so. However, over time and a number of confessions she had come to *formó escrúpulo* about the event and to feel that she needed absolution to restore her spiritual and emotional equilibrium.[23] It must have been disheartening to be told this was not possible until she told her story to the comisario. It must have been similarly difficult for Juana Navarro, who traveled nearly forty miles from her home in Toluca to the town of San Fernando, now a neighborhood in Mexico City, to find a new confessor only to be sent back to Toluca to denounce her old one. Her prior confessor, Fray Sandoval, after four years of regular confession, had begun to fondle her every time he heard her confession. He kept this up for two years and then suddenly stopped. She continued confessing with him for another two years after this behavior ceased, but she later testified that her experience of escrúpulo had grown over time and eventually become too much to bear in spite of their long sacramental relationship. Perhaps she was afraid to tell any other local clergymen, and perhaps she had family or friends with whom she could stay in San Fernando. Whatever the case, she testified that she decided to stop confessing with him and make the long trek to find a new confessor to unburden herself with.[24] One can imagine how alarming it must have been

22  Banc. mss 96/95m 1773, Fray Joaquin García.     23   AGN, Inq. 295, f. 1.
24  "Haciéndole escrúpulo a esta declarante confesarse con este Reo se resolvió a dejarlo y irse a San Fernando."

when this new confessor told her she had to return to Toluca and present a denunciation in person to a comisario who was likely a colleague of her former confessor.[25] In a very different experience, María de Tapia, a young *española* living in the *recogimiento* of Belem, testified against Miguel Alvarez only when compelled to do so by a new confessor. De Tapia initially had no intention of discussing her ambiguous relationship with her former but still beloved confessor, but when her new confessor asked searching questions about their relationship, the details she revealed to him led her to the door of the Inquisition. De Tapia said she had deep respect and spiritual love for the priest now under suspicion, but through the process of her new confessor's inquiries and later those of the comisario, she was forced to describe their relationship as both sinful and heretical.[26]

Even when what was being confessed did not directly involve the penitent, the moment of being told you had just implicated someone else in an Inquisition investigation could also be very troubling. Inquisition testimonies are filled with examples of women expressing unease about a friend or family member's actions, probably without the intention of getting that person in trouble. A mother worrying about something unorthodox her daughter had said,[27] a woman who had come to fear that her friend might be being visited by the devil at night,[28] another woman who had heard a rumor that an acquaintance was using magic[29] – all had the choice of taking their concerns directly to the local comisario or ecclesiastical judge or even going to a priest extra-sacramentum to ask for guidance. Instead, they chose to bring up these concerns in the context of confession, where they had reason to believe that their words would be kept confidential. Seeking relief from escrúpulo and maybe the council of their confessor, these women may have been dismayed to learn they were now obligated to expose their loved ones or community members to the formal scrutiny of the Inquisition. Some of these kinds of orders probably went unheeded, though this entailed great spiritual risk and would also mean not returning to the same confessor who had given the directive. In addition, Inquisition records contain examples of confessors themselves making denunciations when they suspected that their penitents would not or had not done so. In fact, sometimes priests made it clear in confession that if their penitents failed to make a denunciation, they would be obligated to do it themselves. If this took place, the recalcitrant penitent would then be subject to the Inquisition's discipline themselves for disobeying. And if they went on to confess with someone else – hiding the matter about which they had been instructed to speak to the Inquisition – and to take

25   Banc mss 96/95m 1750, Padre Thomás Sandoval.
26   Banc. mss 96/95m, 1694, Br. Miguel Alvarez.   27   Banc. mss 72/57m.
28   AGN Inq. V 1312, exp. 2.   29   Inq. V. 369, exp. 1.

communion, they would then also be guilty of partaking in the Eucharist without absolution.

Though perhaps less disorienting, it was still disempowering for a woman seeking the help of an ecclesiastical judge to learn that she had unwittingly become a witness in an Inquisition investigation. As previously mentioned, this primarily happened when a married woman went to the local diocesan court to present a complaint that her husband had abandoned her. A woman in this position could expect the priest-judge to make an effort to find her husband and, if possible, bring him home and command him to fulfill his matrimonial duties. But when the judge's efforts led to the discovery that the absent spouse was in fact living in another town married to someone else, the petitioner's position would dramatically change. This is what happened to María Bernal, a free mulata who lived in the Real del Rosario. After seeking the help of the local ecclesiastical judge, she was called by the local comisario to testify against her husband in a forum in which her concerns were no longer the priority. It was not helpful to Bernal to have her husband sequestered in the Inquisition's secret prisons, but this was the unintended consequence of seeking the help of the local diocesan court.[30] Other women had the bizarre experience of having both their testimonies heard by the same clergyman wearing two different institutional hats. This was the case for a woman whose name was not recorded in a village near Acapulco. She had approached the ecclesiastical judge about her husband's absence, but because this judge also served as the local comisario, when inquiries determined that a second marriage was involved, he reported the case to his second set of bosses in Mexico City. At this point, acting as comisario and following Inquisitor's orders, he summoned the woman to appear in the same location but with a different stance and a far less flexible format. Forced now to answer only the questions he asked, this woman was no longer free to ask for his help, and the only thing she could expect from the authorities was the likely imprisonment of the man she had sought to bring home.

As these bigamy examples suggest, the experience of testifying before a comisario was not likely to be an easy or beneficial one for laywomen. In addition to facing the intimidating formality and the stance of interrogation – probably only slightly mitigated when the woman was familiar with the comisario – most laywomen made their initial testimonies full of the anxiety of escrúpulo or fear of the unknown. They arrived having been formally called by the office of the Inquisition and not knowing why or having just learned that they would remain in a state of *enhoramala* until they made a denunciation. From there, the experience could be better or

---

30   AGN Inq. V 497, exp. 9.

worse; the type of case it was, the circumstances of a woman's testimony, the social status of both witness and accused, and the results of the investigations into witness credibility would all have an impact on how the comisario and Inquisitors treated her and whether they believed her words.

Comisarios and the Inquisitors who reviewed the documents sent to them sometimes expressed doubt and disdain in the form of marginal notes alongside women's testimony, and these attitudes could be conveyed in the questions they asked. Whereas sometimes comisarios would call such witnesses back to testify repeatedly, Inquisitors may in fact decide to simply disregard their testimonies after examining their social positions, reputations, sexual histories, and religious behavior. The woman who went to San Fernando to find a new confessor was one such witness. Juana Navarro was twenty-six years old when she testified before the comisario of Toluca in 1750. The notary described her as a *mulata soltera*, a phrase that immediately marked her as a woman worthy of suspicion. Her *casta* was thought to imply looser morals, and her status as unmarried but *soltera* – single rather than *doncella*, or virginal maiden – confirmed her as a woman of ill repute. Though she told the comisario that she had regularly confessed with Sandoval in the *Casa Profesa* for four years before he started using the sacrament as a venue to express salacious desires, Inquisitors nonetheless determined that Juana was a woman of *mala fama*, or bad reputation. Even before they wrote these assessments in the marginal notes beside her testimony, the comisario's questions reflected doubts about her character. Inquisitors in Mexico City ultimately dismissed her testimony against Sandoval as "malicious" and "dishonest." This was in spite of the fact that six other women had already testified against him, three of them telling stories very similar to Juana's, and the Inquisitors had taken these other stories seriously.[31]

Sometimes it was not a woman's individual character as much as suspicion about her community's reputation that gave Inquisitors reason to doubt a witness' testimony. In a 1612 denunciation originating in the Indian pueblo of *chilchota* in northwestern Michoacán, a married Tarascan woman named Mónica Zupaqua brought an interpreter with her and appeared before the local comisario. She told the story of a violent sexual assault in the confessional at the hands of Fray Juan de Mendoza. She told the comisario that another confessor had directed her to make this denunciation. However, in his communication with Mexico City Inquisitors, the comisario expressed doubt that this was true. He told his superiors that the Tarascans of this area were known for giving false testimony against priests. In the end, however, the comisario's superiors accepted Mónica Zupaqua's

31 Banc mss 96/95m 1750, Padre Thomás Sandoval.

testimony and directed him to call her back for questioning. Mónica's testimonies were then dutifully filed in Mexico City for reference if another such complaint came through but did not generate a full trial.[32]

Whether women's accusations were believed or not, examiners in New Spain were rarely concerned with women's sexual agency in the situations they described; their primary focus was determining whether what transpired was in fact solicitación or merely a sexual transgression that did not require the attention of the Inquisition. Doña María Antonia Gutiérrez, a Spanish widow from Toluca, received much different treatment from the same comisario in the same case Juana Navarro's testimony was a part of. This was true in spite of the fact that Gutiérrez's own testimony, correspondence from the accused priest, and testimony from acquaintances all suggested that she was involved in a long-term voluntary sexual relationship with Sandoval. Nonetheless, marginal notes described her as a credible witness, and the comisario's questions focused on whether their sexual encounters had actually taken place in a way that could be classified as solicitación. Since it appeared that at least some of the time the pair used the pretext of confession for their liaisons, Inquisitors determined that Sandoval was in fact guilty of a mild form of solicitación. Gutiérrez would pretend to be sick and send word to Sandoval, who would come to her house and abscond with her behind closed doors for hours. Sandoval was spared guilt for more serious levels of the crime because their activities had not taken place in a confessional and no form of confession had actually taken place during the encounters. Throughout this discussion, Inquisitors deemed Gutiérrez's level of participation in these events as irrelevant. She was treated only as witness to a crime of violation in which the victim was the sacrament.[33]

While Inquisitors dismissed Juana Navarro's testimony as malicious and untrue, Gutiérrez's testimony was deemed credible, even though there was evidence that she had been complicit in the sexual relationship with Sandoval. She was a Spanish woman, known to frequent the sacraments, and honored with the title of "doña." As such, her word was given the benefit of the doubt. In contrast, Juana Navarro's social status as an unmarried *mulata* known to have lost her virginity caused greater suspicion.

Though Inquisitors evaluated witnesses according to the racialized social hierarchy that informed their notions of virtue and credibility, marginal notes discussing witness reputations show that casta and social class were not always automatic determinants of reliability. Women described as indias, mestizas, mulatas, and other castas were sometimes believed and sometimes described as virtuous and honest. Neither did being seen as

32   AGN Inq. V. 295, exp. 1.    33   Banc mss 96/95m 1750, Padre Thomás Sandoval.

"española" always protect women from doubt and disdainful treatment by comisarios. This is reflected in the treatment of María Anastasia González, an española whose testimony was utterly disbelieved because of her sexual history; as a result, her reputation as a pious beata was completely dismantled.[34] However, the variable algebra of racial, social, and spiritual status always shaped women's experiences when they testified; comisarios and Inquisitors saw them through hierarchical colonial schema that took all of this into account – in different ways at different moments and in relation to whom and what they were testifying about.

For some women, the line between testifying as witness and being the subject of an investigation was even thinner than for women like Juana Navara, whom Inquisitors simply dismissed as bringing false witness. This risk was present for all kinds of cases: María Anastasia González was called to testify against her confessor for solicitación and ended up accused of heresy herself because of the content of her testimony; María Bernal came under suspicion of heretical marriage practices herself after testifying against her husband because the comisario suspected she had known of her husband's prior marriage when she married him.[35] But this line was most precarious in trials for hidden Jewish practices. Once a formal accusation was levied, others usually followed until most members of the family found themselves imprisoned. In these extensive trials, female relatives tended to quickly fill up the ranks of witnesses.[36] Their testimonies describe a female-centered domestic space in which women shared and preserved information about devotional practices and traditions while attempting to conceal them from outsiders. Once the protective boundaries of this world had been broken, the line between witness and accused blurred quickly. Many women compelled to testify against loved ones were in fact already in the Inquisition's secret prisons awaiting or under-going their own trials. Most of those who had not been accused by the time the Inquisition first called them to testify would be very soon.

The least harrowing type of case for female witnesses was probably bigamy cases, though María Bernal's case shows that even these were not entirely without risk. Wives compelled to testify against their husbands were generally subject to less scrutiny than in other cases, mostly because the Inquisition could theoretically use parish marriage and death records to corroborate the most important elements of their testimonies: whether a marriage had actually occurred, whether a previous spouse had been alive at the time, and whether the officiating priest had followed proper protocol in determining these things. If, on the other hand, this

34  AGN Inq. 1312, exp. 2; Banc. Mss 72/57.    35  Ibid.
36  See, for example, AGN Inq. V. 379, exp. 1; AGN Inq. V. 380, exp. 5; AGN Inq. V. 406, exp. 2;
    AGN Inq. V. 413, exp. 4; AGN Inq. V. 419, exp. 4, and the Judaism cases in Banc. mss 96/95m.

collaboration was not possible, then the wives' testimonies meant fairly little. This left little incentive for comisarios to be concerned with women's credibility, perhaps leading to more neutral, if not always pleasant, treatment.

Even though testifying against one's husband in a bigamy case was quite different than presenting a complaint about an absentee husband to a diocesan judge – in the latter, a woman could demand that the judge temporarily jail her husband and pressure him to reunite with her, whereas in the former she had far less chance of influencing the course of action or punishment – some women did seem to want to see their husbands punished.[37] Even María Bernal, years after the first set of investigations had fizzled out, when it was clear that she would not regain either her spouse or her reputation, initiated yet another bigamy case against her offending husband – this time by going directly to the comisario. Like María Bernal, women who took this path either knew of their husbands' second wives and had already exhausted all other means of seeking reunion or restitution or were from wealthy families and were more concerned about the dishonor of having their husbands live openly with other women than with securing their return or financial support.[38]

These relatively rare examples of women initiating bigamy cases point to the fact that in spite of all of the damaging consequences of being a witness for the Inquisition, some women did try to turn the experience of testifying into an attempt to seek restitution. Some women, even though they had not chosen to testify, behaved more like accusers than witnesses, using the space of a trial or investigation to defend themselves and to seek a certain kind of justice in the telling of their stories. In the context of a solicitación investigation, particularly one long enough to have created a presumption of the priest's guilt, the social distance that may have made it impossible for a woman to resist her confessor's sexual advances in the first place might be lessened to some extent in the context of testifying. She would hear her examiners refer to her ex-confessor as *el reo*, the criminal, and sometimes took the opportunity to assert that he had harmed not only the sacraments and the church but her own body, soul, and social standing as well.

This is unusually visible in the testimony of María Marta Gertrudis, a poor servant woman sometimes called an española and at other times

37  For examples of bigamy cases that began as complaints to diocesan judges, see AHAM caja 80, exp. 53 and AGN Inq. V. 456, exp. 6.

38  For another example of a woman choosing to seek punishment for her bigamous husband, see Banc. mss M-M 1826. In this case, the first wife had remained in Spain when her husband traveled to the New World with the intention of returning. However, the husband decided to stay, and when he could not convince his wife to join him, he remarried in Mexico. This news reached the first wife through relatives, suggesting the new marriage had become public knowledge. The first wife initiated a bigamy case in Mexico by letter, in an attempt to restore her own honor.

a mestiza, who testified against Fray Joaquin García before the comisario of Tulango. Though she was compelled to testify long after she had suffered García's abuse, and Inquisitors ultimately dismissed her testimony because it did not fall into the category of solicitación, she nonetheless used her testimonies as a forum to decry the man who had harmed her. Her words read very much like those of the women who testified before diocesan judges. This is rare among the Inquisition cases I have read, yet its existence suggests that there may have been more like it.

María Marta Gertrudis was the illegitimate daughter of the female cook in a household of wealthy widows in Tulango, where both she and her mother lived. Fray Garcia was a visiting priest from Mexico City who came to the house several times to visit her mistresses. During these visits, Fray García cornered and raped María Marta Gertrudis at knifepoint. By the time she testified against García in 1793, María Marta Gertrudis had lost nearly everything she had, including her place of shelter and employment, the possibility of marriage, her reputation, and her health. She became pregnant as a result of García's violations, and when her pregnancy became public knowledge, her mistress threw both her and her mother out on the street. She turned to her fiancé for help, but he abandoned her upon realizing she was carrying another man's child. To make things even worse, her pregnancy was a difficult one. She narrowly survived the birth, which left her permanently weak and disabled. By the time of her testimony, she was living in poverty with her mother and young daughter.

Though she did not approach the Inquisition of her own volition, once she found herself testifying before the comisario, María Marta Gertrudis defended her honor and accused her assailant in much the same way as women did in diocesan courts. She told the judge that there had been no public recrimination of García and that he had not helped or compensated her in the slightest. At the time, she had sought the help of the local priest named Padre Calero who was hosting Fray García. She told Calero what was going on and pleaded with him to hear her confession so that her employers would stop insisting that she confess with García. Padre Calero refused to hear her confession until after García returned to Mexico. Apparently since the sexual violence had not taken place in the confessional, Calero did not feel obliged to require or make a denunciation but still thought it prudent to wait to hear her confession until his guest left town.[39] María Marta

---

39 Examples of confessors gambling with parishioners' salvation and spiritual well-being in order to protect themselves or other clergymen are particularly chilling in light of the sacramental theologies that undergirded the punitive consequences they were hoping to avoid. Such moments are worthy of study unto themselves, as they raise questions about cynicism and skepticism – if not in relation to fundamental beliefs, perhaps in relation to some of the Inquisition's use of these beliefs. These moments may also be useful entryways into competing claims for supremacy of authority between Inquisitors – whose office lay outside the institutional structures of both the

Gertrudis testified that after maintaining a coercive sexual relationship with her for the duration of his two-year stay in her town and witnessing her social, physical, and economic demise, Fray García gave her two pesos and left town without saying goodbye.

María Marta Gertrudis's testimony was ultimately disregarded, and García's abuses were not counted among the crimes of which he was accused because they did not count as solicitación. But for the duration of her examination, María Marta Gertrudis had the opportunity to denounce the man she felt had destroyed her life. Her strength of voice stands in pronounced contrast to Padre Calero's descriptions of her; in his testimony, he described her as a helpless, miserable, illegitimate servant child who *sufró el castigo del Dios.*[40] María Marta Gertrudis, on the other hand, told her own story with a palpable sense of outrage and clarity, accusing García of "robbing her" of her virginity and honor. María Marta Gertrudis told the comisario that she had refused to confess with García in spite of her employer's insistence because to do so would have been like pardoning him and publicly conceding that he was not the one responsible for her moral, economic, and social ruin.[41] She also described his ultimate disappearance in much the same way that women spoke before local diocesan judges about men who had abandoned them. She told the comisario, "He has neither written me, nor appreciated me, nor given me more than the two pesos that he gave me at the time he left, even having seen that the birth resulted in severe illness to the point that I was close to dying."[42] Her testimony reflects a sense of injured honor, and it is framed as a clear condemnation of the man who was responsible.[43]

It was clearly important to her to speak this way because María Marta Gertrudis uttered these particular words outside her answers to Inquisitors' specific questions. Though her injuries emerge throughout her testimony, she spoke at significant length at the end, when Inquisitors asked if she had anything else to add. It was in these final additions that her testimony took on the tone of an accusation of harm done to her person and the sense of being owed compensation or retribution of some kind.

---

diocesan church and the religious orders, and whose relationship to the Spanish crown and the Peninsular provenance of its highest officials arguably set it further apart from the rest of the church in the New World – and confessors, ecclesiastical judges, and bishops, also charged with struggling against sin and religious error.

40    "Suffered the punishment of God."

41    "Ella no condescendió porque no estará esa disculpa, de que la confesaba, y con eso dixera que no era el, el que la havía perdido."

42    "Ni (me) ha escrito, ni hecho aprecio, ni socorro mas que con los dos pesos que al tiempo de irse (me) dió, aun haviéndose visto de resultas del parto para morir de gravisimimas enfermedades que (me) acaecieron."

43    Banc. mss 96/95m 1973, Fray Joaquin García.

María Marta Gertrudis's use of her testimony is unusual, but there are other examples of laywomen attempting to seek help from the Inquisition. In an effort to escape abusive masters, both male and female slaves sometimes denounced themselves for blasphemous statements.[44] Francisca López, a *negra criolla* and the personal slave of the nun who served as *rectora* of the convent of Santa Mónica in Mexico City, seems to have done this when she voluntarily appeared before the Inquisition to denounce herself for having denied the existence of God and all of the saints after her mistress had given her a particularly severe beating.[45]

There may also have been instances where seeking a priest's help in making a denunciation against another confessor might help a woman escape a difficult situation. This may have been what the convent servant Teresa de Magdalena tried to do with Br. Luis Gomez de León, who delivered a denunciation in her name accusing the convent priest of repeatedly soliciting sexual favors. Gomez de León told the Inquisitors that the accused priest had a great deal of power in the convent and requested that they pursue the matter without letting him know who had accused him so that Teresa de Magdalena could retain her position. It is even possible that Teresa de Magdalena turned to Luis Gomez in the hopes that the offending confessor would be removed without her having to risk losing the employment and shelter the convent provided.

The Inquisition's involvement of laywomen as witnesses could have a long-term impact because of the ways that witness investigations could affect their reputations. This is difficult to trace, but we do have some clues in the case records themselves. Witness investigations were most common in cases of solicitación, most uncommon in bigamy cases, and then varied for other types of cases depending on social status and circumstances. When practiced, the results were recorded in the marginal notes alongside witness testimonies, and these notes reveal a greater level of scrutiny of laywomen than either nuns or men and a particularly high level of scrutiny when the laywoman was testifying against someone of higher social status than herself. Comisarios usually undertook these investigations informally, quietly asking friends, family, and acquaintances of the witnesses, along with local clergymen, about their chastity and marital status, how often they confessed and took communion, and whether they had ever been associated with scandal. In spite of the fact that these investigations of witnesses were meant to be secret, such inquiries, especially coming from a clergyman known to be a representative of the Inquisition, were likely to stir up rumors. For a laywoman, the impact of such rumors could far outlast the length of an Inquisition investigation, affecting her marriage or long-term relationship possibilities, making her more vulnerable to ecclesiastical or civil

44  See Villa-Flores, *Dangerous Speech.*    45  Inq.274, f. 76.

accusation and discipline at a future time, and placing her at greater risk of sacramental abuse at the hands of local clergymen, aware of the likelihood that authorities might not find her to be a credible witness.[46]

Beyond the investigation of witness credibility, just being called to testify could have a long-term impact on women's reputations. Bigamy cases exemplify this, since they rarely involved witness investigations. When wives were compelled to testify against husbands, potentially embarrassing information came to light. Some women were suddenly known as jilted first wives with heretics for husbands, while others went from being thought of as legitimately married to living in concubinage after having been duped into a heretical marriage. This could mean the sudden loss of honor, as well as husband, home, and financial security, if the bigamous spouse was imprisoned.[47] And in all cases, there may have been a certain danger of guilt by association. This was clearly true for cases of judaizante, even if a witness was not formally accused at the time she testified, but it would also have been true for religious errors associated with women, like witchcraft, melancholy, and false visions, and also when witnesses were a part of a close circle of women.

In addition to damaging individual reputations, the methods by which the Inquisition compelled women to testify as witnesses could be very disruptive for families and communities. One profound example of this is the effect of espontaneas in solicitación cases. Espontaneas often mentioned lists of rural indias from towns through which soliciting priests had traveled. Frequently in these cases, the accused could only recall very limited information about these women, even forgetting their names. The comisario would then have to try to find these women so they could be brought to testify. In this process, the comisario called forward women who may or may not have been the subject of solicitación, starting rumors and creating suspicion among family members, as husbands, parents, and other relatives wondered if the woman had been keeping a secret from them. Even when they got the right people, comisarios were examining multiple women from

---

46  On the relationship between reputation and life possibilities, see Twinam, *Public Lives*; Lavrin, "Sexuality in Colonial Mexico"; and Gonzalbo Aizpuru, "Las mujeres novohispanas."

47  This situation varied somewhat when the man accused of bigamy was classified by the court as an indio, since it would not go to trial in the Inquisition. Throughout the colonial period, diocesan and regular clergy were engaged in a struggle against the persistence of the pre-Hispanic practice of bigamy, as well as separation and remarriage, among some Indigenous people. As part of this struggle, diocesan judges acting as "Indian Inquisitors" did sometimes force people to abandon all but an original union and reunite with their first spouses rather than strictly treating the situation as one of heresy. Thus, if a bigamous husband bore the racial category of Indian, this colonial concern might lead to reuniting the original couple.

tight-knit communities about a shameful event from years past – something certain to stir up problems.[48]

Similarly, the stories in which networks of female friends, relatives, and domestic servants all had to testify after one person spoke to a priest or comisario point to the possible damage that could befall a community as a result of Inquisition investigations. The slave's fear of returning to her employers' house in the case against Isabel Cartado is one indicator. Another is the two sisters' reticence to incriminate Padre de Cuellar. He was a well-known community member, and turning him in to the Inquisition put everyone who had confessed with him at risk of being called to testify as well. It is easy to imagine the sense of betrayal, loss of trust, damaged friendships, and suspicions that must have resulted when someone moved from sharing stories to involving the authorities.

The dramatic example of María Anastasia González, who was called to testify against her long-time father confessor, illustrates many of the ways testifying could affect female witnesses and is worth relaying at length. In this vivid and tragic case, women's close relationships with priests and deep connection to the sacraments that had once been a source of comfort and strength in their lives became liabilities, witnesses' reputations were threatened, and one witness even found herself on trial. The investigation process, which in this case dragged on for a very long time, had a clearly disruptive impact on what had previously been a very close-knit community of women and a few trusted clergymen.[49]

At the time that she was called to testify against her former confessor, María Anastasia González was known and celebrated for her piety in her home community in Sayula. However, her encounter with the local workings of the Inquisition led to the complete demise of her reputation, the forced testimony of an entire network of pious women, and ultimately González's own accusation, trial, and punishment. The fact that the comisario had to summon her to testify in an already advanced trial against her former confessor, Father Zendejas, rather than her having come forward

---

48  See for example AGN Inq. V. 357, exp. 9; AGN Inq. V. 279, exp. 4; and Banc. mss 96/95m 1792, Fray Juan de Ortega.

49  In this case, the investigation did eventually lead to a trial. I have considered the content of María Anastasia González's actual trial at length elsewhere; it reveals much about late colonial anxieties about race and the decline of Catholic orthodoxy among American-born Spaniards, as well as the intersection of spiritual and sexual intimacy in confessor/penitent relationships, and it is a fascinating story of an individual woman's assertion of her own faith and sense of religious authority as founded on her personal and mystical experience of God. Jessica Delgado, *The Beata of the Black Habit: María Anastasia González and Late Colonial Anxieties* (unpublished book manuscript, tentatively titled). However, the preliminary investigations are the primary focus here in this chapter. They lasted nearly ten years before María Anastasia González was actually brought to trial.

first was already a strike against her. Her fate was sealed then by the content of her testimony.

Though she had not seen or spoken with Zendejas for several years, she once had a close relationship with him as her father confessor and spiritual advisor. According to both of their testimonies, after some months of hearing her confessions and guiding her in her spiritual practices, Zendejas began to order her to perform sexual acts with him, which he framed as exercises in obedience and penance. Though González did not formally denounce him, she did report experiencing escrúpulo early on in their relationship and bringing her concerns to two other local priests. She remembered these priests telling her not to worry. Unsatisfied, she then took the question directly to God in prayer, who comforted her.

González was a mystic who experienced direct communication from God, the Virgin Mary, and the other saints. It had been one of these visions that had originally directed her to Father Zendejas as guide and confessor. This being the case, González told the comisario that she eventually realized that Zendejas's motives had to be pure since God had chosen him for her. Making this claim was not only heretical – in effect she was saying that sex in the confessional could be divinely ordained – but it also revealed her to be a woman of impure thoughts and sexual past, from the perspective of her examiners.

However, the men present for her testimony had further reason to be alarmed by María Anastasia González's testimony. Even if she ultimately followed her own faith in deciding not to denounce Father Zendejas, her testimony unwittingly accused the other priests she claimed to have spoken to of a serious lapse themselves. By telling her to ignore Zendejas's behavior, they had protected their colleague at the expense of the sacrament and could be accused of heresy themselves. Not surprisingly then, it was these two priests, one of whom had accompanied the comisario in listening to González's initial testimony, who spearheaded accusations against her. In their denunciation, these men claimed that González had denied knowing of anything that would concern the Inquisition, even when the comisario confronted her with detailed descriptions of her and Zendejas's sexual encounters taken from Zendejas's own testimony. They further accused her of false visions and heresy when she asserted that she knew both she and Zendejas were innocent because God had directed her to the offending confessor. Even more damning, the comisario said that during her testimony, González had fallen into a trance and claimed to see visions of Christ and saints speaking with her and comforting her. She spoke in strange voices, experienced convulsions, and ultimately had to be dragged from the room. Ultimately, these priests denounced González for heretical notions, hypocrisy, and false visions.

At the time of this accusation, González was a forty-one-year-old widow who wore the habit of a beata and enjoyed the friendship of a close circle of friends, all women also known for their intense piety. María Gertrudis,

María Josepha, María Ysavel, and María Rosa spent much of their time at María Anastasia González's house, seeking out her prayers and council and, on more than one occasion, placing their young female relatives in her care. Three years later, however, all of these women had testified against her. What they said about her indicated that the investigation had ruined her standing in their community. The first few years after she testified against Zendejas must have been a confusing and painful time, as she became aware of the whispers when she walked by, the lessening of people who sought out her company and advice, and the increasing distance with her closest friends. Unbeknownst to her, several local priests with close ties to all of these women had begun gathering information about her, and the comisario was summoning each of her friends, one by one, to testify against her.

González's fellow beatas' testimonies unmistakably show the decline of her reputation, but what happened to them as witnesses is not quite as obvious. Over time, their descriptions of their friend changed dramatically, reflecting the growing influence of the increasingly sinister rumors they reported hearing about her. But they also expressed an increasing level of fear on their part. These testimonies go from slightly confused concern to swearing that their former confidant was transporting herself into their rooms at night, terrorizing them and bringing them into unwanted contact with the occult. Tears, violent shaking, and expressions of guilt marked all of their later testimonies, as they felt themselves to be somehow complicit in what they now understood as González's thoroughly sinful, hypocritical, and possibly heretical practices.

Inquisitors' marginal notes provide some more clues about what was causing this anxiety. In spite of the fact that these women were all known for their piety, kept close ties with priests in their neighborhoods, and apparently lived chaste and modest lives, Inquisitors ordered the Sayulan comisario to subject each of them to an intense level of scrutiny. Through familiars and local priests, the comisarios systematically requested information about each of their lives along with that of María Anastasia González. And in their correspondence with comisarios, Inquisitors expressed doubt about their testimonies and their pious reputations and even suggested that some of them could have been guilty of similar crimes. The possibility of guilt by association, together with the general suspicion many clergymen held for *beatas*, as laywomen who dedicated themselves to a relatively autonomous spiritual path, created an atmosphere in which these women must have sensed that they too could easily fall prey to accusation. The distance they put between their old friend and themselves and their exaggerated descriptions of her diabolical activities may have been defensive and self-protective reactions.[50]

50  AGN Inq. V. 1312, exp. 2 and Banc. mss 72/57m.

Though testifying as a witness did not usually lead women to be tried and punished for heresy, María Anastasia González's case nonetheless illustrates many of the risks involved. Public involvement with the Inquisition was often damaging for women in one way or another. They often arrived frightened and confused, and in some cases their reputations were put on trial alongside the person their testimonies condemned. They were subjected to differential treatment, their social status, sacramental habits, and sexual history shaping how their testimonies were heard and believed. And their lives, in many cases, would be changed forever.

## Conclusions: Laywomen and Local Inquisitorial Practices

Recent historiography on the Mexican Inquisition has shown us that it was not a monolithic and all-powerful institution of repression; however, viewed through the lens of its ordinary, relatively informal mechanisms of operation and through the experiences of witnesses, it becomes clear that the Inquisition could have a significant impact on people's lives and relationships. Through the activities of priests, confessional practices, and forms of unofficial communication, the Inquisition was episodically present in local communities of New Spain. Women experienced this presence in particular ways because of gendered ideas about sin, scandal, and guilt and the significant role of confession and priests in their lives.

The quiet spectacle of rumor, the destruction of reputations resulting from "secret" investigations of both accused and witnesses, the publication of edicts requiring denunciations, and the active involvement of local priests in the goals of the Inquisition fostered an inquisitorial culture of fear, suspicion, distrust, and mutual surveillance on a local level. Mitigated in part by the social forces of friendship, loyalty, and laywomen's purposeful guarding of secrets, the Inquisition never succeeded in creating an ironclad hold on Mexican communities. But a focus on testimonies, and in particular those of laywomen, does demonstrate that some kind of an inquisitorial culture was dynamically present. Inquisitorial practices were threaded through colonial religiosity – subtle at times and then occasionally exploding into the kinds of anxieties expressed in María Anastasia González's trial. The publication of an edict or a particularly fierce rash of escrúpulo and rumors could bring Inquisitorial workings to the surface. This on-and-off culture of suspicion affected women's experience of and relationship to the church in detrimental ways. Nonetheless, they also participated in it centrally. It was in fact often women's gendered sense of guilt, shame, and fear, along with the vulnerability of their communication habits and networks, that brought the gaze of the Inquisition into their communities, neighborhoods, and homes.

PART II

# Places and Practices of Cloister

The next three chapters look at laywomen's engagements with places and practices intended either to protect society from the contaminating impact of unprotected or uncontrolled women or to sanctify society through the protection and concentration of innocent and virtuous women. Undergirded by the belief that both women's vice and virtue were particularly contagious, these places and practices were connected and were all manifestations of the ideology of *recogimiento*. This ideology was the manifestation of a gendered and racialized theology of containment that shaped women's lives and the way society positioned them. Religious and civil authorities, together with wealthy and pious individuals, developed legal practices, institutions, and resources to contain and quarantine dangerous women, protect virtuous and vulnerable women, redeem repentant women, and maximize the sanctifying power of exceptionally virtuous women.

Confraternities and pious donors raised funds and created endowments to support all of these endeavors. Religious and civil authorities contributed money, regulations, and oversight. Poor, virtuous, and – increasingly over time – racially pure women became the beneficiaries of lotteries, receiving money from *obras pías* to be used as dowries for marriage or profession or to pay for room and board in prestigious lay cloisters where they could be sequestered until they "took state" as a wife or nun. In other contexts, ecclesiastical judges made sure that wayward or disorderly wives were placed in an appropriate institution or under the custody of a private household licensed to serve as a *casa de depósito* for women who needed protection and supervision.[1] These same judges also responded to women's own requests to be transferred to such places when their husbands abandoned them, mistreated them, or were absent because of work, travel, or death. In related practices of spiritual inversion, the recogimiento of some women was compromised in order to facilitate that of others; in the hierarchical economy of female piety, some women worked as servants or were enslaved in convents so that nuns could avoid the labor and contact

---

1   On these private houses, see Penyak, "Safe Harbors."

with the outside world that would have threatened their complete seclusion and the highest qualities of their recogimiento.

For all of these examples, the logic of recogimiento was central. As a concept, a personal quality, a practice, and a term for an institutional cloister, "recogimiento" was a ubiquitous word, the meaning of which was both assumed and contested in New Spain. In the context of ecclesiastical court cases, it served as an umbrella term for cloisters of women – including convents – as well as a specific term for lay cloisters. It also indicated the practice of gathering together and secluding women. And, even more frequently, it evoked a desired and desirable quality in women.

The content of that quality is never completely clear in these documents, however. While the word "recogimiento" was part of a shared and thoroughly accepted vocabulary, people used it and claimed it in different ways. For most religious authorities and elite men and women, a woman was *muy recogida* or lived a life of "mucho recogimiento" only when she was secluded from public view and had limited contact with men – ideally only with male family members, confessors, and an occasional doctor. But women who could not achieve this level of seclusion also claimed these terms for themselves. For poor women and those who worked in the marketplace or as domestic servants, being "muy recogida" meant being modest, obedient, and chaste within the constraints and possibilities of their lives. Even unmarried women living in monogamous, consensual unions claimed that they lived with *mucho recogimiento* to signal that they were free of scandal, knew their place in the gender and social hierarchy, and comported themselves with appropriate humility and obedience.

Over time, working in the wide variety of contexts in which this term was deployed and contested, I came to understand recogimiento as an ideology and more specifically as a gendered and racialized theology of containment. As such, it linked the seemingly distinct institutions of convent, lay cloister, and asylum, together with practices of depósito in private homes. Furthermore, it informed women's interactions with confessors, ecclesiastical judges, and other religious authorities. It also formed the core of women's spiritual status, shaping their life possibilities in relation to their racial, social, and economic status.[2] In other words, more

---

2   I encountered Nancy van Deusen's work on recogimiento in Peru after having spent some years of dissertation research sorting all of this out and having come to see recogimiento as an ideology, not only a set of places and practices. When I read van Deusen's groundbreaking study, it deepened my conviction that recogimiento was a unifying element of colonial women's religio-social experience, and thanks to van Deusen's exploration of the transculturation of the term, its hemispheric and Atlantic implications became clearer to me. Nancy van Deusen, *Between the Sacred and the Worldly: The Institutional and Cultural Practice of Recogimiento in Colonial Lima* (Stanford, CA: Stanford University Press, 2001).

than just a sum of its parts, I have come to see the ideology of recogimiento as foundational not only for the church's practices and doctrines related to women but also for colonial Catholicism itself. Seen in this light, lay-women's engagement with recogimiento – in the form of specific practices and institutions but also in the abstract as an ideology – became for me the primary location from which to start investigating laywomen's participation in the religious culture in New Spain.

Nancy van Deusen describes recogimiento as at once "a theological concept, a virtue, and an institutional practice." As a way of illustrating its historical complexity, she opens her first chapter with the twenty-three early modern dictionary definitions that correspond to the various verbs, nouns, and adjectives related to the word "recogimiento." To summarize this rich body of meanings: the verb *recoger* meant to seclude, separate, gather up, or gather in; the noun *recogimiento* was both a place and practice of shelter and seclusion as well as a value of modesty and chastity; and the word *recogida* was both a term for a woman who lived in an enclosure of some kind and an adjective that meant virtuous, secluded, modest, and humble.[3] These definitions were all associated with female honor and reputation and can be seen in action everywhere that colonial women left testimony about themselves or men left testimony about women. And as an overarching gendered and racialized theology of containment, recogimiento permeated colonial authorities' approaches to the problems they thought women posed for society.

Lay cloisters were, from the perspective of their founders and supporters, a necessary response to women's spiritual and social vulnerability.[4] However, in spite of their social and cultural importance, it has been very difficult for historians to get an accurate sense of the scope of this institutional landscape. Miscellaneous documentation in the form of petitions and oblique references reflects a large number of places known y as *casas de recogimiento*, *casas de recogidas*, and *casas de arrepentidas,* or repentant women throughout New Spain. But there is spotty extant information about many of their origins, internal functioning, and ultimate closings. There were also *colegios de niñas* – literally "schools for girls" – which were sometimes attached to recogimientos and sometimes independent from them. More of the records of the standalone colegios have survived, but it is still unclear how many recogimientos had colegios as annexes. And finally, this institutional landscape included *beaterios*, which were places for women who took religious vows but did not have the dowry or perhaps the *limpieza de sangre* to profess as a nun. Some beaterios are well known to us, but others that

3  van Deusen, *Between the Sacred and the Worldly*, xi, 1.
4  Josephina Muriel, *Los recogimientos de mujeres: Respuesta a una problemática social novohispana* (Mexico City: UNAM, 1974).

evolved either from or toward other kinds of lay cloisters remain relatively obscure.

The cloistering that happened in these institutions could be voluntary or involuntary, but this line was not always clear. Some institutions were theoretically designed for the protection, seclusion, and supervision of virtuous *mujeres desamparadas*, or unprotected women, while others were intended for the voluntary reform of "mujeres perdidas," and still others were established as places of involuntary seclusion and correction of women found guilty of crimes or scandal. In reality, however, both voluntary and involuntary seclusion could take place in each of these kinds of cloisters.[5] Colegios de niñas, though meant for girls, nonetheless frequently housed women of all ages who had arrived as children but never left. And some institutions were known as both recogimientos and colegios.

There was a great deal of overlap between these institutions; some recogimientos meant for repentant women evolved into beaterios or even convents while others became involuntary houses of correction. The majority of the more prestigious colegios and recogimientos became more exclusive over time – at least officially. And many convents served unofficially as temporary or permanent cloisters for a large number of laywomen and girls. Some convent laywomen were enslaved, while others were dependents and companions of individual nuns, and others still were personal servants. Along with the practice of depósito in private homes, all of these institutions existed on a continuum of cloistering practices – connected at one end to the ideal of female containment in a convent or marriage, and at the other end, to the imagined necessity of places like women's prisons, asylums, and hospitals – particularly those designed for *mujeres dementas*, or "demented" women, who deviated significantly from proper feminine behavior.

Most medium to large towns had recogimientos, and some had colegios, beaterios, and convents as well. And the practice of depósito in private homes happened everywhere. The following three chapters explore lay-women engaging with prestigious recogimientos and colegios, private homes that served as places of deposit, correctional and repentant cloisters, and convents as *depositadas* (literally, deposited women), dependents, slaves, and servants. These chapters continue to illustrate the argument made in Part I that women's participation in religious culture paradoxically took place through their engagement with the very ideologies within that culture that worked to marginalize their participation.

---

5  For a discussion of the origins of the convent and other cloistering institutions for women in the sixteenth century as they related to the desire to protect unattached women, see Jacqueline Holler, *Escogidas Plantas*.

# 4

# Cloister for the Poor and Virtuous

On August 19, 1720, a group of pious laymen known as the *Archicofradía del Santísimo Sacramento y Caridad* met in the Mexico City cathedral. The first order of business was a petition from a young woman who sought the help of this religious brotherhood. Doña Margarita Yturri was a woman of Spanish descent whose parents had died and left her with nothing but their good name. She asked the members of the prestigious confraternity for entrance into the school and shelter they had established for virtuous but poor and fatherless girls, saying she was "totally destitute, without remedy or hope." These men decided to grant her entrance into their *Colegio de las Niñas de Nuestra Señora de la Caridad*.[1] As a new *colegiala*, Yturri would be given protection, room and board, education, and a five-hundred-peso dowry for a future marriage or profession in a convent. Her entrance would be marked by a ceremonial appearance in the choir balcony of the colegio's church, announcing her new status to the public. She would be seated with the other residents, separated from the rest of the parishioners by a gate symbolizing her entrance into a cloistered life, wearing a special blue mantle, and holding a lighted candle in her hands for all to see.

Margarita Yturri had previously been living in another institution designed for the protection and seclusion of women, the *Recogimiento y Colegio de San Miguel de Belem*. It was under the authority of the archbishop of Mexico, and his office had paid for Margarita's room and board out of the funds set aside for girls and women with no other source of support. A man described only as "her countryman" petitioned for her entrance when her parents died but in doing so did not relinquish his authority over her destiny. Just a few months before she sought entrance into the Colegio de Caridad, this man pulled her out of Belem, saying he wanted her to "provide company for his wife" – a phrase that usually implied a companionship that included domestic service.[2] In seeking the protection of the archicofradía, Margarita was seeking to remove herself from this man's control by placing herself under the protection of powerful men who

---

1  AHCV 9-I-3, f. 40–60.    2  AHCV 13-IV-3, f. 89–92.

would claim her as their adopted daughter. No countryman, guardian, or family member could remove her from their colegio without their permission, which they would not give unless she herself chose to leave.

Nine years later, this same group of men responded to a different kind of petition: that of a woman who sought license to leave the same colegio Margarita Yturri had wanted to enter. Doña Ana Margarita de Casterón y Trigo's petition expressed regret and sorrow at needing to leave along with gratitude for the years of shelter and protection they had granted her. Nonetheless, she explained, three different doctors had advised her to leave the colegio for health reasons. She assured the men who saw themselves as her surrogate fathers that she would continue to honor the feminine ideals of virtue and seclusion she had learned in their glorious colegio. In fact, she planned to move to the nearby convent of San Bernardo where would live as the dependent of her relative, Madre Francisca María.

Neither these assurances nor Casterón y Trigo's tone of contrition and humility assuaged the feelings of betrayal her petition caused, however. The men in charge of the colegio expressed that by leaving without "taking state," through either marriage or profession as a nun, Casterón y Trigo was behaving in an ungrateful and disobedient manner, which they decried in their written responses to her petitions. Furthermore, they decided to make a public example of her to dissuade other colegialas from following suit. One of them, don Nicolás de Uría, went to the colegio to deliver the message; gathering together all of the residents, he announced that Casterón y Trigo was no longer a colegiala and that he would deliver her immediately to the convent of San Bernardo. However, before doing so, he made clear to all that from the moment she left, Ana Margarita de Casterón y Trigo could never return and would be stripped of all rights and privileges granted to her, including the five-hundred-peso dowry she would have received had she remained under their protection until taking state.[3]

Stories like these, of entrances into and exits from institutions where laywomen lived under the supervision and protection of religious organizations or authorities, represent the experience of hundreds of women in New Spain. The social backgrounds and circumstances of these women varied greatly, as did the kinds of institutions they were entering or leaving. They were all taking part in a broad range of institutional cloistering practices built on the understanding of women's moral qualities and spiritual status as porous and communicable. Their choices in doing so – as limited as they often were – shaped that landscape in subtle ways. By forging opportunities and resisting constraints, they both reinforced and changed aspects of the culture of cloister with which they engaged.

3    AHCV 9-I-3, f. 120–30.

This chapter focuses on the seclusion of women envisioned as virtuous but vulnerable in three relatively prestigious lay cloisters in Mexico City. These institutions represented a middle road between beaterios and institutions designed for repentant, divorced, or recalcitrant scandalous women and focused on both protection and education in varying degrees. The Colegio de las Niñas de Nuestra Señora de la Caridad was run by one of the largest cofradías in New Spain and was designed for poor but virtuous girls, yet in practice, it sheltered many residents long past their girlhood.[4] The Recogimiento y Colegio de San Miguel de Belem was run by the archbishop of Mexico and reflected a broad range of mixed and shifting priorities, including voluntary rehabilitation of fallen women, sheltering the virtuous poor, and educating vulnerable maidens. And the *Colegio de San Ignacio de Loyola, las Vizcaínas* was founded and administered by the Basque *Cofradía de Nuestra Señora de Aránzazu* exclusively for daughters and widows of Basque men and their descendants. However, San Ignacio eventually developed an annex for the education of girls regardless of racial or social status, leading the way for more widespread changes in women's education in the nineteenth century.

These institutions were the three great colegios and officially purely voluntary recogimientos of Mexico City. They were founded at different moments, with different intentions and administrative structures. All of them became recipients of popular devotion and pious donations as symbols of the spiritually beneficial seclusion of women. And all of them became more exclusive over time and administrators attempted to distinguish them from *casas de arrepentidas*, cloisters for "repentant" women. Their histories also became entangled in ways their founders could not have imagined. Though their foundations spanned the length of the colonial period, they all survived to the era of the reform. Under Benito Juarez, Belem and Caridad faced sudden closure as part of state appropriation of church property. The ever savvy Aránzazu cofradía had anticipated this eventuality, however. Its members preemptively converted the brotherhood from a religious to a civic organization and retained control of the cloister, now reframed as a private, but no longer church-supported, school. Because of this, they were in a position to shelter the suddenly homeless residents of Belem and Caridad. Overnight, all of the girls and women, along with their teachers, archives, and libraries, moved to what became known as the *Colegio de las Vizcaínas*, (Basques) which still exists today, now as a co-ed private school.

---

4   I have not found any clear age designation for "niña." Rather, what seems the most significant divisions are those of marriage or sexual activity. Girls entered into the colegios as young as eight years old, but the majority of them entered sometime between twelve and twenty-five. And there were residents who remained until their death.

This merging preserved the histories of these three institutions in a unique way that allows for extended study and comparison.[5]

The Colegio de las Niñas de la Caridad began with a focus reflective of the early colonial period – racially inclusive in the name of creating Christian and culturally Spanish mothers and wives. But this quickly gave way to prioritizing the protection of poor Spanish women. A deep concern with the effects of poverty on Spanish women's virtue led to a project of social and spiritual uplift, creating a spiritual elite among artisan or downwardly mobile Spanish women by endowing them with special privileges. Nominally this project was about creating good Spanish wives, but the structure of the institution and the choices residents made reveals a strong undercurrent of desire to see these spiritual daughters take on the permanent prestige of the convent. Caridad remained small and exclusive throughout its existence, which allowed the members of the archicofradía to regulate and protect their adopted daughters throughout their lives, even beyond their time in the cloister. Powerful in its effects on the lives of colegialas, the wider significance of Caridad's vision was largely symbolic because of its size and exclusivity.

In contrast, the Recogimiento y Colegio de San Miguel de Belem was equally important symbolically but also sheltered a much larger and less permanent population of girls and women. Started in very different time, the late seventeenth century, its founders were motivated right from the start by anxieties about unprotected and unregulated women. Its original architect, Father Domingo Pérez Barcia, was deeply concerned for "all women," although this was probably a code for those who could at least pass as being of Spanish descent. Belem was in some ways the opposite of Caridad. Rather than creating a small female elite to benefit society through example, Belem's founders, Barcia and Archbishop Francisco de Aguiar y Seijas, hoped to create a large shelter that could accommodate redeemable fallen women alongside the vulnerable and virtuous poor as well as those with a desire for the monastic life. Belem's founders felt an urgency related to growing urban poverty and the significant population of single women, many of them mothers. However, Belem became an object of popular devotion, and as this popularity grew, so did its purported racial and social exclusivity. In practice, it continued to act as a safety valve for poor women and children throughout the colonial period, however. In other words, it always housed a more diverse population than its increasingly stringent entrance requirements would suggest.

The Colegio de San Ignacio de Loyola, las Vizcaínas began in the early eighteenth century with no pretenses to inclusiveness, though its founding

---

5   There is a dearth of literature on nonconventual female institutions, particularly that is meaningfully comparative. Chowning, "Convents and Nuns."

confraternity did have broader philanthropic interests in education and the protection of women. The brotherhood that established San Ignacio built its colegio in order to shelter exclusively maidens and "honest widows" of Basque descent. Ironically, however, it arose out of and was supported by Belem early on and throughout its history maintained a special, though fraught, relationship with the archbishop and his recogimiento. Over time, San Ignacio evolved into an ever more school-like institution, giving voice to the confraternity's more expansive concerns and paving the way for the changes in women's education of the nineteenth century in which these elite men would participate.

All three of these institutions provided shelter, protection, and material support along with opportunities for literacy and learning skills that could provide income and increase women's appeal as wives or nuns. They also imposed significant restrictions on the mobility of the residents, separated them from society, and demanded complete obedience. The women who lived there navigated these opportunities and constraints by using these cloisters as temporary havens, paths to increase their status, or an indefinite third option between marriage and the convent.

## Colegio de las Niñas de Nuestra Señora de la Caridad

### *Colonial Hierarchies and Social Mobility*

The founding confraternity of Mexico City's first colegio for laywomen, the Colegio de las Niñas de Nuestra Señora de la Caridad, was among the most illustrious and wealthy in New Spain.[6] This confraternity came into being in 1545 when the *Archicofradía del Santísimo Sacramento* and the *Cofradía de Nuestra Señora de la Caridad* combined to form the Archicofradía de la Santísimo Sacramento y Caridad. It enjoyed close relations with the archbishop and his officials and the patronage of many wealthy individuals, both ecclesiastics and laypersons.[7] One of its top priorities throughout the

---

6  Prior to this there had been smaller "escuelas" for "niñas indígenas" set up in the context of Christianization and early colonization. See chapter 6 of Josefina Muriel, *La sociedad novohispana y sus colegios de niñas* I (Mexico City: UNAM, 1995); and Pilar Gonzalbo Aizpuru, *Historia de la educación en la época colonial: El mundo indígena* (Mexico City: El Colegio de México, 1990). Spanish girls and young women were also educated within convents. See Gonzalbo Aizpuru, *Las mujeres en la Nueva España: Educación y vida cotidiana* (Mexico City: El Colegio de México, Centro de Estudios Históricos, 1987); and Gonzalbo Aizpuru, "Reffugium Virginum. Beneficencia y educación en los colegios y conventos novohispanos," in *Memoria del II Congreso Internacional: El Monacato Femenino en el Imperio Español: Monasterios, beaterios, recogimientos y colegios: Homenaje a Josefina Muriel*, ed. Manuel Ramos Media (Mexico City: Centro de Estudios de Historia de México, Condumex, 1995), 429–41.

7  The substantial monetary gift from the archbishop in 1736 is a good example of this relationship: AHCV 9-I-3, f. 159. For a discussion of this cofradía in the context of others in New Spain, see Asunción Lavrin, "Cofradías novohispanas: Economías material y espiritual," in *Cofradías,*

colonial period was to provide for the shelter, protection, and education of as many poor but virtuous girls and young women as possible. In addition to constructing and supporting their own colegio, they accomplished this goal by developing funds to endow individual *doncellas* chosen by lottery. These funds would provide dowries for marriage or profession or would go for room and board in a colegio or lay cloister.

The archicofradía originally established the Colegio de las Niñas de Nuestra Señora de la Caridad in the early years of the colony to shelter and educate mestiza daughters of Spaniards, separating them from their Indigenous mothers and placing them in the company of virtuous Spanish women who also needed protection. With this in mind, only non-Indigenous servants and employees were initially permitted in the colegio so as to keep the mestizas separate from the influences of their mothers' cultures, and no one was allowed to speak Nahuatl.[8] In the institution's original constitutions and other foundational documents, the founders expressed concern about *flaqueza mujeril*, or women's physical, moral, and spiritual weakness, and asserted that protecting and instructing Spanish and mixed-race women were critical to Spain's success in the New World.[9] Over time, these original intentions changed, however. Reflecting a larger trend in colonial society, the archicofradía narrowed its focus to racially "pure" women. It is not clear when this became official policy, but by the early seventeenth century, the annual *nombramientos*, or naming, of new colegialas listed all of the new residents as *doncellas españolas, virtuosas y pobres* – virtuous and poor Spanish maidens.[10]

By the early seventeenth century, the society of the colegio was also a stratified one. Popularly known as both the *Colegio de la Caridad* and the *Colegio de las Niñas Doncellas*, often shortened to either *Colegio de las Niñas* or *Colegio de las Doncellas*, it housed two categories of full-time residents: colegialas, who were supported by the archicofradía; and *pupilas*, whose parents, guardians, or an outside *obra pía* ("pious work" in the form of a religious fund) paid their way. Collectively they were called *educandas*, and the colegio could house up to fifty of them at a time. Legitimate birth, *limpieza de sangre*, and virginity were requirements for all of them, but only poor *huérfanas* (orphans who had lost at least their fathers) could become colegialas.

The colegio's constitutions from 1600 onward stipulated that colegialas must be *huérfanas de padre*. However, the archicofradía occasionally made

*capellanías y obras pías en la América colonial*, ed. Pilar Martínez López-Cano, Gisela Von Wobeser, and Juan Guillermo Muñoz (Mexico City: UNAM, 1998), 49–64.

8    AHCV 9-III-3, f. 60–62. Muriel, *La sociedad novohispana* I.
9    AHCV 9-III-3, f. 47. The constitution articulated the vision of female cloisters as key tools of evangelization.
10   See AHCV 14-IV-9.

an exception for girls who had only lost their mothers if the father was destitute and claimed that without the mother's guidance he feared his daughter would be "lost." Women and men alike asserted that without fathers, girls were likely to *perderse*, literally, lose themselves or become lost. This phrase implied a loss of virginity but also a more general loss of reputation, moral footing and, along with these, financial and physical well-being. The few petitions claiming that the lack of a mother's guidance would cause the same result are intriguing, as is the brotherhood's acceptance of them. They suggest the presence of a less prevalent but coexisting notion that mothers too played a vital role and that, sometimes, male protection was not sufficient.

Colegialas ranged from eight to forty years of age, though like pupilas, most of them were between twelve and twenty-five. They were chosen from a long waiting list built from petitions of guardians and prospective colegialas. Most petitioners were either widowed mothers who claimed "complete destitution" and "extreme poverty" or the temporary guardians of girls whose parents had died.[11] Colegios received full room and board for as long as they remained, an education, and five hundred pesos for a dowry to be used for marriage or professing in a convent. They were expected to contribute some labor to cleaning and housekeeping. Throughout the seventeenth and eighteenth centuries, the colegio could support between twenty and thirty-seven colegialas at a time.

Pupilas not supported by obras pías came from wealthier families than colegialas and often entered with their own personal servants.[12] However, in some cases the economic difference between pupilas and colegialas was only slight. Sometimes a family with just enough would make sacrifices to send their daughter to live as a pupila. To avoid the possibility of "abandonment" of pupilas by such families or guardians, the archicofradía required payment for a year in advance.[13] Those who entered with the support of an obra pía would be subject to the strength of that fund; some were strong and able to support recipients for years as well as provide a dowry, but others dried up because of mismanagement or scarcity. When that happened, recipients had to leave or forego dowries. But pupilas nonetheless enjoyed daily privileges colegialas did not. Even the pupilas supported by obras pías, who, like colegialas, were generally orphaned and poor, were still exempt from cleaning and other menial labor.[14] This may have led them to assert a kind of class privilege in their interactions with colegialas, who

---

11  **AHCV** 9-I-2 and 9-I-3.    12  Muriel, *La sociedad novohispana* I.
13  This kind of "abandonment" was not uncommon in Belem.
14  Muriel, *La sociedad novohispana* I.

usually came from lower artisan families and had to perform some labor alongside servants and slaves.[15]

In another way, colegialas occupied the position of greater symbolic prestige, however. Being chosen and *dotada* (endowed) as a colegiala meant becoming the adopted daughters of powerful men. Most of the confraternity's writings were directed toward colegialas, and even after marriage, these men watched over their "daughters" more than many fathers were able, making sure husbands did not mistreat them or misuse their dowries. In fact, such conditions were expressly articulated in the contracts drawn up between prospective spouses and the archicofradía. Pupilas did not share in this lifelong status or ongoing protection. Their time in the colegio certainly protected them temporarily from poverty and increased their spiritual and social status. However, their parents or guardians could remove them from the colegio at will, their guardians negotiated marriage arrangements without the assistance of the archicofradía, and they did not retain their titles as did colegialas.

Those poor enough to be chosen as a colegiala could access upward mobility through marriage or profession in a convent. If they stayed in the colegio long enough, they also joined a rarefied class of women – nun-like in their education and reputation for virtue but still marriageable. Though five hundred pesos was not enough to reach the uppermost echelons of society, where an expected dowry or bride inheritance might be three to four thousand pesos, it did make colegialas more appealing to ambitious members of the upper artisan or lower professional classes. Marrying poor but virtuous Spanish girls into upwardly mobile families was one of the confraternity's goals for the colegio and represented the inseparability of spiritual, social, and economic status in New Spain. The other goal was of course to produce nuns. Though some convents required larger dowries than the confraternity provided, most would make an exception for a colegiala from Caridad. In fact, colegialas were highly valued for their prestige and the various skills they brought. Throughout the life of the colegio, a stream of colegialas left to become novices in convents.[16]

Cloisters in the New World generally reflected the social stratifications outside them, but fear of the impact of poor Spaniards, and particularly women, led to some mitigation of class differences at Caridad. Requiring the poorer girls to perform their own chores illustrates a sense of obligation to protect the wealthier ones from manual labor, but by

---

15   For family backgrounds of colegialas, see the petitions presented in the seventeenth and eighteenth centuries in **AHCV 14-IV-9, AHCV 9-I-2, AHCV 8-I-6,** and **AHCV 8-I-11.**

16   See exits and entrances in **AHCV 7-I-2, AHCV 8-I-11, AHCV 9-I-2, AHCV 9-I-3, AHCV 9-I-4,** and **AHCV 14-IV-9.**

giving girls otherwise destined to work as domestic servants or live in poverty the status of colegialas, the archicofradía intervened in the economic hierarchy among Spanish families. Virtue and reputation had class dimensions as well, however. And many of the girls thought worthy of being colegialas came from downwardly mobile families that had enjoyed wealth and status in previous generations. Nonetheless, the colegialas themselves were spared from the insecurity caused by the declension of their families' fortunes.

The archicofradía elected eight to fifteen colegialas to hold special positions within Caridad, adding another level of hierarchy similar to that found in convents. Unlike convents, where the women generally elected their officers, the archicofradía made the ultimate choice. Sometimes they chose from a list of suggestions residents submitted, other times they approved or rejected the women's selections, and other times they simply chose without input from the majority of residents. However, in all cases, the *rectora*, the governing woman within the colegio, cast her vote alongside those of the members of the archicofradía.

These officials held a significant amount of power within the colegio and acted as intermediaries between the community and the archconfraternity. This was particularly true for the rectora, who was the ultimate authority within the colegio beneath the external administration of the archicofradía. Initially rectoras were pious widows who entered the colegio specifically to assume this role. But by the early seventeenth century the archicofradía was electing older doncellas to this position. Rectoras lived in private residences, were allotted more money for their regular maintenance, and were allowed special hours for private prayer in the colegio chapel. The position of rectora as well as the other elected officers tended to rotate among a very select group of women, who often maintained their positions for many years in a row.[17] And finally, there were women who served as teachers. These were sometimes widows who came from outside to teach music, reading, writing, crafts, and basic religious instruction, but they might also come from the long-term colegio population.

Adding another level to colegio society were the temporary residents known as *depositadas*. As early as 1585, members of the archicofradía charged with yearly inspections of the colegio reported that *mujeres corrruptas* (corrupt women) both married and *soltera*, among depositadas were a "great inconvenience" and "bad example" and had caused "dissention" and "great prejudice and corruption of the habits and honesty of the doncellas."[18] Officially, only "doncellas of the necessary quality" were

---

17  See, for example, elections between the years of 1600 and 1700 in **AHCV** 14-IV-9 and elections between the years of 1712 and 1770 in **AHCV** 9-I-3.

18  **AHCV** 9-III-3, f. 48.

allowed to enter as depositadas, but complaints and comments throughout the seventeenth and eighteenth centuries suggest that this rule was occasionally bent.[19] Depositadas had to pay their own way or have it paid by the person who took responsibility for them. During times of scarcity, someone willing to donate necessary funds might find it possible to place a wife or daughter in the protective privacy of the colegio in spite of the rules to the contrary.

Supporting this society at its foundation were servants and slaves, some who worked for the institution and others who served individual pupilas. Caridad's records rarely mentioned these women by name, much less recorded their experiences, but it is possible to know a few things about them. By the seventeenth century, once the ban against Indigenous servants was relaxed, this population included indias, *negras*, *castas* of all kinds, and poor españolas. Servants, slaves, and *criadas*[20] of individual pupilas only found their way into the historical record when they grew too numerous, caused problems, or purchased their freedom.[21] For all of the seventeenth and eighteenth centuries, the archconfraternity maintained three women in separate quarters who did much of the daily cooking and cleaning for the residents. These women regularly appeared in the archicofradía's annual visit records not by name but simply as *las tres mozas*, "the three servant women." They were obligated to attend mass with the residents and abide the same visiting hours and regulations on coming and going. The budget, which was administered by the rectora, allotted thirty pesos for each *moza* for food, clothing, and medicine. For comparison, the same budget allotted seventy pesos for the rectora's needs, between sixty-two and fifty-two for the rest of the officers, and fifty for all other colegialas.[22]

The colegio also maintained additional enslaved laborers, generally described as *negros* and *mulatos*, both men and women, who lived in adjoining residences just outside the colegio. The male slaves performed work that did not require them to enter the colegio or interact with the residents, and the record of them is limited to occasional petitions related to housing, work, and food.[23] The female slaves, however, entered the colegio, worked alongside servants, attended mass, and fulfilled the weekly requirements of confession and communion. They probably served as go-betweens for

19   See especially visit interviews in AHCV 9-I-3 between the years of 1712 and 1750.

20   The term "criada," though literally meaning "raised" from the verb "criar," often referred to someone growing up in a household who performed domestic service. Often the parents of pupilas would send these girls or women to accompany their daughter when they went to live in the Colegio de Caridad.

21   See AHCV 14-IV-7 and 15-IV-9.

22   See visit records of the seventeenth century in AHCV 9-I-2 and of the eighteenth century in AHCV 9-I-3.

23   AHCV 14-III-8 and AHCV 14-IV-8.

cloistered residents as well, protecting the recogimiento of the colegialas and pupilas by delivering messages and running errands outside the colegio.

## The Space of the Cloister

Like other female cloisters, Caridad's architecture and physical layout were designed to facilitate and enforce the ideology of recogimiento. In 1558, the archicofradía began purchasing multiple houses in the center of Mexico City, in the heart of the *traza*, the neighborhood now known as *Centro Histórico*. By the early seventeenth century, architects had turned this stretch of houses covering several city blocks into a large complex that included the main buildings of the colegio and its church. From the outside, it looked like one enormous, fortress-like building, with seamless and unadorned walls. But this impenetrable exterior housed a complex internal world resembling a small city center with an airy plaza and gardens. Inside, residents could walk between several adjoining buildings clustered around three patios and a large garden area. Inside the main entryway, this center was open to the sky so residents could enjoy the outdoors while remaining enclosed and separate from the outside world. Colegialas and pupilas alike – and presumably depositadas as well – slept, bathed, and ate in communal dormitories, wash areas, and cafeteria. The colegio also contained a kitchen, pantry, infirmary, and pharmacy. Students attended their lessons in large rooms designed for that purpose. Children received formal instruction in reading, writing, and basic math, while older residents learned sewing and crafts in the *sala de labores*. All residents attended music lessons in a separate music room or the choir and performed spiritual exercises in the choir and chapel, where they also listened as chaplains gave spiritual *pláticas*, or talks, and doctrine lessons.

There were two physical boundaries between this vibrant internal space of the colegio and the city beyond its heavy walls. The first was a *locutorio*, or parlor space, where official business with outsiders took place. It was guarded by the *portería*, or entryway, with large, heavy doors that opened only during specific visiting hours when residents could communicate with family members and other preapproved visitors through the *reja*, or gate. A woman holding the position of *escucha de reja*, or gate listener, monitored all conversations to ensure proper decorum and modesty. The *portera* guarded the doors and visiting area, making sure visits were conducted appropriately during visiting hours and that the doors remained shut at all other times.

The second boundary with the outside world was the colegio church, which was open to the public for mass, confession, and communion. The constitution required all residents, including servants and enslaved women, to attend mass in the colegio church every Sunday. They sat in either the upper or lower choir balcony, which was separated by gates. These gates effectively prevented colegio residents from interacting with other parishioners but did allow them to be seen, and great care was to be taken with their appearance. Colegialas and pupilas did not partake of confession or communion with the rest of the parishioners. Instead, the constitution stipulated that all confessors enter the colegio through the portería and administer the sacraments in the confessionals located in the locutorio only. They were to advise the rectora beforehand of their arrival, and she was to stay present and watchful while the interactions took place. Only in cases of serious illness could priests enter the inner part of the colegio, and even then, the rectora was to accompany them at all times. This rule placed the rectora in a position that was unusual for laywomen – that of supervising clergymen. These moments may have elevated the rectora's personal sense of authority.

This level of seclusion, with its narrow band of interaction with the outside world, and the architectural features that supported it closely resembled those of a convent. However, one important difference was that residents could sometimes leave the cloister on preapproved and supervised trips to visit family members or to participate in important events outside the colegio. Such outside world visits were infrequent, and some women never experienced them, but for women of marriageable age, they were seen as opportunities to find suitable husbands. Ambitious and reputable families looked to the doncellas of Caridad to find virtuous wives for their sons, knowing that the prestige of the archicofradía and a decent dowry were part of the deal.

All ventures out of the colegio required the permission of the *rector, diputados*, and *mayordomo*, the archicofradía members elected as administrators of the colegio. The rectora and portera were then responsible for ensuring that doncellas left with the correct person at the appointed time, that the gate was shut quickly after them and that they always left one at a time and never in pairs or groups. This rule aimed to prevent mischief, gossip, or the formation of "exclusive and intense friendships" – all things administrators of lay cloisters wrote about as potential dangers to be avoided. If the doncella did not return to the colegio promptly when she was supposed to, she risked punishment, which could include permanent expulsion from the colegio and the loss of all privileges attached to it.

### *Women's Education and Work: Competing Spiritual and Social Visions*

Given the importance the archicofradía placed on marriage, it is striking how different colegialas' daily lives were from those of most wives in New Spain. Caridad's founders spoke about the colegio as a place where young women learned the skills and virtues necessary for Christian marriage and motherhood, and the constitution said that its primary goal for residents was to "marry them and put their lives in order."[24] Yet when they wrote concretely about teaching them "what is essential to women," it was not the skills of household maintenance and child-rearing but rather Christian ideals of female virtue, humility, and obedience – in other words, recogimiento.[25] Servants performed most of the regular cooking and cleaning in Caridad. Though colegialas did contribute to the general upkeep through rotating chores, living in a dormitory and eating prepared meals would not have trained them in the daily skills presumably expected of them as wives and mothers. Unless they married into a family that could afford to delegate this work to domestic servants, this must have been a source of conflict for some women when they arrived to their new home, fairly untutored in mundane domestic tasks.

For the founders of Caridad, "what is essential to women" meant a particular vision of female behavior, which they aimed to teach the residents through a life of seclusion, tranquility, and spiritual discipline – moderated by humility. Like nuns and *beatas*, the young women in Caridad and other colegios and recogimientos spent more hours a day in prayer, doctrinal and scriptural lessons, and other spiritual exercises than anything else. Through this routine, residents gained a more advanced religious education than most laywomen, but it was still distinct from that of novices committed to becoming nuns. Their devotional practices did not include the solitary acts of reflection expected of nuns because the members of the archconfraternity feared these would lead the educandas to an inflated sense of their own sanctity. Rather, the routine included group lessons, recitations, and prayers designed to teach discipline, obedience, and devotion.

There were other ways in which these women's education seemed to prepare them more for convents than marriage, however. In addition to spiritual exercises, younger residents spent part of their day in the *sala de niñas*, learning reading, writing, and basic arithmetic. However, once they reached a certain age, they spent those hours in the *sala de labor* learning rarefied skills. These *labores de mano* were not cooking, cleaning, and other domestic labor but rather embroidery and making fine objects of beauty like paper flowers or silk ornaments. These were tasks nuns performed, sometimes selling their handiwork to bring extra income to their convents. Furthermore, all Caridad residents learned to sing, play musical instruments, and read music. Musical talent was an appealing trait in a wife, to be sure, but it was even more important to a convent community. Many convents were willing to waive or reduce their required dowries for women who were already skilled in music.

24  *Casarlas y ponerlas en orden de vivir.* AHCV 9-III-3, f. 48.   25  AHCV 9-III-3, f. 48.

Throughout the centuries of the colegio's existence, its founders consistently wrote as if turning the doncellas of Caridad into proper Spanish wives was the primary task. However, the structure of their daily lives reflects the hope that many of them would end up taking formal religious vows. It also reflects the notion that for a certain class of women, spiritual status and nun-like qualities were more important, even for marriage, than the mundane skills of running a household. The archicofradía purported to be preparing the residents for marriage and motherhood, and yet the vision of feminine piety taught in its colegio was closely connected to the monastic ideal.

This contradiction was reflective of a broader paradox in colonial society. Religious authorities and pious men and women agreed that educating future wives was an honorable and necessary endeavor, and yet the prestige associated with nuns held a powerful allure. Church teachings celebrated celibacy over marriage. Marital sexuality was understood to be God's merciful provision for those who were not suited to the challenges of monastic life, but the latter was ultimately more pleasing to him. And because the monastic ideal for women was the pinnacle of proper female virtue and piety, it also shaped expectations for the ideal wife. The qualities of recogimiento – seclusion, modesty, obedience, and pious devotion – were called for in both nuns and wives. And in Caridad, these ideals were intertwined in the archicofradía's vision for its spiritual daughters.

### *Discipline and Supervision in the Archicofradía's Cloister*

For all of the archicofradía's interest in and concern over the day-to-day activities of its colegialas, its ability to enforce its vision was limited by the very ideology of cloister; the colegio's administrators never entered its innermost spaces and depended on yearly interviews conducted in the choir and locutorio to learn whether things were happening as they should. archicofradía members were invested in the minute details of the residents' daily routines, behavior, and attitudes, as reflected in the constitutions they authored, but to personally supervise the activities in the colegio would have meant undermining the ideal of recogimiento that lay at the heart of their endeavor.

Instead, the archicofradía expected the rectora and other female officers to carry out its will. The brotherhood elected a rector, mayordomo, and diputados to serve as external administrators, which took the form of annual visits and special proclamations and decisions when there were problems to solve. In between these, the rectora had complete authority in the daily workings of the colegio and was a partner with the archicofradía in many of the external logistics as well. She worked with the rector and diputados to manage the colegio's finances and oversaw the distribution of clothing, food, money, and other goods within the colegio. She decided what time the residents should rise in the morning, retire for the evening, and transition from activity to activity. In most cases, she alone was free to determine when a transgression deserved punishment and the form that punishment should take.

Annual visits were usually relatively uneventful, but they nonetheless reveal that the archicofradía's rules about silence, obedience, and even proper seclusion were not always followed. In spite of strict routines, colegio life was shaped by the vicissitudes of human emotions, behavior, and relationships. Friendships and animosities developed, residents obeyed and respected the rectora to greater and lesser degrees, spiritual devotion waxed and waned, and residents approached their required activities and responsibilities with more or less rigor. Young girls sometimes ran around when they were not supposed to, while others snuck off to explore forbidden places, like the pantry or the servants' quarters. Melancholy women wandered in the gardens when they were supposed to be eating or getting ready for bed. Others remained in their rooms when they were expected in the choir or the sala de labor. Greater scandals occasionally erupted as well in which residents expressed frustration, anger, or resentment, raising their voices at colegio officers or behaving in openly defiant ways. Some women chafed against the restrictions on contact with the outside world and tried to stretch the rules, and the porteras and escuchas were sometimes tolerant and sometimes harsh.

Residents' most frequent complaints to the male administrators during yearly visits related to material need. Ironically, in times of scarcity, it was often the pupilas who complained most of hunger and "nakedness" because either their families had fallen into poverty or the obras pías that supported them had dwindled. But there were certainly lean times for colegialas as well. Complaints about fellow residents were less common but also occurred. And while residents occasionally complained about the portera and escucha, they rarely spoke ill of the rectora. Given the close channel of communication between the rector and diputados and rectora, residents had good reason to fear that such complaints would reach the ears of the woman who had so much power over their daily lives.

In the rare event that these complaints became significant, the archicofradía members charged with the administration of the colegio intervened and exerted their authority. In the visit of 1719, colegialas complained extensively about both fellow residents and colegio authorities, and the rectora and other officials responded in kind. Collectively they painted a picture of chaos in which superiors were ineffective, residents did not respect the officers, and the rules were bent to such a degree that the colegio's status as "a proper recogimiento" was in danger, according to the rector, mayordomo, and diputados who conducted the visit.

The archicofradía decided on a swift and complete change of internal administration, immediately replacing all but one lower officer. Even more striking is that they chose women outside the usual group through which these positions rotated, meaning that residents without any experience in this kind of leadership were now suddenly in control. When the rector and diputados announced these changes to the residents, they scolded them harshly and urged the incoming officers to enforce the constitution more strictly, particularly the rules related to interactions with outsiders.[26]

The brotherhood would also get involved in disciplining individual colegialas when they felt it was necessary. If complaints about individual residents were serious or frequent, the rector and diputados might instruct the rectora to take additional disciplinary measures. In 1719, though infractions of the rules were widespread, the rectora, portera, and escucha spoke about three young women as particularly insubordinate and disrespectful. After installing a new rectora, the rector and diputados instructed her to give these troublesome women three warnings, making it clear that after that, they would be expelled.[27] In other instances, the rector and diputados might suggest a public scolding, and in rare occasions, they could even demand an immediate expulsion. In such a case, the men themselves would ask the colegiala's nearest relative to retrieve her and would order the rectora to release her into the custody of this family member.

For women like Margarita Yturri, who had submitted her own petition to enter the colegio, being expelled could mean losing all material support – a devastating consequence for a young woman in Mexico City. In such a case, the woman in question might seek entrance into Belem as a recogida supported by *la casa* or *providencia divina* (the house or divine providence, both ways of describing the charity of the archbishop's cloister itself), or she might seek less formal shelter in a convent or hospital. But being expelled from the well-known Colegio de Caridad could make these options difficult. To avoid destitution, such a woman may have had to move to a recogimiento of lesser repute, like the *Recogimiento de María Magdalena* or *Misericordia*, which were home to repentant and sometimes imprisoned women. Or she might throw herself on the mercy of the *Provisorato* and ask the judge to place her in depósito in a private home. When depósito was indefinite like this, it likely meant effectively becoming a domestic servant in a respected household in return for protection and shelter. Thus, misbehavior carried a high cost for some women. The loss of spiritual status for those without a family safety net could mean rapid downward mobility in real material terms.

26   AHCV 9-I-3, f. 35–60.    27   Ibid.

In the visit of 1721, there was another rash of complaints, but this time they were primarily directed at the men entrusted with the residents' spiritual and medical care.[28] The main problems that year were with doctors, pharmacists, and priests. The archicofradía members' responses demonstrated a mix of concern for their adopted daughters' welfare and a general reticence to back the rectora in conflicts with other male authorities. Residents complained that the doctor was slow to attend to the sick and the pharmacist did not provide sufficient medicine. Another reoccurring complaint was that the colegio chaplains were barring women's personal confessors from entering to hear their confession, particularly when the confessors were members of religious orders. Only the rectora had the authority to bar people from entering the colegio, so the chaplains' actions amounted to an abuse of their positions and an infringement on her sovereignty. In addition, some of the women whose confessors were barred were choosing to go without confession and therefore communion rather than confess with the chaplains. This undermined the requirement for weekly communion for all residents and put those colegialas remaining *enhoramala* in serious spiritual peril.

In spite of the seriousness of these complaints, the archicofradía was hesitant to act forcefully. Though the rector, diputado, and mayordomo chastised the physician and directed him to make more frequent visits, they did not reprimand the pharmacist. Perhaps they were aware that the lack of medicine was the result of a general scarcity or of the colegio's own limited funds rather than the neglect of the pharmacist.[29] But most striking was these mens' reticence to become involved in the struggle between chaplains and rectoras and, perhaps more importantly, between chaplains and outside confessors. Though later versions of the constitution would address these problems in the abstract by explicitly forbidding chaplains from interfering with the internal government of the colegio, at the time of these complaints, the administrators did not respond. They did not reprimand the chaplains, they did not come to the aid of the rectora, and they did not insist that the residents confess with the chaplains. For the time being, the archicofradía stayed out of the conflict and left the issue unresolved in spite of its significant spiritual implications.[30]

## Leaving Caridad

Conflicts also emerged when colegialas wanted to leave and archicofradía members did not approve. The status and protection afforded a colegiala

---

28 A few scrupulous women reported that some members of their community were still misbehaving: not maintaining silence after bedtime, skipping out on choir and classes, and eating and drinking when and where they should not. But these were isolated complaints, and the archconfraternity members noted them but did not formally respond. **AHCV** 9–1-3, f. 61.

29 AHCV 9-I-3, f. 60–71.    30 **Ibid.**

were meant to be lifelong as long as she fulfilled her obligations. These included obedience to the will of her surrogate fathers, respecting the authority of the rectoras, and following the rules of the constitution. Entrance and continued residence within the colegio were voluntary, but if a woman sought to leave before "taking state," she lost her dowry and all rights and privileges as a colegiala. The brotherhood treated such unauthorized exits as betrayals, formally expelling women who chose to leave "prematurely" and describing their leavings as scandalous, disobedient, and ungrateful. Such expulsions were often public affairs, designed to make an example of women who wanted to leave. Assembling the residents, the rector and diputados or sometimes the rectora would harshly reprimand the offending woman, formally revoke her status, and ceremoniously declare that she would never be welcomed back. Nonetheless, some residents left to live in private homes with relatives or sought informal shelter in convents, beaterios, or recogimientos or colegios, all in violation of the colegio's constitution.

On the other hand, exits for an approved marriage or profession were celebrated affairs. The archconfraternity's members reserved the right to decide and execute their adopted daughters' exit arrangements themselves. In the case of marriage, rather than going directly to a clergyman with the power to give marriage licenses, which was the usual process for a betrothed couple, both parties had to petition the archicofradía for permission to marry. These men were extremely concerned with ensuring a proper marriage and upward mobility for their adoptive daughters; they scrutinized the social and financial status of potential spouses and did not hesitate to deny the request if they felt it was not "convenient." If the members of the archicofradía did approve a match, they themselves would go the provisor on behalf of the colegiala to begin the marriage process. Ultimately, they could not control the actions of a colegiala who was determined to marry against their will, but such a choice would mean expulsion and the loss of her dowry. And it would also require careful planning and persistence in order to make the necessary arrangements while still under the restrictions imposed by the colegio.

Prior to the marriage law reforms of 1778, biological parents and legal guardians did not have the authority to stop a marriage that a clergyman had approved, though they frequently tried and could certainly make the path very difficult.[31] For most of the colonial period, couples with interfering parents could seek the help of local priests or the provisor and his judges, complaining that their families were trying to impede their desired union. If necessary, the couple might resort to a staged "kidnapping," in

31   In 1778 the Ley Pragmática de Matrimonios allowed parents and civil courts to intervene in order to prohibit marriages in which there existed an "inequality" of race and social caste.

which the man absconded with his desired spouse in a public manner and kept her at his house for a number of days, presumably deflowering her. The couple would then appear as penitents before an ecclesiastical judge to confess their sins and ask for the church's dispensation and help in securing the marriage that they now needed in order to redeem the woman's reputation and both of their spiritual well-being.

A colegiala seeking to marry against her adopted fathers' will had limited mobility within which to enact these strategies, but she could still turn to the church court for help. In 1737, archconfraternity members rejected doña Ana Thomasa Tadeo de Ybarrola's desired marriage partner. She turned to the Provisorato Eclesiástico's assistance, thereby pitting the authority of the archbishop and his court against that of the archicofradía. Two years after the archconfraternity had decided Tadeo de Ybarrola's suitor was not worthy, the couple presented their case to the provisor, and he agreed to help them. They then completed the necessary proceedings for marriage, all in secret. This must have been difficult and probably required collaboration of relatives and fellow residents. The couple had to make their plans in spite of the ever-present gaze of the rectora and attentive ears of the portera and escucha and had to organize at least one approved leave for Ana Thomasa Tadeo de Ybarrola in order to secretly appear before the provisor. After the archicofradía had rejected his marriage request, the fiancé would presumably no longer be an approved visitor, so he must have employed someone else to make these arrangements. Passing notes at the gate was forbidden, so these communications had to be done surreptitiously and quietly, or else with the tacit approval of the escucha de reja and portera.

However, they accomplished it, the couple's plan worked; the provisor sent a formal letter advising the archicofradía that he would send his representative to collect Tadeo de Ybarrola and that it should stop trying to impede this marriage. The assertion of ultimate authority in the name of the archbishop was clear but was expressed with careful diplomacy. Addressing the archicofradía members as beloved servants of the church, whose power and authority in the administration of their colegio was never in question, the archbishop's provisor sought to resolve the situation with minimal embarrassment and scandal, as he had no desire to stain or display a lack of respect for the "lofty reputation" of the archicofradía, its "illustrious colegio," or the "virtuous doncellas" the cloister housed. The members of the brotherhood saw the wisdom in this. Though their internal records expressed dismay at having to concede to a marriage of which they did not approve, their communication with the provisor was respectful and reasonably compliant. By pitting one patriarchal religious authority against others, Ana Thomasa Tadeo de Ybarrola was able to choose her own life partner without the public disgrace of being expelled.

Though such flagrant disobedience would normally be openly condemned, the archconfraternity's members feared that making the details
public would encourage other colegialas to employ similar strategies.
At the request of the archicofradía, the provisor informed the rectora
when his representative would be arriving so she could facilitate a quiet
exit witnessed by as few residents as possible. There had been other, less
decorous instances of colegialas leaving Caridad to pursue nonapproved
marriages – one just a few years back, in the very year Tadeo de Ybarrola
had entered Caridad. In 1732, Josepha Delgado left the colegio, "with
scandal, remaining barred from it," to marry without permission of the
archicofradía.[32] The members of the archconfraternity had condemned her
actions but could not undo the damage her dramatic leaving had caused.
For these men, Tadeo de Ybarrola's betrayal stung all the more because she
had been an obedient and devoted colegiala since her entrance in 1732.
Judging from their descriptions of her, she was also highly articulate, self-
possessed, and determined – all skills that eventually served her well in
gaining the support of the provisor.

In the wake of this incident, the archicofradía drafted a new policy aimed
at preventing such occurrences. The members of the brotherhood added an
addendum to the constitution to be read aloud at each annual visit. They
underlined in greater detail how marriages were to be contracted and
warned the residents that pursuing a marriage license without first obtain-
ing their permission or going against their will in the case of their
disapproval would result in formal and permanent expulsion and loss of
dowry. They further specified that the archconfraternity members alone
would arrange and pursue all necessary diligencias, acting on behalf of their
protected daughters.[33]

These extreme measures to control the marriage choices of colegialas and
the high standards they maintained for suitors illustrate the archicofradía's
members' seriousness about their mission. By saving roughly thirty poor
but virtuous Spanish women every decade or so from the "ruin" of the
"extreme need" of their poverty, they were preventing the potential spread
of this damage and converting vulnerable, unprotected women into virtuous forces of sanctification. But all of the resources that went into every
colegiala were only worthwhile if they remained "uplifted" for life. Each
one who "fell," through bad behavior or marriage to someone below her in
*calidad*, represented a failure of this goal. Colegialas like Ana Thomasa
Tadeo de Ybarrola and Josepha Delgado sacrificed not only their dowries
but their reputations as colegialas in order to marry the men they chose.
Perhaps these women felt they had already benefited from their time in the
colegio and did not share in the sense that they were marrying "below their

32  AHCV 9-I-3, f. 115–120.    33  AHCV 9-I-3, f. 158–162.

status." But for the members of the archconfraternity, the goal was to create a spiritual and social elite out of the innocent but wretched girls and women who they allowed into their colegio.

Besides an acceptable marriage, the only other legitimate way to leave the colegio was to profess as a nun. As with marriage, the archicofradía claimed the right to oversee and approve all requests and arrangements for profession. A steady minority of colegialas consistently chose this option. The dowry and skills colegialas received made this possible for women who otherwise would not have had this opportunity. However, despite the similarities between the colegio and convents, not all colegialas were capable of sustaining the intensified version of monastic life they encountered as novices. The demands on those seeking to profess were extremely high and the devotional practices and schedule more rigorous than that of Caridad.[34]

Some colegialas who became novitiates found that they did not have the stamina for convent life. The archicofradía kept track of the those who had left to profess as nuns and sometimes noted that the women had gone to live with relatives before their novitiate period was complete, usually because of concerns for their health. It is not clear what happened to these women's dowries in such instances – whether they were absorbed by the convent or returned to the archicofradía. According to the constitution, a colegiala had to profess as a nun or be married in order to have her dowry applied, so presumably the archicofradía would attempt to recover it if it had already been provided to the convent. And since these women were no longer living in the colegio and had not succeeded in taking state, they had probably also forfeited their colegiala status and with it any future access to their dowry.

At least one woman avoided this fate by petitioning to return to the colegio when health reasons prevented her from completing the novitiate process. In 1731, the archicofradía received a letter from Catarina de San Pedro, the *capellana* and *presidenta* of the convent of Santa Ynez. In it she said that former colegiala doña María de Pevedilla, who had since taken the name of Sor María de Guadalupe, was suffering from fatigue and consistent illness. The presidenta confirmed that Pevedilla was been physically unable to abide the schedule of spiritual exercises and fulfill the responsibilities necessary to complete her novitiate and that all efforts to cure her had failed. María de Pevedilla had served as a *maestra* before leaving the colegio and perhaps did not realize her life at Santa Ynez would be significantly more strenuous than what she was used to. Or perhaps her health had simply deteriorated. Whatever the case, the now very ill María de Pevedilla

---

34  See Asuncion Lavrin, "The Novice Becomes a Nun," in *Brides of Christ*, 48–80. For a discussion of the extreme tests of will novices had to undergo, which could include harsh discipline and punishment, see especially 55–70.

wanted nothing more than to return to "her colegio." The archicofradía reviewed the request carefully and, after some discussion, its members decided that her illness warranted compassion and that they would let her return to her previous colegiala status. In doing so, however, they made every effort to minimize the visibility of her return, noting that the situation was exceptional and could set a bad example for the other colegialas to follow. Once in the colegio, María de Pevedilla's health must have stabilized somewhat because eleven years later, in 1748, she was still serving as maestra and, in 1751, as *vicaria*. By then, she was probably well past marriageable age, but she also knew that the brand of monastic life found in convents was beyond her abilities. Presumably, María de Pevedilla had decided to stay indefinitely at the Colegio de la Caridad.[35]

## Conclusions: A Third Path

The members of the archicofradía did not actively discourage women from choosing to stay in Caridad indefinitely, but neither did they encourage it. On one hand, the more women who stayed until their deaths, the fewer women the archicofradía could protect and uplift. On the other hand, maintaining a convent-like cloister populated by devoted nun-like colegialas accomplished an important, sanctifying purpose as well. And indeed, a significant minority of women chose this third option, many of them serving as nurses, teachers, vicarias, and sometimes rectoras.

While the numbers of women who chose marriage over the monastic life were higher in the eighteenth century than they were for most of the seventeenth century, so was the number of women choosing to stay in the colegio. This probably reflects the larger trend in which elite society gradually came to see marriage as more desirable vis-à-vis monastic life, beginning in the eighteenth century and increasingly in the nineteenth century. But the simultaneous increase of women who chose to stay in the colegio also suggests that marriage was not always a preferable option for the women themselves. Perhaps the increased pressure to marry made it even more appealing to remain indefinitely cloistered while still not taking formal and permanent vows as a nun.

The visit records of the later seventeenth and eighteenth centuries show a gradual increase in the colegialas who found this middle road to be more appealing or possible than marriage or the convent. There were always those women who entered and left quickly to get married, but the average stay in the colegio grew longer over time, and more spaces were occupied until the death of the residents holding them.

35   AHCV 9-I-3, f. 162–65, 211, and 227.

The goal of the archicofradía was not simply to provide honorable seclusion. Its members also had in mind the permanent social and spiritual uplift of a select group of virtuous and poor Spanish young women, some of whom they hoped would join the spiritual elite in the monastic life, while the rest would either increase the ranks of virtuous and pious wives or remain cloistered in Caridad. There was a hierarchy of possibilities: only three of them were acceptable; and the first two were preferable.

For the most part, colegialas adhered to the goals of their surrogate fathers, the majority choosing one of the three acceptable paths. Increasingly, however, they chose to stay, when the members of the archconfraternity would supposedly rather have them choose marriage or to become a nun. For some women, the opportunities within the colegio were preferable to the alternatives. The physical intrusion of direct male authority was minimal, and residents received the benefits of an educational routine rich in both devotional practices and artistic endeavors without the strenuous demands placed on a novice seeking formal profession in a convent. In other words, in a society in which marriage or becoming a nun were hailed as the only two respectable paths for women, a select group of economically disadvantaged Spanish women found in the Colegio de Nuestra Señora de la Caridad a third way to create for themselves a life of material and social security.

## Recogimiento y Colegio de San Miguel de Belem

*The Virtuous and the Fallen: A Place for All Women*

The significance of the Colegio de las Niñas de Nuestra Señora de la Caridad as a place that housed, protected, and regulated poor and virtuous Spanish women was related to its prestige and reputation in Mexican society more than the actual number of women it sheltered. The waiting list of girls seeking entrance into Caridad was much longer than the archicofradía and its institution could accommodate, and the intended recipients of the colegio's protection made up a fairly exclusive group. A second institution developed in the last decades of the seventeenth century whose scope was much greater. Though the Recogimiento de San Miguel de Belem would eventually evolve into a colegio whose official entrance requirements resembled Caridad's more than its own original vision, it would nonetheless remain a much larger institution, housing up to 300 women at one time. As such, it responded to the social problem of women's poverty and vulnerability on a much grander scale than the relatively elite colegio of Caridad.

The shifting ideologies and conventual culture of Belem reflect interconnected concerns about women's virtue and vulnerability. The stories of some Belem residents belong in the next chapter, which looks at women cloistered because they supposedly needed reform, repentance, or correction. Here, my focus is on the way Belem operated – both ideally and in reality – as a prestigious voluntary cloister for virtuous women and girls. Officially, Belem was always a voluntary cloister, but scattered petitions and complaints reveal that family members and judges occasionally sent women there against their will or forced them to stay after they arrived voluntarily but then later wanted to leave. Belem nonetheless retained its reputation as a reputable voluntary institution – not one as exclusive and prestigious as Caridad but still something religious authorities boasted about as a model of chaste and virtuous female cloister.

The recogimiento and later colegio of Belem was founded, supported, and developed by a financial partnership between the archbishop of Mexico and pious and wealthy individuals in Mexico City. The primary architect of its original vision was Padre Domingo Pérez Barcia, an active philanthropist and Jesuit priest. After building a school for poor children in the neighborhood of Belem, he became particularly concerned about the "economic and moral support" of women in Mexico City.[36] In the late 1670s, Archbishop Aguiar y Seijas approached Barcia with the suggestion that they construct a shelter for women. The archbishop was himself a man of charity as well as a strong proponent of the values of feminine recogimiento. Barcia's idea, which the archbishop initially signed on for as well, was to house repentant women alongside those who were virtuous but at risk, without making distinctions between "good" and "lost" women. This alone made the proposed institution quite different from Caridad.[37]

In the early 1680s, Barcia began acquiring houses in the neighborhood of Belem to use for the cloister, which welcomed its first residents in 1683. In 1684, the archbishop completed his first visit to interview the founding women, and in 1686, he gave his formal approval. In the same year, the two men oversaw the construction of an enormous chapel that could house three hundred women. Barcia's vision shaped the original constitution, which stipulated that the Recogimiento de San Miguel de Belem was to remain a voluntary shelter for "fallen" women, widows with children, and married women as well as young maidens "on the verge of losing their innocence" and thus in need of protection. Barcia maintained that it should never become a place of punishment nor develop into a convent or colegio but should forever remain a home for "mujeres desamparadas," be they repentant prostitutes, abandoned wives, single mothers, or virtuous doncellas.[38]

36  Josefina Muriel, *La sociedad novohispana* II, 74.
37  Muriel, *Los Recogimientos de Mujeres*, 75–78. AHCV 13-IV-3.     38   AHCV 13-IV-3.

Unlike Caridad, access to Belem was not limited to huérfanas or women whose poverty made them especially vulnerable, though in the early decades, most of the residents were in fact escaping poverty and destitution. Nonetheless, the original vision for Belem was ambitious and vast. Women who simply "realized" the dangers and risks inherent in their state of unprotected femaleness, whatever their economic or family situation, could find a place at Belem, if they were willing to submit themselves to its authorities, restrictions, and activities. The founding documents proclaimed the idea that the more women who chose to seclude themselves in Belem, the more pleasing the institution would be to God and the greater benefit it would provide society.

Barcia strongly believed that housing virtuous women of "good education" alongside repentant and poor women (two categories that blurred in the founding documents) would uplift the latter and instill humility in the former. The founders hoped that Belem would become a place where such women could become worthy wives and nuns and that their institution would grow in prestige while remaining open to those who needed it most.

The question of caste and race within this vision is ambiguous in the founding documents. This was probably because the Jesuit father wanted the casa to be more accessible than strictly enforced limpieza de sangre requirements would allow for and because there was an unspoken assumption that the most important women to protect were those of Spanish descent. It is unlikely that open acceptance of Indigenous or African women was ever common at Belem, though it is possible that Father Barcia was more radical about this than many of his contemporaries.

Father Barcia and Archbishop Aguiar y Seijas did not always agree on Belem's purpose, and the archbishop ultimately asserted his control in a way that shaped its ultimate direction. Barcia wrote in the founding documents he authored that he did not want Belem to have an established "rule" like that of convents, or the Colegio de Caridad, for that matter, which prescribed a particular regime of spiritual exercises and prayers. Barcia did not want to dictate the devotional practices of the residents, believing instead that their prayers should be voluntary to ensure their sincerity. However, the archbishop did not want to leave the religious life of the institution up to chance; within the first decade, Aguiar y Seijas had established a *reglamento formal*, or formal "rule," of the kind Barcia had not wanted. These assertions of power, often made during periods when ill health limited Padre Barcia's involvement in the administration of Belem, were the early steps toward the office of the archbishop taking complete authority of and responsibility for Belem and its workings.

## Increasing Exclusivity

Aguiar y Seijas' vision of life for Belem's residents was austere and disciplined, and the records of these early decades reflect this.[39] Many women left because they could not stand the rigors of life there, while others complained and petitioned to leave but changed their minds at the last minute, noting that their poverty left them destitute with nowhere else to go. Later generations of women would wax nostalgic about these early years, complaining about the laxness that characterized the institution in their own time and comparing it unfavorably to the stories they had heard about the founding days.[40] Aguiar y Seijas died in 1698, placing the recogimiento entirely in Barcia's hands until his own death in 1713. After some legal wrangling, Belem officially came entirely and indefinitely under the authority of the office of the archbishop in 1726, during the time of Archbishop José Lanciego y Eguiluz. This meant Belem would develop according to the personal priorities of each archbishop and the changing ideas prevalent in each of their administrations about female piety and the church's responsibility to women.

Strictly speaking, Barcia's original vision of a nonexclusive but voluntary recogimiento was short-lived. By 1696, Belem housed one hundred and thirty-three women, not counting the many daughters of these women who accompanied them. Residents included former prostitutes, "mujeres públicas," and "mujeres vergonzozas," who lived and prayed alongside virtuous maidens and widows. By 1720, Belem had become a popular destination of pious donations, its prestige growing as it became known as a place that successfully "laundered the poor and the destitute," turning them into potential nuns and desirable wives for decent families.[41]

This growing prestige led parents and guardians to seek placement at Belem for their daughters and young relatives. Though the original constitution had proclaimed that the recogimiento should never become a colegio, it also said that the daughters of the recogidas should be welcomed and well cared for. This turned out to be an impossible distinction to maintain as the number of daughters became so large that significant resources and attention, including changes in the architecture and daily schedule, went to providing for their proper education, effectively creating a colegio within the recogimiento. By 1730, Belem was flooded

---

39   Archbishop Aguiar y Seijas also undertook significant reforms of the female convents in an attempt to make them more austere and strict in their observance. His involvement in women's institutions is striking given his reputation as a notorious misogynist who ordered that no woman ever be allowed in his physical presence.

40   AHCV 13-IV-3, f. 18–87.

41   Muriel, *La sociedad novohispana* II. See Vizcaínas 13-IV-I for the popularity of Belem as a recipient of pious donations.

with requests by parents and guardians willing to pay for young girls to live there, and internal documents sometimes referred to the institution as the "recogimiento y colegio" or "casa y colegio" de San Miguel de Belem.[42] Indeed, by the mid-1730s, maestras were teaching the younger residents reading, writing, and basic arithmetic.

The early popularity of Belem reflects a larger interest in pious society in the reformation of "mujeres perdidas" seen also in the public response to recogimientos designed for repentant prostitutes and other "fallen" women. Prostitution was not illegal in New Spain, but it was regulated. It was only "allowed" in officially designated houses of prostitution, and women who worked there were envisioned collectively as serving a purpose to contain vice and protect the virtue of other, yet unsullied women. Individually, however, these the church and pious society still targeted these women for reform and repentance, and this process was celebrated and somewhat romanticized. Women caught selling sex privately, on the other hand, either on the streets or out of their homes, would be punished – often by being sent to a recogimiento against her will.[43]

Ironically, Belem's popularity increased its prestige, ultimately leading to more exclusivity. A similar process happened in recogimientos for repentant women, some of which became beaterios where only "virtuous" women were welcome.[44] Gradual changes in the descriptions of the residents reflect this shift. Visit records from 1720 describe Belem as a *casa de mujeres virtuosas*, no longer *repentidas* but still not officially required to be virginal doncellas.[45] By the 1724 visit, however, it had become a *casa de doncellas recogidas voluntariamente* in spite of the fact that there were still a great many widows and women with children living there.[46] Though the early documents were vague on the question of race, later documents explicitly assume that Belem began as a place for "lost" and poor españolas. Though it is perhaps unlikely that mestizas and mulatas (and much less "indias" and "negras") would have been openly welcome alongside españolas in a pious cloister of the late seventeenth century, written proof of limpieza de sangre was not a requirement for entrance until the late eighteenth century. The lack of proof had probably allowed some casta women to enter undetected in the early years.

Juan Antonio de Vizarrón y Eguiarreta, who was archbishop from 1734 to 1746, accelerated the transition from recogimiento to colegio by

---

42 Until about 1750, most of the time the language was still just "recogimiento" or "casa," but "colegio" occasionally appears as early as 1720 and becomes increasingly common in the 1730s.

43 Recogimientos aimed at repentant women and those being punished are the subject of the following chapter.

44 The opposite trend was also visible as well, as some recogimientos became increasingly the destination for women sent against their will for reform and correction.

45 AHCV 13-IV-3.　46 "A house of voluntarily cloistered virginal maidens." AHCV 13-IV-I.

establishing an exclusive music school within the walls of Belem. Girls and women who showed particular musical aptitude were selected from among the larger population to participate in the school. This created an elite class within the institution, as Belem's school of music became increasingly well known, convents accepted its students as novices, and Belem music school girls were paid to perform at religious events throughout the city.

By 1750, Belem's focus had shifted so much toward the education of niñas and doncellas that it became known as the Colegio de Niñas de Belem. In a letter to the king in 1760 requesting financial assistance, Archbishop Manuel Rubio y Salinas wrote that only virtuous, legitimate, Spanish doncellas were allowed entrance to Belem, though this was a bit of an exaggeration to encourage the king's support, as married women, divorcees, and widows continued to petition for and gain entrance into Belem in the capacity of depositadas.[47] However, in 1765, "lost women," widows, and married women were officially excluded from this institution that had largely been built with them in mind. Again, this rule was not universally followed in the case of temporary residents staying there as depositadas, but it did mean that Belem had become publicly known as a colegio where only doncellas could be colegialas. This shift only increased under the Archbishop Francisco Antonio de Lorenzana, 1765–1771, whose charitable priorities lay in strengthening institutions that housed and protected orphans and abandoned children. But it was Archbishop Alonso Núñez de Haro y Peralta, 1771–1800, who instituted the most dramatic reforms aimed at transforming Belem into an exclusive colegio for "españolas doncellas virtuosas" by requiring written proof of both legitimacy and limpieza de sangre.[48]

The move from "mujeres recogidas" to "doncellas colegialas" did not mean that only young women could live there, however. On the contrary, the colegialas of Belem spanned a much greater age range than at Caridad. While some arrived as abandoned infants, many arrived in their mid-twenties, and some women spent their entire lives in Belem. Visit records of the eighteenth century regularly list residents in their fifties and sixties, along with a few women of exceptional longevity in their seventies and even eighties.

*Authority and Supervision*

The presence of girls and women of all ages was consistent throughout Belem's history and figured centrally into the architectural design and

---

47  For example: AGN Bienes Nac. V. 976, exp. 10, f. 1–8 shows a married woman seeking and gaining entrance into Belem in 1773.

48  AHAM caja 20L.

residential organization of the institution. Unlike the Colegio de Caridad, residents of Belem did not live in dormitories and eat in communal dining spaces. Rather, groups of girls lived in separate *viviendas* – or dwelling spaces – each under the care and authority of a *nana*, or house mother. Belem was enormous, and like Caridad, its exterior belied its bustling interior, but its size made this contrast even greater than in the smaller colegio. The viviendas constituted a kind of neighborhood – hidden from outside the cloister – adjacent to the central buildings, which included classrooms and common areas, a large chapel, and the usual gated entryway and locutorio. In the early years when recogidas brought their daughters with them, these children did not live with their mothers but rather in a vivienda with other girls roughly their own age. Other viviendas housed the recogidas themselves. Later, when Belem was officially a colegio, this same structure functioned to educate girls in preparation for marriage. Nanas received and distributed supplies and organized meals, cleaning, and other household tasks in each vivienda. Nanas structured the domestic routines of their houses as they saw fit but ideally with the goal of teaching residents how to be good wives and mothers.

The house system added another layer of female authority to Belem not present at Caridad, and one that was far less visible to the external male authorities, but a system of elected female officers did also exist. The primary authority was called a *prepósita* rather than rectora, and her authority was somewhat less extensive than that of her counterpart in Caridad. She was usually a woman in her fifties or sixties. Once Belem had been functioning for long enough, she was also always someone who had lived there for at least fifteen to twenty years. Given the large number of residents (between one and three hundred, usually hovering around two hundred), it took many women to supervise the doors and gates. Eight to twelve women held the positions of portera, while one escucha listened at each of the four gates. In addition to these important positions, there were a host of other elected posts with responsibilities ranging from keeping track of supplies; maintenance of the choir, library, sacristy, and infirmary; ringing the bells; teaching; and serving as nurses. In this system, the prepósita operated more like a managing supervisor than the immediate and personal authority figure represented by the rectora in Caridad. Thus, female authority was more diffuse and multileveled than in Caridad. First and foremost, it was embodied in the domestic setting by the nana and then more broadly through the various officers in their particular areas of responsibility.

If female authority was less centralized in Belem, male authority and that of the church were more direct and physically present. The archbishop usually appointed the officers himself with very little input from the residents, though a few archbishops allowed the residents to nominate candidates. The visits were more invasive than those at Caridad; the archbishop or a representative personally toured all the communal areas in the entire facility. They did not, however, enter the viviendas. In Caridad, visits lasted two days: one to conduct private interviews with the rectora, officers, and all or some of the other residents, and another to gather everyone together to make announcements and read aloud the constitution and all additional rules and regulations. In Belem, visits took much longer and were very extensive. The archbishop or his representative interviewed colegio officials and all of the residents who had been there longer than twelve years, asking questions about every aspect of cloister life and society. They also took the formal testimony of chaplains, doctors, and pharmacists, along with men of prestige from the community in order to gauge the public perception of the cloister. And they gathered up and reviewed lists of entrances and exits, made new lists, and carefully went over financial and other accounting records.

Belem visits resembled those the archbishop undertook in towns and villages, and they highlighted his direct authority in a similar way. When a significant problem arose, the archbishop would send his representative to announce his solution directly to the community rather than delivering it to the prepósita and letting her convey and implement the new policies as she chose. These mechanisms corresponded to the larger and more disperse structure of Belem, but they also conveyed and conferred less trust and responsibility on the prepósita than the rectora of Caridad and on the residents in general as well.

In addition to the archbishop's greater assertion of authority, the chaplains of Belem were more present and visible in Belem than in Caridad, and this changed the dynamics of the internal female world of the cloister. Belem's doors and gates were guarded just like those in Caridad, and the same kinds of rules regulated the residents' communication with the outside world. But chaplains were regularly allowed into the communal areas of Belem, provided they had a "legitimate" reason to be there. The prepósita or another official was supposed to accompany them at all times, but visit records suggest that chaplains frequently broke this rule.

Chaplains lived in their own viviendas, with separate entrances, but were not outside the cloister walls like those of Caridad. A few times in Belem's history, residents of Belem were in fact forced to move into the houses designated for chaplains when their numbers expanded beyond the capacity of the girls' viviendas.[49] In at least one instance, a chaplain lived in his vivienda with an older colegiala, who had raised him as her son before she arrived to Belem.[50] All of this made Belem less of a completely closed

49   AHCV 5-IV-7.    50   Vizcaínas 13-IV-1.

cloister and more like a world apart – one that included men to a certain degree as well as private domestic space alongside the communal. The greater visibility and involvement of the chaplains in colegio life sometimes became a source of concern for residents or the archbishop. Prefectas sometimes complained that the chaplain was meddling in internal government, and as in Caridad, residents complained that chaplains were barring outside confessors. Chaplains themselves complained about the presence of outside confessors, apparently out of the sense that the cloister was their territory and that outside confessors compromised the girls' seclusion in a way that they did not. But meanwhile, residents reported that chaplains were keeping unsupervised company with the girls and women of Belem, sharing food and enjoying music with them.[51] These complaints reflect similar competition and power struggles as those that existed in Caridad between chaplains, outside clergymen, and the female officers, but they also reveal a vibrant community in which clergymen and cloistered laywomen regularly mingled.

The archbishop and his representatives were particularly concerned about ensuring that everyone living in Belem was doing so voluntarily. During visits, in which they interviewed long-term residents, chaplains, doctors, pharmacists, and men of status from the surrounding neighborhoods, they always asked three questions related to this: (1) whether the interviewee thought all the residents were content, (2) whether she or he had heard that anyone had been compelled to be there, and (3) whether she or he had ever heard anyone express a desire to leave. The archbishop wanted to make sure Belem was not being utilized as a place of punishment or being taken advantage of by guardians who were forcing their dependents to be there. Both of these things would have undermined Belem's prestige and its residents' claims to virtue and spiritual status. But in reality, maintaining Belem as a place of voluntary cloister required vigilance. Records from various judicial authorities, like those discussed in the following chapter, reveal that families and other authority figures did send women to Belem involuntarily. And yet residents were generally reticent to discuss this during the visits.

Another area of significant concern was whether residents were leaving for improper reasons – in particular because of a lack of funds. Interviewers asked whether parents and guardians kept up with payments, whether anyone was going hungry, and whether anyone had left because of poverty. Residents did not hesitate to lodge complaints about these things. It appeared that food scarcity was chronic at Belem throughout its history, largely because many guardians shirked their financial obligations or perhaps were unable to fulfill them. Many residents left for this reason;

51  AHAM caja 20L and Vizcaínas 13-V-1.

hunger made them vulnerable to outsiders who sought to use them as domestic servants. The archbishop did not want Belem to be a poorhouse or temporary way station for needy girls, nor did he want outsiders to poach his true doncellas virtuosas and corrupt the quality of their recogimiento. Rather Belem was intended to be a respectable cloister preparing girls and women for marriage or the convent. Clearly the reality did not always match this goal, however.

Taken together, visit records paint a picture of a large, dynamic, and relatively diverse community of (mostly) women. The impression is that in spite of the archbishop's heavy-handed approach to the supervision of his recogimiento, it remained difficult to know with any confidence what was really going on inside it or to control the conditions effectively. Guardians left women to languish without support or removed them against their wishes. Women came and went without taking state. And it was a bit of a mystery how the viviendas ran and what daily rhythms nanas imposed on the girls and women in each residence. In the end, for all of his assertion of power, the archbishop was less able to regulate and protect his daughters than was the archicofradía in charge of Caridad. In Caridad, the direct and immediate authority of the rectora and the level of her integration into the cofradía's own administration of the colegio allowed for this. In Belem, female officers did not enjoy the same trust or autonomy, and in return, they did not seem to exhibit the same loyalty toward the archbishop or willingness to enforce his rules.

## A Divided Community

Throughout 1720s and 1730s, testimonies gathered in the annual visits consistently described the residents of Belem as "no different from other women except that they desired to separate themselves from the dangers of the world."[52] This may have been a rehearsed affirmation of the founder's vision of Belem as a place without elite pretensions, but it still points to the fact Belem functioned as a safety net for women and families seeking refuge "from the dangers of the world."

Throughout the institution's history, large numbers of residents – infants, elderly women, and everyone in between – were there to escape poverty; but economic need was never the only reason women lived at Belem. From its inception, some women chose to be there because of religious aspirations. And from the 1730s on, many families paid for their daughters to live and be educated there as well. Some of them made sacrifices to do so, and many guardians defaulted on their payments. Sometimes residents had guardians who were only obliquely connected to them. A number of rather chilling exit petitions reveal that someone charged with the care of an orphan had placed her in Belem to be raised when she was very young but then pulled her out years later to work as a domestic servant in their home.[53] But wealthy families also placed their daughters there. The combination of reasons girls and women lived in Belem led to a wide range of social, spiritual, and economic status among the residents.

The diversity among Belem residents led to tensions, most notably between those there out of material necessity and those with serious religious pretensions. Because visits only recorded the words of long-term residents of Belem, they are weighted toward the perspective of women who were supported by "la casa," a dependable benefactor, or an obra pía. From their descriptions, a picture emerges of a rich and active devotional culture alongside declension narratives. Chaplains' testimonies do not reveal any significant changes in sacramental practices, consistently reporting that a sizable number of women took communion on a daily basis and participated enthusiastically in a prescribed schedule of spiritual exercises. But many of the women interviewed, particularly those in their late thirties or older, regularly complained about a lack of spiritual discipline in the general population.

From the 1720s through the end of the eighteenth century, the older women almost uniformly bemoaned the fact that things were not like they used to be. According to them, residents did not attend choir or say their prayers as much as they once did. In addition, though they praised the officers for their best efforts, they reported that the younger residents were still out of control; chaos reigned, noise disturbed the peace, and visiting hours and rules were regularly transgressed.[54] The women presenting these complaints seem to have had a genuine desire to live a cloistered life of religious devotion, quiet, and recogimiento and felt nostalgic for a bygone era of stricter seclusion.

The younger women told a different story, however. Because all those women interviewed had lived at Belem for at least twelve years, the women interviewed in their twenties had all grown up in Belem. Many of them also seemed to have serious religious aspirations. A few longed for the more disciplined past their nanas had described to them, but overall, they appeared less dissatisfied than the older women and believed that most everyone was content. One insightful young woman remarked that "although everyone complains, it seems more from the mouth than the heart."[55]

---

53  AHCV 13-IV-3.  54  AHAM caja 20L; AHCV 13-IV-1; AHCV 13-IV-3.
55  "Aunque todas se quejan mas parece de boca q.e de Corazon." AHCV 13-IV-3.

Visits did not record the perspectives of the large number of women who spent less than twelve years in Belem, but these women's experiences are partially reflected in the entrance and exit records. What stands in contrast to Caridad is how many women left for reasons other than to take state and the relative ease with which they did so. This is not to say that women from Belem never found well-placed husbands or received dowries from religious funds or benefactors that allowed them to profess in prestigious convents. But these numbers were fewer than those who left without taking state.[56] Unlike the ceremonial scolding that Caridad's residents received when they left like this, these departures at Belem were relatively minor affairs. The archbishop's office regularly received exit petitions from residents as well as from their guardians. His response always included an in-person interview, in which he "reminded them of the grave dangers posed by the world." If the petitioners persisted, he would inform them that the resident could not return if she left, but this was done in a private audience rather than a ritual expulsion. The implication was that it was just a matter of losing one's spot in an institution that always had trouble providing for the number of women who required its support.

## A Lively Cloister

Though overall, annual visit records offer only a limited view of daily life inside Belem, more hints than usual emerge from the visits of the 1770s and 1780s when Archbishop Alonso Núñez de Haro y Peralta tried to implement royal orders reforming women's cloisters. Rather than recording the words of the residents, these records summarize the problems the archbishop found and the measures needed to remedy them. Nonetheless, glimmers of a vibrant internal society emerge from the archbishop's efforts to regulate it.

Apparently, by these years, within the thick walls of Belem lay a noisy and busy community. Dogs, cats, and chickens ran freely, and neighborhood children entered at will to play with the younger colegialas. Intense friendships developed between the residents, and young girls wrote passionate, furtive, and forbidden letters to one another. Visitors came to the gates at all hours, and the portera could not hope to regulate their conversations. And the daily routine of the hundreds of residents varied greatly from vivienda to vivienda. Some houses brimmed with servants, while others had none. Some residents were disrespectful to colegio officials, and some officials disciplined too harshly. Outside priests came and went liberally, and chaplains regularly interacted with colegialas outside of confession. Yet as a background to this somewhat chaotic picture, these

56   AHCV 13-IV-3.

records also describe a constant rhythm of prayer; children learning to read, write, and play music; and basically well-functioning individual households where all-female families ate, worked, laughed, and played.[57]

The archbishop ordered a great many changes. Animals and outside children were to be banished. Visiting hours should be strictly enforced. Speech and emotional expression should be regulated and *amistades muy estrechas*, or very close friendships, be avoided, particularly between the younger residents.[58] Passing notes should be forbidden. Servants should no longer live in the viviendas. Chaplains should only enter the communal parts of the colegio when absolutely necessary. And daily schedules should be regularized and regulated.[59]

Whether his efforts to change things were ultimately effective or not, there was one way in which the archbishop's reforms did affect Belem's residents. In 1774, Archbishop Núñez de Haro y Peralta, in obedience of a royal reform meant to minimize "distractions" for religious women "on the road to perfection," expelled most of the laywomen living in convents and forbade any others from entering. Not only did this take away one of the options Belem residents had for leaving (that of moving to convents as dependents or servants), but since the archbishop could find no other place to put all of the displaced *niñas*, he was forced to accommodate them in the already crowded Belem. Although he sang the praises of the girls and young women who had been "educated in the cloister with the holy fear of God," the social circumstances of these girls in fact varied widely. They included *criadas* and *niñas expósitas*, or abandoned girls, some of whom were mestizas and other castas. Certainly, their inclusion into Belem undermined the archbishop's attempts to enforce legitimate birth as an entrance requirement, as many of them were of unknown parentage. Thus, though this period and this archbishop's tenure mark the pinnacle of Belem's official move toward exclusivity and respectability on one hand, the expulsion of laywomen from convents ironically led to a partial return to Father Barcia's original vision as Belem was forced to accommodate more than a hundred girls and young women expelled from ten different convents.[60]

---

57  AHAM caja 20L.
58  Male supervisors of cloisters regularly warned against such closeness but did not make explicit the reason for their concern. This is intriguing and highlights the need to study friendship, love, and intimacy among women in colonial Latin America.
59  AHAM caja 20L.
60  AHCV 5-IV-7. For a discussion of these reforms, see Chowning, "Convent Reform"; Asunción Lavrin, "Ecclesiastical Reform of Nunneries in New Spain in the Eighteenth Century," *The Americas* 22, no. 1 (1965): 182–203; N. Salazar de la Garza, *La vida común en los conventos de monjas de la ciudad de Puebla* (Puebla: Biblioteca Angelopolitana, Gobierno del Estado de Puebla, Secretaría de Cultura, 1990); Rosalva Loreto López, "Familias y conventos en Puebla de los Ángeles durante las reformas borbónicas: Los cambios del siglo XVIII," *Anuario del IHES* 5 (1990): 31–50; María Justina Sarabia Viejo, "Controversias sobre la 'vida común' ante la reforma monacal

## Conclusions: Liminality and Diversity

In the end, Belem's history reflects the broader tension in colonial society between an increasingly exclusive notion of female cloister and a competing vision of the church as responsible for "laundering the poor" and rescuing and controlling as many "mujeres desamparadas" as possible. At Belem, stricter entry requirements must have had an impact, but the difficulty of regulating such a large population allowed officially disqualified women to continue to slip through the cracks, even in later years. And ultimately, the entrance of convent niñas in 1774 meant that these requirements had to be relaxed just at the moment when theoretically they were the strictest.[61]

There was a paradox in Belem's ultimate purpose, as well. Though its founder and the archbishops who subsequently administered it hoped Belem would produce both marriageable women and potential nuns, its central function remained in practice the temporary or permanent protection of women without other options. While a substantial core of residents spent decades there, some arriving as infants and staying into old age, large numbers of women also came and went without ever taking state. In some cases, Belem acted as a kind of way station for girls whose distant guardians chose not to raise them but paid for their upkeep until they reached adulthood, when they then had to fend for themselves.

None of this kept Belem from housing a lively community of monastic devotion, however. Though the women who were the most spiritually disciplined may have longed for a different kind of environment, they nonetheless practiced an intensive regimen of daily communion, prayers, and religious exercises. The most devout women of Belem reported a personal routine that was in fact more rigorous than what the colegialas at Caridad generally described. And officially, even the women who came and went were supposed to be virtuous and of pure blood, thus allowing the institution to maintain a quasi-monastic glamour in spite of its relative ambiguousness as a somewhat liminal space of cloister.

---

femenina en México," in *Actas del II Congreso Internacional del Monacato Femenino en el Imperio Español: Monasterios, beaterios, recogimientos y colegios: Homenaje a Josefina Muriel*, ed. Manuel Ramos Medina (Mexico City: Cóndumex, 1995), 583–92; Isabel Arenas Frutos, "Las 'otras': Niñas y criadas ante la reforma conventual femenina en México y Puebla de los Ángeles," in *España y América entre el barroco y la Ilustración* (1722–1804), ed. Jesús Paniagua Pérez (León: Universidad de León, 2005), 191–210; and Nuria Salazar Simarro, "Niñas, viudas, mozas y esclavas en la claúsura monjil," in *La "América abundante" de Sor Juana*, ed. María del Consuelo Maquivar, 161–90 (Mexico City: Instituto Nacional de Antropología e Historia, 1995).

61 This does not mean that Belem did not continue to be seen as a place where young girls could go to receive a respectable and cloistered education. In 1791, Lic. Don. Fernando Francisco Fernandez de Ibarco, a man who served as a lawyer for the Real Audiencia of Guadalajara, petitioned for his "parienta" doña Vicenta Gertrudis Cortes to enter Belem in order to receive "una educación Cristiana, civil, y recogida." AGN Bienes Nac. V. 584, exp. 25.

## Colegio de San Ignacio de Loyola, Vizcaínas

*Domesticity, Religiosity, and Learning*

In the late 1730s, a special group of Belem colegialas took up residence in their own vivienda built by the prestigious Basque confraternity, the Cofradía de Nuestra Señora de Aránzazu. These girls were a part of the community at Belem, but they were fully supported by the cofradía and were destined to be a part of something greater. It turned out, however, that this destiny was not to be fulfilled for more than thirty years, when a different generation of colegialas living in the same special vivienda would be the ones to participate in the long awaited and much anticipated opening of a brand-new colegio.

In the early morning of September 9, 1767, in the center of Mexico City not far from where Belem stood, Archbishop Francisco Antonio de Lorenzana met the members of the Cofradía de Nuestra Señora de Aránzazu to christen their new Colegio de San Ignacio de Loyola. This cloister was intended exclusively for daughters and widows of men whose families heralded from the Basque provinces of Spain. After the archbishop ceremoniously blessed the colegio's buildings and church with holy water, several carriages arrived from Belem carrying twenty-four young women of Basque ancestry who would become the founding colegialas of the third colegio de niñas in Mexico City.

The visual spectacle of cloistered virgins traveling in protected custody to inhabit a new sacred space, sanctifying the town and neighborhoods through which they traveled as well as the ones surrounding the new colegio – together with elevating the reputation and spiritual status of the Basque community – reflects the collective power of cloistered and gathered virtuous women. But it reveals nothing of how these young women themselves experienced the move. Though the founding documents of San Ignacio claim that its colegialas had lived separately from the general population of Belem, it is unlikely that they were truly segregated given the structure and rhythm of Belem. Therefore, this move probably repre-sented for at least some of these women the loss of friendships and perhaps a fear of the unknown. On the other hand, they had also been taught that this was their destiny and that it was a significant one. Some of the young women must have experienced the ceremonial arrival with excitement and anticipation.

When the young women from Belem arrived, the archbishop opened the colegio doors, and the cofradía members ushered them inside, where they joined forty-six others who had been waiting in the portería. Like all of those who came from Belem, sixteen of the forty-six waiting inside were huérfanas endowed by the cofradía. These young women had arrived from the convents of *Limpia Concepción, Jesús María*, and *San Lorenzo* where they had previously been living. The remaining thirty were *pensionistas*, girls whose parents or guardians were going to pay their way. In total, seventy residents joined the cofradía members in the new colegio's church, where they heard the archbishop say mass and then took communion from his hand, presumably having been properly confessed in preparation for this event. Afterward, each of them kissed that same hand, entered their new home, and said goodbye to the men who remained outside – and with them, the world, for the duration of their seclusion. With that, the great convent-like doors were sealed.[62]

The confraternity, named after Our Lady of Aránzazu, the patroness of the Basque provinces of Spain, had been laboring to establish this colegio since 1729, when it established a fund to support two Basque huérfanas already living in Belem. This number grew alongside the efforts to build the colegio, and in 1737, the cofradía brokered a deal with the archbishop to build a special residence for the women it was supporting at Belem. The cofradía paid for the construction, exclusively for the Basque huérfanas it sponsored, but its members agreed to relinquish all claims to the building once these women left for their new home. Over the years, the recipients of the cofradía's support lived in Belem, presumably sharing the communal spaces with other colegialas but always with the understanding that they would eventually leave to populate the new colegio. In 1750, the physical structure of San Ignacio de Loyola had been all but completed, and the members of the cofradía were confident that its opening was imminent. With this in mind, the brotherhood chose additional huérfanas to support at the Basque vivienda in Belem, raising the number to twenty-four, which was more than the house could comfortably accommodate for any length of time. Bureaucratic problems unexpectedly slowed the plans, and some of these women remained in these cramped quarters until the opening of San Ignacio seventeen years later. Nonetheless, there were a great many huérfanas seeking entrance in the future colegio. Over the years, when one of the residents in the special vivienda left to get married or profess as a nun, another would immediately replace her.[63]

The cofradía of Aránzazu formed at the end of the seventeenth century, receiving official approval from the archbishop in 1696; from the beginning, it asserted its independence and autonomy from the church hierarchy in various ways, including establishing itself without seeking the archbishop's approval first.[64] A certain power struggle characterized the

---

62   AHCV 6-IV-10.    63   AHCV 6-IV-10. Muriel, *La sociedad novohispana* II.

64   Muriel, *La sociedad novohispana* II; Elisa Luque Alcaide, "Coyuntura social y cofradía: Cofradías de Aránzazu de Lima y México," in *Cofradías, capellanías, y obras pías en la América Colonial*, ed. Pilar Martínez López-Cano, Gisela Von Wobeser, and Juan Guillermo Muñoz (Mexico City: UNAM, 1998), 91–108.

relationship between the archbishop and the cofradía throughout the eighteenth century, but the brotherhood counterbalanced its independence with a notorious generosity to the church, and as a result the archbishops treated the cofradía with courtesy and respect. Thus, the archbishop's role in the founding of the colegio was purely symbolic, and like the colegio of Caridad, San Ignacio de Loyola was regulated, supervised, and supported by the cofradía that had founded it.

One area in which the cofradía was particularly generous was in supporting huérfanas and widows, and the colegio was meant for both in equal parts. San Ignacio was never called a recogimiento and always had an educational purpose. Nonetheless the founding documents consistently describe it as a place for "viudas honestas y doncellas" whose ancestors came from the Basque provinces of Spain. Avoidance of the term "recogimiento" was probably because of its increasing association with repentant and fallen women by the time San Ignacio was founded. The cofradía also relied on the steady income provided by the pensionistas, and its members saw no conflict in maintaining the multipronged focus of educating Basque girls, cloistering vulnerable Basque maidens, and protecting and supporting Basque widows.

Visit records are far less revealing for San Ignacio than for Belem and Caridad in terms of conflicts over marriage choices and tensions between female officers, residents, maestras, and confessors. It may be that the cofradía guarded the privacy of its colegio with the same fierce independence it expressed in relation to the church hierarchy. Or it may be that San Ignacio de Loyola was indeed very harmonious as a fairly small and homogenous community.

Along with its founding residents, San Ignacio also took its residential style from Belem. The "honest widows" served as the "maestras" or *primeras* to groups of younger women living together in individual viviendas. San Ignacio was considerably smaller than Belem, however, so this residential pattern created an intimate community of female-headed families in which much of the education took place. Unlike the "nanas" of Belem, the women who served as heads of each household were also trained as teachers and led the daily reading and writing lessons in the houses. They received and managed the ten pesos a month assigned for each resident, whether it came from the cofradía or the guardians of the pensionistas, and organized the household maintenance so as to train the residents to be wives and mothers. There were no servants in the houses. In contrast to Caridad, learning to cook and clean was considered an essential part of feminine education. The youngest residents were exempt from this labor and were supposed to devote all of their time to their studies, and the older ones supplemented their household work by attending music lessons and listening to the spiritual "pláticas" delivered by the colegio chaplains. They also spent time in the "sala de labor," where they learned to make handicrafts and the usual objects of beauty.

Residents also maintained a busy schedule of religious instruction and spiritual exercises under the supervision of a rectora as well as the maestras. The members of the cofradía wrote that their primary goal was to shelter and educate Basque women and girls with the aim of creating exemplary wives, mothers, and perhaps nuns who would "make visible" to all the "blessings that divine providence had showered" on the people of their provinces.[65] Concretely, the vivienda system would prepare young women for marriage and motherhood, but the rigorous spiritual education they received would also expose them to the religious life.

A letter from Sor María Rafaela, the *Madre Vicaria* of the Poor Capuchinas Convent of San Felipe de Jesús, suggests that by the end of the eighteenth century, the girls and women of San Ignacio were considered part of the broader community of religious women and honored as such. In 1793, Sor María Rafaela wrote the rectora of San Ignacio directly, without including the cofradía in its communication, to ask her to add something to the spiritual regimen of the women under her authority. Using language full of respect and veneration and addressing the colegialas as *hermanas espirituales*, or spiritual sisters, she explained that the nuns wanted to establish a reciprocal relationship with the women of San Ignacio to pray for the souls of their deceased members. She proposed to immediately inform the rectora when a nun died, at which point the colegialas should perform three days of specific spiritual exercises for the soul of the deceased. In turn, Sor María Rafaela pledged to do the same for any colegialas who passed away. This letter offers strong evidence that in spite of the cofradía's efforts to instill domestic values, San Ignacio was recognized as a monastic community. Its prayers were efficacious enough to be valuable to a convent of nuns. These habited women considered the residents of San Ignacio to be worthy participants in the spiritual economy of female cloister.[66]

### The Paradox of Recogimiento and Education

The history of Colegio de San Ignacio de Loyola reveals a tension between the exclusive vision of Basque patriotism and paternalism and a larger concern with the vulnerability of girls and women in general. The Basque brotherhood was outspoken about its sense of obligation to women in general alongside its desire to nurture and maintain superior calidad in its *own* women. The special residences in Belem contributed to the growth of Belem, a worthy goal from the brotherhood's perspective and one for

65    AHCV 6-IV-10, f. 170.    66    On spiritual economy, see Burns, *Colonial Habits*.

which the archbishop was indebted. The members of the cofradía decided in 1771 to open a second door to the colegio's church because of its growing popularity. And in debating this decision, these men concluded that the colegio was "public, and destined not only for the particular use of the colegialas, but for common use" as well.[67]

However, this commitment to broader society was tested in 1774, when the Archbishop Alonso Núñez de Haro y Peralta unsuccessfully asked the cofradía to house the non-Basque women he had ordered to leave the convents in implementation of royal reforms. The exchange between the archbishop and the cofradía reveals a careful negotiation around the paradox of protecting all women and worrying about the reputations and purity of some.[68] After ordering that laywomen leave the ten convents under his jurisdiction, Archbishop Alonso Núñez de Haro y Peralta faced the serious problem of what to do with the large number of girls and women who now had no place to go. In his letter to the cofradía, he described the terrible possibility that the "abandonment" of so many "niñas" of both "young and medium age" would cause these young women raised in a cloistered environment with the "holy fear of God"[69] to *perderse miserablemente*.[70] To avoid this danger, he told the cofradía that he was prepared to support them all, in spite of his many other charitable expenses.[71] The problem was that he did not have anywhere to put them. He explained that Belem was already nearly at full capacity, which meant it could only accommodate about a third of those who needed it. Under these difficult circumstances, he asked the cofradía to allow the remaining niñas to live in the Colegio de San Ignacio at his expense. His language in the letter was deferential, and he assured the cofradía that he had no intention of these niñas being admitted as colegialas, only that they receive temporary shelter until places could be found for them. At the same time, while they were there, they would be under the complete authority of the rectora and would follow any rules the cofradía imposed on them.[72]

The confraternity's response was careful and courteous but notably without the contrite, submissive tone the archbishop had taken in his. After complementing his person, admiring his pious desire to *recoger mujeres*, and expressing deep concern over the situation he described, the letter then explained in detail the laws and regulations of the colegio, which made it an exclusive place for widows and huérfanas of Basque ancestry.

---

67  AHCV 6-IV-10, f. 192. "La fundación de dicho Real Colegio que es pública y destinada no solo para la utilidad particular de las colegialas, sino para la de el común."

68  AHCV 5-IV-7.    69  *Santo temor de Dios.*    70  "Lose themselves miserably."

71  "Recogerlas a todas, mantenerlas y vestirlas, no obstante que todavía me hallo empeñado, cargado de otras muchas limosnas, no menos urgentes y por consig.te necesitado a contratar nuevas deudas . . ." AHCV 5-IV-7.

72  AHCV 5-IV-7.

It described the difficulties that would befall the colegio if it suddenly admitted such a large number of women "without the precise requirements of quality" that the founders of the colegio had intended for their institution. With all of this in mind, the members of the cofradía told the archbishop that they could regrettably only accept up to seventy of his niñas and then only if they met the requirements of the colegio, effectively barring most if not all of them, who were unlikely to be of Basque descent.[73]

This response seems to have reminded the archbishop that the colegio of San Ignacio was more like the convents from which he had just removed these niñas than it was like his own colegio of Belem. In his next letter, he completely withdrew his request. Quickly backpedalling, he told the cofradía that he had miscalculated and that the number of vulnerable women with no place to go was not as great as he had originally thought. This being the case, he would in fact be able to incorporate them all into the community of Belem. If necessary, he said, he could use the chaplains' houses, and the chaplains could live elsewhere. Alonso Núñez de Haro y Peralta also expressed sympathy with the cofradía's perspective that "grave inconveniences" would result from the mixing of the different calidades of women.[74] However, this must have caused him personal conflict, since he was also attempting to make Belem increasingly exclusive, and he knew that many of the niñas expelled from the convents could not provide the proof of legitimacy and limpieza de sangre that he had so recently instituted as an entrance requirement for Belem.[75]

This cofradía continued to be a supporter of girls' education and uplift, and this vision culminated in 1793 when the cofradía established the *escuelas públicas de niñas* in the bottom floor of its colegio. These "public girls' schools" were meant to serve *niñas de toda clase*, girls of all kinds, who lived in the neighborhoods surrounding San Ignacio, without regard to ethnicity, family background, or reputation. Older colegialas or widows residing in San Ignacio served as teachers in the escuelas públicas. Though initially the confraternity brought in a nun to serve as "prefecta," or principal, for the public schools' teachers, after a couple of years, the members of the cofradía decided that this position should be held by the laywoman who served as the rectora of the Colegio de San Ignacio de Loyola.[76]

In spite of all these connections between the colegio and escuelas públicas, a series of strict rules guarded their separation. The escuelas were day schools, and their students were forbidden to stay overnight. Under no circumstance was a pupil of the public schools to go upstairs, and

73  Ibid.    74  *Graves inconvenientes.*    75  **AHCV** 5-IV-7.
76  **AHCV** 6-IV-10; **AHCV** 14-V-2.

no colegiala other than the teachers and rectora were to ever venture downstairs. The language with which the members of the cofradía wrote about the pupils shows that though they hoped to provide these *hijas de artesanos* basic literacy and mathematics – skills, a series of income-generating crafts, and an extensive religious education, but they did not intend to level social distinctions. "Honor, honesty, and values important to women" were the key elements of the education the public schools provided, according to the school's constitutions, and "if by luck" any of the pupils were interested in the monastic life, this would be a welcome turn of events, but it was not expected.

The students were to appear in their "common and poor outfits, but clean and combed," taking great care that no one dressed above their status, which "would bring results contrary to the purpose of building these schools." The founders issued important warnings to be careful in dealing with social diversity among the students; teachers should recognize those of higher birth, but not in a way that would cause harm to rest of their classmates. They acknowledged that some of the pupils came from "the highest distinction," and they should be treated "with the delicateness appropriate to their birth, but not in a way that can be perceived by those who did not enjoy such fortune but were rather born of humble parents."[77]

The mission of these schools, which the cofradía members lauded as "one of the establishments most noble, most useful, and most pious" not only in the New World "but also in old Spain," was to give the *pobrecitas niñas* what their parents could not "for reasons of their indigence." While these niñas were in school, the maestras, virtuous colegialas that they were, should endeavor to be "true mothers" and pass on not only the fear and love of God but all the virtues appropriate to their sex.[78] The two-leveled colegio, literally segregating higher status from lower status while still attempting to serve both, is a fitting metaphor for how this cofradía increasingly imagined itself within the ideology of recogimiento.

### On the Forefront of Girls' Education

The archbishop's unfulfilled request in 1774 foreshadowed later events of the mid-nineteenth century when the government of Benito Juárez claimed the properties of both Belem and Caridad and all the residents of these two colegios moved to San Ignacio, which was by then known as the *Colegio de las Vizcaínas*. The government attempted to claim the Basque colegio as well, but the cofradía's tradition of independence from the church, along

---

77  *Con la delicadesa que merece su nacimiento pero de un modo que no les sea sencible a las que no tuvieron la fortuna sino de nacer de Padres humildes.* AHCV 6-IV-10.

78  AHCV 6-IV-10.

with the financial resources and skilled lawyers at its disposal, allowed the brotherhood to reconstitute itself as a civil organization and claim its right to administer a private school. In this new environment, the former cofradía abandoned its efforts to provide an exclusive prestigious education for Basque women and girls, choosing instead to open its institutional arms to all the women and girls of Belem and Caridad. Over the course of a few days, the women and girls of Caridad and Belem all moved to Vizcaínas, where they, along with their Basque counterparts, remained enclosed – a dying breed of cloistered laywomen – as the school around them transformed into a secular and eventually coeducational school.[79]

The history of this great transition is outside the bounds of this study, but it is relevant not only because it reflects the interconnected history of these three colegios and by extension other religious institutions in which laywomen lived but also because it highlights the contradictory desires of the members of the cofradía of Aránzazu in their efforts to educate and shelter girls and women. The ultimate decision of the ex-cofradía to surrender its exclusive pretensions in the broader interest of women's recogimiento and education is less surprising in light of the escuelas públicas that had become an essential part of the work of the colegio. By the mid-nineteenth century, the cofradía had in fact been educating women of all ethnic and social backgrounds for more than fifty years. These public schools put the Basque cofradía at the forefront of women's education, as it sought to instill proper feminine virtue in the broader community. As a day school, it was also a shift away from the model of recogimiento as the most effective way to teach these qualities.

## Final Conclusions: A Space Apart

Residents of all three of these institutions were solidly under external supervision, but the gendered and racialized theology of containment that animated them also facilitated internal female spaces that rescued some women from poverty, provided opportunities for education and economic improvement, and allowed those so inclined to pursue a life of devotion in a semimonastic environment. Voluntary cloister allowed women an option outside marriage, the convent, or the vulnerability of dishonorable singleness and in some cases provided a measure of autonomy in their daily lives that was beyond what many women experienced outside their walls. In some institutions, women in positions of power exercised a significant amount of authority, while in others these offices were more

79    The stories of these women's adjustments and their continued but changed relationship with the church are the subject of a new book project in which I will explore changes in women's education in Mexico in relation to race, class, and religion.

circumscribed by the clergymen or lay brotherhoods in charge of them. While founders imagined these institutions as temporary seclusion on the way to marriage or the convent, a significant minority of the residents of these three places chose to make them their permanent home, thus effectively creating an alternate space of female cloister.

These opportunities were highly conditional, however; they were predicated on proper behavior and increasingly limited to "virtuous," legitimately born, and racially pure *españolas*. And once there, in order to enjoy the benefits of recogimiento, residents had to accept, even embrace, its constraints. Of course, many of these women had few other options; chafe as they might against the control and separation from society these institutions imposed, some women probably still enacted obedience because their lives in the cloister were better than what they faced outside.

In all of these institutions, there was a tension between external male religious authority and internal female rule, but how it was expressed differed. The cofradías were less intrusive in their supervision of the internal life of their cloisters than the archbishop, and the women holding office in Caridad and San Ignacio exercised a more extensive authority than did their counterparts at Belem. On the other hand, the cofradía members were much more controlling of and invested in what women did after they left. The lack of this type of control in Belem allowed guardians to retain more power in the lives of the residents, to the point of sometimes pulling them out of Belem against their will. And in both Belem and San Ignacio, the domestic authority of nanas or maestras mitigated the control exercised by prepósita or rectora and, in the case of Belem, also challenged the archbishop's ability to regulate residents' daily routines.

Also at work in all of these institutions were both cooperation and competition between pious society and the institutional church in relation to the regulation and protection of women. In Caridad, the church hierarchy could assert its dominance over the archicofradía when necessary, particularly in the area of regulating marriage. With San Ignacio, on the other hand, the archbishop's authority was more limited because the Basque cofradía that founded this colegio had both jealously guarded its own autonomy as a brotherhood and had nurtured a patron-like relationship with the church through its wealth and generosity. In Belem, the contributions of pious benefactors, cofradías, and obras pías were essential, but they also challenged the archbishop's ability to regulate the comings and goings of his colegialas and recogidas, and, in addition, they fostered economic inequality among the residents.

Caridad, Belem, and San Ignacio were spaces apart that together with convents and other institutions and practices of cloistering constituted a form of patriarchal control outside the authority of fathers and husbands. These three relatively prestigious institutions offered some women some of the advantages of a convent but with more flexibility and possibility for movement. They always stood in relation to those other institutions and practices, however. Convents drew residents of these recogimientos and colegios as novices, dependents, and servants, and for those residents, this meant either upward or downward mobility in terms of spiritual and social status. Marriage consummated founders' vision of creating nun-like wives and delivering residents from a vulnerable girlhood to pious womanhood, though there was always the possibility that they would instead marry below their station or make the lay cloister their permanent home. And the specter of involuntary cloister hovered always nearby. Disobedience and expulsion for women with few other options could quickly lead to a far less appealing kind of cloister.

The following two chapters make clearer the porousness between voluntary and involuntary cloister, along with dependency, servitude, and slavery, in relation to the gendered and racialized theology of containment that gave rise to all of these places and practices of recogimiento. Engaging with all of these "spaces apart" had high stakes for women. They could offer ways out of difficult circumstances as well as opportunities for rich and vibrant daily lives, but they also subjected women to heightened scrutiny, surveillance, and loss of physical freedom. In all of these contexts, women's efforts, interpretations, and negotiations had an impact on the culture of cloister itself and, with it, the shape of colonial Catholicism.

# 5

# Cloister for the Unruly and Unhappy

In September 1642, Gerónima de Dueñas, together with her children, was living with her mother in Mexico City. She had left her husband, Baltasar de Sierra, because she did not want to move with him to the Pueblo of San Jacinto; he had been spending a lot of time there and was planning to relocate for work. Not wanting to be separated from her community and extended family, de Dueñas chose to stay with her mother and her aunts.

Baltasar de Sierra did not like this arrangement; he called on local judicial authority, accusing her of marital abandonment and seeking to have her cloistered against her will until she agreed to come with him to San Jacinto. Using his authority as husband to dictate the terms of his wife's *depósito* (safe "deposit" in either private home or institution), he sought the help of the *Alguacil Mayor* in forcibly relocating de Dueñas to the *Recogimiento de Magdalena*.[1] He told the Alguacil Mayor that if his wife did not want to *hacer vida maridable* with him, then he wanted this judge to send her to this particular *recogimiento* and bar her from speaking to anyone outside it, particularly her mother or aunts.[2] The Alguacil enforced de Sierra's will. The *rectora* of the recogimiento, María Diaz, received de Dueñas and ushered her inside the "second door" of the cloister with strict orders not to let her have contact with anyone from outside.[3] The record does not show whether her children went with her or stayed with de Sierra or his in-laws.

---

1  Alguacil Mayor was an honorific title referring to higher level judges, something akin to a Chief Justice, for a given place or tribunal.

2  Hacer vida maridable, literally "to do or to make married life," generally implied sharing a home and fulfilling the domestic, sexual, and financial obligations of marriage. In this case, it was all of those things. However, in some instances, husbands and wives accused each other of failing to "hacer vida maridable" even when they did share a residence, thus referring only to the other unmet obligations.

3  The "second door" is a reference to the internal door of a cloister that one entered after passing through the locutorio. It was the door that only cloistered residents could pass through and signified the beginning of their formal seclusion.

Over the course of the following year, female and male family members testified on behalf of de Dueñas, challenging the terms of her cloister, accusing her husband of leaving her "hungry and naked" by neglecting to pay for her necessities, and ultimately seeking her release. De Dueñas herself presented petitions as well, including claims that she had fallen ill and needed to live with her mother to get well and requests to leave the cloister so she could work to "support her children." De Sierra also marshalled testimony on his behalf; he denied or made excuses for financial neglect and insisted on the strictness of her enclosure, and witnesses vouched for his commitment to pay for his wife's food and clothing. While de Dueñas seems to have managed some communications with her family and her husband did eventually start paying for her upkeep again, she never succeeded in leaving the cloister to live with her mother or aunts. The petitions by and on behalf of de Dueñas ended on January 26, 1643.

Three months later, on April 27, 1643, de Sierra petitioned for his wife's release. He told the judge that he now requested his wife's freedom because she had communicated her willingness to go with him to San Jacinto and *hacer vida maridable cumpliendo con la obligación de matrimonio.*[4] The judge granted his petition and ordered the rectora to release de Dueñas from the recogimiento. Having successfully asserted his right to control his wife's movements, de Sierra took his wife into his custody and presumably to San Jacinto. Though this turn of events suggests that remaining secluded in Magdalena may have become intolerable for de Dueñas, the fact that she had refused to live with her husband for almost a year and a half, even when it meant being cloistered and having her communication with her mother and relatives monitored and sometimes prohibited, suggests just how strongly she had initially objected to relocating with her husband. For an extended time, at least, de Dueñas preferred the Recogimiento de Magdalena to accepting her husband's authority on this question.[5]

Stories like that of Gerónima de Dueñas and of recogimientos like the one in which she lived for a time differ from those of the previous chapter, but these institutions and situations were part of the same ecology of cloistering practices and places. The Recogimiento de Magdalena and other cloisters like it were different from places like Caridad, San Ignacio de Loyola, and even Belem because the former were either founded as or came to be places of repentance and correction. In these less prestigious institutions, *divorciadas* and women experiencing marital conflict mingled with former prostitutes and women punished for petty or sometimes violent crimes. And yet, like Caridad, Belem, and San Ignacio, these

4    "To do (make or live) married life, fulfilling the obligation of marriage."
5    AGN, B. Nac., V. 235, exp. 19.

cloisters for repentant women and those in need of correction were also manifestations of the gendered and racialized theology of containment that constituted the ideology and practice of recogimiento.

For women like Gerónima de Dueñas, whose cloistering came in relation to their status and obligations as married women, these institutions were only one option among many; married women experiencing conflict or needing protection were also sent, with or without their consent, to more prestigious recogimientos, convents, homes of relatives, and private households licensed as *casas de depósito.*[6] They did so for various reasons: to escape an abusive husband, to seek shelter when their husband left town, to protest a change of residence, or simply because they did not want to live the "married life" with their spouses anymore. Women accused of publicly scandalous or criminal behavior did not generally have these options, on the other hand. For them, their placement in institutional recogimiento was in most cases an alternative only to jail, compulsory service in a hospital, or an asylum for "demented" women.

Gerónima de Dueñas's story illustrates the difficulty of making clear distinctions between voluntary and involuntary cloistering practices and places. Recogimientos like Magdalena housed women who resisted being cloistered as well as those who had sought shelter and protection of their own initiative. In addition, convents and relatively prestigious recogimientos like Belem sometimes served as temporary homes for women who had not chosen to be there. And truthfully, the notion of voluntary cloister, even in places where authorities tried to ensure that residents were there of their own volition, must be understood in the context of the limits on women's autonomy in New Spain in general. Laywomen sought residence in cloisters in response to family pressures, violence, and scarcity of resources, alongside a desire to protect and improve their spiritual status. Therefore, this chapter does not attempt to draw a line between voluntary and involuntary cloister. Rather it explores laywomen's engagement with places and practices of enclosure through a focus on women whose seclusion was the result of marital conflict or because patriarchal authorities thought they needed containment, correction, and repentance.

Like the previous chapter, this one argues that women shaped the practices of cloister through their interpretations of them. This was not always empowering or even necessarily beneficial, however. Some women did manage to protect or improve their personal spiritual status or material circumstances through the available opportunities. But facing the nexus of patriarchal control in the form of husbands and ecclesiastical judges, along with rectoras willing to enforce these men's will, most women ultimately failed, as de Dueñas arguably did, to better their lives in any significant way. And for some women, the constraints of poverty and authorities'

---

6   For more discussion of private casas de depósito, see Penyak, "Safe Harbors."

racialized and sexualized perceptions of their spiritual status meant that there was even less room to use recogimiento to their benefit. But successful resistance was not the only way women participated in and shaped religious culture. Women's engagements with and interpretations of the practices of seclusion and recogimiento affected the reality of those practices, even when the result was not necessarily an improvement. The negotiations themselves can reveal how women came to understand themselves in relation to dominant notions of repentance and protection and illustrate some of how they related to the gendered and racialized theology of containment that shaped so much of their lives.

In their testimonies, choices, and strategies, women articulated their own understandings of recogimiento, marital obligations, and correct feminine behavior. Even in submitting and succumbing to the ideology of female cloister, they had an impact on it. Like the women who chose the unofficial middle path between convent and marriage by remaining indefinitely in the recogimientos of Caridad, San Ignacio, or Belem and in doing so transformed what was intended to be a temporary liminal state into a permanent lifestyle, so did women like Gerónima de Dueñas and others redefine elements of cloistering practices by trying to engage with them on their own terms, even when they were ultimately unsuccessful in their particular aims.

## Corrective and Redemptive Recogimiento

The range of cloistering practices for women in New Spain implied a spectrum of agency and coercion tied to a continuum of perceived virtue and vice among women. The ideology of recogimiento constructed all women as contagious – in either their saintliness or sinfulness. Where women lay on this continuum determined what kind of enclosure was needed to activate and protect their collective sanctifying potential or to contain and prevent their contaminating one. Cloistering good women not only protected their virtue but also concentrated the sanctifying power of their chastity, modesty, and piety, spiritually invigorating the communities that lay immediately outside their enclosure. Cloistering sinful women, on the other hand, stopped the potential spread of scandal and sin, protecting the adjacent society from the dangers of contagion and sometimes making redemption possible. But as the ambiguity of Belem illustrates, there was a slim margin between virtuous and vulnerable and between vulnerable and dangerous; slipping backward could happen easily, whereas climbing forward took great effort. Such downward movement then correlated to an increase in poverty, violence, racialized suspicion, and patriarchal domination, both in the circumstances of women's lives and in the structures and mechanisms of recogimiento they encountered.

The analytical lens of race is essential to keep in mind in relation to the institutions and practices of cloister, and yet the racial and casta identities of the women involved are often unclear. The petitions and complaints related to depósito often do not identify the perceived or actual casta or racial status of the women involved. When it was mentioned, the women were usually identified as nonwhite, suggesting that there was a tendency not to mention racial identity when the women were perceived to be of Spanish descent. However, it would be a mistake to assume that this was always the case, and indeed sometimes it becomes clear that it was not. But given the purported racial exclusivity of places like Caridad, Belem, and San Ignacio de Loyola, it is significant that nonwhite women had access to or were forced to reside in other recogimientos that explicitly served a corrective purpose. In other words, there was a connection between race, class, and lower spiritual status on one hand and the coercive and corrective elements of these institutions on the other.

In addition to the Recogimiento de Santa María de la Magdalena, there were many other institutions that fell into the category of redemptive or corrective recogimientos in New Spain. Some of the most prominent in Mexico City were *Nuestra Señora de la Misericordia*, *Jesús de la Penitencia*, and *Santa María de Egipciaca*. The *Casa de las Recogidas* in Puebla was also well known and frequently utilized, as was the *Casa de Recogidas de Irapuato y Salamanca* in Guanajuato, the *Casa Depósito de Mujeres Perdidas* in Veracruz, the *Recogimiento de Mujeres* (also in Veracruz), the *Casa de Recogimiento* in San Luis Potosí, and the *Casa de Corrección para Mujeres Prostitutas* in Tamaulipas. In addition, there existed recogimientos officially designated for married, divorced, and widowed women, such as *Santa Mónica* of Mexico City.

The extant foundation records of these corrective or redemptive recogimientos are far less complete than the protective ones, namely Caridad, Belem, and San Ignacio. Nonetheless, what has survived does consistently reflect a combined vision of redemptive and protective purpose.[7] Founders and major donors imagined these institutions as places where repentant prostitutes and other sinful women could seek enclosure and regain their honor, where poor women of ambiguous reputation could be taught and protected, and where recalcitrant women would be imprisoned in order to protect society from their corrupting influence and contagion.

This original vision differs from the available documentation that reveals the actual circumstances of women's comings and goings, however. The scattered judicial record of women's presence in these types of cloisters reflects a reality that appears more consistently protective and corrective

---

7　The best treatment of these foundational records remains Josephina Muriel's 1974 *Los recogimientos de mujeres: Respuesta a una problemática social novohispana*.

than redemptive. Ecclesiastical and civil judges who sent women to these recogimientos were motivated by a broadly defined desire to protect society from scandal, but they enacted this desire primarily by upholding the patriarchal power of husbands and policing poor women rather than by actively redeeming "fallen" women. There also seems to be a shared understanding in petitions both by and about women that the practices of depósito and the existence of institutional recogimientos were necessary for the physical and material protection of women unable or unwilling to live with their husbands. However, I have found very few examples of "repentant" women voluntarily entering these institutions in order to leave behind sinful ways. In other words, the founders' stated primary motivations do not seem to reflect women's understandings of these institutions in this regard. Rather, women who approached judges to request entry into these cloisters were most often escaping marital conflict, trying to mitigate a temporary or indefinite lack of male protection, or avoiding accompanying their husbands on an unwanted change of residence.

Some of this might be due to a bias in the sources, however. While wives and daughters appear in the judicial record seeking cloister in these institutions as well as being sent against their will by the men in their lives, this same record rarely shows single, fatherless women seeking entrance into these redemptive/corrective institutions. Single mothers struggling to make ends meet, financially independent women whose public labor compromised their reputations, and widows whose independence might make them suspect in the eyes of neighbors or judges tended to be among the ranks of women cloistered against their will rather than among those voluntarily entering. However, there would be little reason for these women to generate legal documentation by seeking to take advantage of these cloisters' redemptive possibilities. If there was no transfer of guardianship and no mandate from a judge, then the only documentation created would probably have been in the cloisters' own internal records of requests, entrances, and exits. Unlike the largely intact archives of Belem, Caridad, and San Ignacio, lists of residents and their comings and goings have rarely survived for the institutions discussed in this chapter. In other words, it is conceivable that a record of women seeking redemption or a change in lifestyle through voluntary cloister in these kinds of recogimientos has simply been lost to historians.

Absent this evidence, and judging by the extensive record of women seeking out cloister for pragmatic and protective reasons on one hand and being sent there for discipline and correction on the other, there seems to have been a significant disjunction between the founders' original redemptive visions for these cloisters and the reality of women's actual use and experience of them. But even within this representation of reality, the fact that women were not rushing to take advantage of the redemptive vision that founders of rehabilitation recogimientos had in mind does not mean that piety and the theological aspects of recogimiento were not in play for those who sought cloister for other reasons. Protecting their reputations, seeking to live in peace and free of public scandal, submitting to restrictions on their movements, and performing obedience were all part of many women's notions of what it meant to maintain spiritual health and protect their spiritual status. Some women who sought recogimiento may have even imagined themselves as enacting a kind of preemptive repentance as a protective measure.[8] And though some clearly railed against the specific terms of their seclusion that the patriarchs in their lives imposed, they rarely questioned the notion that some form of depósito and recogimiento was morally necessary, as well as logistically practical and maybe even essential for their material survival.

## Depósito and Marriage

Depósito, the practice that led to de Dueñas's involuntary imprisonment, is a clear example of the complexity of cloistering practices. Used as a general term for placing women under official and external supervision, depósito always implied a change of guardianship for women who had been living under the authority of a husband or father, whether it took place in a private home or an institution. Voluntary or not, wives and daughters officially traded one authority for another when they entered depósito.

Marital discord and disruption was the primary reason women sought out depósito. They might be escaping an abusive husband, protecting their reputations when their husbands had left, died, or were traveling for an extended time, or resisting their husband's authority on some matter — often having to do with relocating away from or closer to one of their extended families. Women might request depósito with a relative or in a "home of satisfaction" or an "honest home," usually licensed as an official casa de depósito, where they would be protected and perhaps employed, or they might ask to live in an institutional cloister. Women also petitioned to leave institutional cloisters in favor of depósito in private homes for various reasons: when their husbands defaulted on payment, because they had fallen

---

8   I use the term "preemptive repentance" not to suggest insincerity but rather to acknowledge that women who fell short of ideal virtue were always at risk for punishment or involuntary containment. "Preemptive repentance" therefore could be sincere, strategic, or both, but the phrase is meant to highlight the importance of its public and performative nature that was intended to prevent harsher consequences in the future. Though this practice could have particular meaning for women in this context, it was something men engaged in as well. The function of judicial oversight and punishment in New Spain in general was structured on a penitential model. Thus, preemptive confessions, like the espontanea submitted to the Inquisition, were a recognized way of garnering some amount of mercy.

ill or were being mistreated, or because they simply found a better arrangement. Ecclesiastical judges regularly placed women in temporary depósito – institutional or domestic – while they were awaiting the resolution of betrothal disputes. And depósito was also something domestic, religious, and secular authorities imposed on married and betrothed women against their wills as disciplinary or supposedly protective measures.

Gerónima de Dueñas's case illustrates the possibilities of both self-defined and imposed depósito; de Dueñas and her female relatives struggled to redefine recogimiento and depósito as things that could legitimately happen in de Dueñas's mother's home, where they argued she would live virtuously and chastely but could still provide for her children. When this argument didn't work, they accused de Dueñas's husband of leaving her "hungry and naked," charges he denied. Ultimately, de Dueñas conceded to "hacer vida maridable" with her husband, but by then it was probably clear to her that she could not find a judge that would rule against her husband and allow her to live with her family of origin.

In theory, husbands were expected to provide for wives placed in depósito. This was true whether husbands had petitioned to have their wives cloistered or women had sought a separation and requested depósito themselves. When husbands sought to place their wives in depósito, they often made it clear to judges that they were prepared to pay regularly and promptly for the upkeep of their estranged spouses. This was the case for Bartholome Mendiola, who appeared before the juez provisor in January 1700 to complain that his wife had abandoned him and to ask the judge to present her with an ultimatum; either she return to live with him or be cloistered in the Recogimiento de la Misericordia. If she chose the latter, he assured the judge that he would pay the recogimiento weekly without fail for her upkeep.[9] In some cases, however, men were unable to pay and sought the support of the institutions themselves. Juan Cienfuegos had previously sent his wife, María Josefa Sevilla, to the Recogimiento de la Misericordia, motivated by her excessive drinking, but after a short time, she had returned home promising to abstain. In August 1790, Cienfuegos appeared once again before the juez provisor asking to have her returned, complaining that she had returned to her problematic drinking. This time, though, Cienfuegos informed the judge that he did not have the ability to support her fully while also providing for the family members who were his responsibility. He asked for financial assistance from Misericordia in the amount necessary to pay for her food. Though the judge did order Sevilla sent back to Misericordia, the recogimiento denied her husbands' request for assistance for lack of available funds.[10]

Women who chose to cloister themselves – particularly in order to escape marital abuse – did not always seek out their husbands' support, however. In September 1708, Theresa de Guertas presented a petition before the Provisorato requesting entrance in the Recogimiento de Belem for herself and her daughters. She told the ecclesiastical judge that she had narrowly escaped death at the hands of her abusive and compulsively gambling husband and had no place to go and no money for housing. Though she promised to find a way to provide food for herself and her daughters, she sought the charity of the house for "casa y recogimiento," indicating that she either did not want to or thought it was not feasible to try to press her husband into supporting them.[11]

Even when husbands were expected to provide support, they did not always follow through on this obligation. Married women living in recogimientos frequently complained that their husbands had neglected to pay for their food, clothing, and maintenance. Like Gerónima de Dueñas, these women often used this as justification for requesting a change in their depósito. María Petra Lucía, whose husband had accused her of adultery and successfully petitioned to have her cloistered in the Recogimiento de Magdalena, presented such an argument to the juez provisor of the Archbishopric of Mexico in 1744.[12] Though she denied her husband's accusation of infidelity, the main reason for her petition was his failure to pay her way. She asked the judge to order her husband to pay for food, clothing, and board or to allow her to leave and be placed in a private residence.[13]

In December 1699, María Altimarano had also requested a change in depósito because of her husband's refusal to financially support her institutional cloister. She sought an audience with the treasurer of the cathedral and asked to leave the Recogimiento de Misericordia, where she had been for seven months, and move to a private household. She testified that the juez provisor had sent her to the recogimiento when her husband presented his own complaint – most likely of abandonment – but that she had suffered grave physical abuse at his hands. She claimed to be able to present physical evidence of his violence as well as the testimonies of witnesses. She further reported that she had not asked anything of her husband in the months she had been living at the recogimiento. For these reasons, she asked the cathedral treasurer to aid her in leaving Misericordia and moving to the home of Thomas Xuarez, who was willing to support and house her in return for "providing company for his wife." Altimarano's efforts worked; on December 23, her husband, Salvador Ramirez, removed her

---

11   AGN, C.Reg.Sec., Caja 0947, exp. 3.
12   María Petra Lucía's petition does not state how long she had been in Magdalena.
13   AGN, Mat., Caja 5981, exp. 33.

from the recogimiento and turned her over to Thomas Xuarez. Thomas Xuarez affirmed that he would assume custody and guardianship of Altimarano but explicitly stated that his wife would be the one to ensure that she was properly cloistered.[14]

Gaining the financial support of someone other than one's husband was an alternative to living in an institutional cloister for some women. Sometimes women sought depósito in the household of relatives who were willing to support them or for whom they would perform some work in return for room and board. But in other cases, unrelated men claimed responsibility for women in the form of depósito, most often saying that they would "provide company for" their wives. This was probably a euphemism for domestic service in which the wife would act as the immediate authority, guaranteeing the depositada's proper recogimiento in return for her household labor. It may also have also implied mutual surveillance, however – a way of protecting wives' reputations as well as that of depositadas when husbands were away from home. Husbands generally retained the right to approve or veto their wives' placement before it was complete. Allowing them to live outside an institution – either with relatives or as a cloistered domestic servant in another, unrelated man's household – freed husbands from the obligation to provide financial support, but they did also forfeit a certain amount of their authority over their spouses.

The case of María Manuela Perez Muñoz and Antonio Heres de Medina is a particularly vivid example of this relationship between the financial responsibility and authority of husbands in the practice of depósito. On January 21, 1766, Perez Muñoz asked the provisor to allow her to leave the Recogimiento de Misericordia, where she had been for four months, for a private residence. Perez Muñoz's husband, Heres de Medina, had sent her to the recogimiento but claimed that he did not have any way of paying for her room and board. After some months of living with scarcity, Perez Muñoz had found an alternative arrangement; she wanted to live in the household of a man named Luis Miguel de Luyando, whose wife, Doña Francisca de Berrio, agreed to assume care of her at her own personal financial expense.

The details of what this agreement entailed unfortunately remain a mystery to us, but it was notable for the woman of the household to explicitly promise to take on this financial burden. Perhaps de Berrio and Muñoz had a personal relationship that was not acknowledged in the petition, or perhaps de Berrio was simply taking on Muñoz as servant, using money that was considered her own within the confines of her husband's authority.

14   AGN, Mat., Caja 2086, exp. 35.

Whatever the case, the judge agreed, and Muñoz went to live with Luyando and de Berrio. Muñoz's husband, Antonio Heres de Medina, did not appear to respect the terms of the arrangement, however. On February 18, 1766, María Manuela Perez Muñoz returned to the provisor to complain that her husband continued to bother her at her new residence. She argued that "until he is capable of maintaining me with shelter, clothes, and necessities" and as long as her new mistress was the one supporting her, Heres de Medina should stop attempting to see or communicate with her.

The judge complied and ordered Heres de Medina to stay away from his estranged wife. This ultimate loss of access and authority proved to be intolerable to Antonio Heres de Medina. He appeared before the court on the February 25 saying that he was now capable of providing for his wife in his own home and that he wanted to reunite with her. María Manuela Perez Muñoz objected to this turn of events, apparently preferring her new living arrangements. The following day, she appeared before the judge to assert that because her husband had sent her to Misericordia without just cause and had effectively abandoned her financially, she no longer wanted to live with him. She asked the judge to approve her indefinite separation from her husband and allow her to live with Luyando and de Berrio. The judge did not agree that Heres de Medina's actions justified separation. Instead, he reinstated Heres de Medina's authority and ordered the couple to reunite, "living quietly and peacefully, in obligation of their state [of matrimony]."[15] In other words, if the husband could not financially provide for his wife, he relinquished his marital rights over her person and labor. But if he complied with this obligation and did not behave egregiously in the form of extreme violence or neglect, judges would see him as justified in reclaiming these rights.

In addition to illustrating the tensions and connections between financial dependency, financial obligation, and patriarchal authority, the case of María Manuela Perez Muñoz and Antonio Heres de Medina also raises the possibility of bonds between women that are not visible – and perhaps even purposely hidden from the transactional interactions documented in these petitions. It is possible that Doña Francisca de Berrio and María Manuela Perez Muñoz had a relationship of friendship and affection, or even patronage, that led the former to convince her husband to take the latter into her home and led her to specify that she would do so at her own personal expense. If so, this would further explain Perez Muñoz's desire to stay in her household of depósito. Normally, the relationships implied by the phrase "keeping my wife company" are obscured by the prominence of the men represented as authorities in these petitions; judges, husbands, and heads of other households trade responsibility and guardianship of the women to be

15  AGN, C.Reg.Sec., Caja 5799, exp. 30.

deposited. Nonetheless, it is quite possible that the most important relationships in terms of affective ties as well as day-to-day relations of power may have been those between women.

Most women, if they had the option, sought depósito in the home of a relative rather than arrange to live with people outside their families or in an institutional cloister. Like Gerónima de Dueñas, these women described these living arrangements to judges as valid situations of depósito. However, whether this type of depósito was found acceptable depended on the circumstances of the case. In cases where husbands accused their wives of abandonment, neglecting their obligations, or causing undue conflict and chaos, judges tended to prefer depósito in an institution or in a reputable household under the authority of a nonrelative. Even when husbands and judges approved of placing women with relatives, they continued to scrutinize the situation and worry that the estranged wife's movements and behavior were not reliably monitored and controlled.

In the spring of 1673, Teresa Gomes de Pastrana and Lorenzo Lopez de la Torre, a married couple in Mexico City who had recently separated, had a conflict over the location and terms of Gomes de Pastrana's chosen depósito. Gomes de Pastrana had sought separation and ultimately divorce, and her husband had initially approved her request to live with her mother, Luisa de Soria Sanador. The conditions of this relatively comfortable arrangement were that Gomes de Pastrana was not to ever leave the house except to hear mass or receive the sacraments and, even then, only in the company of her mother. All parties had agreed to these terms "on penalty of excommunication". But on the May 10 and 13, Lopez de la Torre sought an audience with a canon of the Cathedral and Procurador Vicario to complain that his wife had continued to leave the house daily and that her mother was not honoring her obligation to control her daughter's movements. His petitions suggested that he had previously presented his case elsewhere to no avail; he stated that no resolution had been reached in spite of his complaints before other judges. Furthermore, he said that if the situation did not change, he wanted to send his wife to a different depósito, "of his choosing." He indicated that he was in fact already seeking out an alternative arrangement.[16]

A common conflict in such cases was animosity between husband and in-laws. Unlike Lopez de la Torre, Baltasar de Sierra, whose case began this chapter, had disapproved of his wife living with her mother and aunt from the beginning because he saw his in-laws as obstacles to domestic harmony. Like de Sierra, many men complained that their wives' families were "sowing the seeds of discord" and "causing conflicts and fights" or even that they had suffered physical violence, verbal abuse, and public

16    AGN, Mat., Caja 4756, exp. 85.

humiliation at the hands of their in-laws. It was not unusual for aggrieved husbands to ask judges to prohibit wives from communicating with their families of origin, especially their female relatives. And, indeed, it was frequently mothers and sisters who came forward to testify on their daughters' and siblings' behalf, accusing the husband of abuse, neglect, or false testimony.[17]

Conflict about the level of supervision in a private residence depósito sometimes took place even when the deposited wife was living in a casa de depósito with nonrelatives. In 1642, the same year that Gerónima de Dueñas entered the Recogimiento de Magdalena, Nicolas de Bernavides asked a juez provisor in Mexico City to remove his wife, Clara de Miranda, from her current residence, where she was living in depósito in "a reputable household," and place her indefinitely in "the new recogimiento of this town," most likely the Recogimiento de Magdalena.[18] Miranda was seeking a divorce, and though Bernavides had attempted to compel her to "live married life with him," he had eventually accepted that it was not possible. But Bernavides was not comfortable with the current arrangement. He told the judge that he did not want to let her "obtain the maliciousness of living in complete liberty," which he argued she was doing in her too-lenient depósito, in spite of it being in a licensed casa de depósito. Thus, he sought to have her indefinitely cloistered in an institutional setting.[19]

Evidence from cases heard in the Toluca Valley suggests that judges tended to be more supportive of wives who sought their help and protection in situations of abuse and neglect before leaving the company of their husbands.[20] This worked best, however, when the husband was also seen as shirking his obligations to such a degree that he himself faced imprisonment. If a wife sought a separation for reasons like those of Gerónima de Dueñas and others who resisted their husbands' decision to relocate to another town, husbands remained free to exercise their veto power in the location of their wives depósito and the ability to place restrictions on their communication and movement. This was the case in the 1744 conflict between Juan Joseph Baron de Lara and his wife, Ana María Beltran. She did not want to move to the Pueblo of Guautitlan and fiercely resisted his

---

17 See Chapter 2.
18 This was most likely Recogimiento de Santa María de la Magdalena, as I have seen it referred to as the "new recogimiento in this city" in the years 1642 and 1643. Josefina Muriel dated the founding of Magdalena as 1692, and other scholars have cited her. However, I have found multiple instances of women going to a Recogimiento de Magdalena in Mexico City from 1642 onward and other mentions of a new recogimiento in the year 1642. Muriel's source is a brief mention of the founding in a document that I have not been able to find. It is possible that the author of the document mistakenly wrote "92" instead of "42" or that the writing was not legible enough to distinguish a "9" from a "4."
19 AGN Mat., Caja 5928, exp. 30.     20 See Chapter 2.

insistence that she come with him. There is no indication that Beltran attempted to live anywhere else, but her husband claimed that she constantly fought with him about it, "abusing him in word and deed, provoking his ruin."[21] In his petition to the provisor, Baron de Lara said he could no longer tolerate the fighting and her desire to leave his company. He asked that she be placed in the Recogimiento de Misericordia and promised to financially maintain her while she was living there.[22]

Sometimes seeking depósito was clearly a part of women's strategies for navigating domestic conflict and was not intended as a long-term solution. Ecclesiastical Judge Dr. Alejo Antonio Betancourt in Toluca, in 1775, was willing to comply with the wishes of Juana Manuela Morales, an *India tributaria*, that she be deposited in a secure house of good repute and send her husband, Nicolás Guadalupe, to the local jail for abusive treatment. As often happened, however, after her husband was in jail briefly, Morales expressed a desire to reconcile and return home with her husband. Though Morales may have intended only to scare her husband into better treatment, asking the judge to place her in depósito and leaving the choice of location up to him also had the effect of garnering Betancourt's trust and protection.[23] In 1766, Gertrudis Valero y Leyva appeared before the provisor in Mexico City to say that she wanted to reunite with her husband. She stressed that she was living in the Recogimiento de Misericordia of her own accord – that her husband had not sent her nor had any judge – but that she had entered the cloister because of a conflict that she and her husband had not been able to resolve. This was probably particularly important to emphasize in her case because of the specifics of her request: she was asking to leave immediately in order to resolve her differences with her husband with the intention of reuniting with him as soon as possible. However, in the meantime, she wanted to live in an apartment that she had the means to rent. She promised that she would do so "without leaving the house ... as if in depósito" until she and her husband resolved their conflict.[24]

Wherever women ended up, actively and voluntarily seeking depósito did not negate the loss of freedom this cloistering practice implied, nor did it necessarily end husbands' authority over their wives. In 1688, Juana de Medina sought shelter in Belem after fighting with her husband on Christmas Eve. In another version of in-law conflict as well as conflict over a change of residence, Medina's husband, Manuel Antonio de Minaya, wanted them to leave his wife's uncle's house where the couple had been

---

21    "Hazerme malos tratamientos de obras, y palabras infamatorias, provocandome a mi perdición . . .
      que el animo de mi esposa . . . no es otro que el foment de pleito . . . "
22    AGN, Mat., Caja 5981, exp. 33.    23    AHAM, Caja 114, exp. 26.
24    AGN, C.Reg.Sec., Caja 5799, exp. 3.

living, but Medina refused. When Minaya stormed out of the house, Medina physically went to Belem and sought shelter. She was probably only seeking temporary protection from her husband's anger and a way to show her objection to his desire to move out of her extended family's home. But Minaya exerted his authority in a way that radically changed his wife's life. Before being convicted of murder and sent in exile to the Philippines, Minaya made arrangements to prevent Medina from ever leaving Belem or even talking to her mother, in spite of his indefinite absence. In this case, Medina's preemptive efforts to secure protection from her husband through the proper channels did not mitigate her husband's authority. Though she had of her own volition entered Belem, a cloister that was supposed to be exclusively voluntary, she was treated as a woman deserving punishment. Even her husband's own murder trial and punishment did not dissuade the authorities from upholding his right to control his wife's mobility and communication. Medina's increasingly desperate efforts to free herself from this control, which included a failed escape and a suicide attempt, pushed her further down the continuum of virtue and vice. She was not an innocent doncella; rather she was a failed wife whose husband had ordered indefinitely cloistered. And because of her perceived disobedience to this mandate, an ecclesiastical judge eventually sent her to prison, leaving behind even those recogimientos that at least in theory allowed for the possibility of repentance.[25]

Along with complaints that husbands were not paying for their subsistence, another common reason women gave in their petitions to move from recogimientos to private depósito was that of illness. Reports that a recogida had fallen gravely ill while living in an institutional setting and claims that she could not get well inside the cloister are common stories in cases of women placed in recogimientos against their will as well as those of colegialas in voluntary cloisters and even novices in convents.[26] Sometimes it was family members who petitioned to be able to receive the ailing recogida into their care so they could "curarla."[27] Other times, a recogida would be moved to a hospital – either permanently or temporarily, particularly when she did not have family to take responsibility for her.[28] And depending on the kind of illness and the circumstances, moving to a private home could be understood as an indefinite relocation or simply a temporary one from which she would be expected to return as soon as she got well.

In a reversal of this dynamic, family members occasionally petitioned to have women enter recogimientos because they were ill and the said family

---

25  Villa-Flores, *Dangerous Speech*. Taken from AGN, Inq. 677, 6, f. 228–71 and AGN, Inq. 520, 169, f. 267v–68v.
26  AGN, B.Nac., Exp. 19; AGN, Car.Pres., Caja 0861.
27  AGN, Acord., Contenedor 12, V. 29, exp. 8.    28  AGN, Acord., Contenedor 4, V. 7, exp. 5.

members lacked the means to care for or cure them. This was the case in 1683 when José Gonzalez requested entry for his wife, María de Mena, to the Recogimiento de Magdalena. He argued that his wife's mother could not care for her – that in fact María de Mena "hated her mother's presence" – and that he himself could not cure her. His proposition to send her to Magdalena included weekly payments for her sustenance and necessary medicine.[29]

In circumstances like that of María de Mena, presumably the recogida would not be required to do the kind of labor that may have precipitated or at least worsened the illness other recogidas suffered; in contrast, for those women sent involuntarily to recogimientos, this labor was often a factor in their petitions. A mestiza named Gertrudis de Vivero, described as "presa" rather than "recogida," in the Recogimiento de Magdalena, submitted a petition in 1690 to be deposited in an "honorable" house because of serious illness. Though the petition does not say why she was in Magdalena in the first place, since she was described as imprisoned rather than recogida, it is likely that she had been sent by a civil or ecclesiastical judge for a crime rather than having been sent there by her husband or having entered voluntarily. She presented testimony to the fact that she was gravely ill, and though she did not have a particular place in mind, she appealed to the judge to allow her to be placed somewhere at his discretion.[30] Ignacia Balbina Lopez, cloistered in the Casa de Recogidas in Puebla, appealed in 1783 to the Señor Fiscal del Crimen to allow her to serve the remainder of her sentence – which included labor – in a private home because she had fallen ill. When the judge denied her request to leave, she asked instead for a change in the nature of the work she was doing to something less physically demanding.[31] Gregoria Josepha de Roxas, cloistered in Misericordia at the order of the provisor, appeared before him in November 1698 to request a relocation to the home of Antonio de Contreras, who would "guard her depósito and faithfully entrust her to serve in the company of his wife." The reason de Roxas gave was that she had fallen very ill, which she claimed was notorious among the other residents in Misericordia. Her petition suggests that she thought it more possible to get well living as a servant in Contreras' household, under the supervision of his wife, than continuing to reside in Misericordia.[32] And María Foronda, cloistered in Magdalena in 1759 while she waited for her husband to complete the necessary legal actions to complete their divorce, asked the provisor to intervene. She claimed to have become very ill in Magdalena and said that she was unable to get well there; her petition

---

29   AGN C.Reg.Sec., Caja 5827, exp. 57.     30   AGN, Cár.Pres., Caja 0861, exp. 12.
31   AGN, A.May.,V. 8, exp. 86, f. 152.     32   AGN, C.Reg.Sec., Caja 1814, exp. 17.

suggested that she could find another more suitable depósito once the divorce had been approved.[33]

These examples of women seeking to leave recogimientos for private houses because of deprivation, scarcity, or illness should not obscure the fact that not all women resisted institutional cloister. María Francisca Picaso y Medina asked the provisor to imprison her abusive husband and send her to live in the Recogimiento de Misericordia in 1752.[34] Theresa de Guertas sought entrance in Belem for herself and her daughters to escape her husband's abuse.[35] This seems to have been the case even for many of the women who eventually asked to leave recogimientos – either to reunite with their husbands or to seek depósito in private households – as so many marital dispute cases from Toluca illustrate.

However, some women also willingly accepted "recogimiento perpetuo," or permanent cloister, and some even sought it out as their first choice. In 1759, María Nicolasa Morgada sought indefinite enclosure in one of the recogimientos of Mexico City. Her husband, Roque de Castro, had presented a bitter complaint of abandonment to the provisor and delivered an ultimatum to his wife that she either stay with him or go to a recogimiento. Morgada responded by seeking an audience with the same judge and requesting that he sanction their separation and allow her to live in a cloister. In her testimony, she said that she and her husband had spent twenty wonderful years together in which they had "experienced a mutual correspondence, love, and union." However, her husband was spending more and more time in Guanajuato for reasons of work, and though she testified that she knew this was necessary, she could not follow him for health reasons, and she accepted the option of finding a permanent home in a cloister.[36]

A few years earlier, in 1756, Juan Eligio appeared before the provisor to request that his wife, Damiana de los Dolores, be allowed to live indefinitely in a recogimiento. In his petition, he conceded that his spouse had previously requested this but that he had resisted it, even seeking judges' help in forcing her to stay with him. But at this point, he had decided that he "did not want to live in constant war" with her and that if they stayed together it would be nothing but endless conflict and unhappiness. He framed his petition not as a request that she be sent away, however, but rather one of resignation, giving his permission to allow his wife to live in permanent recogimiento.[37]

Without her testimony, it is hard to know whether Damiana de los Dolores was seeking recogimiento because of marital strife or whether she

---

33  AGN, Mat., Caja 5782, exp. 39.    34  AGN, C.Reg.Sec., Caja 0725, exp. 15.
35  AGN, C.Reg.Sec., Caja 0947, exp. 3.    36  AGN Mat., Caja 5782, exp. 41.
37  AGN, Mat., Caja 2384, exp. 30.

was motivated by a desire to live a cloistered life for its own sake. This was not uncommon; women whose children had grown or who were childless sometimes sought permission to live in a cloistered environment and take vows of chastity and obedience. Some of these women expressed that this had been a longstanding desire of theirs but that marrying young and bearing children had kept them from pursuing it.[38] In the case of Ana María de Gansias, perhaps a desire for the conventual life coincided with an abusive marriage. In 1752, she denounced her husband, Juan de Silva, for abuse, but she did so from the Convent of Nuestra Señora de la Concepción, where she had already been living for some time. Perhaps this petition was in response to attempts on the part of her husband to get her to return to their home and marriage.[39] Whatever the case, it is striking that de Gansias is noted as a "reclusa en convento," a laywoman acknowledged as residing indefinitely in a convent, cloistered and protected.[40]

Laywomen living in convents required the approval of an ecclesiastical judge and, officially, both the mother superior or prioress and the clerical leadership of the convent itself. Sometimes laywomen residing in convents were from families that had donated generously to that convent, while other times, a particular nun took responsibility and guardianship for a "depositada." In 1684, the prioress of the Convento de San Bernardo, Gertrudis de San Jose, offered testimony for the Archbishop Francisco de Aguiar y Seijas, giving her blessing and approval for the convent to house Josefa de la Cruz. Cruz had sought shelter with her sister, a nun living in San Bernardo, to escape her husband's physical violence and had officially petitioned the archbishop for license to enter the convent, saying that her life was at risk. The prioress testified that no harm would befall the convent as a result, that she welcomed Josefa de la Cruz, and that she and the depositada's sister would assume full responsibility for her recogimiento.[41]

Female authority and relationships between women were clearly important in institutional settings, but this was true also for depósito in private homes, as some of the stories discussed earlier in this chapter illustrate. Be they mothers, other female relatives, or wives serving as guardians and employers, it seems to have generally been women who acted as the immediate authorities and supervisors of deposited women. This role came through in Lorenzo de la Torre's complaint that his mother-in-law had not been vigilant enough about restraining her daughter's movements[42] and in the way Thomas Xuarez described his own wife

---

38  As was the case for María Anastasia Gonzáles, whose story appears in Chapters 1 and 3.
39  This petition is archived without context or response, and I have not been able to find other materials related to this case.
40  AGN, Temp.Conv., V. 74, exp. 15.    41  AGN, Temp.Conv., Caja 6226, exp. 91.
42  AGN, Mat., Caja 4756, exp. 85.

as María Altimarano's keeper.[43] When María Petra Lucía asked the juez provisor in 1744 to allow her to leave Magdalena because her husband was failing to make payments, she explicitly asked to live in depósito with a woman, Doña Ana Monrior, whom she said had given her a room and food – presumably in return for domestic service, though this is not explicitly stated.[44] And when Doña Maria Manuela Pérez Muñoz moved from Misericordia in 1766 to a private depósito in the house of Luis Miguel de Luyando, she explicitly stated that she would do so "at the expense of his wife, Doña Francisca de Berrio."[45]

## Cloistering Repentant and Disorderly Women

The history of recogimientos for "repentant" women is difficult to trace. The records, as well as the secondary literature, are contradictory – alternately identifying particular institutions as having been established for repentant public women, recalcitrant prostitutes, divorcees seeking to live a chaste life, and women having been sent by angry husbands or other male family members.[46] However, it is clear that at least part of the intention and practice of some recogimientos was related to the idea of repentance, and in fact the term *Casas de Arrepentidas* was used to refer to some recogimientos. The Recogimiento de María Magdalena in Mexico City and María Egipciaca in Puebla were especially associated with repentance and redemption, for instance. Named after two saints known for dramatic conversion away from lives of sin, these two recogimientos were meant to house prostitutes and "public women," among others, who had willingly renounced their wayward ways and may have even come to have religious pretentions.

Some of the residents in these kinds of place may have experienced a religious vocation, but their previous life made it impossible to achieve the status of a beata, except through the path of repentance, reconciliation, and institutional enclosure. These desires are difficult to see in the historical record of entrances and exits. In some of these houses, nuns and pious widows served as the rectora, with the intended effect of improving the character of the recogidas. And occasionally, when husbands or fathers sent women to a recogimiento against their wills, these men cited the hope that the "colegialas" or more virtuous residents would be good influences on her. This is what Mariano Galban did in his request to send his wife, María

---

43   AGN, Mat., Caja 2086, exp. 35.    44   AGN, C.Reg.Sec., Caja 6150, exp. 1.

45   AGN, C. Reg.Sec, Caja 5799, exp. 23.

46   Isabel Juárez Bacerra, "Reformación Femenina en Nueva Galacia: La Casa de Recogidas de Guadalajara," *Revista Historia* 2.0 3, no. 5 (June 2013); Dolores Pérez Baltasar, "Orígenes de los recogimientos de mujeres," *Cuaderno de Historia Moderna y Contemporanea*, 6 (1985): 20.

Josefa Zespedes to Misericordia in 1768 because of the constant fighting he accused her of instigating. The provisor granted this license and echoed Galban's hope that the residents of Misericordia would encourage and teach Zespedes to behave as God commanded.[47]

The majority of petitions I have found, however, show women either being sent to these places against their will or having cloistered themselves in the face of marital conflict. This stands in stark contrast to the petitions and requests for Belem, Caridad, and San Ignacio. Some of this, however, might have to do with the history of the institutions and the way these records were kept. Occasionally, the records of Caridad and San Ignacio mention the population of depositadas, and yet I have found very few petitions or other records that indicate their entrance, suggesting that their presence in these places came about through informal means rather than by court order and that the records for such entrances were not kept by the cloisters themselves in a way that led them to be housed with the other extant documentation. The records of depositadas in Magdalena, Misericordia, and to a certain extent even Belem have generally come to be stored with other criminal and judicial records, which over the course of the nineteenth and twentieth centuries became organized by categories more than by the institutions themselves.[48]

All of this suggests that it is possible that records of unmarried women who voluntarily chose to enter these recogimientos may have gotten lost; if a judge had not sent them against their will – either because of a crime or at the request of a family member – and if they had not required a legal process to approve their separation from their husband and his authority, then perhaps they could have sought entrance in a way that did not leave the same kind of documentation. This is certainly suggested by the evidence of depositadas (as well as servants) in places where they do not show up by name or where I have found no record of official entrances.

In other words, the relative historical visibility of laywomen's active engagement with cloisters may have less to do with the type of institution in question or the reason for depósito in and of itself than with the degree of patriarchal authority present in women's lives. The extent to which a

---

47  AGN, C.Reg.Sec., Caja 6621, exp. 69.

48  The range of collections in which these records appear is instructive. At the National Archives of Mexico, these include Acordada, Ayuntamientos, Arzopispos y Obispos, Bienes Nacionales, Capellanías, Cárceles y Presidios, Civil, Clero Regular y Secular, Colegios, Consolidaciones, Correspondencias de Diversos Autoridades, Criminal, Iglesias, Indios, Jesuitas, Judicial, Matrimonios, Obras Pías, Obras Públicas, Protomedicato, Real Audiencia, Real Cédula, Templos y Conventos, Temporalidades, Tierras, and Tributos. And there is no internal organization in which these types of cases are distinguished from any other. The records for Belem housed at the Vizcainas archives are robust, but they do not include the judicial record of petitions by and about women entering and leaving.

woman lived under the authority and protection of an individual man – be it a husband, a father, another male relative, or even an employer or nonfamilial guardian – probably determined whether or not entering a recogimiento required a formal petition. It is not hard to believe that women without male support or supervision might simply turn up at the door of a cloister or seek an audience with the rectora directly to ask for shelter. And some of these women may have been seeking to leave a life of prostitution or other illicit practices and offered their labor to pay their own way. All of this is to say that single women seeking voluntary cloister for redemptive purposes could very well be dramatically underrepresented in the historical record.

Involuntary cloistering practices were utilized in large part to establish, reestablish, and defend men's domestic authority over women – most often wives but also daughters, as well. Though judges did sometimes send women to cloisters for immodest, unchaste, or sexually scandalous behavior without having been requested to do so by husbands or fathers, the majority of the petitions of this nature that I have found were instigated by husbands. In these instances, the judges were relatively silent, and husbands took on the role of moralizing and arguing for the need to control and contain the scandal that had manifested in their wives' behavior.

As the preceding discussion of depósito shows, men frequently cited abandonment or refusing to "hacer vida maridable" as the justification for involuntary depósito of their wives. This could include everything from resisting an unwanted change of residence, going to live with relatives, disappearing, or simply refusing to comply with the husband's sexual demands. But simple noncompliance with marital obligations was not the only reason why husbands asked judges to cloister their wives. Disorderly behavior in the form of excessive jealousy, constantly instigating arguments and conflict, and even verbal and physical abuse were also reasons men gave in asking judges to cloister their wives. And it is in these kinds of cases that the language of control, scandal, and correction is most obvious.

Francisco Xavier de Aparicio, an español, presented a petition in March 1744 that sounded like an exhausted plea for help. According to him, his wife, María Ana Joaquina de Rueda, was out of control and had been for some time. Constant fighting, verbal and physical abuse, abandoning him with their two small daughters, insisting that she did not want to be with him – these things had been happening for at least the past four or five years. Four years prior, the aggrieved husband had sent Ana Joaquina de Rueda to jail for a time. After she was freed and had apparently returned to the same chaotic behavior, Aparicio had her placed in depósito at the Recogimiento de Misericordia in the hopes that the company of the other "recogidas" would change her. But though she had lived there for two months, she was not grateful when he received her back into his home.

Rather she apparently screamed at him and told him that she had not wanted to return to him and that "to look at him was like looking upon demons." She then went to go live with her sister, leaving him once again with their two daughters.

In language that emphasized both punishment and repentance but also spoke to the specific pain and damage his wife's freedom was causing him, Aparicio proposed yet another solution; he asked the judge to send her to the "Casa de Sallago," a colloquial name for the Hospital del Divino Salvador, for "demented" women.[49] "I pray to the greatness of your excellency to give me the paper I need to turn my wife over (to the hospital)." He explained that as things stood right now, she was free to "go out" (salirse) whenever and with whomever she wanted. Seeing this, Aparicio told the judge, he had been "out of [his] mind." He went on to say that "even if she was with her brothers, or with my brothers, I would not be satisfied. Being unable to tolerate such ingratitude, I ask your greatness, by the blood of God, for the remedy of sending her to the Casa de Sallagos so that, because of this punishment, my wife will finally live as God commanded."[50]

It is striking that while Aparicio began with sending his wife to jail, he then proceeded to place her, first, with "other recogidas" and then later other recogidas deemed to have lost their minds. Each step of this narrative is telling. His initial instinct was to punish her. It was unusual for judges to send women to jail for marital disputes unless adultery was involved, and Aparicio's petition does not suggest that it was. Yet, in this instance, the husband felt that prison was the appropriate response, and the judge supported him. However, Aparicio then came to believe that the reforming possibilities of a recogimiento might be more effective. It is striking that this step came *after* jail and that Aparicio narrates the story as a progression of ever more serious attempts at changing his wife. Then, when María Ana Joaquina de Rueda returned from Misericordia, she claimed that it had never been her will to leave and suggested that while she wanted to live with her sister, she would be willing to go back to the recogimiento rather than stay at home with him. Upon hearing this, Aparicio then decided that a hospital for "demented" women was the only place he would feel satisfied sending her. In making his case to the judge, he did not directly say that his wife was insane, though his description of her behavior seems to have been intended as evidence of this. But whether she was "demented" or not, he referred to her sequestration in the hospital as "punishment" and explicitly said that he hoped that when she experienced the severity of this punishment, she would finally reform and "conform to a correct life."[51]

---

49   It was so named because of its founder, Jose de Sáyago (or Sallago), who first began to shelter women considered insane in his own home. Thus, the hospital literally began as the "Casa de Sáyago."

50   AGN, Mat., Caja 6126, exp. 68.     51   "Por fin reduzca a vida recta."

Aparicio had reason to hope that repeatedly sending his wife to various institutions of imprisonment and cloister might have the effect he desired; the archives contain many examples of women agreeing to their husbands' demands after having been worn down by extended periods of enclosure. This was the case for Magdalena Dominga Rodríguez, who agreed in March 1691 to live with her husband after two years and four months in the Recogimiento de Magdalena. She had previously refused to do so and was in the cloister for that reason. Though the extant documentation does not reveal whether she had chosen to go to Magdalena as an alternative or whether her husband had placed her there, it could have been the case that Rodríguez would have preferred to live with relatives or in a private depósito. Whatever her initial desire was, it is striking both that she changed her mind and became willing to live "married life" with her husband, and that it took more than two years for her to do so.[52]

María Ana Joaquina de Rueda, the unruly wife of Francisco Xavier de Aparicio, did not return from her time in the "Casa de Sallagos" a changed woman – at least not indefinitely. Ten years after his petition to have her sent to the hospital for "demented" women in the hopes that she would finally change, Aparicio came before the juez provisor once again to ask the judge to cloister his wife. This time, he sounded defeated and had given up all hope of reforming his wife. He told the judge that he had been married to Reuda for twenty years and that in that time he had suffered greatly. In particular, he claimed that she had not fulfilled her obligations for the past two years of living together, which was probably a way of saying that the two had not had sexual relations. But the final straw was when his wife began accusing him of having an adulterous relationship with one of her friends and instigating constant fights because of her suspicions. In this 1754 petition, Aparicio requested that she be sent to Misericordia again, presumably indefinitely, so he could "live quietly, in peace." He had resigned himself to being unable to control her while she was with him, and argued that it was necessary for his own spiritual and mental well-being that she be cloistered and kept away from him.[53]

While these petitions most frequently show husbands acting as the primary keepers of their wives' marital and other obligations, ecclesiastical judges did see themselves as guardians of public morality, and this included the obligation to try to reform or punish women engaged in illicit sexual relations. Scholars have convincingly shown that consensual sexual relations outside marriage were far more common than the official prohibitions against them might suggest; in fact, it is probably not an exaggeration to say that they were the norm for most communities. But this fact did not reduce the stigma present when such relations became notorious or

---

52  AGN, Mat., Caja 4994, exp. 13; 1691.  53  AGN, Mat., Caja 5410, exp. 37.

otherwise scandalous, nor did it mean that accusations of such behavior were not still dangerous for the people engaged in them if a vigilant observer decided to alert an authority. Accusations might come from particularly zealous priests, pious laypeople, jealous lovers, would-be suitors, or disapproving relatives. Ecclesiastical court records illustrate the range of these possibilities, and while recogimiento petitions do not tend to be as detailed about the origins of the accusations, they do show judges acting as final arbiters of female morality.

This may have been particularly true in the case of Indigenous women, whom judges of the Provisorato de Indios felt a particular responsibility to supervise. María Teresa, labeled "india" by the notary recording her petition before the Cathedral canon and juez provisor, wanted to leave the Recogimiento de Misericordia and be placed in depósito in a private home. The judge had sent her to Misericordia because she had allegedly had an illicit sexual relationship with a mestizo named Gerónimo de Figuero. María Teresa's language is ambivalent about her innocence or guilt, but she highlights the facts that she was poor, had a child on her own, and had spent a great deal of time in the recogimiento already. Her petition is remarkably free of any language of repentance or living modestly; rather she simply asks to live in a private depósito, citing her suffering as justification. The petition was forwarded to the provisor, but the record ends there.[54]

Even in the case of married women being sent to recogimientos against their will, someone other than their husbands could have been the ones to present the original denunciation that led to a judge's ultimate decision to cloister them. In the case of María Micaela, an anonymous denunciation to the *Alcalde Ordinario* of the Villa de San Miguel led to her placement in the nearby Casa de Recogimiento.[55] Apparently María Micaela had committed adultery in a rather flamboyant way. Her husband, Vicente Silva, had accidentally locked himself out of the house upon leaving, and when he returned home later that day and knocked, she refused to let him in. When he tried to break the locks, he discovered that another man was in his house and was acting "in such possession of the house, as if he was the actual husband." According to the denunciation, María Micaela was also given to drinking and was living openly in "perfect abandonment of her husband." Someone in their community had objected to the scandal and had brought it to the attention of the Provisorato. In

---

54    AGN, Civ., Caja 2349, exp. 48.
55    Though the record does not mention casta categories for anyone involved in this case, most women listed without last names were Indigenous women. The record only mentions the cloister in question as "Casa de Recogimiento."

response, the judge sentenced María Micaela to be cloistered for six years and forbade her to communicate with the man she had been involved with.[56]

## Criminalizing Poor Women

When María Teresa argued for her release from Misericordia, she did not confirm or deny the charges of sexual misconduct originally levied against her, but she clearly stated that she had been sent to the recogimiento "because she was poor."[57] This statement points to a reality of recogimientos that is not immediately obvious from petitions related to marital discord and sexual scandal, and that is the fact that civil judges and authorities often used these religious institutions to police and control the illicit economic activities of poor women, many of them Indigenous. Ecclesiastical judges and male family members, sometimes with the help of secular judges as well, sent women to recogimientos for domestic problems and sexual misconduct, and women sought shelter in them for these reasons. But one particular judicial body also sent women to recogimientos for a range of other kinds of crimes – most notably the making and selling of prohibited liquors but also theft, fencing stolen goods, and selling in general without a license. Occasionally a charge of murder or other kinds of violence shows up in these documents as well, but these crimes usually resulted in jail time rather than cloister at a recogimiento.

The court most active in these types of cases was the *Tribunal de la Acordada*, which was charged with adjudicating cases of prohibited liquor, among other things. Sometimes these kinds of cases show up before other civil judges and authorities, but the Acordada had primary responsibility for them. The women this court sent to recogimientos for selling prohibited liquor were frequently single mothers trying to support children and other family members. Their ages ranged – young teenage mothers to very old widows and single women with children appeared among the accused – and their sentences were often harsh – sometimes as much as six or more years.

Taken together these types of cases seem to reflect an attempt to control and police poor women and cloister them under the same kind of moral rubric as women sent to recogimientos for marital disobedience or sexual misconduct. The language used in these types of cases was distinct from those other situations, however. Judges called women "reas," or criminals, and referred to their time in the recogimiento as the time they were "condemned" to be cloistered – or "serving" sentences. Even the adjectives

56  AGN, Acord., Contenedor 3, V. 4, exp. 8.
57  "Por ser una pobre." AGN, Civ., Caja 2349, exp. 48.

judges used to describe the cloistered women were distinct; they often referred to these women as "presas" rather than "recogidas" – imprisoned rather than cloistered. It was clear that these women were being incarcerated, and the language used in these cases reflected punishment more than redemption.

However, the women in question were *not* being sent to prisons, and they could have been. The choice of a recogimiento was presumably meaningful, even if the judges were rarely explicit about their reasoning. When women served their four-, five-, and six-year sentences for selling prohibited liquor in recogimientos rather than jail, they would have been in the company of women sent there by husbands for disobedient behavior as well as women who had chosen to be there. Theoretically, they would have also been exposed to a convent-like daily rhythm of devotional activities and lived in a convent-like cloistered environment. This was notably different than what they would have encountered at prisons. It is also notable that men accused of the same crimes *were* sent to jails and presidios. In other words, even these civil judges from the Tribunal de la Acordada seemed to believe that women convicted of wrongdoing, no matter the kind, ought to be contained somewhere where redemption was at least a part of the institution's mission.

For poor women, and particularly those of Indigenous and African descent, the differences between recogimientos and jails were mitigated by the fact that their sentences generally included labor demands. There is very little extant documentation describing the internal operations of these corrective and redemptive recogimientos, but women cloistered as punishment for economic crimes often complained of burdensome labor requirements in addition to other problems. This stands in contrast to the petitions that wayward wives generally presented, in which they primarily suffered from a lack of food and proper clothing as well as separation from their families of origin. Together, these petitions suggest that poor and nonwhite women probably provided the bulk of the daily physical labor required for the internal life of these cloisters. Though we do not have explicit descriptions of a hierarchical division of labor, it is most likely that poor, criminally accused women found themselves at the bottom of this ranking, followed by other involuntarily cloistered women. Those who sought recogimiento voluntarily seem to have been spared from much this hard or unpleasant work.

In May 1780, Maria Juliana Pedrosa petitioned the Judge of the Acordada for her early release. She had served two years of a four-year sentence for selling prohibited liquor. She told the judge that she was ill, and she pleaded with him for mercy, calling him someone "whose generous and compassionate heart quickened to protect the poor and *desvalidos*" (helpless, invalid, vulnerable, and disgraced). She said that she "was one of the many who had experienced his kindness," acknowledging that he had shown her mercy in the past. This was her second time being cloistered in the Recogimiento de Egipciaca as a *tepachera* – a maker and seller of the illegal liquor known as *tepache*. The first time was in 1773, and this same judge had allowed her to leave after serving only four months. But in 1777, she was again caught selling tepache and sentenced to four years this time. Her petition was long and flowery, and though she could not write even enough to sign her name, her spoken words were eloquent and elaborate. She focused on the judge's merciful disposition and her own fragility and illness. Her efforts were to no avail, however. The judge recommended to his superiors that Pedrosa serve out her full sentence, noting that his lenience in the past had only led to her returning to her crimes.[58]

In 1781, a nineteen-year-old woman, Josefa Vasquez, petitioned the *fiscal* – the official in charge of public prosecution – to release her mother, who had been convicted of selling tepache and sent to the Recogimiento de Magdalena in Mexico City. She explained that her mother, Tomasa Ciprés, had sold the prohibited drink in order to support her and her two brothers after their father's death had left them all destitute. Josefa Vasquez went on to say that for the past four months, her mother had suffered multiple serious illnesses and injuries as a result of a fall. The doctor of the recogimiento testified that Tomasa Ciprés was indeed in danger of losing her life if she stayed in the cloister. The Juez Provisional de la Acordada granted her release and ordered that Ciprés be transferred to a hospital, where she could receive the medical care she needed.

In 1782, a seventy-year-old widow, an "India" named María Josefa Angulo, asked the *Juez de Bebidas Prohibidas* of the *Acordada* to allow her to serve out the remainder of her sentence in a private home. She had been caught with a "small amount of *pulque*" and sentenced to four years. She had so far spent four months in jail and two months in the Recogimiento of Egipciaca, where she was supposed to remain for the rest of her sentence. She appealed to the judge, emphasizing her advanced age and explaining that she still had to support her children. She told him that having to provide for her children was what led her to sell pulque "for a short amount of time." In her petition, she further claimed that she had not been aware of the penalty of doing so and promised that she would not return to this illicit business if he showed her mercy and let her serve the rest of her sentence in a private depósito. The judge listened to her plea but then disputed her claims of ignorance and her attempts to minimize her crimes, recommending to his superiors that the elderly woman serve her full four years cloistered in the recogimiento.[59]

---

58   AGN, Acord., Contenedor 3, V. 5, exp. 1.     59   AGN, Acord., Contenedor 3, V. 4, exp. 83.

The following year, also in Puebla, in the Recogimiento de la Misericordia of that town, Juana Alcala, requested temporary release because she was suffering from tuberculosis.[60] Alcala had also been convicted of selling prohibited liquor and did not dispute the length or justice of her imprisonment. Rather, she simply expressed that she was gravely ill and promised to serve out the rest of her sentence once she was well; she asked to be released "on bail and for a certain amount of time" in order to be cured. A doctor verified her illness, citing the "excessive work" expected of Alcala in the recogimiento, which he stated was exacerbating her already quite grave illness, and he recommended her immediate release.[61]

In 1791, Josefa Sánchez was convicted of robbery and selling stolen goods and sent to the Casa de Recogimiento of San Luis Potosi. She presented a petition to the judge of the Acordada, saying that her case had not been handled properly and that she had not been able to tell her side of the story. According to Sánchez, she had nothing to do with the robbery, which had been undertaken by her brothers who lived and worked in a different household than she did. She claimed that her brothers had taken advantage of her own position as a domestic servant and had robbed the household where she worked. Her employers presumed that she was involved, and the man of the house had beaten her savagely and then denounced both her and her brothers to the court. Sanchez's brothers were serving ten years in the Presidio, while Sanchéz herself was sent to the cloister. In her petition, she maintained her innocence and sought her own release, separately from her brothers.[62]

## Conclusions: Laywomen & Recogimiento

In September 1783, the Viceroy Don Matias de Galvez ordered the governor of Puebla, Don Gaspar de Portolá, to pay a visit to the Recogimiento de Santa María de Egipciaca to investigate the reasons why so many women had asked to leave because of a lack of food. When he did so, the governor discovered alarming scarcities of the materials for basic needs in Egipciaca; Portolá recommended further investigation into the funds and rents that were intended to pay for the care of the cloistered women. By this time, Egipciaca, along with other recogimientos, were in practice increasingly holding women convicted of crimes – be they sexual or economic in nature. But women escaping bad marriages and those sent by angry, dissatisfied, or jealous husbands and paternalistic judges still made up a part of the population and were still officially the women for whom these institutions

---

60 This recogimiento had the same name as the one in Mexico City. It was common for these institutions to be named similar things in various towns and cities.

61 AGN, Acord., Contenedor 4, V. 7, exp. 5.    62 AGN, Acord., Caja 326, exp. 8.

were built. The governor's reference to funds and rents designated for the upkeep of Egipciaca speaks to the fact that these recogimientos remained the recipients of charity and donations from pious laymen and women as well as from some clergy.[63]

Forming part of the same institutional landscape as the colegios and prestigious recogimientos, places like Magdalena, Misericordia, and Egipciaca served women who fell in a different part of the virtue-to-vice continuum. But like those women served by those schools and more exclusive cloisters as well, these recogidas were seen as needing containment – be it for the protection of themselves or the protection of society from the effect of their behavior. Some women sought this containment as the only available alternative to life circumstances that had become untenable. Other women resisted it or attempted to mitigate aspects of it.

Many women experienced recogimiento through the practice of depósito in a private home rather than an institution. Their stories are part of a larger history of domestic service in Latin America, but they are not only that. Women who went to live under other men's roofs – be it to serve a lonely upper-class wife with whom they may have been in a relationship of mutual chaperonage, to provide labor for a wealthy man of status, or to live as a dependent of extended family members – were all participating in the practice of depósito and the ideology of recogimiento. Like those who lived in institutional cloisters, some did so voluntarily and others did not. Many women seemed to prefer depósito in a private household, even when domestic labor was involved. This may speak to the preference for a relative amount of freedom, or it may reflect the scarcity and otherwise harsh conditions of the less prestigious cloisters. The large numbers of women seeking entrance into Belem would suggest that it was not necessarily the institutional seclusion itself that caused so many women to object to being placed in places like Magdelena, Misericordia, or Egipciaca.

The final part of this institutional landscape and world of cloistering practices for laywomen is the history of the role of servants, slaves, and dependents living in convents. Though this chapter has offered some glimpses into this world, the next chapter will examine more fully how laywomen actually upheld the ideology and practice of cloister for the nuns who were the paragons of female virtue. Nuns' collective virtue was thought to be contagious enough to serve as an evangelizing force for Indigenous Christians in need of models and an inspiration to the colonial society in general. But this would not have been possible without the "other women," who moved between the convents and the outside world, facilitating a more perfect recogimiento for the elite women they served and accompanied.

63   AGN, A.May., V. 8, exp. 1783.

# 6

# In the Convent but Not of It

In 1705, Madre Francisca de Santa Teresa, an ailing nun living in the convent of *Nuestra Señora de la Encarnación* in Mexico City, petitioned Archbishop Juan de Ortega Montañes for permission to buy a slave named María de la Cruz. Her reasoning was different from that of most other such petitions; most nuns emphasized the need for a slave to provide personal service so they could better focus on their demanding spiritual obligations, but Madre Francisca's petition cited both "love" that she felt for the enslaved woman already serving her and María de la Cruz's desire to remain in the convent. Madre Francisca told the archbishop that her brother, Domingo Martínez de Castro, had "lent" her de la Cruz when the little girl was five or six years old and that for the next fourteen years, the nun had "dressed, fed, raised, and cured her of many illnesses" and had "covered her with love." Now at age nineteen or twenty, Martínez de Castro wanted to take her back into his own service. According to Madre Francisca, María de la Cruz had begged her not to let anyone remove her from the convent. Madre Francisca sought permission not only to buy her but also to guarantee that in the event of her own death, ownership of de la Cruz would transfer to the convent without the possibility of a future sale. All parties agreed, and the sale and contract took place that same year.

Five years later, having survived her illness, Madre Francisca presented another petition to the archbishop. She did so along with the abbess and *vicaria* of her convent as well as de la Cruz herself, now a twenty-four or twenty-five-year-old woman. The petition explained that de la Cruz had saved the two hundred pesos necessary to buy her freedom and wished to do so. It further expressed that the convent was willing to accept the payment and relinquish all present and future claims to María de la Cruz's person and labor. It took three more years to process the request, but at twenty-seven or twenty-eight years old, she purchased her freedom, receiving the archbishop's declaration and license that officially ended her status as a slave. The record does not say whether she left the convent or stayed on in the capacity of a hired servant, dependent, or lay sister.[1]

---

1   AHAM caja 24, exp. 32.

The story of Madre Francisca and María de la Cruz bristles with unanswered questions about relations of power and affection between nuns and their servants and the possibilities and limits these convent-bound laywomen lived within. Residing in the individual cell of Madre Francisca since she was five or six, what was the girl's real relationship to her mistress? How did she experience her childhood and adolescence in the convent community? Was there a moment when she transitioned from a quasi-adopted daughter status to that of personal servant, or had she always taken part in the work and social interactions deemed appropriate for domestic slaves of particular ages? How much had she participated in the devotional life of the convent, and what did these spiritual practices mean to her? As a personal servant, what was her relationship to the slaves and servants who pertained to the convent as a whole and slept in their own communal quarters without the possible benefits and added struggles of the one-on-one relationship María had? Had she truly asked to stay in the convent, and if so, why? When faced with the possibility of an uncertain future in the home of a man she barely knew – one who may very well have soon sold her to a stranger – had María chosen to stay with what was at least familiar to her? Or was this simply an argument put forth by Madre Francisca to justify her purchase? And why did the nuns eventually allow María de la Cruz to buy her freedom and leave the convent if she so chose? Was this part of a behind-the-scenes agreement between Madre Francisca and her servant/companion, or had the convent simply come to need two hundred pesos more than Madre Francisca needed the enslaved woman's services? And did María de la Cruz have somewhere to go after claiming her freedom, or did she remain in the convent, as either a paid servant or dependent?

These unanswered questions point to the subjects this chapter will explore; women like María de la Cruz who labored for nuns and convents experienced religious seclusion in ways particular to their status as slaves or servants, but these experiences were also connected to the those of other convent laywomen. Enslaved women, hired or contracted servants, dependents known as *niñas* who were raised and educated in convents, widows, and temporary residents known as *depositadas* who sought shelter or were sent to reside among nuns temporarily together formed a population that outnumbered professed and habited religious women in many convents.[2] In addition, some of these women who wore habits were in fact lay sisters, wearing white rather than black veils.[3]

2   This was not true for reformed convents of nuns known as "discalced," or barefoot, in reference to strict interpretations of the vows of poverty.
3   Lay sisters occupied an intermediary place in convent society. They were more like nuns than other convent laywomen, but they paid a smaller dowry to enter, were excluded from voting in convent elections, and were expected to perform more labor than black-veiled nuns, often placing them alongside convent servants and slaves in their lighter tasks.

Though convents were designed to protect and nurture the spiritual, racial, and economic elite among women, by tradition, they also carried an obligation to educate and protect girls and young women.[4] In addition, by the seventeenth century, most nonreformed convents in New Spain housed large and diverse populations of laywomen who were in fact an essential part of convent life and the opportunities they provided for the exceptional but culturally significant women who professed as nuns. In turn, convents and nuns constituted a primary way that these laywomen experienced the institutional church in their lives; for them the cloister both blurred and highlighted the lines between "secular" and "religious" life and status. Their presence was controversial throughout the colonial period and, in some cases, officially forbidden, though tolerance remained the unspoken rule in many convents. Church authorities became increasingly concerned about the presence of laywomen over time, however. In the second half of the eighteenth century, ecclesiastical and royal reforms attempted to reduce the number of convent servants and expel all other laywomen from convents. Though these reforms had a significant effect, they were never successful in completely doing away with convent laywomen, and by the 1790s, the waves of reform had mostly subsided.[5]

The subject of nuns and convents in colonial Mexico has inspired a rich and sophisticated body of scholarship, in which there has been a deepening interest in the daily life of convent society.[6] As a part of this focus, scholars have recognized the role of convent laywomen, but there have been very few focused studies on them.[7] This is not because of scholarly neglect but

4   For a discussion of these contradictions, see Pilar Gonzalbo Aizpuru, *Las mujeres en la Nueva España: Educación y vida cotidiana* (Mexico City: Colegio de Mexico, Centro de Estudios Históricos, 1987); Nuria Salazar Simarro, "Niñas, viudas, mozas y esclavas en la clausura monjil," in *La "América abundante" de Sor Juana*, ed. María del Consuelo Maquivar (Mexico City: Instituto Nacional de Antropología e Historia, 1995), 161–90. For a discussion of education in convents in general and how it changed in the eighteenth century, see Gonzalbo Aizpuru, "Reffugium Virginum," 429–41.

5   Nuria Salazar Simarro says, "La tolerancia permitió la presencia de niñas y mujeres mayores en los claustros hasta 1774," which is the year that King Charles III ordered the expulsion of laywomen from all convents. Salazar Simarro, "Niñas, viudas, mozas," 169. This order followed earlier ones to expel laywomen from reformed convents. The bishops of Puebla and the archbishop of Mexico also led their own reform campaigns that preceded, followed, and supported the king's orders. Margaret Chowning says, "In time, enforcement of the vida común reform" (of which expelling laywomen was only one part) "began to relax, as had happened with so many previous convent reform efforts; by the early 1780s, there were already signs of diminishing official enthusiasm for the vida común, and by the late 1780s and early 1790s, it was, for all intents and purposes, abandoned." Chowning, *Rebellious Nuns*, 156.

6   Chowning, "Convents and Nuns"; Lavrin, *Brides of Christ*.

7   Nuria Salazar Simarro and Isabel Arenas Frutos have both written article-length treatments of convent laywomen: Salazar Simarro, "Niñas, viudas, mozas" and Arenas Frutos, "Las 'otras,'" 191–210. For a good discussion of convent servants, see Lavrin, *Brides of Christ*, 160–70. Pilar Gonzalbo Aizpuru has contributed significantly to our understanding of schoolgirls in convents

because convent records reveal little about these women beyond their numbers and varying auspices for being there. Sixteenth-century chronicles, the writings of ecclesiastical authorities, and the documents produced by nuns' responses to reformers reveal that the presence of laywomen was important to many nuns' visions of their way of life. A few scholars have employed these sources to discuss the significance of convent laywomen to the cloistered societies they were a part of and to the debates around monastic reform in general.[8]

This chapter builds on this small body of work but seeks to shift the direction of analysis toward the experiences and contributions of convent laywomen themselves. It focuses on the seventeenth and early eighteenth centuries, before the intensification of efforts to implement the *vida común* attempted to do away with individual living quarters and eliminate or reduce the numbers of laywomen residing in convents.[9] Set within the larger context of laywomen engaging with the ideology and practice of *recogimiento*, it understands convents as part of the landscape of female cloister – intimately connected to *colegios*, *beaterios*, and the entire range of recogimientos for laywomen as well as to the practice of *depósito* in private homes. Utilizing ecclesiastical court petitions and testimonies about convent laywomen, the goal here is to understand laywomen's interactions with nuns and convents as a part of the broader history of laywomen's participation in the ideology and practice of recogimiento and in colonial religious culture more generally.

For many laywomen, convents represented an extension of the opportunities and constraints represented by institutional cloisters meant for laywomen, but with even greater distinctions of race, class, and spiritual/social status. Laywomen's positions within convent society mirrored the

through her ongoing work on education, which includes various studies of convents, colegios, and recogimientos as sites of education for girls and young women. In this same vein, several essays in the collection published as a result of the 1995 conference in honor of Josefina Muriel address the subject of education in convents and colegios and the relationship between these and other female cloisters. See Gonzalbo Aizpuru, "Reffugium Virginum," Isabel Arenas Frutos, "Innovaciones educativas en el mundo conventual femenino. Nueva España, siglo XVIII: el Colegio de Niñas de Jesús María," and Carmen Castaneda, "Relaciones entre beaterios, colegios y conventos femeninos en Guadalajara, época colonial," in *Memoria del II Congreso Internacional: El Monacato Femenino en el Imperio Español: Monasterios, beaterios, recogimientos y colegios: Homenaje a Josefina Muriel,* ed. Manuel Ramos Media (Mexico City: Centro de Estudios de Historia de México, Condumex, 1995), 429–41, 443–54, 455–76.

8  Salazar Simarro, "Niñas, viudas, mozas"; Arenas Frutos, "Las 'otras'"; and Sarabia Viejo, "Controversias."

9  For sustained discussions of these reforms and their impact on convents in New Spain, see Lavrin, "Ecclesiastical Reform"; Salazar de Garza, *La vida común*; Loreto López, "Familias y conventos"; Chowning, "Convent Reform"; Sarabia Viejo, "Controversias"; Salazar Simarro, "Niñas, viudas, mozas"; and Arenas Frutos, "Las 'otras'."

complexities of the social hierarchies outside it, and these complexities shaped convent laywomen's experiences of cloister. Exploring these experiences and realities, this chapter argues that by their very presence, laywomen living and working in convents challenged the ideology and practice of female enclosure, even as they facilitated it and participated in it. This paradoxical engagement with the gendered and racialized theology of containment that lay at the heart of the practice of recogimiento shaped the significant role that convents played in colonial religiosity.

Cloistered institutions for laywomen were limited in the number of women they could house, and the most prestigious ones were exclusive in relation to racial, social, and spiritual status. Ironically, then, convents meant for the spiritually elite housed a broader range of women than did lay recogimientos meant for voluntary residents. They also served as a place of employment or enslavement for the same populations of women who made up the – often involuntary – residents of less prestigious recogimientos.

Through the practice of cloistering girls and women as "niñas," convents offered a less exclusive option for a quasi-monastic life than colegios and prestigious recogimientos did for some women. This was true in spite of the fact that convents were officially reserved for the spiritual, racial, and social elite, and lay cloisters were supposedly designed to help less fortunate women. By the seventeenth century, *limpieza de sangre* and legitimate birth were requirements for residence in colegios, and by the mid-seventeenth century, for most voluntary recogimientos as well.[10] This, of course, was true for women seeking to profess in convents as well, but not for those raised, educated, and sheltered as "niñas." For convent servants, a position with no racial requirement, the cloister provided employment, room, and board. On the other hand, the labor in convents could be heavy, hierarchical relations were ever-present and sometimes brutal, and pay and provisions could be minimal.

For enslaved women, working in a convent may or may not have been less onerous than other living and working environments, but the fact of their enslavement and status as property shaped their experiences regardless of other factors. The opening story of María de la Cruz raises the possibility of affection and at least unidirectionally perceived family ties between enslaved women and nuns, but there is also much documentation of nuns' harsh and abusive treatment of enslaved women and servants. And even if María de la Cruz's connection to Madre Francisca de Santa Teresa did include mutual affection, it was still necessary for the enslaved woman to earn, save, and pay 200 pesos in order to be freed of her legal status. Whatever her personal relationship was to her mistress, her official position

---

10    See Muriel, *Los recogimientos de mujeres*; Muriel, *La sociedad novohispana*; and Gonzalbo Aizpuru, "Reffugium Virginum."

as a slave was inescapable. Some nuns performed their piety through acts of "humility" centered on placing enslaved women and servants above them by washing their feet, serving them, and even asking enslaved women to inflict physical punishment upon them. But the efficacy and power of such acts of voluntary debasement were predicated on the hierarchical status the privileged nuns were momentarily relinquishing. The enslaved women who took part in these interactions did not gain spiritual status through them, nor did doing so change their material reality in any reliable way.

Convent laywomen's relationships to church teachings and rituals varied by their social circumstances prior to arriving at the convent as well as by their status as servants, slaves, niñas, or temporary depositadas. Nonetheless, laywomen of all of these categories sometimes took refuge in monastic spirituality, and their devotional practices may have provided some measure of relief from the harsher and more arduous aspects of their daily responsibilities and experiences. Many convent laywomen's devotional lives were active and full. In most convents, all residents – including servants and slaves – were required to confess weekly and expected to take communion afterward. Though labor demands limited their time, enslaved women and servants could theoretically take part in at least some of the scheduled devotional activities. And some women in service positions went beyond these minimal possibilities – making time for prayer and spiritual exercises in spite of their demanding schedules. By sharing aspects of the nuns' spiritual routines, some convent laywomen aspired to, and in a few rare cases, even achieved elements of the lifestyle and respect that cloistered religious women enjoyed.

The presence of servants, slaves, dependents, and other laywomen strengthened nuns' claims to spiritual and social privilege, but it also challenged and troubled the ideal of seclusion that was the basis of that privilege. Racialized relations of power and prestige were an explicit part of religious women's immense spiritual status in colonial society, but as in the world outside the convent, hierarchy did not necessarily imply segregation. By performing labor deemed inappropriate for elite women, convent laywomen provided necessary services that allowed religious women to focus on their devotional lives. But in addition, by offering companionship, entertainment, and news of the outside world, laywomen made the rigors of seclusion more viable for many cloistered nuns. Both in and outside the convent, vertical ties of patronage, obligation, and even affection mingled with horizontally shared experiences. The former complicated the possibility of class- or caste-based identity and solidarity, but these must certainly have at least sometimes been a source of community and survival strategies, even if rarely documented.[11] Alongside the tensions,

11  For a discussion of the ways horizontal and vertical ties intersected in colonial Mexico, see Douglas Cope, *The Limits of Racial Domination: Plebeian Society in Colonial Mexico City, 1660–1720* (Madison, WI: University of Wisconsin Press. 1994).

hierarchical power relations, and potential for status-based solidarity, the relative intimacy and daily contact between laywomen and nuns also presented challenges to the ideals of strict cloister for nuns. As women understood as racially inferior, economically marginal, and possibly sexually impure, the presence of servants, slaves, dependents, and temporary residents challenged the spiritually and socially exclusive vision of convents that religious authorities increasingly sought to uphold.

The material circumstances and experiences of laywomen within convents varied greatly. The type and amount of labor they performed, the extent to which they were excluded from or incorporated into the convent's devotional rhythms and social networks, and the character of their personal relationships with one another and with nuns and novices were all factors that shaped the quality of their devotional and daily lives. For convent laywomen, nuns and convent administrators held a great deal of power. Professed religious women could treat personal slaves and servants with harshness and disregard and could demand submissive deference from all laywomen sharing their personal living quarters. On the other hand, some nuns saw particular laywomen as members of their extended families – a family that was hierarchical in structure but was also a context for intimacy, affection, protection, and favors. As mentioned previously, some nuns even developed pious practices that incorporated social reversals through which to strengthen and demonstrate their own humility. These could be simple acts of charity, such as giving up their food so that their dependents could be better nourished, but also included serving, praising, and grooming their servants in performed imitation of Christ's treatment of sinners. In some instances, nuns even asked slaves and servants to administer physical discipline on them as part of their religious practices, out of the belief that accepting punishment from a social inferior demonstrated a profound depth of Christian humility. Neither such ritualized inversions nor cross-status intimacies and friendships implied an overall criticism of the social hierarchies of colonial society replicated within the convent itself, however. Instead, they simply made these hierarchies more complex and widened the range of experiences possible for laywomen living in convents.

Convents held paradoxical meanings in colonial society as a result of conflicting ideas about which women deserved church protection.[12] On one hand, convents were officially places where the rare "jewels" of society were kept separate from the world so that they could devote themselves to the spiritual service of the community through prayer and devotional acts. On the other hand, in practice, they also provided shelter for abandoned and orphaned girls, widows, and other vulnerable women, along with

---

12    These conflicting ideas are also visible in changes in entrance requirements for colegios and recogimientos.

education for girls whose parents sought it for them.[13] Both of these functions grew out of the ideology of recogimiento for women, and both were part of the unofficial contract convents had with the society that supported them. While nuns needed laywomen in order to complete the rigorous spiritual obligations from which society as a whole was thought to benefit, the convent could also provide avenues through which women formally excluded from religious life could pursue aspects of it. Niñas, though perhaps racially impure, too poor for a dowry, or tainted by illegitimate birth, could nonetheless take informal vows if they proved themselves worthy. This was an option sometimes extended to servants and slaves as well. And even without taking vows, all convent laywomen participated in aspects of the cloistered devotional life convents nurtured.

The contradictions inherent in the purpose and meaning of convents in colonial society added to the controversy that surrounded laywomen's presence. Even before the period of the major monastic reforms, religious authorities frequently strove to limit the number of laywomen residing in convents. Nuns, on the other hand, were divided on the issue: reformed orders, known as *discalced* or "barefoot" orders, observed their vows of poverty and seclusion in a more rigorous way. This meant fewer servants, eating and sleeping in communal arrangements, and less opportunities for laywomen to be a part of the convent community. The nonreformed convents, the *calced* or "shoed" orders, generally maintained the perspective that the presence of large numbers of laywomen was not only acceptable but beneficial. In both types of convents, some nuns insisted that without servants, the devotional rigor expected of them would be impossible and that they also had an obligation to protect the vulnerable women who came seeking their protection. The steady stream of laywomen seeking entrance to convents gave strength to these arguments, even though some members of the more lenient convents disagreed and periodically sought to reform their own communities from within. Neither they nor ecclesiastical

13   The contradiction between the idea that laywomen should not be allowed in convents in order to protect the seclusion of nuns and the idea that convents provided an ideal education for girls was visible even in the founding documents of some convents. Salazar says, referring to the case of the Concepcionistas, "que llegaron a la Nueva España a solicitud de fray Juan de Zumárraga para apoyar la educación de la mujer, pero cuya regal expresamente ordenaba: 'no entren dentro de la claúsura niños ni niñas, por la inquietud que esto trae consigo.' También se aponían a ello las 'Constituciones'." But as she notes, "Las constituciones del arzobispo entraban en contradicción con las de los fundadores, que incluían en el monasterio las funciones de un colegio que llamaron de Nuestra Señora del Rosario." In addition, prelates often took advantage of their position and placed their young relatives in the care of nuns, as happened in the early days of Jesús María, where it was also the case that exceptions were made for a few orphans. Salazar Simarro, "Niñas, viudas, mozas," 163–64. These kinds of exceptions continued and multiplied, and by the seventeenth century, a number of convents had niñados, and it was a regular practice for parents to send daughters to receive an education.

authorities ever managed to completely exclude laywomen from convents in the colonial period, however.

### Niñas, *Legas*, and *Educandas*

Though her request angered her benefactors, when doña Ana Margarita de Casterón y Trigo asked to leave her home in the *Colegio de las Niñas de Nuestra Señora de la Caridad* to live under the protection of Madre Francisca María in the convent of San Bernardo, she was following a path taken by many girls and women in colonial Mexico.[14] Known as niñas, in spite of the fact that some of them were old enough to be grandmothers, large numbers of dependent laywomen lived in convents before royal and ecclesiastical reforms succeeded in reducing this population. For most of the colonial period, convents served as informal orphanages for abandoned girls, permanent shelters for young *mujeres desamparadas*, and schools for girls whose guardians sent them to be educated and perhaps to eventually profess. In fact, convents, together with colegios, provided the primary context for an ongoing feminine education.[15]

Only the most fortunate of the schoolgirls and other niñas could become black-veiled nuns, but professing as white-veiled sisters was a somewhat more accessible option. Sometimes referred to as lay sisters or *legas*, other times simply called *monjas profesas de velo blanco*, these women still had to demonstrate limpieza de sangre and legitimate birth, but they paid a smaller dowry upon profession.[16] They took religious vows, were subject

14    Vizcaínas 9-I-3, f. 120–30.
15    Escuelas de primeras letras did also provide some girls with a basic education, particularly in the late eighteenth century. See Dorothy Tanck de Estrada, *La educación ilustrada, 1786–1836: Educación primaria en la ciudad de México*, fourth edn. (Mexico City: El Colegio de México, Centro de Estudios Históricos, 2005). However, other scholars have found that for most of the colonial period, parents inclined to seek education for their daughters saw convents as the most appropriate environment for doing so because religious training and the instillation of values of recogimiento were thought more important than literacy or other academics per se. Gonzalbo Aizpuru, "Reffugium Virginum" and *Las mujeres en la Nueva España*. For a broader discussion of education among Indigenous communities, see Tanck de Estrada, *Pueblos de indios y educación en el México colonial, 1750–1821* (Mexico City: El Colegio de México, Centro de Estudios Históricos, 1999).
16    There is some confusion in both scholarly work and convent records themselves in the categories of lay sisters and white-veiled nuns. My sense is that not all women referred to as legas were in fact white-veil wearers and that, in some convents, "monjas profesas de velo blanco" actually formed a second tier of nuns while there were other women in the same convent thought of as "lay sisters" or legas. Other scholars have found that the white-veil wearers were the lay sisters in the convents they studied. The confusion comes from the facts that records of various kinds use both the terms "monjas profesas de velo blanco" and "legas de velo blanco" and that there are also references to convent laywomen taking vows but not wearing habits. For a sampling of the variety of usages, see Lavrin, *Brides of Christ*, 35, 52, 116–17, and 122; Salazar, "Niñas, viudas, mozas," 178–80; and Arenas Frutos, "Las 'otras,'" 200, and then compare these discussions and the documents they cite

to the same rules as their more prestigious spiritual sisters, and were expected to participate fully in the devotional life of the convent. They could not vote, however, which meant they had little say in the administration and organization of the convents, and they had more labor requirements than black-veiled nuns, which must have cut into their prayer time. Nonetheless, they were nuns in all but a technical sense and were sometimes called nuns *de segunda clase*, ranking below senior and junior black-veiled nuns.[17] There were probably informal social differentiations among wearers of the white veil as well, since not all of them had originally entered the convent as either niñas or new legas. Some convents allowed certain classes of servants to become legas after a certain number of years of work.[18] That some women would choose the option of living as a white-veiled sister in a convent of nuns rather than opting for a beaterio, where they could live as cloistered religious women without the "second-class" status, may have spoken to the prestige and mystique of convents.[19]

A great many niñas could not profess as either black- or white-veiled sisters, however, even if they could arrange for a dowry, because they could not prove limpieza de sangre and legitimate birth. Unlike the residents in most colegios, convent niñas were not all, or even mostly, *españolas*. In part because there was never official ecclesiastical agreement on the acceptability of admitting niñas into convents, the practice was not externally regulated – at least not effectively so. This allowed the entrance of orphans and poor girls and women with some kind of connections to nuns as well as abandoned infants and children the nuns took pity on.[20] Though this

---

with documents found in AHAM Fondo Cabildo, Sección Hacedúria, Serie Administrador de aniversarios and AHAM Fondo Episcopal, Sección Secretaría arzobispal, Serie Conventos and Serie Visitas. For quick reference to the phrase "monja profesa de velo blanco," see the entry for AHAM caja 10, exp. 41 in Gustavo Watson Marrón et al., eds., *Guía de documentos Novohispanos del Archivo Histórico del Arzobispado de México* (Mexico City: Archivo Histórico de Arzobispado de México, 2002), 245.

17   Arenas Frutos, "Innovaciones," 445.

18   Margaret Chowning found that the convent of la Purísima Concepción had a practice in which donadas, a certain type of servant that will be discussed further on in this chapter, could become white-veiled legas after ten years of service to the convent, thus effectively working for their dowry. Nuria Salazar Simarro has also found evidence of donadas in New Spanish convents taking vows to become lay sisters. Chowning, *Rebellious Nuns,* 185–86, 194; Salazar Simarro, "Niñas, viudas, mozas," 178.

19   It may also speak to the greater risks involved in being a beata. Their relative freedom from male ecclesiastical oversight in comparison with nuns also led to greater suspicion. While beatas were often highly respected pious figures, they also fell afoul of the Inquisition and other ecclesiastical authorities disproportionately more often than nuns did.

20   Pilar Gonzalbo Aizpuru argues that "conventos resultaron mucho más igualitarios que los colegios, ya que en ellos entraban seglares indias, mulatas, mestizas y españolas y la diferencia en el trato dado a niñas y criadas dependía tan solo de las circunstancias en las que hubieran ingresado, de los lazos de amistad o parentesco con las religiosas y del talente de las monjas, ya que

made convents less exclusive places for laywomen and girls seeking shelter and education, this openness did not translate into a facility to profess for *mestizas* or other *castas* or even españolas whose parents were not married.[21] Nonetheless, there was never a shortage of girls and young women who arrived as niñas and remained indefinitely without ever taking formal religious vows.

Some convents were founded with the purpose of educating girls in mind. Among these, some established a separate school attached to the convent that boarded and taught a small number of *educandas*, or schoolgirls, usually between the ages of six and eleven.[22] Many of these "teaching convents" were among those that practiced a communal way of life and had a strict interpretation of cloister. In these contexts, the schoolgirls' instruction was the responsibility of one or more nuns on a rotating basis. The educandas' living quarters were ideally separate from the main body of the convent in order to limit contact with nuns who slept in communal dormitories and ate in dining halls. In practice, however, this type of separation was difficult to maintain because so many niñas were related to nuns in the convent, having accompanied their sisters, cousins, or even young aunts as they entered as novices. Some of these niñas therefore ended up boarding with their relatives and participating in convent activities to the extent that they could.

Once their school years were over, educandas were supposed to choose whether they wanted to get married or – if they were eligible – stay and profess. In practice, however, many stayed on under the designation of niñas, perhaps postponing the "decision" indefinitely until it was considered too late to find a husband.[23] Indeed, some educandas had nowhere to go, having entered the convent as orphans or abandoned children, and for those who had arrived with a particular nun when they were very young, the convent was the life they knew. Official ecclesiastical regulations and law frowned upon the presence of children considered too young for instruction, but in practice, young

---

nunca existío reglamento o normas reguladoras del trato que recibirían educandas y criadas." Gonzalbo Aizpuru, "Reffugium Virginum."

21   Money and powerful connections might buy "proof" of legitimate birth, as it did for the famous Sor Juana Inés de la Cruz, but most niñas lacked both of these. For some examples, besides Sor Juana, see Lavrin, *Brides of Christ*, 22.

22   For instance, Nuestra Señora del Rosario and La Purísima. On the school in La Purísima, the ideal and difficulty of keeping the girls separate from the nuns, and the family relations between many of the educandas and religiosas, see Chowning, *Rebellious Nuns*, 160. Pilar Gonzalbo Aizpuru says that even in these separate convent schools, there was not usually a fixed schedule of classes. This could also have allowed more flexibility in terms of niñas participation in convent life. Gonzalbo Aizpuru, "Reffugium Virginum."

23   Lavrin, *Brides of Christ*, 23; Salazar Simarro, "Niñas, viudas, mozas," 166.

children did join the convent community before they were old enough to attend classes.[24]

Convents without separate schools attached to them still participated in the education of young girls in New Spain. Pilar Gonzalbo Aizpuru has found that prior to the late eighteenth century, large numbers of parents felt that living among nuns was the best way for their daughters to learn the values and qualities considered most important for women.[25] Some institutions did so in faithfulness to the original mission of their founders, while in others, the presence of educandas was in apparent contradiction to constitutional stipulations that children and other "seculars" be prohibited from living in the convent. Where no convent schools existed, instruction happened in a less formal way, with individual nuns taking responsibility for the education of the niñas they were also in effect raising. Like residents in colegios, girls in convents learned the skills thought necessary to make them good wives or nuns: basic reading and writing together with music, embroidery, making artificial flowers, and other fine crafts were interwoven into an education in Christian doctrine and practice.

The convents with the largest number of niñas actually living among the nuns were those that practiced the *vida particular* rather than the vida común.[26] In these convents, nuns who had the resources to do so owned individual living quarters of differing size and layout and furnished them to varying degrees of austerity or luxury, depending on their tastes, convictions, and family wealth. They shared these "cells" with niñas and personal servants and sometimes less wealthy nuns. Some of these households

---

24  Salazar talks about a contradiction in the regulations related to very young children. The III Mexican Provincial Council of 1585 said that under no circumstances should young children be allowed in convents or monasteries, but later their admittance became commonplace. She notes that in 1708, Andrés de Borda wrote a compendium of monastic "norms of conduct" for convents of nuns, in which he said that children under the age of seven were allowed to come and go because their age was "before the use of reason," and therefore they would not incite the nuns to sin. Salazar Simarro, "Niñas, viudas, mozas," 166–67.

25  Gonzalbo Aizpuru, "Reffugium Virginum." Gonzalbo Aizpuru notes that what was most important to parents seeking education for their daughters was not systematic instruction in literacy, math, or music, though those subjects were generally taught in one form or another. Rather, learning the values of prayer, quiet, obedience, and seclusion was considered most vital. It was these priorities that made an education in a monastic environment so appealing and created the large demand for space in the convent for schoolgirls. Also see Gonzalbo Aizpuru, *Las mujeres en la Nueva España*.

26  For example, Margaret Chowning found that even in the late 1780s, after reformers had begun expelling niñas from convents in dioceses of Mexico and Puebla, a census of the convent of Nuestra Señora de Salud in Pátzcuaro, Michoacán, "indicated that 184 girls and women lived in the collection of houses and patios that comprised the convent, but only 30 of them were nuns: There were 51 'niñas' (14 of whom were at least 40 years old and 5 of whom were over 60), 24 other laywomen living temporarily in the convent for a variety of reasons (though mainly to provide service to the nuns), and 79 servants, including 1 slave." Chowning, *Rebellious Nuns*, 160–61.

consisted of just a few people, while others resembled large extended families, with dependents, servants, and slaves living in two-story apartments with multiple rooms.[27] In some of these arrangements, two religious women shared household tasks, including the responsibility of educating the niñas in their charge.

Though late eighteenth-century reformers attempted to make the vida común mandatory in all Mexican convents, they were never in fact able to completely do away with the vida particular as a way of life. In the 1770s and 1780s, many niñas were indeed expelled, and others moved to their own dormitories in convent schools, but by the 1790s, enforcement of these new regulations had been relaxed, and some niñas managed to outlast the first waves of reform. Nuns and niñas alike resisted these dramatic changes as they were imposed, and the intimacies and family ties they had developed are visible in the language of their passionate objections.[28] Using terms like *hija de corazón* and *nanita de mi vida* in both complaints and correspondence, the nuns expressed love and affection for the niñas they had cared for.[29] As this language suggests, nuns often treated these girls as their adopted children, and nuns bathed, dressed, fed, and nursed their beloved young niñas.[30] Critics of the girls' presence argued that fixing niñas' hair and adorning them with beautiful clothes and jewelry, decorating their rooms, and finding ways to purchase gifts for them were all too common distractions for nuns who should be focusing on their prayers.[31] When niñas got into trouble or were threatened, their guardians were known to "fight with all of their strength" on their behalf.[32]

This was not always the case, however. The distinction between servant and niña was sometimes less than clear, and some niñas occupied a more ambivalent place in a nun's household. Convent records list some niñas as entering convents with a nun "to keep her company," a phrase that usually implied domestic service obligations, while others who arrived as educandas attached themselves to a particular nun in relationships of both dependency and service.[33] In both kinds of situations, these girls were sometimes called niñas and other times, *criadas*. Criada could refer to someone raised or cared for (from the verb *criar*) by an individual or family, but the term usually implied a service obligation as well. Convent inventories tend to

---

27  For descriptions, examples, and discussion of living quarters, see Lavrin, *Brides of Christ*, 173–75 and Salazar Simarro, "Niñas, viudas, mozas," 187.

28  Arenas Frutos, "Las 'otras'"; Lavrin, *Brides of Christ*, 282–83.

29  Isabel Arenas Frutos, *Dos arzobispos de México: Lorenzana y Nuñez de Haro, ante la reforma conventual femenina (1766–1775)* (León: Universidad de León, 2004), appendix 9. Also cited in Arenas Frutos, "Las 'otras,'" 197.

30  See Arenas Frutos, "Las 'otras,'" 194.

31  Salazar Simarro, "Niñas, viudas, mozas,"163–67; Gonzalbo Aizpuru, *Las mujeres en la Nueva España*.

32  Arenas Frutos, "Las 'otras.'"    33  Gonzalbo Aizpuru, *Las mujeres en la Nueva España*.

make a distinction between criada and *moza*, the general term for servant, but also between criada and niña. They sometimes counted criadas in both the number of niñas living in the convent as well as the number of servants. In fact, when necessary, the term "criada" could serve as a flexible middle ground between the two; if reformers were looking to reduce the number of niñas, a girl or woman "accompanying" a nun could conveniently become a criada, but if the concern was the number of servants, a criada, unlike a moza, could easily be called a niña in census records.[34]

The informal hierarchies through which niñas of these varying circumstances experienced the dynamics of convent life remain opaque, and yet they must have shaped their daily lives in many ways. A woman from a wealthy family placed in the convent as a child to be raised by her doting aunt who was a nun occupied a different place in the convent community than a niña abandoned in the convent doorway as an infant or sent by poor relatives to be educated, who then stayed on in return for work. Each convent developed its own society, however, and though all of them tended to reflect the hierarchies of colonial society, exceptional situations could also develop behind their protective walls. Some of the niñas whom nuns regarded as surrogate daughters, true confidants, and companions may have originally been *abandonadas* who then grew up to find favor in the eyes of a particular nun, or they could have been poor huérfanas who started out as humble members of a nun's household but then grew in their mistresses' affections until they were the center of the nuns' attention.

Nonetheless, the material conditions of niñas within convents often depended on their social connections outside them. Wealthy patrons sometimes placed niñas in convents to be raised by or to "accompany" a favored nun and, in doing so, committed to providing money to the convent for their upkeep.[35] This meant more food, clothes, even jewelry, and perhaps a few toys for some niñas while others had to rely on the generosity of the nuns in whose care they found themselves. When doña Ana Margarita de Casterón y Trigo went to live with Madre Francisca María, she gave up the dowry she would have received from the cofradía that supported her as a *colegiala* of the colegio of Caridad because she was not entering as a novice. Presumably, Madre Francisca María planned to support young Margarita, perhaps in return for some

---

34 This is visible particularly in the expulsion records but also visita records. For example, see records discussed in Arenas Frutos, "Las 'otras,'" 203–4, and "Innovaciones educativas," 445–46. See also Gonzalbo Aizpuru, "Reffugium Virginum," 435, for a discussion of the blurring of the lines between various categories of convent laywomen.

35 Salazar Simarro, "Niñas, viudas, mozas," 163–64.

labor.[36] More privileged niñas, with individual patrons, may have also had an easier time becoming nuns if that turned out to be their choice.[37]

Whatever their relationships with nuns or their positions in convent households, niñas participated in the daily rhythm of devotional practices. They attended mass, participated in at least some of the collective prayers and singing, observed holy days, and completed the required amount of confession and communion. Some of those who shared living quarters with black- or white-veiled nuns also rose before dawn in imitation of their guardians to practice the mental prayer and rigorous spiritual acts of the professed religious women. Nuns acted as mentors in religious life, teaching niñas Christian doctrine, leading them in their devotions, and hoping to inspire spiritual dedication and discipline.[38]

Niñas were not formally expected to sustain the same level of rigor in their spiritual exercises as were novices, but given their experiences and exposure to the cloister, it is not surprising that some of them developed religious vocations and craved formal acceptance and fuller involvement in the spiritual life of the convent. Nuns and parents alike celebrated the possibility that girls educated in convents might grow up to become nuns, in spite of the fact that many such girls lacked the necessary dowries, proof of racial purity, and legitimate birth to attain even white-veiled status.[39] And, of course, some did choose the path of the novitiate, during which they were to be harshly tested and challenged as a part of their initiation into a different status in the community.[40]

Of course, former colegialas and residents of beaterios and some respected recogimientos frequently entered convents as novices rather than niñas, having received a dowry from their former institution or a wealthy patron, or as a huérfana chosen to benefit from a particular *obra pía*. Unlike the choice Ana Casterón y Trigo made, cofradía men and ecclesiastical authorities celebrated these moves and took them as a sign of success for the institutions they were supervising. Creating nuns out of poor but virtuous

---

36   Vizcaínas 9-I-3, f. 120–30.

37   Salazar notes a few examples of particularly well-connected niñas, some of whom arrived as educandas and some of whom went on to be nuns. Salazar Simarro, "Niñas, viudas, mozas," 165.

38   Gonzalbo Aizpuru, *Las mujeres en la Nueva España*, 221.

39   Margaret Chowning found that in the reformed convent of La Purísima, there was an expectation that many of the girls living and being educated in the convent would choose to become nuns. "As one visitor later put it, it was natural that, entering the school at an early age, the niñas would 'come to love the convent and the Religiosas, and these tender first impressions would last until, perhaps, they themselves became Religiosas.'" She goes on to say that at the time of Archbishop Hoyos y Mier's 1775 visita, there were four novices and at least three nuns who had previously lived in the convent as niñas and that two of the niñas living there at the time would go on to become nuns. Chowning, *Rebellious Nuns*, 160.

40   Lavrin, "The Novice Becomes a Nun," in *Brides of Christ*, 48–80.

girls was, from their perspective, certainly as good as, if not better than, preparing them for a successful and reputable marriage. In spite of the intentions of the administrators of these semimonastic institutions, however, when these particular novices entered their new homes, they brought a certain amount of social and economic diversity to the population of professed religious women. Though they may have acquired the dowry necessary to profess, they were not originally from families that could afford dowries, and thus they also would not be able to afford large cells, fine cloth, jewelry, or personal servants. They may even have had to impose on another nun because they could not afford to buy their own living quarters.

On the other hand, previously cloistered laywomen had more experience living in monastic environments than many of the more economically privileged women who arrived straight from their family homes. Of course, not all colegialas and *recogidas* found it possible to make the transition to becoming a black- or white-veiled cloistered religious woman, as illustrated by the example of María de Pevedilla discussed in the previous chapter. Pevedilla left the colegio of Caridad to profess in the convent of Santa Ynez, only to fall severely ill during the strenuous novitiate process. The convent *presidenta* confirmed that the novice was unable to complete the necessary spiritual exercises to become a full member of the community and recommended that she be allowed to return to the Colegio of Caridad.[41] Nonetheless, most colegialas and recogidas probably had a clearer sense of at least some of the rigors, isolation, and obedience that marked the path of a novice than many other young women who sought to take it. They might also have been more aware of the opportunities for creative and spiritual expression, intellectual development, and certain forms of independence offered by a female culture of cloistered devotion.

Whether they started out with the intention of becoming a nun, decided after their school years to become a novice, or remained unprofessed but living in convents into their old age, those women known as niñas were united by diverse circumstances and desires that all led to monastic seclusion. Religious aspirations, parents' vision of a proper feminine education, a lack of resources, an understanding of themselves as needing protection and shelter, a belief that they would not find a suitable spouse, or perhaps even a secret distaste for marriage led a steady stream of laywomen to occupy convents as niñas throughout most of the colonial period.

When monastic reforms of the late eighteenth century turned many of these niñas out of convents, nuns responded with great resistance. If there was similar opposition outside convents, it did not leave much of a record, but given the numbers of girls and women without resources who relied on convents for shelter and protection, these reforms must have caused

41   AHCV 9-I-3, AHCV f.162–165, AHCV 211, and AHCV 227.

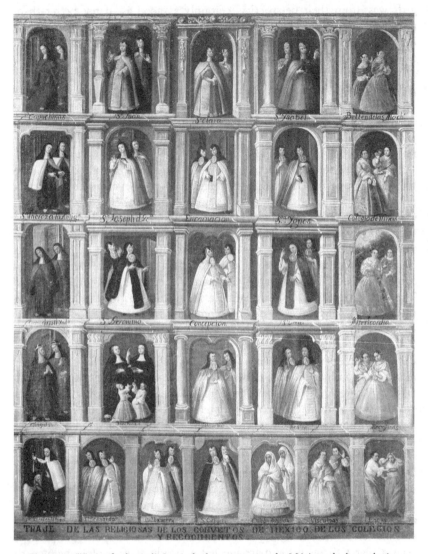

Figure 1 "Traje de las religiosas de los conventos de México, de los colegios, y recogimientos." Eighteenth century. Anonymous. With permission from the Museo Nacional del Virreinato. Tepozotlan, Mexico.

disturbances that reached beyond the convent walls. When Archbishop Alonso Núñez de Haro y Peralta ordered the expulsion of niñas from the nonreformed convents in his diocese, he was confronted with the problem of what to do with the large numbers of girls and women with no families who had only known a cloistered life. He asked the cofradía of Aránzazu to house some of them in its colegio, but when the men of the Basque brotherhood prevaricated, the archbishop responded that there were not as many to place as he had originally counted and so he could probably find space for them at the colegio of Belem.[42] This may in fact have been true because a significant number of the niñas ordered to leave did not actually do so.[43] Exceptions were made for some who were "of advanced age," suffered illness, or had special talents that benefited the convent, like exceptional secretarial skills or musical gifts.[44] Some niñas were converted to criadas in the records and thus counted among the few necessary servants convents continued to claim. Though the numbers of niñas did drop in the 1760s and 1770s, by the last decade of the eighteenth century, the practice of housing and educating girls and young women in convents returned, though perhaps not quite as intensely as before because of slow changes in ideas about feminine education.[45]

Overall, in practice and in the collective imagination, convents remained home to a great many "niñas," young and old, who probably felt the convent to be as much their place as that of the nuns they shared it with. An anonymous painting of the clothing of cloistered women hangs in the *Museo Nacional del Virreinato* in Tepozotlan, Mexico, with the words *traje de las religiosas de los conventos de México, de los colegios y recogimientos* along the bottom edge.[46] The painting portrays nuns, colegialas, and recogidas as all occupying the same sacred landscape. Pictured in neatly ordered rows, representations of cloistered women from all the various institutions appear framed by archways. The frames include discalced and calced convents and convent schools as well as colegios and recogimientos for laywomen. Even the asylum, the *Casa de Locas*, is included.

One of the images includes two black-veiled nuns talking to one another with two young girls standing at their feet. The girls appear as if they are the nuns' daughters, each attached to one of the nuns, interacting with each other as playmates whose mothers are busy talking together about adult matters. One of the nuns gesticulates with one hand while she holds a book

42 AHCV 5-IV-7.    43 Arenas Frutos, "Las 'otras,'" 202–5, and "Innovaciones," 446.
44 Salazar Simarro, "Niñas, viudas, mozas," 169.
45 Gonzalbo Aizpuru, *Las mujeres en la Nueva España* and "Reffugium Virginum." In the latter, Gonzalbo Aizpuru argues that though music, reading, writing, and arithmetic were indeed taught to girls in convents and colegios throughout the colonial period, they were not widely considered the most important elements of female education. To parents and society, "oración y silencio, clausura y penitencia, recogimiento y obediencia" were central not only to conventual life but to an ideal feminine education as well. Though pedagogues were writing about the importance of systematic learning, Gonzalbo Aizpuru argues that the shift toward the implementation of things like formal classes and schedules did not take hold until the late eighteenth century and then only slowly. As a part of this shift, however, convents became gradually less important for girls' education.
46 "The dress of religious women of the convents of Mexico, the colegios, and the recogimientos."

Figure 2 Detail from "Traje de las religiosas de los conventos de México, de los colegios, y recogimientos." Eighteenth century. Anonymous. With permission from the Museo Nacional del Virreinato. Tepozotlan, Mexico.

in her other; the other listens and rests a loving hand absentmindedly on her child's head. Both the children are wearing fancy dresses with ruffled sleeves and holding what appear to be toys.

The painting illustrates not only the range of clothing, wealth, and discipline thought to characterize the various institutions but also a perceived continuum of female seclusion between nuns, recogidas, colegialas, and niñas. Church authorities and colonial culture in general both recognized this connection between the various ways women could live a voluntarily cloistered life. Though the presence of niñas caused reoccurring anxiety in the former, society's expectations ultimately prevailed. Convents provided opportunities for shelter and education for a more diverse group of young and old laywomen than the colegios officially designed for them. These opportunities were experienced within the racial and social hierarchies that existed outside the convent and reproduced within it, but emotional and filial bonds between nuns and niñas complicated them as well. These same ties were an important part of cloister life. Though ecclesiastical authorities worried that they undermined its purpose, for many women living in convents, these bonds probably made seclusion bearable and certainly fuller and more interesting.

## Depositadas and Widows

There was another group of women whose residency was more transient than that of niñas and who left even less historical record; depositadas, known as such because they had been "deposited" in convents, were in some ways an even greater challenge to the ideology of cloister than niñas, but they also centrally took part in practices that ecclesiastical courts and other authorities used to regulate and protect women through seclusion. Some depositadas asked ecclesiastical authorities for permission to seek temporary shelter in a convent, while others were sent because their husbands or other male relatives had requested they be cloistered there. Some were escaping an abusive marriage or seeking shelter and protection after their husbands died or abandoned them. Others were betrothed or awaiting ecclesiastical dispensation to get married, and staying in a convent was thought to secure their reputation and guarantee their future spouse's claim on their virginity. Jealous husbands sometimes sought *depósito* for wives they suspected of infidelity or while they were long absent. Others seeking a permanent separation from their wives asked judges to place their spouses in convents in order to guard their own honor as husbands who continued to have a claim on their estranged wives' chastity.

Most information about depositadas comes from ecclesiastical court records rather than from convent archives.[47] However, their presence is

---

47  For examples of requests from family members and women themselves to be placed in depósito in a convent, see AGN Bienes Nac. V. 235, exp. 19, f. 1–17; AGN Bienes Nac. V. 584, exp. 24; AGN Bienes Nac. V. 976, exp. 10, f. 1–8.

also visible in the occasional complaints about them by male religious authorities. Archbishop José Lanciego y Eguiluz, for one, wrote with concern about this population of sexually experienced women living among nuns, undermining the purpose of the cloister. Throughout his time as archbishop, he periodically tried to expel them from convents with varying degrees of success.[48]

Widows were among this population of depositadas but could also sometimes occupy a more permanent and respected place in convent communities. Like the prohibitions against niñas living among nuns, those excluding widows were not always followed. Throughout the colonial period, a small minority of black-veiled nuns came from the ranks of highly pious widows, some of whose wealth helped open the convent doors for them and some of whom had been important donors when they were married.[49] It was more common for widows to become legas than full voting members of the community, but even so, some widows entered with the stated hope of taking vows. In theory, widows had to prove themselves more than *doncellas*, and some probably could not pass the community's tests.[50] Others probably decided that simple residence was enough but found ways to remain indefinitely – some by contributing money, others by offering domestic service, and still others by linking themselves to the patronage and protection of a particular nun.

A convent was not the worst kind of depósito a woman could find herself in. Many women asked to be placed in a convent and expressed distress when they had to settle instead for a less reputable cloister for laywomen or a private home. When doña María Luisa approached the ecclesiastical judge in Toluca, part of her complaint against her husband was that he had convinced previous judges to place her in "denigrating depositos" in disreputable recogimientos and private homes where she was probably forced to perform domestic service. When women had the chance, they often asked judges to send them to a convent, where their reputations were less vulnerable than in these other kinds of places.

Though ecclesiastical authorities were concerned about niñas distracting nuns from their prayers and widows who wanted to profess were subject to harsh standards and scrutiny, depositadas were particularly subversive of what male religious authorities thought of as proper seclusion because of their temporary status. Widows turned nuns, or even repentant women living in Magdalena houses or cloisters for divorcees, were sexually experienced and thus worldly women, but they were seeking indefinite enclosure. Whatever their past had entailed, they were committing to a monastic life of celibacy and seclusion. Depositadas, on the other hand, sought only

48   Salazar Simarro, "Niñas, viudas, mozas," 167–69.
49   Lavrin, *Brides of Christ*, 23–24; Salazar Simarro, "Niñas, viudas, mozas," 167–69.   50   Ibid.

temporary shelter, and as such, their needs and goals were different. They did not represent either repentance from sexual impropriety or a move from a married, sexually active life to a religious one. Those women who were there voluntarily may have seen the convent as a means of moral and physical protection but did not necessarily understand their residency as a commitment to a new way of life. And those placed against their will must have seen it as a kind of prison, or at least a severe imposition. Whatever the case, as temporary residents, depositadas challenged the separation of the nuns from the outside world in a particularly significant way. Not only did they bring life experience of a different sort than did the niñas, but they also brought news and information to a greater extent than did visitors who spoke with the nuns through the gated doors of the convent during supervised visiting hours.

More than niñas, depositadas linked the inner life of the convent to the outside world. Like niñas, depositadas were expected to participate at least minimally in the devotional rhythms of the convent by attending mass, partaking of the sacraments of confession and communion, and participating in collective prayers and singing. Whether they should be required or allowed to complete the private spiritual exercises that were a part of the nuns' daily routines or how often they ought to perform the sacraments and attend mass was undoubtedly a source of controversy in many convents. However, even if their participation in the spiritual life of their temporary community was limited, when depositadas left convents, they did so having gained an insight into some of the mysteries of cloistered life. Asunción Lavrin says that the separation of nuns from the world and the invisibility of their daily lives were central to their mystique and to society's sense of the convents' spiritual power and that this differed from male monasteries whose members were regularly seen in public roles and settings.[51] Depositadas must have brought reports of what they had seen in convents back to their communities, be it examples of impressively rigorous piety surpassing people's expectations or disappointing mediocrity and even moments of scandal, disorder, and conflict.[52]

---

51 "The physical but hidden proximity of the women living in the adjacent cloisters infused nunneries with an aura of respect and mystery that was lacking in male convents, inasmuch as monks were part of the world, and their own visibility in the streets made them familiar and accessible." Lavrin, *Brides of Christ*, 2.

52 On the idea of nuns as exceptional women and this being a source of their spiritual power, Asunción Lavrin says: "The spiritual prestige of convents was based on the projection of the image of nuns as privileged persons. The Brides of Christ, the chosen ones, were those who could stand the rigor of a disciplined life without sex, and devote themselves not only to their own personal salvation, but also to help and benefit others with their prayers. Such prayers had a special value in the period under review, and people understood their relation to nunneries as one of exchange of material support for the spiritual benefits derived from the salvific mediation of the brides of

## Servants and Slaves

Convents were also home to other laywomen who bridged the cloister with the outside world but who occupied a more clearly subordinate position in convent life than niñas and depositadas. Servants and slaves, whether employed or owned by the convent or individual nuns, were bound by contracts of servitude; though some of them did achieve respect and even lay-sister status, their official role in convent life was to labor for the more privileged residents. Servants were *indias, negras, mulatas, mestizas*, and poor españolas. In the sixteenth century, convent slaves could be both Indigenous and African women, but by the seventeenth century, they were almost exclusively negras or mulatas. Servants and slaves were a part of convent societies from the earliest foundations in the sixteenth century throughout the colonial period, though their numbers rose and fell with the waves of reform and varied between the calced and discalced convents. Like with niñas and other dependent laywomen, there was generally a significant gap between written rules about their presence and actual practices.

Servants often accompanied nuns when they arrived as novices, while others arrived separately. Some servants were sent by their own families, employers, or nuns' wealthy patrons to accompany and aid individual nuns, while others offered their services to the convent as a whole. While it seems clear that many women were forced into their positions as convent servants, there are also examples of women arriving of their own accord, escaping poverty, seeking shelter, or even running away from another employer.[53] Their ages varied greatly, from young children to middle-aged women. Some were orphans with no real outside connections or protections, some were criadas raised by families not their own, and others were long-term domestic servants employed by the families of the nuns they served. Some servants were women who turned to domestic service as adults, when poverty or abandonment by a spouse left them few options.

Enslaved women and girls also frequently entered convents alongside a particular nun when she professed. Others arrived as purchases or donations from secular individuals or other monastic institutions. Like servants, slaves were also a wide variety of ages. Many came as infants or toddlers and spent their whole childhoods in the service of a particular nun or the convent as a whole, while others arrived as schoolchildren, teenagers, or adults. Some remained until they were of very advanced age.

Both servants and slaves also brought their own children with them. Children of servants could remain in the same positions as their mothers, but some managed to move up the social ladder within the convent or leave.

Christ. This mystique was in the minds of those who helped create these institutions and those who wished to profess in them." Lavrin, *Brides of Christ*, 5.

53    Salazar Simarro, "Niñas, viudas, mozas," 177.

The children of slaves, on the other hand, were treated as part of the convent's inventory and retained or sold at the will of the nuns who owned them, unless an outside party had a claim to them through a will or postponed purchase.

Servants known as *donadas*, though not property in the same way that slaves were, had nonetheless been "donated" by guardians, patrons, or sometimes themselves for a term of perpetual, permanent service. Asunción Lavrin calls them "servants by another name, almost close to slavery," which was particularly true for those donated by others.[54] But as Lavrin also discusses, some donadas came of their own accord out of a desire for the religious life. Women willing to commit to a life of service might eventually obtain the status of a white-veiled sister without having to pay a dowry, at which point their labor obligations could be reduced to make room for a fuller spiritual life.[55] Or if their racial status precluded this possibility, they might be allowed instead to take informal vows and be recognized as an unprofessed lay sister, who wore yet another kind of habit but continued on with the same service obligations. This was an option occasionally extended to other classes of servants and even slaves who were impressively pious.[56] Donadas had sometimes been "given" to convents at birth, as a promise or devotional act of their parents, and convent records sometimes refer to these women as wearing the "habit of a donada" right from their entrance. This was the case of a woman of mixed African and Spanish ancestry, known as Sor Leónor de los Angeles. Sor Leónor's father dedicated her to God when she was a child, after she was miraculously rescued from drowning. He took her to Santa Clara, where she took on the habit of a donada. She became famous for her intense piety, healing, and prophetic gifts and was the subject of posthumous hagiography.[57] In a very real sense, donadas occupied an intermediary space between servant and nun.

54 Larvrin, *Brides of Christ*, 161.
55 Margaret Chowning has found that in the convent of La Purísima, donadas could take up the white veil after ten years of service. Chowning, *Rebellious Nuns*, 185–86, 194; Nuria Salazar has also found instances in which after a set term of service, donadas could become lay sisters. Salazar Simarro, "Niñas, viudas, mozas," 178. Asunción Lavrin writes about instances in which donadas continued their service obligations indefinitely but from the beginning held a position like that of a beata. "Donadas had no special rights in the convent, but were recognized as perpetually devoted to religion. Once dedicated by this special bond, they did not leave the cloisters. The convent thus gained her service forever. However, the possibility of being received as a donada was extraordinary for the humble woman." This option was open to non-Spanish women, including those classified as indios and women of African descent. For examples of "Indian" donadas, see Lavrin, *Brides of Christ*, 250–51, 254. For those of African descent, see Lavrin, *Brides of Christ*, 32–33.
56 Salazar Simarro, "Niñas, viudas, mozas," 178–79; Lavrin, *Brides of Christ*, 165–70.
57 Asunción Lavrin tells this story in greater length in Lavrin, *Brides of Christ*, 33. She takes it from Fr. Agustín de Vetancurt, *Memologio Franciscano*.

Many enslaved women spent their childhoods in convents, having been sold or donated as infants or toddlers. In 1680, the Jesuits at the college of San Pedro y San Pablo in Mexico City sold a one-year-old *"mulatilla"* named Antonia to a nun at the convent of Nuestra Señora de la Encarnación.[58] Ten years later, these same priests sold a nine-month-old, Laureana, who they referred to as a *mulatilla blanca*, to another nun in the same convent.[59] Both children were taken from their parents, who served the college in different capacities, to be raised in the convent for the eventual purpose of being the personal servants of the nuns who purchased them. They sometimes moved directly into these nuns' living quarters, where presumably they would have been cared for with the help of another servant or niña, or they were placed in the care of another slave or servant who worked for the convent until they were old enough to work for the nuns who claimed their labor. María de la Cruz, whose story opened this chapter, was five or six years old when she came to work for Madre Francisca de Santa Teresa, having been "lent" by the nun's brother.[60] She spent the remainder of her childhood and adolescence sharing the nun's living quarters, establishing – according to Francisca – an intimate, familial bond with the nun who later sought to buy her in order to keep her from being reclaimed.

Some slaves arrived as adolescents and adults, bringing with them a variety of experiences, both monastic and otherwise. This was the case with the fourteen-year-old mulata named Catalina who arrived at Nuestra Señora de la Encarnación in 1673. She had lived with her older sister Inés and their mother, Magdalena, in the home of the Salazar Varona family until she was four years old and Don Joseph Salazar and his wife had both passed away. Don Joseph's last testament and will stipulated that owner-ship of the four-year-old Catalina and fourteen-year-old Inés should pass to his daughter, Madre Teresa de San Joseph of the convent of Nuestra Señora de la Encarnación, and that Magdalena should accompany them to care for the young Catalina. Things did not come to pass exactly as planned, however, as Magdalena and her two daughters went instead to the homes of Joseph's two sons, both priests in Mexico City. Ten years later, the two priests, Joseph and Alonso, "donated" Catalina, claiming that they had inherited her from their deceased parents. So, after having spent her child-hood in the company of her mother and sister, first in the service of a secular family and then one or both priests, the teenage Catalina left them and the outside world to live cloistered as a personal servant to a nun, apparently for the rest of her life. Catalina would have been twenty years old when the toddler Antonia arrived at the convent, and thirty-one and thirty-two when she met the infant Laureana and the five-year-old María de la Cruz. Catalina may have been asked to help care for these children when Madre Theresa

58  AHAM caja 12, exp. 6.    59  AHAM caja 18, exp. 14.    60  AHAM caja 24, exp. 32.

was busy with prayers and did not require her services. If she lived into her fifties, she may very well have also lived to see María de la Cruz obtain her freedom.

Though some nuns may have "dressed, bathed, and nursed" young convent slaves with their own hands, these girls and women were still legally considered property and were treated as such. Convent inventories list the persons of enslaved women right alongside furniture and real estate, and the language of sale or donation records read like any other slave sale documents from the time period. In transferring the ownership of the infant Laureana to Madre María de la Santisima Trinidad y San Miguel of Nuestra Señora de la Encarnación, the deed of sale stated that Laureana was to be henceforth Madre María's slave "for her to have and possess and do with as she will, *como cosa suya*" (literally, "as her thing" – as her property).[61] This included selling her if need be, as was the case when the archbishop granted the ailing Sor Josefa de la Encarnación permission to sell her slave in 1684 to pay for convent repairs and improvements she had promised God she would undertake before she died.[62] It also meant that should Madre María die, Laureana would be passed on to another nun, along with the nun's cell, clothing, and furniture or would serve or be sold by the convent as a whole.

On the other hand, convent records and nuns' petitions to buy personal slaves also justified their purchases in language that echoed larger concerns about female vulnerability and the importance of protecting the honor of young women, even if they were slaves. The year Laureana was sold to the Vicaria of Nuestra Señora de la Encarnación, the convent purchased five other young "mulatillas" from the same Jesuit colegio to serve in the capacity of general convent servants. The petition claims that the community wanted to purchase these girls in order to save them from the spiritual dangers that so often befell women and that they would certainly encounter if they were sold into secular society. It goes on to employ language common in discourse about slavery in general in the Americas and Europe at this time: in return for these women's labor, the nuns committed to providing them a good, Christian education, which would guarantee not only their feminine honor but also a "good death" and eternal salvation. As a part of this commitment, the contract stipulated that these five slave girls could never be sold to laypersons. However, if the need arose, the convent could sell them to another monastic community, which would presumably also provide for religious instruction and access to the sacraments, including the last rites and a Christian burial considered necessary for a "good death."[63] Convents did not always keep these commitments, however. Sor Josefa de la Encarnación did not stipulate that her slave be

61  AHAM caja 18, exp. 14.    62  AHAM caja 14, exp. 6.    63  Ibid.

sold to another convent but rather to someone who would pay the price needed for the obra pía she had promised. And convents did sometimes sell their slaves to laypeople, just as they sold property and gave low-interest loans.[64] It seemed that many nuns felt that the selling of enslaved women could serve God as much as the sheltering of them, as long as the former brought funds for pious works.[65]

Though the presence of servants and slaves was controversial, ecclesiastical authorities also recognized the "benefits" of seclusion for women who worked as servants. Discussions about how to remove servants from convents, which ones could stay, and what to do with those who left echoed ecclesiastical judges' concern about disciplining, regulating, and protecting vulnerable women from the dangers of the world on one hand and protecting society from the damage caused by women who fell prey to them on the other.[66] Servants and slaves were supposed to observe the same level of seclusion and to seek permission from an ecclesiastical authority to leave the convent for any reason. In 1664, the priest Br. Luis Gómez de León delivered a denunciation to Inquisitors in Mexico City in the name of Teresa de la Magdalena, a mestiza and personal servant to Madre Magdalena de San Gerónimo of the Conceptionist convent in Mexico City, because the servant could not leave the convent.[67] The accusation was against the convent confessor who had apparently been using the confession to solicit sexual favors from Teresa de la Magdalena. Br. Luis Gómez said the accused confessor had a great deal of influence within the convent, and he was afraid the servant would lose her position if the confessor learned of her denunciation. He asked the Inquisitor to pursue the matter in such a way that the accused would not find out, so Teresa de la

---

64    Salazar Simarro, "Niñas, viudas, mozas," 181.

65    Pilar Gonzalbo Aizpuru notes that in the 150 expedientes from Bienes Nacionales in the AGN dealing with laywomen living in convents in the late eighteenth century, she only found mention of five slaves. Gonzalbo Aizpuru, "Reffugium Virginum." Lavrin notes that there is evidence that the practice of having slaves in convents may have been slowly waning in the eighteenth century. Lavrin, *Brides of Christ*. In the Archivo Histórico del Arzobispado de México (AHAM), there are thirteen documents related to nuns buying, receiving, donating, and occasionally freeing slaves between the years of 1602 and 1711. Only two of these expedientes were before 1670, eight of them were between the years of 1670 and 1695, and three of them were after 1695. A number of them talk about more than one slave, and most are dealing with the same convent, so this points to a fairly significant number of slaves joining the convent of Encarnación in the second half of the seventeenth century. These documents can be found in the Fondo Cabildo and the Fondo Episcopal, and they are: caja 2, exp. 29; caja 4, exp. 36; caja 11, exp. 5; caja 11, exp. 10; caja 11, exp. 34; caja 12, exp. 6; caja 14, exp. 6; caja 18, exp. 14; caja 19, 32; caja 24, exp. 32; caja 24, exp. 33; caja 25 exp. 10 and caja 197 exp. 8.

66    For instance, see the letters written by Archbishop Alonso Núñez de Haro y Peralta in 1774. Vizcaínas 5-IV-7.

67    AGN Inq. V. 510, Testimonio del Br. Luis Gómez de León contra un confesor cuio nombre no supo.

Magdalena could retain the benefit and protection of being "recogida." The fact that Br. Luis Gómez raised the importance of this servant woman remaining "recogida" rather than employed – and instead of the convent's need for her labor – suggests that the priest and Inquisitors shared the assumption that convents were places of spiritual and moral protection even for the laywomen who worked in them.

Whatever rhetorical or ideological strategies nuns and male ecclesiastical authorities may have employed to justify the presence of servants and slaves, these women performed labor that was essential for the smooth functioning of convents. Even in reformed convents, the smaller number of servants and slaves performed labor considered too difficult or demeaning for discalced nuns. They also performed a range of daily tasks linking convents to the outside world that were necessary but that would have compromised the cloister if the nuns had to do them. This included opening and closing the convent doors, receiving deliveries, and leaving the convent to run errands or send messages. Particularly in moments where some urgent and immediate communication was necessary, servants and slaves were essential for protecting the nuns' seclusion.[68]

The positions held by servants and slaves and the types of labor they performed varied depending on the convent as well as the particular position of the slave. In general, servants and slaves cooked, cleaned, helped in the infirmaries, cared for children, and carried heavy loads, including helping deliver materials to male slaves working on construction, and completed many outside world tasks. In the less rigorous convents, where servants and slaves could be very numerous, they also helped the white-veiled sisters and the recently professed junior nuns with their lighter tasks, like closing and locking windows at night, bringing food to other residents, and tidying up the books in the library.[69]

---

68   See the example cited in Salazar Simarro, "Niñas, viudas, mozas," 173.

69   Asunción Lavrin finds five hundred servants and one hundred nuns in the convent of Santa Clara in Querétaro in the 1660s. Lavrin, *Brides of Christ*, 161–64. Rosalva Loreto López finds the numbers significantly less but still high in Puebla a century later: in Santa Catalina, there were ninety servants to ninety-six nuns (and seventy-two niñas); in Santa Inés, there were sixty-five servants to sixty-three nuns (and sixty-one niñas); in Santísima Trinidad, there were sixty servants to sixty-four nuns (and sixty-three niñas); and in San Jerónimo, there were seventy-six servants and seventy-six nuns (and seventy-four niñas). Reflecting the effects of monastic reforms, which began most intensely in Puebla, there were no servants in the Conceptionist convent, La Concepción. Rosalva Loreto López, *Los conventos femeninos y el mundo urbano de la Puebla de los Ángeles del siglo XVIII* (Mexico City.: El Colegio de México, Centro de Estudios Históricos, 2000), 90. These numbers probably rose after the waves of reform subsided, however, in the 1780s and 1790s. In 1851, Margaret Chowning finds thirty-five servants to fifteen nuns in the Conceptionist convent of la Purísima Concepción of San Miguel de Allende and says that this is double what it was in the colonial period. So even this strict and rigorous convent employed at least fifteen servants. Chowning, *Rebellious Nuns*, 156, 243.

In convents where the vida particular was observed, personal servants and slaves generally shared a cell with individual nuns, performing whatever services the religious women demanded. These included everything from laundry, cooking, and cleaning to tending to the young niñas to assisting the nuns in their devotional practices. Being involved in a nun's spiritual disciplines could include simple tasks like awakening her at four in the morning to start her prayers, lighting candles, or even accompanying her in her devotions. But it could also include more difficult, tension-filled, and intimate labor, like helping the nun to administer her physical self-discipline by whipping her and then later tending to her wounds.[70]

Servants and slaves were also entrusted with the care of spaces and objects that were central to the devotional life of the convent. This opened an opportunity for those with a religious vocation to develop particular practices and disciplines and, in some cases, be recognized and honored for them. They maintained the altars, images of saints, and other parts of the chapel, church, and choir areas, rang the church bells, and even collected alms and other donations.[71] Servants and slaves participated in cofradías that formed within convents, like that of Nuestra Señora del Rosario in the convent of La Concepción in Puebla, sometimes taking on positions of particular responsibility.[72] Stories of slaves and servants being favored through gifts of prophecies, visions, or miraculous healings surface in convent writings as examples of how God chooses the most humble of his servants to demonstrate his love and power. These stories point to the fact that these women were occasionally celebrated by the convent communities as examples to follow.[73] Some also took informal vows and reduced their service obligations to allow time for more prayer, and a few were even allowed to wear habits. Racialized notions of virtue and piety made it harder for women of lowly and non-Spanish birth to achieve this kind of recognition. However, it also meant that women who "overcame" the perceived handicap of their race and social position to reach such devotional heights may have been particularly admired.[74]

---

70  Lavrin, *Brides of Christ*, 164–65; Fr. Joseph Gómez, *Vida de la venerable Madre Antonia de San Jacinto* (Mexico City: Imprenta de Antuerpia de los Herederos de la Viuda de Bernardo de Calderón, 1689), 11–13; Carlos de Sigüenza y Góngora, *Parayso occidental plantado y cultivado por la liberal benéfico mano de los muy católicos y poderosos reyes de España nuestros señores en su magnífico real convento de Jesús María de Mexico* (Mexico City: UMAM-Condumex, 1995, 1684), 108.

71  Salazar Simarro, "Niñas, viudas, mozas," 171, 174.     72  Ibid., 171, 175.

73  Ibid., 171–184. See also the examples of María de San Juan reported by Sigüenza y Góngora and Juana Esperanza whom Fr. José Gómez talked about. Lavrin, *Brides of Christ*, 167–79; Sigüenza y Góngora, *Parayso occidental*; Gómez, *Vida de la venerable Madre*.

74  Lavrin says, "The flowering of spirituality in women of low social status provoked admiration and even reverence, not only in New Spain but elsewhere in the colonies. The basic assumption was that it was highly improbably that a black servant or slave would have the sensitivity, resolve, or even the special vocation required to profess. When one of them proved to possess such

Being a part of the community and participating in its sacramental life brought convent women into regular contact with the priests who served as confessors for the convent. This contact was more frequent than it would have been if they lived outside the convent and had the potential to be more intensive and focused, as well. Regular confessors became the spiritual directors of individual nuns, novices, lay sisters, and probably niñas as well, but this relationship could also develop with servants and slaves. Such a relationship carried with it not only spiritual mentorship and guidance but also heightened scrutiny of their thoughts, words, and actions. Because of the religious environment in which they lived, confessors would expect that convent slaves and servants knew and understood more about Christian doctrine than laywomen of similar economic and social status living outside the convent, from whom the priests might expect a certain level of ignorance.

Rafaela Hernández, an orphaned española working as a convent servant in 1777, came under intensified scrutiny upon arriving at Santa Catarina de Sena. She was twenty-one years old when her confession with the convent chaplain came to the attention of the Inquisition; at that time she had been in Santa Catarina for less than a year. She had entered the convent as a way to escape poverty, providing service to the community as a whole rather than one particular nun. The religious environment had proved to be a significant change for her, challenging the skeptical and instrumental view she had privately held about important elements of Christian doctrine.

Fr. Vicente de Santa María presented Inquisitors the self-denunciation Hernández had dictated to him in the course of a general confession, explaining that she could not leave the convent to present it herself. It was a serious crime the Inquisition was considering her for and one that she had no idea she was guilty of until she had spoken her spiritual doubts to her confessor. According to her confession, "ever since the age of reason" Rafaela Hernández had doubted certain core tenants of the Christian faith. It just never made sense to her that Mary could have had a child while still being a virgin or remained so afterward as a married woman, nor that the sacraments of baptism, communion, confession, or confirmation could really contain the divine significance attributed to them. She saw Mary's pregnancy as well as the sacraments as physical "acts of man." She did not understand how the host of the Eucharist could really be the body of Christ or how sins were forgiven by telling them to a priest or how a soul could be saved through the acts of baptism

---

qualifications, the response was one of awe and a display of respect for the way in which the will of God was made itself known. The lower the venue the higher the moral lesson derived from it." Lavrin, *Brides of Christ*, 167 and note 81.

and confirmation, and she did not believe that a baby could be born without sex. But she had never worried about these doubts before she came to the convent. In fact, until a short time before her confession, she had not realized that having mental doubts of this kind was a sin. To make matters worse, she had actually uttered her heretical thoughts out loud a few times, although she swore that she had only done so to herself, in private, with no one else within earshot.

But in recent months, presumably because of the religious education Hernández was receiving in the convent, she had become convinced of the error of her previous thinking. As a part of that process, she had also realized the importance of examining her consciousness and making a thorough confession of all past thoughts, words, and deeds. With this in mind, she approached Fr. Vicente de Santa María and asked to make a general confession of her life up to that point. In the course of this confession, she revealed the lifelong doubts that had come to disturb her consciousness. But in doing so, she was not aware that she was admitting to *herejía mixta*, a crime that carried the punishment of excommunication and had to be dealt with by the Inquisition. Fr. Vicente told her that he could not absolve her and that she had to face the Holy Office. Hernández agreed to let him present her denunciation for her, and as part of that, she swore that she had recognized her mistake and currently had no more lingering doubts about Christian doctrine.

Rafaela Hernández fell prey to the Inquisition's methods of gathering information that linked religious instruction, *escrúpulo*, and confession. This could have happened outside the convent as well if she had encountered a diligent confessor or been privy in some way to an edict read in or near her town. But working in a convent increased the chances of becoming caught in this web. Her particular confessor appeared to be genuinely interested in the health of her soul, as he had counseled her for months before her general confession. He also defended her to the Inquisition, arguing that she was truly remorseful and was sincere in her new certainty of faith; he argued that she deserved mercy since her previous doubts came from ignorance rather than willfulness or malice.

Not all convent confessors were so concerned with the spiritual or emotional well-being of the servants they confessed, however. The power dynamics in the confessor–penitent relationship were potentially very different for servants and slaves than they were for religious women and even niñas, and the potential for abuse was high. Servants and slaves were a captive audience of the clergymen who regularly served the convent given the weekly requirement for confession. Furthermore, unless they enjoyed a trusting relationship with a protective nun, servants and slaves had very little ability to complain if the confessor's behavior was troubling. This kind of vulnerability is visible in the case of María Josefa Fernández, the servant whose experience with a soliciting convent chaplain was discussed in Chapter 1. Her response to the chaplain, García, showed a clear awareness of what was needed for a good confession as well as anxiety about the response of her mistress if Fernández had missed communion. She was trapped between her economic dependency on the convent, the apparently stern nun she worked for, and her spiritual dependency on the chaplain.[75]

Both Rafaela Hernández's and María Josefa Fernández's stories are ones in which convent servants appear to have been steeped in doctrine and to have experienced great anxiety about spiritual matters. In the case of Hernández, this anxiety seems to have been created, or at least significantly heightened, by the increased exposure to religious instruction she experienced in the convent. Fernández's experience illustrates the many ways that these women's positions made them vulnerable to scrutiny on the part of nuns, priests, and the convent community in general as well as subject to abuses of power. It also reveals the kind of dependency these women experienced and the importance of maintaining harmony in their relationships with the nuns they worked for.

Whether they were employed or enslaved, mozas and esclavas were dependent on the supposed generosity of the nuns for basic necessities. Servants sometimes received a small amount of money for their work, but often room and board was considered sufficient for a servant's pay. Nuns living in individual cells received an allowance, which was meant to cover food for their entire "family," including their servants and slaves. Thus, depending on the way a nun managed her household, servants and slaves might eat last and then only what was left over after everyone else had eaten, while other nuns instituted a practice of *imitato Cristo* in which the lowliest members ate first to demonstrate and cultivate the nuns' own humility and virtue. Convent servants living in their own communal quarters either received daily rations of food or ate what was left over or shared with them from the nuns' plates. Most convents provided slaves and servants with a minimal supply of clothing, but anything beyond that would have to come from gifts or their own labor.[76]

To supplement the sparse means the convent provided, many servants and slaves found ways to work extra hours manufacturing food, sweets, or other items, like artificial flowers, to be sold. Nuns often performed this work as well, and the selling of these things was an important source of income for the convent, so there must have been a certain amount of conflict when a servant or slave tried to sell the products of her labor for her own use. Nonetheless, servants and slaves did manage to produce enough to save

---

75 Banc. mss. 96/95m, 1773, Fray Joaquín García.
76 For a discussion of gifts and sharing of this kind, see Lavrin, *Brides of Christ*, 161.

money to buy medicine, clothing, or extra food beyond what the convent provided for them. Some even tried to send a bit of money to their families. Occasionally, slaves like María de la Cruz were able to save up enough money to buy their freedom.

María de la Cruz's story suggests the intertwining of affective or familial bonds with those of servitude and ownership. Much of slaves' and servants' work was done in a domestic context, and these women did sometimes develop intimate relationships with nuns and the rest of the "families" with which they lived.[77] However, like their relationships with confessors – and like those of enslaved and employed domestic workers outside convents as well – intimacy could clearly coexist and comingle with abuse. Even without abuse, any intimacy that developed within the context of servitude and slavery was fundamentally shaped by hierarchical power relationships.

In the case of María de la Cruz and Madre Francisca, if we are to believe the nun's claims that there existed a great love between them, perhaps it was facilitated by the fact that Madre Francisca did not actually own María de la Cruz for most of her life. However, this kind of "borrowing" slaves from a family member, sometimes for the lifetime of the slave, was not an unusual practice in convents.[78] It is worth being suspicious of Madre Francisca's narrative and her insistence that María de la Cruz was like a daughter to her; nonetheless, the fact that she so readily agreed to relinquish ownership suggests some level of genuine affection. On the other hand, María de la Cruz had to buy her freedom rather than receiving it as a gift from the woman who claimed to love her as a mother. It was not unheard of for nuns to free their slaves without payment after they had served them for a time.[79] It is conceivable that Madre Francisca could not do so because of the stipulation she had put in place to prevent María from being returned to her brother in the case of her death, which granted the convent the future rights to María's labor. Perhaps legally, then, the convent as a whole had to be compensated for María's freedom if it was to relinquish those rights. Whatever the case, this relationship appears to have been marked by a complex mixture of power and affection that was shaped by the relations of property, servitude, and intimacy in which María de la Cruz had lived since she was a young child.

---

77    For examples of domestic and intimate relations that included servants whipping nuns and nuns washing the feet of their servants, see Lavrin, *Brides of Christ*, 164–65. For another servant beating a nun as part of her religious practices, see Salazar Simarro, "Niñas, viudas, mozas," 172. For an example of intimacy with slaves and criadas, see Salazar Simarro, "Niñas, viudas, mozas," 173.

78    See the example cited in Lavrin of the Canon Don José de Villegas Jara, who lent two of his slaves to Sor Lorenza de la Presentación of Santa Catalina de Sena. See also several other examples illustrating the variety of arrangements made in terms of nuns buying, selling, lending, borrowing, and freeing slaves. Lavrin, *Brides of Christ*, 165–66.

79    Salazar Simarro, "Niñas, viudas, mozas," 171–84.

Intimate quarters and the passage of time did not always prevent violence, however. In 1605, Francisca López, a "negra *criolla*" who was the personal slave of Catalina Pérez, the *rectora* of Santa Mónica, appeared before the Inquisition as a result of the abuse her mistress had visited upon her. As other enslaved women did in colonial Mexico, Francisca López denounced herself for blasphemous words uttered in despair at the treatment she had received from Catalina Pérez.[80] In her confession, she told Inquisitors that she was *desesperada* with her life in the convent and that she had told Catalina that she was looking for someone to buy her so she could leave.[81] In response, the nun had beaten her fiercely and sent her out of her quarters. While Francisca was sitting wounded near the sacristy door, another slave belonging to Catalina Pérez walked by. This woman was a mulata named María with whom Francisca regularly had conflict and whom she blamed for the abuse she received from Catalina.[82] Out of her anger, Francisca insulted María, calling her a "mulata *desvergonzada*" (shameless), to which María responded that Francisca was a "desvergonzada" and that the fact that her former owners had sold her did not speak well of her.[83] At this, Francisca told the Inquisitors, the anger that had built up within her burst out of her lips in the form of a blasphemous statement; she rejected "God and all of his saints and he who gave [her] will."[84] She said this in the presence of four other convent servants who witnessed her exchange with María.[85]

Francisca's story is worth pondering at some length. It reflects not only violence on the part of a nun against an enslaved woman with whom she shared living quarters, but it also depicts severely strained relations between enslaved convent women. She explained to Inquisitors that though she had not exclaimed the blasphemous words at the time of her actual beating, it was the sight of "María Mulata," whom she claimed was "so happy that [Catalina] had beaten her," and hearing her insults that had finally pushed her over the edge. María's testimony confirmed that the two slaves were enemies and that María enjoyed the favor of Catalina at the expense of Francisca. In contrast, the testimonies of the four convent servants who witnessed Francisca's outburst showed attempts at solidarity and concern for her wellbeing. They all said that Francisca was badly beaten

---

80  On uses of blasphemy, see Javier Villa-Flores, *Dangerous Speech: A Social History of Blasphemy in Colonial Mexico* (Tucson, AZ: University of Arizona Press, 2006).

81  "Le avian dho a la dha rectora su ama que esta andava buscando quien la comprasse por que estava desesperada en el dho convento."

82  "Viendo passar a María mulata esclava assimismo de la dha su ama con quien ha tenido y tiene cada dia muchas pesadumbres paresciendole que ella avia sido causa de que la acotassen."

83  "Que era una desvergonzada y que no por buena la avian vendido."

84  "Con el enojo que tenia reniego de Dios y de todos sus santos y de quien me dio la anima."

85  For another example of a nun abusing her servant, see Lavrin, *Brides of Christ*, 165.

and clearly in a state of despair and that she had repented right away and appeared to be sincere. They also noted that María had clearly provoked Francisca, even though Francisca's own story identifies herself as the instigator of the exchange of verbal insults.

It is possible that Francisca had purposely resorted to blasphemy as a way of seeking an audience with the Inquisition in order to convey her unhappiness in the hopes that these ecclesiastical authorities might order and arrange for her to be sold to someone else. This was a strategy that slaves occasionally utilized, but it was a risky one.[86] The blasphemous words had to appear spontaneous and to arise from a momentary loss of reason brought on by deep, intolerable despair, but they also must be accompanied by the appearance of true remorse if the guilty party was to escape with only minimal punishment. If this had indeed been Francisca's plan, perhaps she chose her timing to ensure that she had sympathetic witnesses. Perhaps she even discussed it with the convent servants, Maríana de los Reyes, Agustina Mendez, Elena de San Juan, and Catalina de las Virgines, before she had her outburst.

Convent mozas and esclavas, like the four who witnessed Francisca's blasphemous words, usually lived in separate, inferior quarters, either dormitories or small individual rooms; however, this did not preclude the possibility of regular exchange with the wider population of the convent. Personal servants would be called to assist convent servants in regular tasks and would of course share the experience of communal prayer, mass, and song; some nuns professed when they were very young or entered originally as niñas or educandas and may have grown up with convent servants their own age. Some of these playmates grew up to challenge the spoken and unspoken prohibitions against cross-status friendships, much to the concern of ecclesiastical authorities. Religious authorities were in fact quite worried about the "intense friendships" that could develop between convent women.[87] Archbishop Aguiar y Seijas, in his 1693 convent visits, used strong language urging abbesses to prevent relationships he referred to as "devotions" between convent women of different social levels. He was concerned about horizontal "devotions" between niñas or between nuns as well, but what most concerned him were the friendships that crossed social hierarchies. He claimed that the internal authority figures would be

---

86  Kathryn Joy McKnight, "Blasphemy as Resistance: An African Slave Woman before the Mexican Inquisition," in *Women in the Inquisition: Spain and the New World*, ed. Mary Giles (Baltimore, MD: Johns Hopkins University Press, 1999), 229–53; Solange Alberro, "Juan de Morga and Gertrudis de Escobar: Rebellious Slaves," in *Struggle and Survival in Colonial America*, ed. David G. Sweet and Gary B. Nash (Berkeley, CA: University of California Press, 1981), 165–88; Javier Villa-Flores, *Dangerous Speech*; and Solange Alberro, *Inquisición y Sociedad*, 455–79.

87  "Amistades muy estrechas." These concerns and this language are visible in many visit records of convents, colegios, and recogimientos. For example, see AHAM caja 20L; Vizcaínas 9-I-3.

vigilant about the relationships that niñas and religious women had with servants "[b]ecause they caused extremely grave inconvenience and notable scandal and spiritual ruin."[88] Alonso Nuñéz de Haro y Peralta echoed these concerns in 1776 when he warned against "intense friendships."[89]

However, there is at least one documented case of what appears to be romantic love between a nun and servant that developed through their daily contact in the convent. María Josefa Yldefonsa de San Juan Bautista Alvarez professed in the convent of Jesús María in México when she was fourteen years old.[90] As a young novice, she developed a connection with a convent servant named Gertrudis Rodríguez. The two became very close, and by Yldefonsa's own description, her attachment to Rodríguez became stronger than her commitment to her vows. At sixteen years of age, soon after Yldefonsa had completed her final vows, Rodríguez became determined to leave the convent, and Yldefonsa promised her "that she would not leave her, that she would go out to the street to live with her."[91] To do so, she employed the services of a silversmith named José Thomas Roberto Barreto, whom she had heard was versed in magic. Barreto told Yldefonsa he could help the two women escape and could set them up in a house together, where they would be protected by means of his magic. Barreto told Yldefonsa all of this through clandestine communications at the convent gate: he passed her a book with blank pages upon which words magically appeared when she read them at night.

It was this use of magic that ultimately brought the two women's relationship to light. María Yldefonsa was eighteen years old when she testified about her devotion to Gertrudis Rodríguez, describing it as a *mala amistad*, a phrase

---

88  "Por ser de gravísimo inconveniente y notable escándalo y ruina espiritual." Archivo Histórico de la Secretaria de Salud, Fondo Jesús María, sección legajos, exp. 17. Cited in Salazar Simarro, "Niñas, viudas, mozas," 177.

89  AHAM caja 20L.

90  AGN Inq. V. 1319, exp. 6. Stephanie Kirk discusses this case at length in her exploration of the possibility of romantic love and sexual relations between women in convents. Kirk discusses the Inquisitor's response to María Gertrudis, connecting their distrust of her testimony to the suggestion of same-sex relations it contained. She looks at *mala amistad* as a charge levied on Yldefonsa as a result of testifying against a man for magical practices, whereas I explore it here primarily as something she herself asserts in relation to her past connection with a convent servant. We both note that it was largely Yldefonsa's description of that relationship that led Inquisitors to believe she suffered from delusions, but for me, what is most striking in the Inquisitor's responses is the extent to which they focused on her as mentally unstable *rather* than as a sexual criminal, even if they suggested that it may have partially been her "illicit communication" with the servant that caused the instability. This appears to be the only case of its kind that either of us has found. Stephanie Kirk, "The Community of Lovers: Mala Amistad in the Convent," in *Convent Life in Colonial Mexico: A Tale of Two Communities* (Gainesville, FL: University Press of Florida, 2007), 51–80.

91  "A la moza solo le aseguró que no la dexaría y que saldría a la calle a vivir con ella."

usually reserved for illicit sexual relationships.[92] Inquisitors in turn pondered whether Yldefonsa had lost her reason as a result of her "desire to leave the cloister in order to be in the bad company of the servant with whom she had illicit communication."[93]

Emotional attachments of a different kind may have also developed between the nuns who served as *maestras de mozas*, or teachers of servants, and their pupils. These "lessons" could be fraught and especially brutal when the nuns resented the task and felt it was beneath them, but they could also facilitate regular personal interactions that were different from the usual contact nuns had with servants and enslaved women. Fr. Alonso Franco recognized and celebrated the "special patience" required of the maestra de mozas, indicating it was a position some nuns saw as a burden, but for which others took special pride in the virtues it necessitated and revealed.[94] Whatever her attitude toward them, the slaves and servants taught by this nun would certainly have developed a particular relationship with her. The maestras de mozas taught servants and slaves the same doctrine and collective prayers niñas and educandas learned, and though they were not required to teach them literacy, this was sometimes a part of the lessons as well, to better facilitate religious instruction. It was probably the maestra de mozas who would have noticed a slave or servant with a particularly strong religious vocation or who could affirm a miraculous vision one of her pupils might have had.[95]

Like other convent laywomen, servants and slaves were expected to follow the basic rhythms and requirements of the "rule" of the convent they were a part of, which meant regular participation in sacraments, prayers, singing, and celebrations. Servants and slaves who shared living quarters with nuns might have taken part in their particular spiritual practices as well, including daily mental prayer, saying the rosary, or devotions to a favorite saint. While some nuns probably excluded their servants from such activities, believing them appropriate only for the

92   "Mala amistad" usually referred to an ongoing and explicitly sexual relationship that was outside marriage.

93   In response to Inquisitors' question about what her motives were for wanting to leave the convent, she said: "con motivo de tener la que declara una mala amistad con una moza llamada María Gertrudis Rodríguez y haver determinado esta salirse de el conv.to quiso la declarante salir tambien por no separar de ella." Asked if she communicated the particular details of the magic José said he would use, María said: "a la moza solo le aseguró que no la dexaría y que saldría a la calle a vivir con ella, por que tenía facilidad para verificarlo." In debating María's sanity Inquisitors pondered whether she suffered "el engano de una fantasía lastimada por enfermedad o por la misma demensia de los deseos que tubo de salir de la claúsura para estar en la mala companía de la moza con que tubo ilícita correspondensia."

94   Sigüenza y Góngora, *Parayso occidental*, 108.

95   In discussing the story of María de San Juan, Lavrin notes that the abbess and later a "nun with visionary gifts" affirmed the servant's devotion and her mystical dream. Lavrin, *Brides of Christ*, 168.

spiritual elite, others probably ran their households like a family in which spiritual education was a part of daily life. Not all convents had a maestra de mozas, and nuns were expected to make sure that their individual servants and slaves received a proper Christian education. Some nuns were probably demanding teachers, requiring their pupils or servants and slaves to follow a set spiritual regimen, while others may have encouraged the particular devotions that appeared to come naturally to the women in their charge. A few examples appear in chronicles of nuns comforting servants or slaves after having spiritual experiences the latter did not understand.[96] In these stories, the servants appear to look to these nuns as spiritual mentors, suggesting that this was part of how the professed nuns understood themselves. In these narratives, nuns are presented much like spiritual directors (a role usually reserved for confessors), from whom their subordinates could and should seek counsel and guidance.

## Conclusions: The Liminality of Convent Laywomen

Convent laywomen were an integral part of convent communities. They made cloister possible, facilitating the practice of female seclusion, even as their multiracial and economically diverse presence challenged the exclusivity and "purity" of the convent community. Though not all of them benefited from the protective possibilities of recogimiento, they were all subject to its regimentation. Ecclesiastical authorities sometimes counted servants and slaves, along with niñas, widows, and depositadas, among the women they were supposedly protecting, and these laywomen were subject to spiritual and sacramental vigilance.

A wide range of experiences were possible for these women, including opportunities for a rich devotional life, some education, protective ties to nuns, and even gaining respect, spiritual status, and prestige. For servants and slaves, however, these opportunities could not change the central fact of servitude that fixed their place within the convent hierarchy. For many of them, this meant harsh labor demands, physical brutality, humiliation, and forced separation from family members. Slaves were treated as property, whatever other kinds of status they may have secured for themselves, and this meant that they were radically unfree; they were not free to leave, to stay if they were being sold, to keep their children with them, or to remain with parents or other loved ones. They were also at the whims of the nuns who owned them and had the power to negotiate their situations. Many servants were effectively trapped in convents as well, even though their legal status was not that of enslavement. For the most vulnerable among

---

96  Lavrin, *Brides of Christ*, 168; Salazar Simarro, "Niñas, viudas, mozas," 174.

them, escape may have been the only way to leave, and society provided so few options for them that even this was not likely to be a viable choice.

For all convent laywomen, nunneries represented a way to participate in female seclusion as a devotional practice, but whether this allowed them to access the benefits this seclusion could offer or primarily subjected them to its restrictions and burdens depended on the position they held both within and outside convent society. The variety of these positions mirrored the social hierarchies outside the convent, but with added complexities that were particular to a female society of cloister. From the perspective of convent laywomen, nuns must have seemed almost like a class of female clergy who exercised significant authority. And yet laywomen also understood that these prestigious women were themselves subordinate within the structure of the church. This dual hierarchy added layers to the vertical ties of patronage, protection, and even intimacy as they intermingled with relations of servitude and unequal status.

Convents were for nuns, so it seemed. However, most of them housed twice as many laywomen as nuns, and these laywomen both populated and gave texture to convent society. Ecclesiastical and royal objections to and worries about their presence show that from the perspective of male authorities, these women threatened and challenged the ideology and practice of female enclosure. However, the fierce reactions of nuns to reformers' attempts to remove convent laywomen suggest that they were also central to it, not insignificant participants or by-products of the needs of individual convents.

Convent laywomen comprised a diverse group of women who actually made possible the creation of female religious communities. These communities were hierarchically organized, and though society understood laywomen as legitimate beneficiaries of some of what convents had to offer – protection, feminine education, and pious seclusion – they were not equal members in it, and their presence was always controversial. Quite often perceived of as racially inferior, most laywomen were clearly marginalized within the vision of convents as homes for the spiritually and socially elite; and yet these homes would not have functioned without their labor and participation. Religious women's authority and status rested in many ways on the presence of laywomen, and in turn, the power and prestige of nuns shaped convent laywomen's daily experience of the church and religious culture.

# Conclusion
## Laywomen Making Colonial Catholicism

In New Spain, women, along with men, built the religious culture in which they lived, and this included laywomen. This should not be a controversial or novel claim, and yet it appears to be. To read almost anything about laywomen's engagement with the church in colonial Mexico is to imbibe a story of women who are, at best, creatively responding to something completely outside of their making. It is difficult to get beyond this depiction: sources reinforce it; historiography consolidates it; even popular assumptions and "common sense" seem to confirm it. Indeed, I am not sure how much I have managed to change that perception myself in these pages. But my intention has been to show that women's "responses to" religious authority, church institutions, theological concepts, and spiritual practices are only one part of the story of women's participation in religious culture. First, because these responses were not merely responses. They were active engagements, and they formed a part of a dialogue. And second, because that dialogue, which included men and women, laypeople, clergy, and nuns in both ordinary and extraordinary interactions, is itself what shaped and forged the contours of colonial Catholicism.

To suggest that women made colonial Catholicism along with men within a dialogic process is not to say that this dialogue was between equal partners. The disparity of power and autonomy between women and men, and in particular between laywomen and religious authorities and male lay leaders, is part of what makes it seem like women were forever responding to something that they did not author or create. But the point of this book has been to insist that this was not and could not have been the case. Learned men wrote theological texts, but the application of these texts took place within human interactions of which women took part. Church authorities claimed ultimate authority to interpret doctrine, regulate church rituals, and try to enforce public morality, but the authority of individual priests and judges and the efficacy of ecclesiastical justice depended on communities' sense of these authorities' legitimacy. And this legitimacy was conferred and contested by ordinary people, in a cumulative way, through interactions of which women were a part.

Gender norms, laws governing relationships between men and women, and the symbolic, spiritual, and theological significance of all of these regulations were clearly undergirded by a long tradition of patriarchy and misogyny that had profoundly deep roots by the colonial era. Women did not have equal mobility, choices, or capacity to exert power within this system. But this tradition and system had been and were nonetheless enacted through particular moments, choices, interpretations, and actions. And women participated in these. In other words, women and men both engaged with *it* – the "it" being the enormity of the Christian patriarchal tradition in the early modern world. And through these engagements, colonial religious culture was formed, re-formed, and changed.

Seen this way, the assertion that laywomen along with everyone else "made" colonial Catholicism is not a radical claim. In fact, it is such an obvious one that it seems almost banal, and yet it needs to be asserted. Women's authorship of culture – religious or otherwise – in most historical times and places prior to the nineteenth century (and some would argue long past it) still bears the burden of proof in our scholarship and too easily slides back into invisibility if we historians do not remain vigilant about the way we write about power, institutions, and authority.

However, the goal of these chapters has not merely been to prove this modest claim – that women participated in the making of the religious culture they were a part of – rather, the goal has been to discover and reveal something of *how* they did so. As for all but the most elite historical protagonists, this is not an easy task and not a new one; social historians have been hard at work for decades trying to illuminate the subtle, cumulative processes through which people incrementally made the world around them in various times and places. This book is a part of that larger task. I wanted to understand and explain some of the specific mechanisms, ideas, and processes by which and through which women helped make colonial Catholicism. I wanted to place their interactions with the church and the society it permeated within the context of a dialogic exchange that affected everyone and shaped everything that was a part of religious culture. In the process, I developed a few concepts and theories that helped me visualize the field within which women interacted with various aspects of the church and the dynamics through which they participated in various manifestations of religious culture. I have also chosen particular sites of interaction as vantage points. All of these choices necessarily shaped my view and presentation of these processes.

Four interconnected "theories" or underlying arguments animated each of the previous chapters, and it is appropriate here, by way of conclusion to underline them in a fairy pedantic way. The first is my proposal that there existed something usefully called spiritual status that was gendered, and which was something women could accumulate and lose. The second is that the following were shared understandings in colonial society: sin, scandal, and the emotional experiences of guilt and shame were contagious; the individual "self" was porous and capable of having an impact on the communal whole; and women were particularly contagious beings by nature. The third is that these shared beliefs and concepts gave rise to a broad ideology of recogimiento, which I also called a gendered and racialized theology of containment, and which placed women on a continuum of virtue and vice, envisioning some form of seclusion as necessary for all of them. And finally, the fourth is that this ideology of recogimiento not only animated places and practices of female cloister, but also lay at the very heart of colonial Catholicism. Early modern Christian theology linked sexuality, the body, and the eternal soul, and racialized colonial hierarchies heightened the earthly stakes of this link. These connections placed the control of women's bodies and souls at the very center of the Spanish imperial effort and the day-to-day workings of its lived theologies.

These proposals, along with the vantage points represented by the subjects of each chapter, illuminate particular aspects of laywomen's roles in the making and shaping of colonial Catholicism, but they also must certainly obscure others. Other schema and vantage points are needed in order to fill out the picture, and I hope other scholars will pursue them. What these particular ones I have chosen offer us is a way of seeing women's interpretive work at a level that is fairly finely grained. Using these ideas as frameworks, women's choices and actions come into better focus.

Women were often unaware, just as men were, of the larger impact of their choices and actions. They were probably not intentionally forging new meanings for the mandate that women be secluded, modest, and obedient – at least not usually. They were probably not intentionally creating alternative sacramental practices of unburdening or consuming the Eucharist that would bypass some of the constraints of the doctrinal proscriptions – at least not framed in that way. And they were almost certainly not purposely turning religious misogyny and the concept of female contagion on their heads when they argued that religious authorities had an obligation to help them regain their honor by correcting and punishing the men who had harmed them, precisely *because*, by being harmed, these women had unwittingly become sources of harm for others.

In other words, most laywomen, most of the time, were probably not trying to make, shape, or change colonial Catholicism. Nonetheless, through all of these ordinary acts of negotiation, interpretation, and survival, they were indeed doing just that. Simply put, these interactions and the dialogue they were a part of were some of the ways that women participated in, and, indeed, authored and created, the religious culture that they were, always, already a part of. In other words, through this participation, in partnership with laymen, clergy, and religious women, laywomen made and shaped the religious worlds in which they lived.

# Bibliography

## Primary Sources

### Archival Collections
#### Bancroft Library, Berkeley, CA

Mexican Inquisition Original Documents
**Cited as "Banc."**

*Center for the Study of Mexican History, Condumex (CEHM), Mexico City, Mexico*
Biblioteca (Bib.)
Miscelanea (Misc.)
Consulta (Cons.)
Sección Folletos (Sec. Fol.)

*Historical Archives of the Archbishopric of Mexico (AHAM), Mexico City, Mexico*
Fondo Juzgado Eclesiástico de Toluca
Fondo Episcopal
Fondo Cabildo
All cited as "AHAM"

*Historical Archive of the Colegio Vizcaínas (AHCV), Mexico City, Mexico*
El Colegio de las Niñas
El Recogimiento y Colegio de San Miguel de Belem
El Colegio Real de las Vizcaínas
All cited as **"AHCV"**

*National Archives of Mexico (AGN), Mexico City, Mexico*
Ramo Arzopispos y Obispos (Ar.Ob.)
Ramo Acordada (Acord.)
Ramo Alcaldes Mayores (A.May.)
Ramo Ayuntamientos (Ayunt.)
Ramo Bienes Nacionales (B.Nac.)

Ramo Capellanías (Cap.)
Ramo Cárceles y Presidios (Cár.Pres.)
Ramo Civil (Civ.)
Ramo Clero Regular y Secular (C.Reg.Sec.)
Ramo Colegios (Col.)
Ramo Consolidaciones (Cons.)
Ramo Correspondencias de Diversos Autoridades (C.Div.Aut.)
Ramo Criminal (Crim.)
Ramo Iglesias (Igl.)
Ramo Indios (Ind.)
Ramo Inquisición (Inq.)
Ramo Jesuitas (Jes.)
Ramo Judicial (Jud.)
Ramo Matrimoniales (Mat.)
Ramo Obras Pías (O.Pías)
Ramo Obras Públicas (O.Púb.)
Ramo Protomedicato (Proto.)
Ramo Real Audiencia (R.A.)
Ramo Real Cédula (Ced.)
Ramo Templos y Conventos (Temp.Conv.)
Ramo Temporalidades (Temp.)
Ramo Tierras (Tier.)
Ramo Tributos (Trib.)

*National Library of Mexico (BN), Mexico City, Mexico*
Fondo Reservado: Colección La Fragua (LAF)

## Published Primary Sources

Carta, Gabino. *Práctica de confessores*. Mexico City: Viuda de Bernardo Calderon, 1653.
Escriche, don Joachín. *Diccionario razonado de legislación y jurisprudencia*. Madrid: Viuda e hijos de D. Antonio Callejo, 1847.
Gómez, Fr. Joseph. *Vida de la venerable Madre Antonia de San Jacinto*. Mexico City: Imprenta de Antuerpia de los Herederos de la Viuda de Bernardo de Calderón, 1689.
Sigüenza y Góngora, Carlos de. *Parayso occidental plantado y cultivado por la liberal beneficio mano de los muy Católicos y poderosos Reyes de España nuestros señores en su maginífico real convento de Jesús María de México*. Mexico City: UMAM-Condumex, 1995, 1684.

## Secondary Sources

Alberro, Solange. "El matrimonio, la sexualidad y la unidad doméstica entre los cripto judíos de la Nueva España, 1640–1650." In *El placer de pecar y el afán de normar*, edited by

Sergio Ortega Noriega and the Seminario de Historia de las Mentalidades, 103–66. Mexico City: Instituto Nacional de Antropolgía e Historia, 1987.

"Herejes, brujas, y beatas: mujeres ante el tribunal del Santo Oficio de la Inquisición en la Nueva España." In *Presencia y transparencia: la mujer en la historia de México*, edited by Carmon Ramos Escandón, 79–94. Mexico City: El Colegio de México, 1987.

"Juan de Morga and Gertrudis de Escobar: Rebellious Slaves." In *Struggle and Survival in Colonial America*, edited by David G. Sweet and Gary B. Nash, 165–88. Berkeley, CA: University of California Press, 1981.

*Inquisición y Sociedad en México 1571–1700.* Mexico City: Centro de Estudios Mexicanos y Centro Americanos, 1988.

*Seis ensayos sobre el discurso colonial relativo a la comunidad doméstica: matrimonio, familia, y sexualidad a través de los cronistas del siglo XVI, el Nuevo Testamento, y el Santo Oficio de la Inquisición.* Mexico City: Departamento de Investigaciones Históricas, INAH, 1989.

Arenas Frutos, Isabel. *Dos arzobispos de México: Lorenzana y Núñez de Haro, ante la reforma conventual femenina (1766–1775).* León: Universidad de León, 2004.

"Innovaciones educativas en el mundo conventual femenino. Nueva España, siglo XVIII: el Colegio de Niñas de Jesús María." In *Memoria del II Congreso Internacional: El Monacato Femenino en el Imperio Español: Monasterios, beaterios, recogimientos y colegios: Homenaje a Josefina Muriel*, edited by Manuel Ramos Media, 443–54. Mexico City: Centro de Estudios de Historia de México, Condumex, 1995.

"Las 'otras': Niñas y criadas ante la reforma conventual femenina en México y Puebla de los Angles." In *España y América entre el barroco y la Ilustración (1722–1804)*, edited by Jesús Paniagua Pérez, 191–210. León: Universidad de León, 2005.

Arrom, Silvia Marina. "Las Señoras de la Caridad: pioneras olvidadas de la asistencia social en México, 1863–1910." *Historia Mexicana* 57, no. 2 (Oct.–Dec. 2007): 445–90.

"Mexican Laywomen Spearhead a Catholic Revival: The Ladies of Charity, 1863–1910." In *Religious Culture in Modern Mexico*, edited by Martin Austin Nesvig, 50–77. Lanham, MD: Rowman and Littlefield Publishers Inc., 2007.

Bakewell, Peter, and Jaqueline Holler, *A History of Latin America to 1825*, third edn. Malden, MA: John Wiley & Sons, 2010.

Bartra, Roger. *Transgresión y melancholia en el México colonial.* Mexico City: UNAM-Centro de Investigaciones Interdisciplinarias en Ciencias y Humanidades, 2004.

Bauer, Arnold, ed. *La Iglesia en la economía de América Latina, siglos XVI al XIX.* México: Instituto Nacional de Antropología e Historia, 1986.

Bazarte Martínez, Alicia. *Las cofradías de españoles en la ciudad de México.* Mexico City: UNAM, 1998.

Behar, Ruth. "Sexual Witchcraft, Colonialism, and Women's Powers: Views from the Mexican Inquisition." In *Sexuality and Marriage in Colonial Latin America*, edited by Asunción Lavrin, 178–208. Lincoln, NE: University of Nebraska Press, 1989.

Bilinkoff, Jodi. "Confessors, Penitents, and the Construction of Identities in Early Modern Avila." In *Culture and Identity in Early Modern Europe: Essays in Honor of Natalie Zemon Davis*, edited by Barbara B. Diefendorf and Carla Hesse, 83–100. Ann Arbor, MI: University of Michigan Press, 1993.

*Related Lives: Confessors and Their Female Penitents, 1450–1750.* Ithaca, NY: Cornell University Press, 2005.

Boyer, Richard. *Lives of the Bigamists: Marriage, Family, and Community in Colonial Mexico.* Albuquerque, NM: University of New Mexico Press, 1995.

"Women, 'La Mala Vida,' and the Politics of Marriage." In *Sexuality and Marriage in Colonial Latin America*, edited by Asunción Lavrin. Lincoln, NE: University of Nebraska Press, 1989, 252–86.

Boyle, Margaret. *Unruly Women: Performance, Penitence, and Punishment in Early Modern Spain.* Toronto: University of Toronto Press, 2014.

Bowers, Kristy Wilson. *Plague and Public Health in Early Modern Seville.* Rochester, NY: University of Rochester Press, 2013.

Brading, D. A. *Church and State in Bourbon Mexico: The Diocese of Michoacán, 1749–1810.* Cambridge: Cambridge University Press, 1994.

Bristol, Joan Cameron. *Christians, Blasphemers, and Witches: Afro-Mexican Ritual Practice in the Seventeenth Century.* Albuquerque, NM: University of New Mexico Press, 2007.

Burns, Kathryn. *Colonial Habits: Convents and the Spiritual Economy of Cuzco, Peru.* Durham, NC: Duke University Press, 1999.

Carballeda, Angela. "Género y matrimonio en Nueva España: las mujeres de la elite ante la aplicación de la Pragmática de 1776." In *Las mujeres en la construcción de las sociedades iberoamericanas*, edited by Pilar Gonzalbo Aizpuru and Berta Ares Queija, 219–50. México: El Colegio de México, Centro de Estudios Históricos, 2004.

Castañeda, Carmen. "Relaciones entre beaterios, colegios y conventos femeninos en Guadalajara, época colonial." In *Memoria del II Congreso Internacional: El Monacato Femenino en el Imperio Español: Monasterios, beaterios, recogimientos y colegios: Homenaje a Josefina Muriel*, edited by Manuel Ramos Media, 455–76. Mexico City: Centro de Estudios de Historia de México, Condumex, 1995.

Chowning, Margaret. "Convents and Nuns: New Approaches to the Study of Female Religious Institutions in Colonial Mexico." *History Compass* 6, no. 5 (2008): 1279–1303.

"Convent Reform, Catholic Reform, and Bourbon Reform in Eighteenth-Century New Spain: The View from the Nunnery." *Hispanic American Historical Reviews* 85 (2005): 1–37.

"La femenización de la piedad en México: Género y piedad en las cofradías de españoles: Tendencias coloniales y pos-coloniales en los arzobispados de Michoacán y Guadalajara." In *Religión, política e identidad en la época de la independencia de México*, edited by Brian Connaughton. Mexico City: UAM, 2010.

"The Catholic Church and the Ladies of the Vela Perpetua: Gender and Devotional Change in Nineteenth-Century Mexico," *Past and Present* 221 (Nov. 2013).

"Liberals, Women, and the Church in Mexico: Politics and the Feminization of Piety, 1700–1930." Paper presented at the Harvard Latin American Studies seminar, Cambridge, MA, 2002.

*Rebellious Nuns: The Troubled History of a Mexican Convent, 1751–1863.* New York, NY: Oxford University Press, 2006.

"Sensuality and Sentiment: The Transnational Church and Latin American Nationalisms, Commentary." Comments presented at the Tri-annual Meeting of the Berkshire Conference of the History of Women, Claremont, CA, June 2–5, 2005.

Christian, William. *Local Religion in Sixteenth-Century Spain.* Princeton, NJ: Princeton University Press, 1981.

Chuchiak, John. "Secrets behind the Screen: Solicitantes in the Colonial Diocese of Yucatan and the Yucatec Maya, 1570–1785." In *Religion in New Spain*, edited by Susan Shroeder and Stafford Poole, 83–110. Albuquerque, NM: University of New Mexico Press, 2007.

Cope, Douglas. *The Limits of Racial Domination: Plebeian Society in Colonial Mexico City, 1660–1720.* Madison, WI: University of Wisconsin Press, 1994.

Costeloe, Michael. *Church Wealth in Mexico: A Study of the Juzgado de Capellanías in the Archbishopric of Mexico, 1800–1856.* London: Cambridge University Press, 1967.

"Rosa de Escalante's Private Party: Popular Female Religiosity in Colonial Mexico City." In *Women in the Inquisition: Spain and the New World*, edited by Mary Giles, 254–69. Baltimore, MD: The Johns Hopkins University Press, 1999.

*The Great Festivals of Colonial Mexico City: Performing Power and Identity*. Albuquerque, NM: University of New Mexico Press, 2004.

Dávila Mendoza, Dora. *Hasta que la muerte nos separe: El divorcio eclesiástico en el arzobispado de México, 1702–1800*. Mexico City: El Colegio de México, 2005.

"Vida matrimonial y orden burocrático. Una visión a través de el quaderno de los divorcios, 1754 a 1820, en el arzobispado de la ciudad de México." In *Historia, género y familia en iberoamérica (siglos XVI a XX)*, edited by Dora Davila Mendoza, 161–208. Caracas: Konrad Adenauer, 2004.

de Boer, Wietse. *The Conquests of the Soul: Confession, Discipline, and Public Order in Counter-Reformation Milan*. Leiden: Brill, 2001.

de Bujanda, Jesús M. "Recent Historiography of the Spanish Inquisition (1977–1988): Balance and Perspective." In *Cultural Encounters: The Impact of the Inquisition in Spain and the New World*, edited by Mary Elizabeth Perry and Anne J. Cruz, 221–47. Berkeley: University of California Press, 1991.

Delgado, Jessica. "Foregrounding Marginal Voices: Writing Women's Stories Using Solicitation Trials." In *Imagining Histories of Colonial Latin America: Synoptic Methods and Practices*, edited by Sylvia Sellers-Garcia and Karen Melvin. Albuquerque, NM: University of New Mexico Press, 2017.

"Virtuous Women and the Contagion of Sin: Race, Poverty, and Women's Spiritual Status in Colonial Mexico," unpublished essay.

"Confesar, Comulgar, y Solicitar: Solicitation and the Sacraments in Women's Lives, New Spain." Paper presented at the Annual Meeting of the Latin American Studies Association, Montreal, Can., Sept. 6–8, 2007.

"La Beata del Habito Negro." Paper presented at the Annual Meeting of the American Society for Eighteenth Century Studies, Las Vegas, NN, March 31–April 3, 2005.

"The Beata of Sayula: Colonialism, Sexuality, and Religious Authority in Eighteenth-Century New Spain." Paper presented at the Tri-annual Meeting of the Berkshire Conference of the History of Women, Claremont, CA, June 2–5, 2005.

"Contagious Sin and Virtue: Race, Poverty, and Women's Spiritual Status in Colonial Mexico," Paper presented at the Annual Meeting of the American Academy of Religion, Chicago, November 2012a.

"Public Piety and *Honestidad*: Women's Spiritual Status in Colonial Mexico," Paper presented at the Annual Meeting of the American Academy of Religion, Chicago, November 2012b.

*The Beata of the Black Habit: María Anastasia González and Late Colonial Anxieties*, unpublished book manuscript.

Delgado, Jessica and Kelsey Moss. "Race and Religion in the Early Modern Iberian Atlantic," in *The Oxford Handbook of Religion and Race in American History*, edited by Kathryn Gin Lum and Paul Harvey. Oxford: Oxford University Press, 2018.

Delumeau, Jean. *Catholicism between Luther and Voltaire: A New View of the Counter-Reformation*. London: Burns and Oats, 1977.

Dopica Black, Georgina. *Perfect Wives, Other Women: Adultery and Inquisition in Early Modern Spain*. Durham, NC: Duke University Press, 2001.

Farriss, Nancy. *Crown and Clergy in Colonial Mexico, 1759–1821: The Crisis of Ecclesiastical Privilege*. London: Athlone, 1968.

Few, Martha. *Women Who Live Evil Lives: Gender, Religion, and the Politics of Power in Colonial Guatemala*. Austin, TX: University of Texas Press, 2002.

Firey, Abigail, ed. *A New History of Penance*. Boston, MA: Brill Press, 2008.

Foucault, Michel. *History of Sexuality, V. I.* New York, NY: Random House, 1978.

Fracastorii, Hieronymi. *De Contagione Et Contagiosis Morbis Et Eorum Curatione, Libri III*, translation and notes by Wilmer Cave Wright. New York, NY: The Knickerbocker Press, 1930.

Gauderman, Kimberly. *Women's Lives in Colonial Quito: Gender, Law, and Economy in Spanish America*. Austin, TX: University of Texas Press, 2003.

Gerhard, Peter. *A Guide to the Historical Geography of New Spain*. Norman, OK: University of Oklahoma Press, 1993.

Gilchrist, Roberta. *Gender and Material Culture: The Archaeology of Religious Women*. London: Routledge, 1994.

Giles, Mary, ed. *Women in the Inquisition: Spain and the New World*. Baltimore, MD: Johns Hopkins University Press, 1999.

Giraud, Francois. "La reacción social ante la violación: del discurso a la práctica. (Nueva España, Siglo XVIII)." In *El placer de pecar y el afán de normar*, edited by Seminario de Historia de las Mentalidades, 295–352. Mexico City: Joaquin Mortiz/Instituto Nacional de Antropología e Historia, 1988.

Gonzalbo Aizpuru, Pilar. *Familia y orden colonial*. Mexico City: El Colegio de México, 1998.

*Historia de la educación en la época colonial: El mundo indígena*. Mexico City: El Colegio de México, 1990.

*Historia de la vida cotidiana en México, Vols. I–III*. Mexico City: El Colegio de México, Fondo de Cultura Económica, 2004.

*Las mujeres en la Nueva España: Educación y vida cotidiana*. Mexico City: El Colegio de México, Centro de Estudios Históricos, 1987.

"Las mujeres novohispanas y las contradicciones de una sociedad patriarchal." In *Las mujeres en la construcción de las sociedades iberoamericanas*, edited by Pilar Gonzalbo Aizpuru and Berta Ares Queija, 121–40. Mexico City: El Colegio de México, Centro de Estudios Históricos, 2004.

"Reffugium Virginum. Beneficencia y educación en los colegios y conventos novohispanos." In *Memoria del II Congreso Internacional: El Monacato Femenino en el Imperio Español: Monasterios, beaterios, recogimientos y colegios: Homenaje a Josefina Muriel*, edited by Manuel Ramos Media, 429–41. Mexico City: Centro de Estudios de Historia de México, Condumex, 1995.

"Violencia y discordia en las relaciones personales en la Ciudad de México a finés del Siglo XVIII," *Historia Mexicana* 51, no. 2 (2001): 233–59.

González Marmolej, Jorge René. *Sexo y confesión: La Iglesia y la penitencia en los siglos XVIII y XIX en la Nueva España*. Mexico City: Instituto Nacional de Antropología e Historia, 2002.

Greenleaf, Richard. "Historiography of the Mexican Inquisition: Evolution of Interpretations and Methodologies." In *Cultural Encounters: The Impact of the Inquisition in Spain and the New World*, edited by Mary Elizabeth Perry and Anne J. Cruz, 249–73. Berkeley, CA: University of California Press, 1991.

"The Inquisition and the Indians of New Spain: A Study in Jurisdictional Confusion," *The Americas* 22, no. 2 (Oct. 1965): 138–66.

"The Inquisition in Eighteenth Century Mexico." *New Mexico Historical Review* 60 (1985): 29–60.

"The Mexican Inquisition and the Indians: Sources for the Ethnohistorian." *The Americas* 34, no. 3 (Jan. 1978): 315–44.

*The Mexican Inquisition of the Sixteenth Century*. Albuquerque, NM: University of New Mexico Press, 1969.

*Zumárraga and the Mexican Inquisition, 1536–1543.* Washington, DC: Academy of American Franciscan History, 1962.

Griffiths, Nicholas, and Fernando Cervantes, eds. *Spiritual Encounters: Interactions Between Christianity and Native Religions in Colonial America.* Birmingham, AL: University of Birmingham Press, 1999.

Gruzinski, Serge. "Individualization and Acculturation: Confession among the Nahuas of Mexico from the Sixteenth to the Eighteenth Century." In *Sexuality and Marriage in Colonial Latin America,* edited by Asunción Lavrin, 96–117. Lincoln, NE: University of Nebraska Press, 1989.

Gutiérrez, Ramón. *When Jesus Came, the Corn Mothers Went Away: Marriage, Sexuality, and Power in New Mexico, 1500–1846.* Stanford, CA: Stanford University Press, 1991.

Haliczer, Stephen. *Sexuality in the Confessional: A Sacrament Profaned.* New York, NY: Oxford University Press, 1996.

Holler, Jacqueline. *"Escogidas Plantas": Nuns and Beatas in Mexico City, 1531–1601.* New York, NY: Columbia University, 2005.

Hordes, Stanley. "The Inquisition as Economic and Political Agent: The Campaign of the Mexican Holy Office against the Crypto-Jews in the Mid-Seventeenth Century." *The Americas* 39, no. 1 (July 1982): 23–38.

Hughes, Jennifer Scheper. *Biography of a Mexican Crucifix: Lived Religion and Local Faith from the Conquest to the Present.* Oxford: Oxford University Press, 2010.

Hunefeldt, Christine. "Los beaterios y los conflictos matrimoniales en el siglo XIX, limeño." In *La familia en el mundo iberoamericano,* edited by Pilar Gonzalbo Aizpuru, 227–64. Mexico City: Instituto de Investigaciones Sociales, Universidad Nacional Autónoma de México, 1994.

Ibsen, Kristine. *Women's Spiritual Autobiography in Colonial Spanish America.* Gainesville, FL: University Press of Florida, 1999.

Israel, Jonathan. *Race, Class, and Politics in Colonial Mexico, 1610–1670.* New York, NY: Oxford University Press, 1975.

Jaffary, Nora E. *False Mystics: Deviant Orthodoxy in Colonial Mexico.* Lincoln, NE: University of Nebraska, 2004.

Juárez Bacerra, Isabel. "Reformación femenina en Nueva Galicia: la Casa de Recogidas de Guadalajara," *Revista Historia* 2.0 3, no. 5 (June 2013).

Kagan, Richard. *Lucrecia's Dreams: Politics and Prophecy in Sixteenth-Century Spain.* Berkeley, CA: University of California Press, 1990.

Kanter, Deborah. *Hijos del Pueblo: Gender, Family, and Community in Rural Mexico, 1730–1850.* Austin, TX: University of Texas Press, 2009.

Katzew, Ilona. *Casta Painting: Images of Race in Eighteenth-Century Mexico.* New Haven, CT: Yale University Press, 2004.

Krause, Virginia. *Witchcraft, Demonology, and Confession in Early Modern France.* New York, NY: Cambridge University Press, 2015.

Kirk, Stephanie. *Convent Life in Colonial Mexico: A Tale of Two Communities.* Gainesville, FL: University Press of Florida, 2007.

Klor de Alva, Jorge. "Colonizing Souls: The Failure of the Indian Inquisition and the Rise of Penitential Discipline." In *Cultural Encounters: The Impact of the Inquisition in Spain and the New World,* edited by Mary Elizabeth Perry and Anne J. Cruz, 3–21. Berkeley, CA: University of California Press, 1991.

———. "'Telling Lives': Confessional Autobiography and the Reconstruction of the Nahua Self." In *Spiritual Encounters: Interactions Between Christianity and Native Religions in Colonial America,* edited by Nicholas Griffiths and Fernando Cervantes, 136–62. Lincoln, NE: University of Nebraska Press, 1999.

Lavrin, Asunción. *Brides of Christ: Conventual Life in Colonial Mexico*. Stanford, CA: Stanford University Press, 2008.

"Cofradías novohispanas: Economías material y espiritual." In *Cofradías, capellanías y obras pías en la América colonial*, edited by Pilar Martínez López-Cano, Gisela Von Wobeser, and Juan Guillermo Muñoz, 49–64. Mexico City: UNAM, 1998.

"Ecclesiastical Reform of Nunneries in New Spain in the Eighteenth Century." *The Americas* 22, no. 1 (1965): 182–203.

"Introduction: The Scenario, the Actors, and the Issues." In *Sexuality and Marriage in Colonial Latin America*, edited by Asunción Lavrin, 1–46. Lincoln, NE: University of Nebraska Press, 1989.

"La sexualidad y las normas de la moral sexual." In *Historia de la vida cotidiana en México II La ciudad barroco*, edited by Antonio Rubial García and Pilar Gonzalbo Aizpuru, 489–517. Mexico City: El Colegio de México, 2005.

"Sexuality in Colonial Mexico: A Church Dilemma." In *Sexuality and Marriage in Colonial Latin America*, edited by Asunción Lavrin, 47–95. Lincoln, NE: University of Nebraska Press, 1989.

*Sexuality & Marriage in Colonial Latin America*. Lincoln, NE: University of Nebraska Press, 1989.

"The Church as an Economic Institution." In *The Roman Catholic Church in Colonial Latin America*, edited by Richard Greenleaf, 182–94. New York, NY: Knopf, 1971.

*Alone at the Altar: Single Women and Devotion in Guatemala, 1670–1870*. Stanford, CA: Stanford University Press, January 2018.

Leonard, Irving A. *Baroque Times in Old Mexico*. Ann Arbor, MI: University of Michigan Press, 1966.

Lewis, Laura. *Hall of Mirrors: Power, Witchcraft, and Caste in Colonial Mexico*. Durham, NC: Duke University Press, 2003.

Lockhart, James. "Capital and Province, Spaniard and Indian: The Example of Late Sixteenth-Century Toluca." In *Provinces of Early Mexico: Variants of Spanish American Regional Evolution*, edited by Ida Altman and James Lockhart, 99–123. Los Angeles, CA: UCLA Latin American Center Publications, 1976.

*Nahuas and Spaniards: Postconquest Central Mexican History and Philology*. Stanford, CA: Stanford University Press, 1991.

Loreto López, Rosalva. "Familias y conventos en Puebla de los Angeles durante las reformas borbónicas: Los cambios del siglo XVIII." *Anuario del IHES* 5 (1990): 31–50.

*Los conventos femeninos y el mundo urbano de la Puebla de los Ángeles del siglo XVIII*. Mexico City: El Colegio de México, Centro de Estudios Históricos, 2000.

Luque Agraz, Elin, and Mary Michele Beltrán. *El arte de dar gracias: Selección de exvotos pictóricos del Museo de la Basílica de Guadalupe*. Mexico City: Universidad Iberoamericana, 2003.

Luque Alcaide, Elisa. "Coyuntura social y cofradía: Cofradías de Aránzazu de Lima y México." In *Cofradías,capellanías, y obras pías en la América Colonial*, edited by Pilar Martínez López-Cano, Gisela Von Wobeser, and Juan Guillermo Muñoz, 91–108. Mexico City: UNAM, 1998.

Martinez, María Elena. *Genealogical Fictions: Limpieza de Sangre, Religion, and Gender in Colonial Mexico*. Stanford, CA: Stanford University Press, 2008.

Martinez, María Elena, Max-Sebastián Hering Torres, and David Nirenberg, eds. *Race and Blood in the Iberian World*. Zurich: Lit Verlag, 2012.

Martinez-Alier, Verena. *Marriage, Class, and Colour in Nineteenth-Century Cuba: A Study of Racial Attitudes and Sexual Values in a Slave Society*. Ann Arbor, MI: University of Michigan Press, 1989.

Martínez López-Cano, Pilar, and Gisela Von Wobeser, and Juan Guillermo Muñoz, eds. *Cofradías, capellanías y obras pías en la América colonial.* Mexico City: UNAM, 1998.

Mayer, Alicia, and Ernesto de la Torre Villar, eds. *Religión, Poder, y Autoridad en la Nueva España.* Mexico City: Universidad Nacional Autónoma de México, 2004.

McKnight, Kathryn Joy. "Blasphemy as Resistance: An African Slave Woman before the Mexican Inquisition." In *Women in the Inquisition: Spain and the New World*, edited by Mary Giles, 229–53. Baltimore, MD: The Johns Hopkins University Press, 1999.

Megged, Amos. *Exporting the Catholic Reformation: Local Religion in Early Colonial Mexico.* New York, NY: Brill Press, 1996.

Mellot, David. *I Was and I Am Dust: Penitente Practices as a Way of Knowing.* Collegeville, MN: Liturgical Press, 2009.

Melvin, Karen. *Building Colonial Cities of God: Mendicant Orders and Urban Culture in New Spain.* New York, NY: Cambridge University Press, 2012.

Mills, Kenneth, William B. Taylor, and Sandra Lauderdale Graham, eds. *Colonial Latin America: A Documentary History.* New York, NY: SR Books, 2002.

Morril, Bruce T., Joanna E. Ziegler, and Susan Rodgers, eds. *Practicing Catholic: Ritual, Body, and Contestation in Catholic Faith.* New York, NY: Palgrave Macmillan, 2006.

Moss, Kelsey. "Instructions in Faith: Constructing Religious and Racial Difference through Evangelizing Discourse in the Early Americas," presented at the AAR annual meeting, Atlanta, GA, November 2015.

"On Earth As It Is in Heaven: Constructions of Race & Religion in the Colonial Americas from Encounter to Enlightenment," dissertation, Princeton University, Princeton, NJ, 2018.

Moss, Kelsey, and Jessica Delgado. "Race and Religion in the Early Modern Iberian Atlantic," in *The Oxford Handbook of Religion and Race in American History*, edited by Kathryn Gin Lum and Paul Harvey. Oxford: Oxford University Press, 2018.

Muriel, Josefina. *Conventos de Monjas en Nueva España.* Mexico City: Editorial Jus, 1946, 1995.

*La sociedad novohispana y sus colegios de niñas I.* Mexico City: UNAM, 1995.

*La sociedad novohispana y sus colegios de niñas II.* Mexico City: UNAM, 2004.

*Los recogimientos de mujeres: Respuesta a una problematica social novohispana.* Mexico City: UNAM, 1974.

Nesvig, Martin Austin, ed. *Local Religion in Colonial Mexico.* Albuquerque, NM: University of New Mexico Press, 2006.

Nutton, Vivian. "Seeds of Disease: An Explanation of Contagion and Infection from the Greeks to the Renaissance," *Medical History* 27 (1983): 1–34.

Osmond, Rosalie. *Mutual Accusation: Seventeenth-Century Body and Soul Dialogues in Their Literary and Theological Content.* Toronto: University of Toronto Press, 1990.

O'Banion, Patrick J. *The Sacrament of Penance and Religious Life in Golden Age Spain.* University Park, PA: Pennsylvania State University Press, 2012.

O'Toole, Rachel Sarah. *Bound Lives: Africans, Indians, and the Making of Race in Colonial Peru.* Pittsburgh, PA: University of Pittsburgh Press, 2012.

Pabel, Hilmar, and Kathleen Comerford, eds. *Early Modern Catholicism: Essays in Honor of John W. O'Malley.* Toronto: University of Toronto Press, 2001.

Penyak, Lee M. "Safe Harbors and Compulsory Custody: Casas de Depósito in Mexico, 1750–1865," *The Hispanic American Historical Review* 79, no. 1 (Feb. 1999): 83–99.

Pérez Baltasar, Dolores. "Orígenes de los recogimientos de mujeres," *Cuaderno de Historia Moderna y Contemporanea* 6 (1985): 20.

Perry, Mary Elizabeth, and Anne J. Cruz, eds. *Cultural Encounters: The Impact of the Inquisition in Spain and the New World.* Berkeley, CA: University of California Press, 1991.

Pescador, Juan Javier. "Entre la espada y el olvido: pleitos matrimoniales en el provisorato eclesiástico de México, siglo XVIII." In *La familia en el mundo iberoamericano*, edited by Pilar Gonzalbo Aizpuru, 193–225. Mexico City: Instituto de Investigaciones Sociales, Universidad Nacional Autónoma de México, 1994.

Pizzigoni, Caterina. *The Life Within: Local Indigenous Society in Mexico's Toluca Valley, 1650–1800*. Stanford, CA: Stanford University Press, 2012.

ed. *Testaments of Toluca*. Stanford, CA: Stanford University Press, 2007.

"'Como frágil y miserable': Las mujeres Nahuas en el valle de Toluca." In *Historia de la vida cotidiana en México: El siglo XVIII: Entre tradición y cambio*, edited by Pilar Gonzalbo Aizpuru, 501–30. Mexico City: El Colegio de México, 2005.

"'Para que le sirva de castigo y al pueblo de exemplo'. El pecado de poligamia y la mujer indígena en el valle de Toluca (siglo XVIII)." In *Las mujeres en la construcción de las sociedades iberoamericanas*, edited by Pilar Gonzalbo Aizpuru and Berta Ares Queija, 193–218. Sevilla-México: Colegio de México, Centro de Estudios Históricos, 2004.

Premo, Bianca. *Enlightenment on Trial: Ordinary Litigants and Colonialism in the Spanish Empire*. New York, NY: Oxford University Press, 2017.

"'The Little Hiders' and Other Reflections on the History of Childhood in Imperial Iberoamerica." In *Raising an Empire: Children in Early Modern Iberia and Colonial Latin America*, edited by Bianca Premo and Ondina González, 238–48. Albuquerque, NM: University of New Mexico Press, 2007.

Salazar de Garza, Nuria. *La vida común en los conventos de monjas de la ciudad de Puebla*. Puebla: Biblioteca Angelopolitana, Gobierno del Estado de Puebla, Secretaría de Cultura, 1990.

Salazar Simarro, Nuria. "Niñas, viudas, mozas y esclavas en la clausura monjil." In *La "América abundante" de Sor Juana*, edited by María del Consuelo Maquivar, 161–90. Mexico City: Instituto Nacional de Antropología e Historia, 1995.

Sampson Vera Tudela, Elisa. *Colonial Angels: Narratives of Gender and Spirituality in Mexico, 1580–1750*. Austin, TX: University of Texas Press, 2000.

Sarabia Viejo, María Justina. "Controversias sobre la 'vida común' ante la reforma monacal femenina en México." In *Actas del II Congreso Internacional del Monacato Femenino en el Imperio Español: Monasterios, beaterios, recogimientos y colegios: Homenaje a Josefina Muriel*, edited by Manuel Ramos Medina, 583–92. Mexico City: Condumex, 1995.

Sarrión Mora, Adelina. *Sexualidad y confesión: la solicitación ante el Tribunal del Santo Oficio (siglos XVI–XIX)*. Madrid: Alianza Universidad, 1994.

Schlau, Stacey. *Gendered Crime and Punishment: Women and/in the Hispanic Inquisitions*. Boston, MA: Brill, 2013.

Schwartz, Stuart. *All Can Be Saved: Religious Tolerance and Salvation in the Iberian Atlantic World*. New Haven, CT: Yale University Press, 2008.

Seed, Patricia. *To Love, Honor, and Obey in Colonial Mexico: Conflicts over Marriage Choice, 1574–1821*. Stanford, CA: Stanford University Press, 1988.

Sluhovsky, Moshe. *Believe Not Every Spirit: Possession, Mysticism, and Dicerment in Early Modern Catholicism*. Chicago, IL: University of Chicago Press, 2007.

Spurling, Geoffrey. "Honor, Sexuality, and the Colonial Church: The Sins of Dr. González, Cathedral Canon." In *The Faces of Honor: Sex, Shame, and Violence in Colonial Latin America*, edited by Lyman Johnson and Sonya Lipsett-Rivera, 45–67. Albuquerque, NM: University of New Mexico Press, 1998.

Starr-Lebeau, Gretchen. "Lay Piety and Community Identity in the Early Modern World." In *A New History of Penance*, edited by Abigail Firey, 395–419. Boston, MA: Brill Press, 2008.

Stern, Steve. *The Secret History of Gender: Women, Men, and Power in Late Colonial Mexico*. Chapel Hill, NC: University of North Carolina Press, 1995.

Suárez Escobar, Marcela. *Sexualidad y norma sobre lo prohibido: la Ciudad de México y las postrimerías del virreinato*. Mexico City: Universidad Autonoma Metropolitano, 1994.

Szuchman, Mark, ed. *The Middle Period in Latin America*. Boulder, CO: PUB CO, 1989.

Tanck de Estrada, Dorothy. *La educación ilustrada, 1786–1836: Educación primaria en la ciudad de México*, fourth ed. Mexico City: El Colegio de México, Centro de Estudios Históricos, 2005.

——— . *Pueblos de indios y educación en el México colonial, 1750–1821*. Mexico City: El Colegio de México, Centro de Estudios Históricos, 1999.

Taylor, William B. "Baroque Religion and Art." Lecture, University of California, Berkeley, CA, Oct. 31, 2006.

——— . *Drinking, Homicide, and Rebellion in Colonial Mexican Villages*. Stanford, CA: Stanford University Press, 1979.

——— . *Magistrates of the Sacred: Priests and Parishioners in Eighteenth-Century Mexico*. Stanford, CA: Stanford University Press, 1996.

——— . "Our Lady in the Kernel of Corn, 1774." *The Americas* 59, no. 4 (April 2003): 559–70.

——— . *Shrines and Miraculous Images: Religious Life in Mexico Before the Reforma*. Albuquerque, NM: University of New Mexico Press, 2010.

——— . *Theater of a Thousand Wonders: A History of Miraculous Images and Shrines in New Spain*. New York, NY: Cambridge University Press, 2016.

Tentler, Thomas. *Sin and Confession on the Eve of the Reformation*. Princeton, NJ: Princeton University Press, 1977.

Tortorici, Zeb. "Contra Natura: Sin, Crime, and 'Unnatural' Sexuality in Colonial Mexico, 1530–1821," Ph.D. dissertation, 2010.

Traslosheros, Jorge E. *Iglesia, justicia, y sociedad en la Nueva España: La audiencia del Arzobispado de México 1528–1668*. Mexico City: Universidad Iberoamericana, 2004.

Twinam, Ann. "Honor, Sexuality, and Illegitimacy in Colonial Spanish America." In *Sexuality & Marriage in Colonial Latin America*, edited by Asunción Lavrin, 118–55. Lincoln, NE: University of Nebraska Press, 1989.

——— . *Public Lives, Private Secrets: Gender, Honor, Sexuality, and Illegitimacy in Colonial Spanish America*. Stanford, CA: Stanford University Press, 1999.

van Deusen, Nancy. *Between the Sacred and the Worldly: The Institutional and Cultural Practice of Recogimiento in Colonial Lima*. Stanford, CA: Stanford University Press, 2001.

Villa-Flores, Javier. *Dangerous Speech: A Social History of Blasphemy in Colonial Mexico*. Tucson, AZ: University of Arizona Press, 2006.

Villa-Flores, Javier, and Sonya Lipsett-Rivera, eds. *Emotions and Daily Life in Colonial Mexico*. Albuquerque, NM: University of New Mexico Press, 2004.

Voekel, Pamela "Liberal Religion: The Schism of 1861." In *Religious Culture in Modern Mexico*, edited by Martin Austin Nesvig, 78–105. Lanham, MD: Rowman and Littlefield Publishers Inc., 2007.

Walker Bynum, Caroline. *Holy Feast and Holy Fast: The Religious Significance of Food to Medieval Women*. Berkeley, CA: University of California Press, 1987.

Watson Marrón, Gustavo, Gilberto González Merlo, Berenise Bravo Rubio, and Marco Antonio Pérez, eds. *Guía de documentos Novohispanos del Archivo Histórico del Arzobispado de México*. Mexico City: Archivo Histórico de Arzobispado de México, 2002.

Wiesner-Hanks, Merry E. "Ideas and Laws Regarding Women." In *Women and Gender in Early Modern Europe*. Cambridge: Cambridge University Press, 2008.

Witschorik, Charles. *Preaching Power: Gender, Politics, and Official Catholic Church Discourses in Mexico City, 1720–1875*. Eugene, OR: Pickwick Publications, 2013.

Wood, Stephanie. "Corporate Adjustments in Colonial Mexican Indian Towns: Toluca Region, 1550–1810." Ph.D. dissertation, University of California, Los Angeles, CA, 1984.

"Matters of Life at Death: Nahuatl Testaments of Rural Women (Central Mexico), 1589–1801." In *Indian Women of Early Mexico*, edited by Susan Schroeder, Stephanie Wood, and Robert Haskett, 165–84. Norman, OK: University of Oklahoma Press, 1997.

*Transcending Conquest: Nahua Views of Spanish Colonial Mexico*. Norman, OK: University of Oklahoma Press, 2003.

Wright-Rios, Edward. *Revolutions in Mexican Catholicism: Reform and Revelation in Oaxaca, 1887–1934*. Durham, NC: Duke University Press, 2009.

*Searching for Madre Matiana: Prophecy and Popular Culture in Modern Mexico*. Albuquerque, NM: University of New Mexico Press, 2014.

# Index

Other Books in the Series (continued from page ii)